Used from Broadway to Britain's West End, QLab software is the tool of choice for many of the world's most prominent sound, projection, and integrated media designers. *QLab 4: Projects in Video, Audio, and Lighting Control* is a project-based book on QLab software covering sound, video, lighting, and show control. With information on audio, video, and lighting system basics and the more advanced functions of QLab such as show control, network capabilities, projection mapping, video effects, and cue cart integration, each chapter's specific projects will allow you to learn the software's capabilities at your own pace. In addition to the text, a companion website hosts project files, instructional videos, and more.

New to this edition:

- Fully updated with features new to QLab 4
- Full color illustrations
- Tools of the Trade, focusing on supplementary applications and techniques for improving your workflow
- New design-focused projects illuminate ways to utilize QLab as a creative tool by the theatrical designer
- Dozens of Design Tips for maximizing your efficiency
- New chapters on using QLab in conjunction with lighting systems
- Foreword by Projection Designer Daniel Brodie (Broadway: Motown the Musical, Disney's Aladdin, large-scale video designs for Kanye West, Mariah Carey, and the Bonnaroo Music and Arts Festival).

Jeromy Hopgood is a Professor of Entertainment Design & Technology at Eastern Michigan University. In addition to his teaching, Jeromy has designed more than 150 plays, musicals, dance, and opera productions over the last decade. His work in scenery, lighting, projections, and sound has been showcased at professional theatres across the Southeast and Midwest United States. He worked at the Williamstown Theatre Festival in its Tony-Award-Winning season and is an artistic associate at the Michigan Shakespeare Festival, where he is the resident scenic designer and technical director. Professor Hopgood is a long-standing member of the United States Institute of Theatre Technology. In addition to presenting panels on projection design, media, and educational theatre at numerous USITT annual conferences, he is also a regular presenter at Live Design International.

QLab 4

Projects in Video, Audio, and Lighting Control

Second Edition

Jeromy Hopgood

Routledge
Taylor & Francis Group

NEW YORK AND LONDON

Second edition published 2018
by Routledge
711 Third Avenue, New York, NY 10017

and by Routledge
2 Park Square, Milton Park, Abingdon, Oxon, OX14 4RN

Routledge is an imprint of the Taylor & Francis Group, an informa business

First edition published by Focal Press 2013

Library of Congress Cataloging-in-Publication Data
A catalog record for this book has been requested

ISBN: 978-1-138-03640-6 (hbk)
ISBN: 978-1-138-03641-3 (pbk)
ISBN: 978-1-315-17855-4 (ebk)

Typeset in ITC Stone Sans and Eurostile by
Servis Filmsetting Ltd, Stockport, Manchester

Visit the companion website: www.routledge.com/cw/hopgood

Contents

Contents

Contents

Contents

Contents

Contents

Contents

Contents

Contents

Contents

Contents

Contents

Contents

Foreword

From black box theaters to Broadway, cues are being fired and organized in Figure 53's excellent application, QLab. What started in 2006 as a simple way to cue and fade audio playback has grown into a staple of the live entertainment industry, now being used in classrooms, cruise ships, mega churches, and arenas alike, controlling not just audio, but video, projections, and network show control protocols and even running the lighting rig.

As a multimedia artist with a wide range of projects myself, from concerts to Broadway to industrials to installation and gallery work, I have used QLab on many occasions as an indispensable tool to produce my effects and show control sequencing. On some shows, I utilize nearly every function of it, providing video playback for projection mapping, controlling audio levels, and sending lighting commands, while on other shows I might just be using it as a hub to control the other show control computers, such as Watchout rig or ETC Eos lighting desk.

Just as the magic that we see on stage is powered by the unseen machinations of designers and technicians such as myself, behind QLab's friendly and simple user interface lies an astonishingly powerful tool capable of sequencing and managing even the most complicated technical shows. Fortunately, Jeromy Hopgood has provided a text resource matching the excellence and beguilingly elegant simplicity of the software itself. In fact, I was fortunate enough to use *QLab 3 Show Control* as a primary text for a Projection Design course I taught at Pace University. Jeromy carefully laid out every part of QLab 3 in great detail, providing my students with a perfect reference.

This new version expands on the approach of the first one, adding new projects and designer tips while streamlining the examples without sacrificing clarity or utility. One of the major themes I have learned in my career is that it isn't just what you know, but also how you go about applying it. Fortunately for the reader of this new edition, they are given the opportunity not only to add to their knowledge base but also how to apply it to their projects. I look forward to the continued success of both QLab and this accompanying text.

Foreword by Projection Designer Daniel Brodie (Broadway: Motown the Musical, Disney's Aladdin, large-scale video designs for Kanye West, Mariah Carey, and the Bonnaroo Music and Arts Festival)

Acknowledgments

As a theatre artist and a teacher, I constantly extoll the virtues of collaboration to my students. Writing a book is a similar undertaking, in that there are countless people who work together towards a common goal. There is no way I would have been able to finish this book without the help of so many people along the way.

To Stacey, Meredith, and the rest of the team at Routledge, many thanks for helping turn this into a reality. As always, thanks are due to the amazing group at Figure 53, who continue to answer so many questions and requests and without whose support this text would not have happened. Special thanks to Mic Pool, Rich Walsh, Jeremy Lee, Sam Kusnetz, and Andy Lang for always being willing to field a question – no matter how obvious the answer seems. To Daniel Brodie, an exceptional projection designer and all-around good guy, thanks for taking time from your busy schedule to write the foreword for this edition.

I have had the pleasure of working closely with the folks at TLS Productions, Inc., in Michigan for the better part of the last decade. Thanks to Dustin Miller of TLSP for his editorial assistance and general wealth of knowledge when it comes to macOS nomenclature. There are a number of colleagues who answered questions, explained things that I didn't understand, and generally were there to offer support at the right moment: Wendall Harrington of Yale, Alex Oliczewski of the Ohio State University, Daniel Fine of the University of Iowa, David Stoughton of Illinois Wesleyan, and Jake Pinholster of Arizona State University. Thanks also to Ellen Lampert Greaux and the good people at Live Design for always being so supportive of my work.

It has been a pleasure to serve as a professor at Eastern Michigan University over the last nine years. I am proud of the work we do here and so happy to call EMU my home. To my ED&T and Theatre students, thanks for being such an inspiration and helping keep my batteries re-charged. You are why I do this work. Thanks, especially, Kathy Stacey, Don Ritzenheim, and the College of Arts and Sciences for supporting my research. To John Charles, Melanie Bond, and Madeleine Huggins, in particular, there aren't enough words in the English language to say how much you have helped me over the years.

Finally, so many thanks are due to my family for their love and support in everything I do. So many times, the work that we do in this field can really take a toll on family life. I'm so lucky to have the team of Katie, Kira, and Isabella to keep me going. Thanks, ladies, for all that you do and for understanding the hours of time I spent at the laptop. I truly am the luckiest guy on the planet.

Preface

If it is true that an artist is only as good as their tools, then we are all very lucky to be living in this time period with so many excellent design and technology tools at our disposal. These days, the entertainment industry seems to evolve at a breakneck pace, with new resources and even fields popping up all around us. As a designer, I know that I am always looking for a new tool to speed up my workflow and assist me in turning my concepts into reality. For me, few have been such a game-changer as QLab.

Back in 2008, I started showing some of my design students this new application that offered Mac users an alternative to SFX for sound playback. It was a robust program with an interface that my students took to effortlessly. What's more, Figure 53 (the makers of QLab) was a small company that really got how customer service needed to work for those in show business. I quickly implemented QLab control systems into my performance spaces and classrooms. With each subsequent version of QLab, more features have been introduced, from video to show control – and lighting. Over the years, even though the company has grown, it has maintained that same commitment to customer service and its user community that it had back when there was just one person on the payroll.

In 2013, I released *QLab 3 Show Control*, a text I envisioned as one part handbook, one part workshop. The concept was to create a practical book that would function both as an instructional manual with hands-on projects and a useful quick reference guide. In addition to the book itself was a collection of supplemental material on a companion website with instructional videos and dozens of downloadable project packets for the reader to work through on their own. In the years since the book's release, I have been pleasantly surprised at the number of people who have reached out to me with stories of how it has pulled them out of a bind or helped figure out a nagging problem.

In late 2016, Figure 53 launched QLab 4 with a number of changes to the software, most notably the inclusion of lighting control. This new book addresses the changes in QLab since Version 3 and offers a number of new projects and exercises. Furthermore, this edition adds dozens of new Design Tips to help the designers better understand how to work with QLab and develop their own sense of workflow. The chapters are broken down in concise numbered sections that allow you to easily identify and focus on a topic. Like the QLab 3 text, this edition also makes use of a companion website with instructional videos and project packets. By downloading the project packets from the companion website (focalpress.com/cw/hopgood), not only can you read through the projects in the text, but also tackle them at your own pace on your computer.

QLab 4 is a requirement for the projects accompanying this text. To download a copy, visit figure53.com/qlab/download. One of the things that makes QLab so great is a strong user base that loves to share their own experiences and assist one another. The QLab Discussion List, housed on Google Groups, is a great place to access years of data and connect with other QLab users. To see the discussion list, visit figure53.com/support and click on the Discussion List button by the QLab icon.

Finally, one of the difficulties of writing about digital technology in the print medium is how very quickly software can change in relation to a book's print cycle. In an effort to keep up with major software updates (which often come out every 6–10 months), visit my Entertainment Design & Technology blog at jeromyhopgood.wordpress.com, where I will post important update information as it is available.

PART I
QLab Basics

What's New in Version 4?

While there are a number of additions to the software, there aren't so many changes that longtime users will be lost the first time they open it. The interface has undergone a redesign featuring a new font and icons, but the layout remains consistent to that of QLab 3. The following section breaks down many of the new additions in Version 4 (referred to as V4 hereafter) and gives you a taste of what to expect.

1.1 – Workflow Changes

One of the greatest strengths of QLab is its simple, logical layout and how the workflow can be tailored to meet the user's needs. Through software updates over the years, QLab has always responded to feedback and tried to make each update more user friendly and, more importantly, *time saving*. QLab 4 offers a wealth of workflow changes geared to allowing the user to customize their experience and maximize productivity.

Cue Templates

Cue Templates is a new function of V4 that allows the user to customize the default settings for newly created cues. Let's say you're a supervisor for a facility with multiple performance spaces. Using the Cue Templates function, you could create a master file that already has the default patch and levels for sound and lighting in those spaces so that users don't have to start from scratch each time.

Record Cue Sequence

One of the most exciting additions for designers is the ability to record a cue sequence. This function watches and records the timing of a cue sequence as you play through it manually. Once you stop the recording, QLab automatically

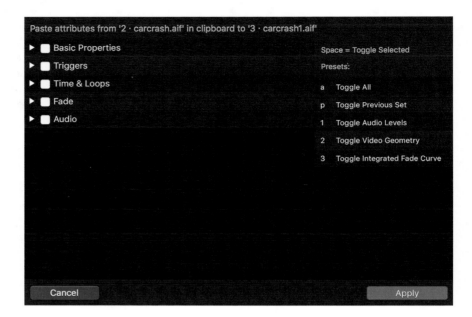

Figure 1.1
The Paste Cue
Properties window.

creates a Group Cue populated with Start Cues that match the playback timing you just created.

Paste Cue Properties

Dubbed "fancy paste" by the Figure 53 team, this new tool allows you to copy some or all of the properties from one cue and paste it into one or more subsequent cues (Figure 1.1). This applies to any or all of the parameters available in the Inspector. This function alone could literally save hours of programming time.

Batch Editing

Another handy addition is the ability to "batch edit" cues. By selecting multiple cues, you can now edit the cue parameters of all selected cues in the Basics and Triggers tabs of the Inspector. Likewise, for Light Cues, you will be able to adjust instrument levels for multiple cues through the Levels tab.

Pop-Out Inspector, Cue Lists, and Carts

With the release of Version 4.1, the Inspector can be "popped out" into its own free-standing window, allowing you to move it and resize as desired. In addition, Cue Lists and Carts can be opened as their own separate windows by using the "Open in New Window" button inside the Lists, Carts, and Active Cues panel.

Keep Audition Window on Top

Version 4.1 introduced the ability to keep the Audition Window "always on top." In previous versions, when selecting a cue in the workspace, the workspace would be moved to the top layer, thereby covering up the Audition Window. By clicking a "keep window on top" checkbox on the Audition Window interface, the Audition Window will always remain floating on the top layer, no matter what else is selected.

1.2 – New Playback Options

QLab 4 also introduces a series of new playback options for cues, changing the traditional playback methods that have been standard in the program for a number of years. These additions continue in the tradition of allowing maximum flexibility for programming to meet the unique needs that arise for live performance environments.

Cue Triggers

All cues have a number of ways in which they can be triggered, from the Go button to hotkeys, wall clock, MIDI, Timecode, or more. V4 creates a unique new tab in the Inspector called Triggers (a change from QLab 3 where trigger controls were included in the Basics tab). In addition to the basic trigger functions, QLab 4 also adds the ability to fade and stop or change levels of other cues once the current cue is triggered. This allows one cue to affect the output of multiple others in the same workspace without adding additional Fade Cues. Figure 1.2 shows the new possibilities for Fade and Stop or "ducking" other cues upon triggering a new cue.

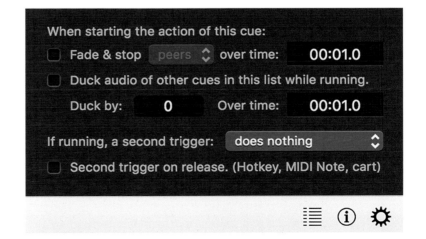

Figure 1.2 The Triggers Tab, with Fade and Ducking capabilities.

Negative Post-Wait

In addition to a regular post-wait (i.e., amount of time after the cue has completed its action), you can now specify a negative post-wait. This sets the trigger for the next cue in the cue sequence as a number of seconds before the current cue ends.

New Fade Curve Shape and Audio Domain

In addition to the standard linear curve, custom curve, and S-curve shapes, V4 introduces a new default **Parametric Fade Curve**. This curve allows for a more mathematically precise control over your fade shapes. In addition to this new curve shape, all audio fades now have a drop-down menu for changing the scales used in QLab for measuring fades – Slider, Decibel, or Linear. Each of these offers unique approaches to controlling the way in which QLab fades audio.

Looping

With the release of Version 4.1, Audio and Video cues can be looped, even when slices have been added to the cue. As such, the Devamp cue now allows you to specify devamping for either the slice or entire cue.

1.3 – Integrated Lighting Control

The most talked about new feature of QLab 4 is the addition of **Lighting Cues**. QLab has long had the ability to interface a lighting console via MIDI or, more recently, OSC. With V4, though, the software has become a legitimate lighting desk all on its own. Lighting Cues can send signals in two ways. The first is over the Art-Net protocol, using a Wi-Fi or Ethernet connection to transmit data to lighting equipment. Since most lighting equipment requires a DMX control signal, this means your QLab lighting rig will likely need to incorporate an Art-Net interface node to translate the Art-Net to DMX signal. The second method, introduced with QLab Version 4.1, is sending DMX signals through the use of a USB-DMX interface. Supported interfaces can be found in Figure 53's QLab4 documentation.

QLab has a built-in **Lighting Definitions** tool that contains some preinstalled definitions (similar to Personalities for conventional lighting consoles) and allows the user to create their own unique definitions for lighting instruments and accessories. These definitions are used in the **Lighting Patch** to assign instruments to their addresses. Finally, the **Lighting Dashboard** is a graphic interface that shows the current live levels of all the lighting instruments in your workspace and allows you to make changes to their parameters in real-time

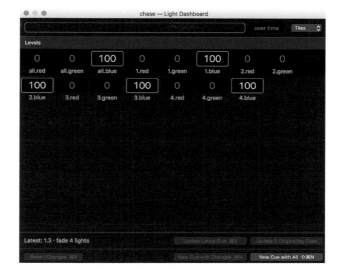

Figure 1.3
The Lighting Dashboard with sliders enabled to control lighting instruments.

(Figure 1.3). Through these simple interfaces, you can create robust lighting designs that integrate seamlessly with the rest of your sound and video. You will find specific details in Part IV: QLab Lighting Control.

1.4 – Cue Carts

Leading up to the release of QLab 3, Figure 53 introduced a new application called QCart. This program was designed to serve as a simple audio cart – a device that allows the user to instantly play back audio files at the push of a button. The layout of this program was similar to a drum machine, a grid of cells into which you insert audio files. The sound was played back by clicking on the cell or triggering it via hotkeys, MIDI, etc. With the release of QLab 4, Figure 53 integrated **Cue Carts** into the application, but greatly expanded on the way in which it functions. Now, in addition to audio, any Cue Cart can hold every type of cue (with the exception of Group Cues). A cart is a collection of cues that operates in a non-linear function with no Playhead, Auto-follows, or Auto-continues. It is simply a grid-style interface that allows easy triggering of cues (Figure 1.4). For a detailed examination of this new function, see Chapter 3.

1.5 – Audio Improvements

At first glance, many of the changes made to the audio functions in QLab may not be immediately apparent. While there may not be quite so many additions

Figure 1.4
A Cue Cart with numerous cue types assigned.

to audio functions as other areas, the changes that have occurred are substantive in how QLab can interface with audio networks and in its precision control of cues.

64-Channel Output

The previous version of QLab featured 48 channels of audio output. While this is a large number of outputs for many systems, modern networked audio/video systems, such as Dante, MADI, and AVB, utilize a larger set of channels. To compensate for this, QLab 4 increased the audio output from 48 to a maximum of 64 channels.

Mic Cues

Mic Cues now utilize the specific channels of their patched audio device, allowing for easier use of Audio Units that sometimes require a specific number of inputs or outputs. This gives more precise control when working with Mic Cues in your design.

Precision Slice Control

Slices now offer twice the precision control in QLab 4, with the minimum slice time reduced from 0.1 seconds to 0.05 seconds. This gives the programmer the ability to create highly precise divisions within any Audio or Video Cue.

1.6 – Video Improvements

While QLab has long had video capabilities, the release of Version 3 marked a giant leap forward for the possibilities of dealing with video content in a flexible manner. QLab 4 keeps the robust video architecture of its predecessor, while offering up some powerful new ways to address video in your design.

HAP Codec Support

QLab offers video playback for any of the file formats supported by AVFoundation. Version 4 now supports file playback for the **HAP** format. HAP is an excellent codec designed for digital video artists and VJs with the goal of achieving higher-performance video playback in OpenGL-based applications. One noticeable benefit of this addition means that videos with transparencies (also referred to as Alpha Channel) can now be created using the HAP Alpha format, in addition to ProRes 4444. The addition of HAP support brings QLab into a group of other media programs such as d3, Isadora, and Watchout.

Copy/Paste Surface Geometry

This new function will certainly be a crowd pleaser for all of the projection designers using QLab. With V4, it is now possible to copy the geometry from one surface and paste it onto another. This is accomplished inside of the Video section of Settings. Once Video Settings are selected, a new menu item appears in the menu bar called **Video Tools**. Once selected, you can simply copy the surface geometry onto your clipboard, select a new surface and then paste the geometry in place. This saves hours in the too-often tedious process of setting up complex geometry for multiple surfaces.

Set Durations for Still Images and Text Cues

Another exciting new video function is the ability to assign a cue duration to still images and Text Cues (formerly called Title Cues). In the past, it was necessary to use one or more Fade Cues to program a Video or Text Cue. QLab 4 allows the programmer to simply input the cue duration in either the Basics tab of the Inspector or in the Action column of the cue row. Note that this creates a stop for the Video Cue and does not allow for adding a slow fade. This could prove to be incredibly useful in the instance of stacking cues on top of one another. Now, instead of having to add a Fade Cue to take out the Video Cue hidden on a bottom layer, the programmer could simply add a cue duration that stops the cue's playback once it is covered by the cue on a higher layer.

1.7 – QLab Remote

One of the wonderful new utilities Figure 53 brought us around the time of the V3 release was the QLab Remote, available for download on Apple's App Store. This iOS application allows the user to remotely connect with QLab to view and edit a QLab workspace. With the release of QLab 4, there is now an update to the QLab Remote with a number of changes that drastically improve the look and function of this app, enabling a greater level of control.

Brand New Design

More than just a new look, the redesign for the QLab Remote enables better control on both the iPhone and iPad. It also enables the use of Split View mode on the iPad. Users of the old version will find that this new design makes its use on an iPhone much easier to manage, especially with the ability to resize the control panel within the app and hide the Toolbox.

Adjust Video Surface Control Points

One omission from previous versions of the QLab Remote was the ability to edit video surfaces. In the new version, you now have control over editing video surfaces from your Apple mobile device. This is a huge advantage for fine-tuning control points on a surface, as you can now stand on stage and edit the control points up close instead of having to do so from the control booth or screen sharing your workspace to a laptop. Figure 1.5 shows the control interface for this function.

Figure 1.5
Editing video control surfaces on the QLab Remote is a snap in this new release.

Access to Light Levels in Inspector

Another useful addition to this version is the ability to access and control the levels of lighting instruments in real time. Like the video surface controls previously mentioned, this enables the designer to have closer access to the stage and frees them from having to remain tethered to the tech table.

Cart Integration

QLab Remote allows you to interact with the Carts built into your workspace, making your mobile device into a portable Cart interface (Figure 1.6). One interesting possibility might be the addition of an iPhone to an actor or dancer's costume to allow for a more interactive control of design elements in real time.

Create and Reorder Cues

Past versions of the QLab Remote lacked the function to do much in the way of cue creation or reordering of the workspace. This new version allows you to create new cues and reorganize your cue order in both cue lists and cue carts. This moves the app away from merely functioning as a remote control into the realm of a true editing interface.

USB Support

Version 4.1 introduced support for connecting to the QLab Remote with a USB cable instead of Wi-Fi. When using the USB, available workspaces show up on the QLab Remote in a separate section labeled "USB."

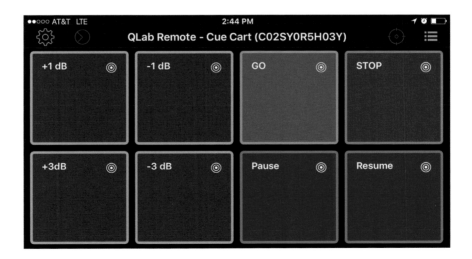

Figure 1.6
Accessing a Cue Cart through the QLab Remote on an iPhone.

1.8 – Summary

QLab 4 certainly offers up a wide range of new options for how the software can be used. From the addition of lighting control, to expanding on the already strong foundation of audio, video, and show control, Version 4 will provide a wealth of possibilities for live performances, installations, and special events. The remainder of the book is broken down into five parts, each focusing on an in-depth analysis of the program and its applications in the areas of audio, video, lighting, and show control.

Getting to Know QLab 4

Before getting into the details of how to use QLab 4 to create a design, it is important to understand the basics of the software, from installation to setup. This chapter addresses all of those preliminary considerations before jumping into how the software functions. For this chapter, we work from the assumption that this is your first time to use QLab 4.

2.1 – QLab 4 System Recommendations

The question I most often get asked when teaching QLab is invariably, "Can I run QLab on my PC?" The simple answer is, no. Due to the fact that QLab is built on the architecture of the Mac OS, it only works on Macintosh computers. Version 4 requires the Apple OS 10.10 (or later) operating system – more commonly referred to as Yosemite. "Hackintoshes" and virtual machine environments to emulate a Mac on a PC are also not supported.

RAM

When considering RAM, the rule of thumb is always equip your system with enough to exceed your current needs (especially when working with audio and video playback). This is particularly true today, as the manufacturing techniques are changing for some Apple computers to make it more difficult (and, in some cases impossible) to upgrade the factory-installed RAM on your own. 4GB is a good baseline for RAM, and the current minimum amount installed in new Macs. Since QLab is a 64-bit application, it is capable of taking full advantage of the total amount of RAM on your computer.

Processor (CPU)

The processor can be equated to the brain of your computer. For AV applications like QLab, it is often the case that the most powerful processor is preferable. The question you have to ask yourself is how will you be using QLab? Since the software can be used in varying configurations for sound, video, lighting, and show control applications, your CPU needs truly depend on the way you're using the software. For basic audio, lighting, or show control cues, the standard configuration processor (currently i5) is fine. Once you start running multiple audio and/or video cues simultaneously, though, your system will benefit from looking at a more powerful processor (currently an i7 or Xeon variety).

GPU

The GPU, or graphics processing unit, is an important consideration for those using video in QLab (for those building an audio-only rig, then GPU is mostly a non-issue). The biggest concern when picking your Mac for QLab use tends to be whether your GPU is discrete or integrated. A discrete GPU is a processor that has its own RAM (called VRAM) independent of the computer's RAM. In this case, the GPU basically has its own memory for performing rendering and video applications. An integrated GPU does not have its own RAM and utilizes a portion of your Mac's RAM to execute its functions. This is why it is advisable to avoid a Mac with integrated GPU if you anticipate ever using your QLab rig to run a video-intensive show. If you have to use a computer with integrated GPU, be sure to equip it with the maximum system RAM possible, however, since increasing the system RAM will allow the computer to allocate a larger portion to VRAM.

Hard Drive

Every computer comes equipped with a hard drive (sometimes referred to as a hard disk). This is the location where your computer stores data for retrieval in applications. There are a number of different types of hard drives on the market, but the two main considerations when picking a hard drive on your Mac are HDD (hard drive disk) or SSD (Solid State Drive). An HDD is the classic "platter style" disk drive, with a spinning disk onto which data is recorded. The SSD is sometimes also referred to as Flash memory because it operates in a similar fashion to "Flash drives," memory sticks with no moving parts. If given the choice, always equip your QLab computer with an SSD because this type of drive is much faster at accessing your data and has no moving parts to break. Figure 53 recommends against the use of the Apple Fusion Drive (a hybrid drive that combines an SSD with an HDD), as the operator has no control over which data is stored on which portion of the drive. These drives also frequently reorganize data storage, shuffling data between the two drives, which can cause undesirable effects in QLab playback.

2.2 – Understanding QLab 4 Licensing

QLab 4 introduces a series of changes to the licensing structure that are completely different in many ways from past iterations. The following section explains the software licensing for V4 and some of the ways in which it differs from the older licensing.

How Do Licenses Work?

In the simplest terms, a QLab license is simply a key that unlocks all of the functions of the free version of the QLab 4 software. All new QLab licenses are based on an accounts-based licensing system through the QLab Store. These licenses are now attached to the email address you use to purchase the software license through their secure online store. This means that licenses can be managed online, allowing for remote deauthorizing of licenses, something that has never been possible before. Once you have set up an account with QLab, you can log in to your account and see your licenses, purchase history, and more.

The Free Version

One of the biggest reasons for QLab's popularity over the years is Figure 53's commitment to having a free version of QLab available for basic playback functions. This remains true for QLab 4, where the free version allows for basic functions in sound, video, lighting, and networking. It bears mentioning that this version works well for basic stereo output audio functions, but for anything other than the most basic video and lighting functions, you will need to upgrade to a licensed version. The chart below explains some of the features available with the free version.

SOUND CONTROL
2 channels of Audio output (with 2 channels of audio per file)
Audio waveform view
Unlimited slices per Audio Cue
Sample accurate playback sync
Unlimited Audio Fades (with Live Fade previews)
Remote control via OSC, MIDI, MSC, and iOS app

VIDEO CONTROL
1 Single-screen Video Surface
1000 video layers
Full Surface Video Cues
Remote control via OSC, MIDI, MSC, and iOS app

LIGHTING CONTROL
16 Patchable DMX addresses
Remote control via OSC, MIDI, MSC, and iOS app

Professional Licenses

For more robust applications, you need to look at the different Pro licenses available for QLab. As mentioned earlier, customer service has always been a benchmark of the QLab name. Nowhere is this truer than in their pricing and options for professional licensing. Understanding that no two installations are alike, Figure 53 has broken down the QLab software into separate licensing packages so that the customer who needs only professional audio capabilities doesn't have to pay for an entire system of functions they will never use. Unlike previous versions, licensing is now split into seven different packages that combine different possibilities of Audio, Video, and Lighting. For those familiar with the old licensing, one notable absence is the "basic" licenses previously offered with V3. QLab 4 licenses now lack a basic tier and split all functions into three professional licenses called QLab 4 Audio, QLab 4 Video, and QLab 4 Lighting. Each of these licenses currently retails at $399. There is a slight discount for purchasing multiple license types. For instance, if you want to bundle two licenses together, the price is $749. The QLab 4 Bundle, which combines all three licenses, is currently $999. For a comparison of the features in each different licensing package, visit the QLab website at **http://figure53.com/docs/qlab/v4/general/features/**

Rent-to-Own

For those in the professional sector who find a need for the software in limited runs, there is also the ability to rent at a modest price (currently $4/$7/$10 per day, depending on selected tier). Rentals give the full capability of the license for a predetermined amount of time programmed directly into a rental license. When you reach the end of your time period, the license will time out. One important new feature to rentals is that they now function as "rent-to-own," meaning that once you have rented the software for 110 days, your account will be credited a standard license of the same type you rented. This new approach is great for tighter budgets and rewards loyal customers. As a result, rentals no longer can be installed on an unlimited number of computers. Rental licenses are basically time-limited standard licenses now and are subject to the same three-computer restrictions of a normal license. QLab's licensing agreement allows for one license to be installed on three computers, provided that one is for the live show, one is for a redundant backup, and one is an off-site programming unit for the designer.

Academic Licensing

Figure 53 offers a substantial discount for academic licensing (students, teachers, and institutions). In order to qualify for academic pricing, you simply have to contact **support@figure53.com** from an educational email address and attach a copy of your academic identification. Once you have done so, you will be able to see academic pricing through your account login. Current academic pricing is $349/$679/$799 for purchases and $3.50/$6.80/$8 per day, depending on selected tier.

Site Licenses

Another new feature with V4 is site licenses. Site licensing allows you to install one license across multiple computers, priced by the seat. It is helpful for large numbers of computers managed by a single organization, such as a computer lab or classroom or a large multi-space venue. Licenses currently are sold as permanent Pro Bundle licenses or as a one-year Pro Bundle. If you plan on keeping the licenses on computers without routinely erasing them, you simply log into your Figure 53 account on each Mac and install the site license like a normal license. In the case of using computers that you have to regularly erase, Figure 53 offers a software tool specially built to make this process easier to manage.

Using QLab 3

For those who own QLab 3, the license will still continue to operate as usual. If you choose to upgrade to V4, you will receive a voucher for a substantial discount on QLab 4. After purchasing, you will still maintain the old V3 licenses in addition to the new V4 licenses you purchase. For those with a QLab 4 license only, QLab 3.2 and higher can be unlocked with a QLab 4 license. This effectively enables you to use either version with one license.

2.3 – Installing the Software

QLab software is accessible only via download through Figure53.com. Whether you will be using the free or Pro version of QLab, the first step will be downloading the software from their website. There is only one program to download – adding a license simply unlocks additional features on the Free version.

When you click on the download icon, the software will appear in your downloads folder as a program icon called QLab. Drag the icon from your downloads folder onto your desktop or into your Applications folder. Once you have done so, you are set up and ready to go. There is no further installation process necessary.

2.4 – Adding a License

Provided you are interested in using the advanced applications in the Pro version of QLab (many of which will be required for the projects throughout the book), you will then need to visit the Figure 53 website again to download your license. As mentioned earlier in this chapter, there are a number of licensing options depending on your needs. Whether you go with a license purchase or a rental, both types of licensing are available for purchase through the QLab Store. For purchase, you simply select which license package you prefer and pay through their secure server. For the rental, you indicate the type of license, starting date, and the number of days required for your purposes. For both methods, you will receive an email that includes both your receipt and instructions for logging into your QLab account. Licenses for V4 (and V3 if you modernize your account) are now all handled through your QLab account. You must log in to your account and then authorize the computer to use a license through QLab.

To make certain that your license was correctly installed, simply open up the QLab software and click the word **QLab** in the menu bar at the top of the screen. In the drop-down menu, click on **Manage Your Licenses....** This will open an interface called Licenses and Activations that shows you the licenses installed on your computer (see Figure 2.1). It will indicate the type of license bundle, license terms, name of licensee, and end date (should it be a rental).

Removing Licenses

In addition to seeing the installed license, the "Manage Your Licenses..." function will show a button labeled "Remove." This button is important to remember should you be installing the software on multiple computers. Standard licensing allows that you can install the software onto one main computer, one backup computer, and one editing computer (for a total of three authorized installations). These licenses are intended to be used for a show computer, a redundant backup of the same show, and a remote editing workstation. The license does not allow for using these licenses on multiple

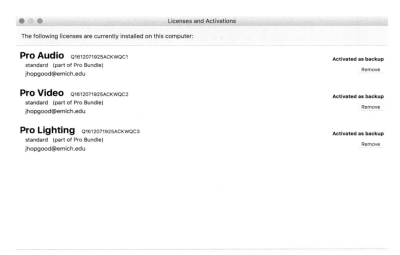

Figure 2.1
QLab licensing
window featuring
different license
types.

different shows at once. As a professional designer, one might install the soft-ware onto a number of different computers. Should you forget to deauthorize, though, you could lose access to one of your potential licenses. In the past, there was no way to remotely deauthorize these licenses. With QLab 4 licenses, however, you can now remove a license from any Mac connected to the Internet by logging into your Figure 53 account on the website.

Modernizing QLab 3 Licenses

Since the QLab 3 licenses were never account based, the process for removing licenses always required a manual deauthorization. QLab 4 has now introduced the ability to modernize V3 licenses, making them account based to allow for precise tracking of which computers have licenses installed and what types. If you choose to modernize your QLab 3 license, you simply deauthorize licenses on all computers except for one and then choose "Manage Your Licenses…" from the QLab menu on that computer. Inside the Licenses and Activations window, you will then be able to click the "modernize" button, and it will modernize your V3 license for all new installs.

2.5 – Organization and Work Flow

No matter how you plan on using QLab, you will quickly discover that having an established organizational method will make the process of programming, trouble-shooting, and playback much easier. Unless you are creating your cue list from the ground up on the computer to be used for playback (and, really, even then), it is important to create a logical file storage method and remain consistent across each computer you use. In order to aid in this, I always create a show folder to be saved onto the desktop of my computer. I will typically name this folder for the show or project that I am working on. Depending on the number and/or type of files associated with the project, I might add a number of sub-folders inside of the master show folder.

Let's look at a hypothetical show featuring music, still imagery, and videos. For this show, called *The Distant Thunder*, I create a master folder on my desktop called "Distant Thunder." Within this folder, I create three sub-folders called "Music," "Stills," and "Videos." This will help me organize the project as I go along and save a lot of time during the process of creating a cue list since everything will be in a logical location. I typically try to take it one step further and make sure that I name (or re-name) any files associated with the project as something very descriptive.

For example, let's assume that there will be numerous different sound cues of thunder in our "Distant Thunder" workspace. For each of the thunder cues, I would make certain that they are numbered chronologically (i.e., Thunder1. wav, Thunder2.wav, and so on) so that when the time comes to program, I don't spend all my time listening to them to decide what order they should be placed in for playback. It could be as simple as this or as complex as naming one "John_is_shot_and_dies_painfully.wav." Ultimately, this system should be unique to you and your thought process, as it is intended to exist only for your benefit or those working on the project.

Another thing to consider is that once a show is saved on one computer, should you move the show file to another computer, QLab will be looking for the same paths for playback. In other words, if you created your show folder on the desktop of one computer, then moved it to the Downloads folder of another computer, your cue list would not function properly (since all of the file paths would have been listed as Desktop, not Downloads). Likewise, over time your show folder might become cluttered with deleted files, unused choices, or multiple takes. If you are transporting this over to another computer for play-back, you likely will not want to bring along those unused files. Since QLab 2, there has been a useful function called **Bundle Workspace** that aids in both of these problems.

Once you are finished with your project and ready to transfer the Workspace from one computer to another, simply click the **File** button on the Menu bar and select the **Bundle Workspace** option in the drop-down menu. This function creates a new folder for your workspace and a copy of all the files referenced within it. All cues in your cue list(s) will then be updated and saved with the new media files in the bundled folder. This can then easily be transferred to the new computer for playback. I strongly recommend always saving these to the desktop, as it is the easiest logical location to drop the file for other computers.

2.6 – Templates

Templates are an easy way to create a default workspace that can be used as a starting point for a new show. Creating a template is easy. All you have to do is start creating a workspace that has all of the default settings, patches, cues, etc., that you want included in the template. This includes everything from your workspace settings to device patches, lighting definitions, Script Cues, cue lists, and more. Once you have the workspace set up the way you like it, simply go to the File menu and select "Save As Template" from the drop-down menu (Figure 2.2). You will be asked if you want to create a new template or replace an existing one. Name the template anything you choose, and it will be saved into QLab's template library.

If you want to create a new workspace from a template, choose "New From Template" in QLab's File menu, or use the keyboard shortcut of ⇧⌘N (Shift-Command-N). This will open up the template library for you to choose from.

2.7 – Workspace Settings

One area to look at before jumping into programming is how to establish preferences for how QLab will behave once you begin to use it. The following section details how to do just that, by using workspace settings. Workspace Settings is a tool for establishing the settings related to one particular work-space, not to QLab as a program. This means that any workspace settings saved with a workspace will travel with it should you move it to another computer. It is always important to look at workspace setting *before* starting a project, as there are several functions that, when enabled, will make your programming

Figure 2.2 Saving a document as a Template.

Figure 2.3 The Workspace Settings icon is located in the lower right corner of the program window.

much easier. Keep in mind, though, that you may well find yourself returning to the workspace settings to make adjustments.

To access the workspace settings, click on the gear-shaped icon in the lower right hand corner of the program window (see Figure 2.3). Once you click on the icon, a new window entitled "Untitled Workspace 1 – Settings" will open. The page is separated into two columns: the left column contains the menu for selecting various preference settings; the right column's content changes for each menu item clicked on the left. It is important to note that, once established, settings will remain in place for all future files added to your workspace. In the section below, we will go through each of the basic settings possibilities to get you ready to start working in QLab. Some will be covered in detail in later chapters. I would recommend opening your workspace settings inside of QLab to reference while reading along.

A. General

The General Settings are just that – settings related to the general function of your QLab workspace (Figure 2.4). These are basic functions that generally allow you to control the visual appearance of cue lists and control playback positions or save you from the legwork of cue numbering. Most of these are self-explanatory. The General Settings are divided into six rows, indicated below.

Cue Triggering:
- The first checkbox allows you to fire a trigger when the workspace is first opened. A number of designers use this as a trigger for a Script Cue used to

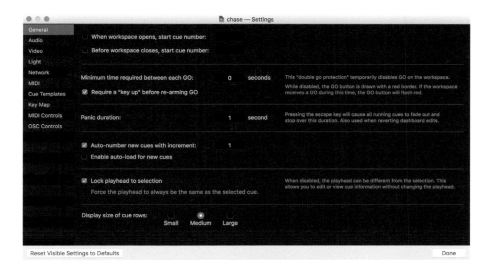

Figure 2.4 The General Settings window.

change certain parameters for the workspace. Consider a show with voice-over recordings specific to an actor in the performance. What do you do if there is an understudy standing in for that performance, though? An easy option is to write a Script Cue that disables all of the Audio Cues for the actor who is out and enables the ones recorded for the understudy. By setting the Script Cue as the one to be triggered each time you open the workspace, this ensures that you will have to answer who is playing which role for that performance and activate the appropriate cues for playback.

- The second checkbox is the opposite function, triggering a cue when your workspace closes. In this case, when you close the workspace, QLab will ask you if you do indeed want to trigger the cue. If you say yes, the cue will trigger and, upon finishing its playback, your QLab workspace will close. In addition, you can choose to circumvent playback of the closing cue and simply close your workspace.

GO Button Settings:

- The next area is what is sometimes referred to as "Double GO Protection." The default minimum time set between GO (firing a cue) is set as 0 seconds. In some situations (provided you don't have rapid-fire cues), you might want to set a slight buffer of 0.5 seconds to defuse any accidental "double-clicks" from the operator. If you use this function, a red box will appear around the GO button to let the operator know that GO has been temporarily suspended. Should the GO be activated during this time period, the area around the GO button will flash red as an indication that the command cannot be followed.

The second checkbox is a protection for the keyboard shortcut assigned to the GO that forces QLab to wait for the key to be released before allowing another GO. This is important when using an X-Keys programmable keyboard device (or any other hardware that does not produce a "key-up" event). If you intend to use this type of peripheral device, simply deactivate the "key-up" checkbox and you will be ready to go.

Panic Duration:

- This function allows for setting the panic duration. In QLab 4, when you press ESC, the panic command will begin, fading out all running cues over the default duration so as to not abruptly stop (particularly useful in live settings). This setting allows you to change the time from the default of 1 second to any duration.

Cue Numbering and Auto-Load:

- The next setting controls the increments of auto-numbering. When checked, you can establish a numbering increment for new cues. The default is 1, meaning that each cue inserted will progress chronologically by adding 1 to the previous number. Sometimes, it is wise to leave a numeric buffer between inserted cues.
- The following checkbox enables auto-load for cues, meaning that all new cues added to the workspace will have the "auto-load" function enabled.

Lock Playhead:

- The general preferences also allow you to control the behavior of the playback position in QLab. The playback position is an indicator that shows what cue is selected for playback once the operator hits GO. By default, the playback position changes to any cue you might click (for instance to edit the settings in a subsequent cue). If you deselect this checkbox, though, you can keep the playback position independent of any cue you select.

Cue Row Sizing:

- Finally, the last of the general preferences simply allows you to change the size of cue rows from small to medium or large.

B. Audio

This settings tab controls all of the Audio Patches, Mic Patches, volume limits, and default levels for new audio cues added to your workspace. In addition, it allows for the editing of external audio devices for Audio Cues or Mic Cues, routing signals, adding effects, and more. The use of Audio settings is covered in depth in Part II of this book, QLab Audio Control.

C. Video

The Video settings tab allows for the control of Video Surfaces and Camera Patches. A Video Surface is the representation of a real-world area for displaying video content, like a projection screen, wall, or geometric surface. This Video Surface might use one or more display devices (called screens) attached to it to create the desired effect. The Video Surfaces settings show all of the available surfaces attached to your workspace and allow you to edit these or create new ones.

The Camera Patches settings show the number of video devices available for inputting live video into a Camera Cue. QLab 4 can connect to up to eight different video input devices, which are all assigned in the Camera Patches area of Video Settings. The use of Video settings is covered extensively in Part III: QLab Video Control.

D. Light

QLab 4 has added the ability to control lighting systems. As such, there is an entirely new settings tab dedicated to lighting control (Figure 2.5). The Light Settings tab is divided into two sections: Patch and Definitions. The Patch tab allows you to view and edit lighting instruments and groups in your workspace. The Definitions tab allows the user to view and edit a lighting definition for instruments in the workspace, including instrument name, manufacturer, and control parameters. The use of Light Settings is featured in Part IV: QLab Lighting Control.

E. Network

Network Cues (formerly known as OSC Cues) enable QLab to send three different types of messages over your Mac's network connection: OSC messages, QLab messages, and UDP messages. The Network Settings window allows you to configure network patches for up to 16 different network destinations (Figure 2.6). The operator can assign naming, select the network interface type, input the IP address and port number for the network destination, and include a passcode (where necessary).

F. MIDI

Through the use of the MIDI Cue, QLab can send MIDI voice messages, MIDI Show Control (MSC), or MIDI System Exclusive (SysEx) messages. In addition, there are also MIDI File Cues, which are used for playing a MIDI file. Both of these cue types require the use of a MIDI device or network connection. This connection is called a patch. The MIDI Settings window is used for assigning an output patch for MIDI devices. The window is divided into two rows, one for

2.5 a

Figure 2.5
The Light Settings
interface, showing
Patch (a) and
Definitions
(b) tabs.

2.5 b

Figure 2.6
The Network
settings tab with
multiple network
patches.

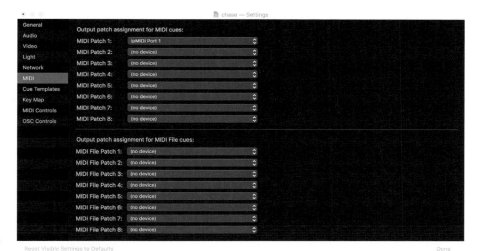

Figure 2.7
The MIDI settings tab showing output patches for MIDI and MIDI File Cues.

MIDI patches and one for MIDI File patches (Figure 2.7). In each instance, you can patch up to eight different MIDI devices or network paths.

G. Cue Templates

In previous versions of QLab, settings like Audio, Mic, Video, Titles, Fade, MIDI, Timecode, Group, Wait, and Script each had separate areas for creating or adjusting default settings for new cues. In Version 4, Cue Templates is the new feature that provides one convenient location for applying these settings. Upon selecting Cue Templates from the left column, a new window will open on the upper right side of the workspace settings featuring an expansive list of cue templates for each cue type available in QLab. The window below this list is called the **Inspector**. The Inspector is an interface that allows you to see and edit attributes within QLab. This interface will be the common tool used in your workspace to change cue settings for all cue types. The number of tabs shown on the Inspector varies, depending on the cue type selected. By selecting a cue type from the Cue Templates upper window, you can create and adjust the default settings for any cue type you select. Figure 2.8 shows the Cue Templates settings for Fade Cues, in which I create a default parametric curve shape with a default time of 6 seconds. Cue Templates are addressed in detail in other chapters.

H. Key Map

One of the most versatile of QLab's functions is the ability to use **Hotkeys**, customized keyboard shortcuts used for triggering certain control or editing

Figure 2.8 Using the Cue Templates settings to establish a default parametric fade curve over a 6-second duration.

functions. The Key Map window shows the default, factory-assigned shortcuts and allows you to change them as needed. For instance, the standard button used for firing GO is the computer's space bar. You can reassign any of the play-back controls to any key on the keyboard (alphanumeric, Space bar, or Control-alphanumeric). The ESC button is pre-programmed to panic all (meaning fade out any cue playing over a brief timespan) or to immediately Hard Stop All if you double-tap the escape button. These settings are the only control hotkeys that cannot be changed.

The Key Map window (Figure 2.9) is divided into two columns – control and editing. The Control hotkeys are used for playback functions, such as GO, pause, resume, Panic, etc. The Editing hotkeys are used to quickly edit cue parameters for a selected cue in your cue list, such as editing cue number, name, notes, target, etc. A mastery of these hotkeys will drastically reduce your programming time and improve your workflow.

I. MIDI and OSC Controls

The MIDI Controls and OSC Controls settings allow the user to set up certain QLab commands that will be triggered via "musical" MIDI controls, MIDI Show Control (MSC), or Open Sound Control (OSC). Essentially, all of these functions exist to allow for QLab to communicate with, control, or be controlled by OSC or MIDI devices (or other instances of QLab running on networked computers). These functions are covered in greater detail in Part V: QLab Show Control and Networking.

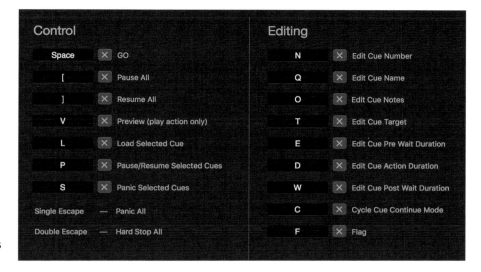

Figure 2.9 The Key Map window, used for setting keyboard shortcuts inside QLab.

2.8 – QLab Preferences

In addition to the use of Workspace Settings, QLab also has application-wide preferences that apply to any workspace created on your computer. Unlike the Workspace Settings, these preferences are unique to your computer and do not travel to another Mac should you transfer the workspace. QLab preferences are accessed through the menu bar by selecting *QLab > QLab Preferences.* Once you select this function, a new window will open called "QLab Preferences," as seen in Figure 2.10. This window is divided into five separate rows with a horizontal line separating them.

At Launch

The upper row of preferences details the software behavior when you first launch QLab. The first preference has a drop-down menu featuring five different choices for launch behavior. The following list describes the preferences and their behaviors.

- **Restore most recent workspaces.** This preference will open the workspace or workspaces that were open the last time QLab was used.
- **Create a new blank workspace.** This preference is the standard setting from QLab 3, in which the program creates a new blank workspace on startup.
- **Create a new workspace from default template.** This preference opens whatever template you have set as a default on startup. To set a workspace template as your default, select *Manage Templates* from the QLab menu, then select a template and click "Set as Default."

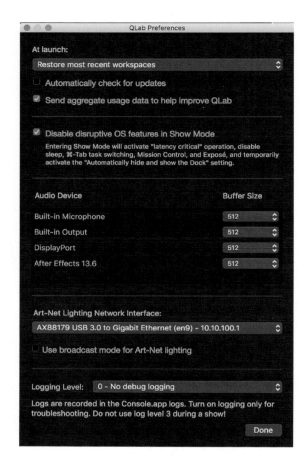

Figure 2.10 The QLab Preferences window, used for establishing application-wide preferences used in any QLab workspace on your Mac.

- **Show the workspace template picker.** This preference opens a template picker menu at launch, allowing you to select a workspace template from the template list.
- **Do nothing.** This preference causes the program to do nothing upon launch.

Updates

The next line in startup actions is called automatically check for updates. When this checkbox is selected, QLab will go online and determine if there is a new version of the software available for download. If there is one available, QLab will prompt you to download and install the update. Updates are never automatically downloaded. It is generally not advisable to change versions of QLab during production since there can sometimes be unforeseen problems that arise from changing to a different version of the software.

Send Aggregate Usage Data

At the time of this writing, this particular preference is not enabled inside of QLab 4. Figure 53 has included the checkbox as a place keeper for the software to enable tracking QLab behavior in order to assist in problem solving for the software. The Figure 53 website indicates that the software "will never include personally identifiable data, media files, or other information proprietary to your designs."

Disabling OS Features

One useful new function of QLab 4 is the ability to disable certain OS functions that have been known to create problems for playback on a Mac. In the past, there was a long list of OS functions that needed to be disabled in order to safely use a Mac as a show computer (see Section 2.9 for a detailed list). With QLab 4, though, there is a quick checkbox that will disable some of the most potentially dangerous OS features while QLab is operating in Show Mode. A list of the disabled features is included below:

- **App Nap:** App Nap is a feature introduced in OS X Mavericks that causes unused applications to go into a paused state in order to reduce power usage and prolong battery life on laptops.
- **Sleep:** Your computer's sleep functions are determined in the Mac's Energy Saver preferences, allowing the computer to go to sleep after a certain period of inactivity. QLab can override your computer's sleep settings.
- **⌘ Tab:** On a Mac, the ⌘ Tab shortcut allows you to move between applications open on your desktop. QLab can disable this shortcut, as it can lead to undesired outcomes when accidentally used during a show.
- **Mission Control:** QLab can also block access to Mission Control, Spaces, and Exposé and temporarily activate the "Automatically hide and show the dock" setting.

Audio Device Buffering

The default buffer size for any audio device connected to QLab is 512 samples. This QLab preference allows you to adjust the buffer size to samples of 16, 32, 64, 128, 256, 512, and 1024. The buffer size is directly connected to latency and audio quality of audio devices, a topic covered in Part II.

Art-Net Lighting Network Interface

As mentioned in Chapter 1, an Art-Net interface is required for sending Lighting Cues out from QLab. This QLab preference allows you to indicate a specific device to be used for sending Art-Net messages. This preference will likely go unnoticed for many users, as QLab can automatically find an interface on its own when left on the "automatic" setting. If you are using a complex network that utilizes more than one network interface connected to different networks with similar addressing schemes, you might need to choose a specific interface. In most instances, though, this will be unnecessary.

Broadcast Mode

Many Art-Net lighting devices support a process called polling, a method by which devices are discovered on the network. If you are using a device that does not support this method of discovery, click the checkbox that reads "Use broadcast mode for Art-Net lighting." Doing so enables QLab to send all lighting data to every device in your network. Clicking this box will also allow QLab to communicate with other software using Art-Net on the same computer. If your device supports polling, it is best to keep this button unchecked, as it will reduce unnecessary network traffic on your system while using Light Cues.

Logging Level

The last row of the QLab preferences window deals specifically with logging debug data. Logging is a method of collecting data for trouble-shooting purposes. This can be particularly useful if you encounter a situation where QLab is behaving in an unexpected fashion and you want to contact Figure 53's support team. There are four different levels of logging available through the drop-down menu: Level 0 – Level 3. Level 0 includes no debug logging at all, and each step up the chain will increase the amount of logging possible. Under normal circumstances, no debug logging should be necessary. In fact, the addition of greater levels of logging can hinder smooth playback of your workspace. As such, it is never recommended to use Level 3 during a show setting.

2.9 – Preparing Your Computer for Running a Show

As mentioned earlier, there are a number of OS functions and processes that your Mac runs in the background on a regular basis. While some of these are essential, others can create an unnecessary drag on system resources for a show computer. It is possible to disable many of these functions to maximize the amount of your computer's resources available to QLab operations. The "Disable disruptive OS features in Show Mode" button inside QLab Preferences will take care of many of these problems without making them apply to all other computer functions. The following section details a few other options and tips for setting up your Mac as a show computer.

Design Tips ▽

Using Terminal

Many of the following tips feature the use of Terminal on your Mac OS and work from the assumption that you have a passing familiarity with this program and its uses. Terminal is an application that lives in your Utilities folder inside Applications. It is a simple command line interface used to provide text-based access to your computer's operating system. For those unfamiliar with Terminal, I recommend doing some research to discover a bit about its function and commands, as it is a powerful timesaving tool when used in conjunction with QLab and other applications. Keep in mind that all commands in Terminal are quite precise. Every character, including spaces, matters to the execution of the command. As such, make sure to pay particular attention to the Terminal commands listed below, and enter them exactly as shown.

Internet Related Concerns

One of the most important things to consider about a show computer is that it should ideally be on a closed network, separate from the possibility of interacting with devices outside of its show network. This is, of course, not always a possibility. Whenever possible, however, following the tips listed below will ensure a safer environment for your show computer.

- **Stay offline when possible.** The process of going online can create unforeseen difficulties, from viruses to slowing down communication on your show computer. The best practice to protect your show computer is simply disconnecting it from the Internet altogether. In addition, if your computer has to be connected to a network to interface with other equipment, make sure that your network is a closed local area network (LAN) that is not connected to the Internet.
- **Turn off Wi-Fi.** There are a number of reasons for using your Wi-Fi, such as creating a closed network in order to screen share or using the QLab remote app. That said, if you are not using Wi-Fi, go ahead and disable the antenna on your computer. This is done by clicking on the Wi-Fi icon on your Mac's menu bar and selecting "Turn Wi-Fi Off."
- **Using online storage programs.** There are a number of online backup and file storage options on the market that are useful for file sharing and off-site access to files. While it may be tempting to rely on these services as a time-saver, it is important to recognize that any background application running on a show-critical computer has the potential for creating numerous problems. Some designers use programs such as Dropbox to transport their show files and media bundles, but it is essential that all files must be

transferred to the show computer's onboard storage and the file sharing software be completely deleted from the computer before using it for show playback.

- **Disable Internet accounts.** There are a number of different Internet accounts that your Mac can use to sync Mail, Calendars, Contacts, etc. It is important that a show computer has disabled these accounts from accessing the Internet, which can have negative effects on your processing (even if your computer is not connected to a network). To disable Internet Accounts, open *System Preferences > Internet Accounts > choose an account, and uncheck all services.* Do this for each account on your Mac.

- **Log out of iCloud.** iCloud is Apple's proprietary cloud storage and cloud computing service connected to media, accounts, passwords, and more. While there are a number of excellent tools associated with iCloud, the system is notoriously persistent at attempting to contact Apple's servers and data centers. When setting up a Mac as a show computer, it is best to simply log out of iCloud. This is done through *System Preferences > iCloud > click on the "sign out" button.*

- **Disable software update.** Once your computer is set up for tech, it is best to avoid any changes to your system altogether. This makes it essential to disable your Mac's software update. This can be done through System Preferences or Terminal. To do so, open *System Preferences > App Store > uncheck the "Automatically check for updates" checkbox.* In Terminal, simply enter this command and press enter: sudo softwareupdate --schedule off

Delete All Extraneous Software

While there are several programs you will need on the computer used for content creation and programming, it is rarely the case that you will need the same programs on your show computer. Deleting any unnecessary applications from your Mac will not only free up storage space, it will also eliminate the possibility of one of these applications interfering with your show playback. Applications are deleted on a Mac by dragging them to the Trash and then emptying the Trashcan (*Control-Click on Trash icon and select "Empty Trash"*).

Disable Notifications

Notifications are an excellent tool for the standard Mac user, but they can certainly get in the way and tie up some background resources if left activated for a show computer. To eliminate this, go into Terminal and input the following command: launchctl unload –w /System/Library/LaunchAgents/com.apple.notificationcenterui.plist

Disable Screen Saver

It is never desirable to have a screen saver pop up in the middle of show playback (especially if the screen saver happens to pop up in your projection design). As such, it is always a good idea to disable your screen saver. This is done through *System Preferences > Desktop and Screen Saver > Screen Saver > select "Never" on the drop-down menu reading "Start after:."*

Disable Spotlight

Spotlight is a system-wide desktop search function built into Apple's macOS and iOS platforms. It routinely indexes all of the files on your computer and all files on attached disks. This process, however innocuous, can create a momentary inability for QLab to access your files and can lead to stuttering or late cue playback. In order to avoid this, Spotlight should be disabled on all show computers. The best method for disabling Spotlight is through Terminal. Though there are Spotlight settings inside of System Preferences, this only changes the categories that appear in Spotlight searches without stopping the disk indexing process. To do this, input the following command into Terminal: sudo mdutil -a -i off

Disable Time Machine

As mentioned earlier, backups can lead to complications, especially when a backup gets initiated during show playback. This is why backups should always be performed manually. Similar to Spotlight, Time Machine (the Mac system backup utility) uses indexing and background processes that can negatively affect your show playback. To avoid this, input the following command into Terminal: sudo tmutil disable

Video Concerns

There are a few steps for setting up your computer that are specific to those doing video work with QLab. If you are only doing sound or lighting, then there is little need for addressing these issues. The following list covers a few concerns that should be addressed for those using QLab for projections.

- **Disable Mirroring.** When using multiple displays on your Mac, there are different options for displaying content. These displays can either be set up to mirror the content of your main monitor or to act independently and allow each monitor to display its own unique content. This is the setting required for using QLab so that the QLab workspace can be seen on your main monitor and video content can be displayed on the attached displays. In order to set this up, you must disable Mirroring (which is the default setting when new displays are connected to your system). This setting is found in *System Preferences > Displays > Arrangement > uncheck "Mirror Displays."*

- **Monitor Arrangement.** When setting up an additional display without mirroring, your Mac views the new display as an extension of your main desktop. Your cursor can travel from one desktop to another by simply sliding the mouse placement off the primary screen and onto the other display. In the Arrangement tab under Displays, you can grab the additional displays and rearrange their placement around the primary display to indicate which side of the primary monitor will lead to the connected display. The default orientation places a new display to the right of the primary display (meaning that once your cursor reaches the right edge of the main screen it will pass over onto the left edge of the second display). One down side of this setup is that your cursor will be displayed over projected video content should you accidentally slide the mouse onto this screen. As a preventative measure, I like to arrange my secondary display to the upper right hand corner of my primary display so there is a smaller window through which the cursor can pass (Figure 2.11).
- **Dock Placement.** In the same Arrangement window, you will notice that one of the displays features a small white bar along the top of the screen. This icon indicates which is set as the primary display. The primary display is where your Dock, Active application windows, and desktop icons appear.

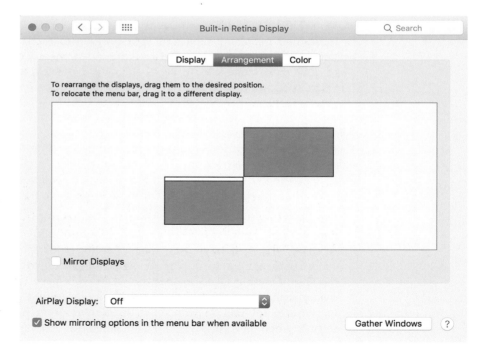

Figure 2.11
Setting the screen arrangement with a secondary display in the upper right corner of the primary display.

It is important to make sure these options remain on the display used for your QLab workspace and not for those used for video output.

- **Menu Bar Placement.** By default, your Mac will add a menu bar to the top of all displays. This can be an unintended addition to your projection design, but luckily there is a quick fix. There are two ways to disable this function. The first is done in *System Preferences > Mission Control > uncheck the box that reads "Displays have Separate Spaces."* The same thing can be accomplished through Terminal by inputting the command defaults write com.apple.spaces spans-displays -bool TRUE

- **Graphics Switching.** Many MacBook Pro laptops have two graphics systems – an integrated graphics processor and a discrete graphics processor. The discrete graphics processor is the higher performance choice of the two. Many people are unaware of a process called graphics switching that occurs with these models, allowing the computer to automatically switch between the two types of graphics processing in order to prolong battery life. Current models of MacBook Pros indicate that discrete graphics processing remains on at all times when connected to an external display; however earlier models may not follow this protocol. As such, I always err on the side of caution and disable graphics switching. This little function is hidden away inside *System Preferences > Energy Saver > uncheck the checkbox reading "Automatic graphics switching."*

- **Black Out Desktops.** One feature that can be problematic is using an image for a desktop background. If QLab is not displaying a video image, any attached displays will show the desktop background. While it is possible to change the desktop background through the Desktop and Screen Saver settings in System Preferences, QLab makes this process much easier through its own Tools menu. Simply click on *Tools > Black Out Desktop Backgrounds.* Keep in mind this will remain in effect until reset. To achieve this, open *Tools > Restore Saved Desktop Backgrounds.*

Design Tips ▼

Backup Systems and Saving Protocol

If you spend enough time working on projects that depend on technology (and, really, what field doesn't now?), you will experience the regrettable sensation of losing work due to a technology malfunction of some sort. It may be the software or even your computer crashing, but it's always a frustrating scenario when you lose any of the hard work you have put into a project. While this experience is virtually unavoidable, there are a number of steps you can take along the way to make sure your loss is minimized.

1. **Be organized.** This sounds like a no-brainer, but I'm amazed by the number of designers I encounter who simply have a collection of files on

(Continued)

their computer. In media terms, these files are referred to as your assets. When creating a design, start off by organizing your assets from the beginning. Create a show folder with a number of sub-folders housed within. Include folders for audio, video, stills, etc. Furthermore, organize those at a deeper level. For instance, your video folder might have sub-folders inside called "research" or "final renders." When naming your files, use something descriptive so that it can easily be identified. While this may not seem to be directly related to backup, it is a time-saver for re-assembling your work once a workspace has been corrupted or you have to start from scratch.

2. **Save frequently.** Clearly, this is an area that everyone knows. Unfortunately, it is also the one that most of us ignore. In QLab, the shortcut to save is ⌘S, or Command-S. Saving isn't just related to in-application work, however. To truly be covered, you should also have multiple backups of your work, which leads to our next point.

3. **Back up your work.** Backing up can become a laborious task, but you will regret not having done so should your show computer crash and you are left without one. Backing up comes in a number of different ways. To truly be secure, you should have multiple backups of your workspace, your assets, and your computer itself. For your work-space, I recommend saving a new file each day using the date (i.e., Macbeth-Mar15), and sometimes I will even make multiple numbered variations for long days of work. By doing this, you are creating a dated series of backup workspaces to fall back on should your current file malfunction. In this way, at least you are only one day behind rather than starting from scratch. For your assets, always make a backup copy on a portable drive on a regular basis. For your computer, creating a Time Machine backup is always a good idea. Just make sure you have configured your computer to do only manual backups so it doesn't interrupt your QLab playback.

4. **Use online file storage.** Online file storage services, such as Dropbox or Google Drive, are excellent resources for designers working in media. I know a number of designers who build their show file and store assets in Dropbox to ensure access options. By adding the Dropbox application onto your Mac, you set up the option of syncing a local folder with the online file storage. Provided that you start with files on Dropbox (during the tech process) and then transfer them to local storage on the show computer, this is a good option. Note that the Dropbox software should always be deleted, as you would with any other non-essential software, and the computer should be removed from the Internet.

Understanding the QLab Workspace

The QLab workspace is a powerful interface for creating and implementing sound, video, lighting designs, and more. One of its strengths is the simple layout and accessibility of tools, enabling users to quickly familiarize themselves with its use. The following chapter details the QLab workspace and enables you to quickly get up to speed on the software's many functions. For those familiar with QLab 3, the layout should be familiar, with only a few key changes.

3.1 – Understanding Cues and the Cue Structure

Cues are the foundation of most traditional control systems for live performance, be it lighting, sound, effects, or projections. In theatre, the time-tested model is assigning cue numbers specific to each type of event to occur during the live performance, then allowing the stage manager to call them out and the operators to hit a go button, thereby triggering the cue. Within QLab, the structure is quite similar in that the workspace is composed of multiple cues with varying specific functions combined for playback purposes. Understanding this structure and how cues function within the QLab system is essential to mastering the software.

What Is a Cue?

In the simplest terms, a cue is a QLab command with an assigned function. For instance, an Audio Cue is a command assigned to play back a given audio file. A Fade Cue changes the attributes of other cue types, such as changing the volume of an Audio Cue or moving the position of a Video Cue. A MIDI Cue sends a MIDI message and so forth. Once you insert a cue into your workspace, it automatically becomes part of a cue list. The **Current Cue List** is shown in the middle row of the page, the largest allocation of space in the workspace. In this window, cues are shown in their playback order featuring a wealth of information about the individual cues in the cue list. An individual cue and all of its listed information (going horizontally across the screen) is referred to as the **Cue Row.**

Visually, each cue row features all of the necessary information about the given cue and all of its properties. The cue row contains (in order from left to right):

1. **Cue status.** This is the first column to the left side of the row, listing information such as whether the cue is on deck, active (running), broken, or flagged. There are particular icons to indicate each of these different statuses (see Figure 3.1).

   The **playhead**, a large gray arrowhead pointing towards a cue, denotes the playback position of the cue list. This icon indicates which cue is on standby to be played when the Go button is pressed. It will always be located first in the cue row.

   Once you press Go, the playhead will move to the next cue in your cue list, and an active cue icon will appear beside the cue being played back. This icon is a small green arrowhead pointing towards the active cue. If you see a small gray slope icon, this means that a cue has stopped playback but the action has an effect that is still tailing out.

   A red x icon indicates a broken cue, or one with some programming error that disables its playback. Whenever you see this icon, the cue will not be able to perform its intended function until the error has been addressed. If you hold your cursor over the broken cue icon, a message will pop up giving an explanation of the problem.

   A red circle with a slash running through it is a sign that an **Override** is blocking your cue's output. Overrides are a method of temporarily blocking QLab from inputting or outputting certain message types. When the Override Controls are activated, there will also be a message in red text in the footer of your workspace indicating what message type is off. More information on the Override function is located in Section 3.8 of this chapter.

   A yellow circle with a triangle inside indicates that a cue has been loaded and is ready for playback. Finally, you might see a flag icon beside a cue. Flags are used as a visual reminder that also appears in the Warnings list. Flagging is addressed in detail in Section 3.2 below. For now, know that flagging a cue will not change its intended behavior.

Figure 3.1 Status Icons: Playhead, Go, Tail Out, Broken Cue, Override, Loaded, Flag.

2. **Cue type.** Each cue performs a specific function, whether it is audio play-back, video, lighting, fading, or sending MIDI signals. The second column in the cue row indicates the type of cue by inserting an icon as a graphic representation of the type of cue.

3. **Cue number.** Each cue will have a unique number to identify it for play-back. When a cue is created, QLab uses a chronological numbering system based on your preferences established in the Settings menu. Typically, cues will be numbered by a sequence of 1. You can later change the cue number, but no two cues can have an identical number. Likewise, should you choose to assign letters to your cues, you can. Just be aware that there is no built-in system for assigning letters and each cue would have to be named manu-ally or by using scripts. Finally, cues do not have to be numbered in order to function. Just keep in mind that certain triggering functions may require the use of cue numbering

4. **Cue name.** The fourth column lists the cue name. The cue name will default to the name of its target file. If you choose to do so, however, the cue name can be changed to anything. Simply double-click the cue name, type in a new one, and press enter.

5. **Cue target.** The fifth column indicates the cue target – the file or QLab cue accessed upon playback. A target may be a file (such as an audio file) or another cue in the workspace.

6. **Cue timing and duration.** The following three columns entitled Pre-Wait, Action, and Post-Wait all relate to the cue timing and duration. Pre-Wait refers to the amount of time set to insert a wait before the action (i.e., adding a 1-second pause before a scream is heard). The Action column lists the duration of the cue (how long it will play). Finally, the Post-Wait refers to the amount of time set to be inserted as a wait after the action occurs. One interesting new addition to QLab 4 is the ability to include a negative post-wait, giving the ability to trigger the next cue a number of seconds before the current cue ends playback.

7. **Continue mode.** The final column in the cue row indicates the cue's continue status. Frequently, a number of cues need to be arranged in such a fashion as to have multiple cues fire simultaneously or to have a subsequent cue start the exact moment one ends. To address these needs, QLab allows three options: Do not continue, Auto-continue, and Auto-follow. Do not continue is the default setting, and as such, there is no icon to indicate this setting. Auto-continue (firing both cues simultane-ously) is indicated by a downward arrow with a triple arrowhead, whereas Auto-follow (firing the subsequent cue once the first is completed) uses a single down arrow with a circle at the top. These icons are illustrated in Figure 3.2.

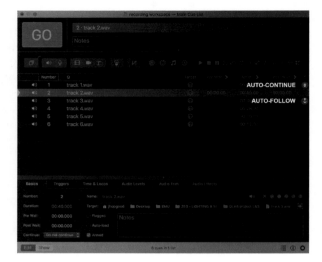

Figure 3.2
Continue Mode
Icons: Auto
continue on top,
with Auto-follow
below.

Design Tips ▼

Using Time Display Modes

For Pre-Wait, Action, and Post-Wait columns, time information can be displayed in one of two different modes: Time Elapsed or Time Remaining. The default setting for new cues is Time Elapsed, showing the amount of time that has passed in the cue's playback. The alternate method shows the amount of time remaining, more like a countdown. To toggle between these different modes, simply click on the angled bracket icon beside the Pre-Wait, Action, and Post-Wait headings. You can assign different time display modes for each of the three columns. Personally, I prefer setting Pre-Wait and Post-Wait as Time Remaining and the Action as Time Elapsed, as this makes more sense to me. Whatever method you choose, consistency is recommended so you don't confuse your operator.

How Do Cues Operate?

Cues operate under a very simple set of rules that correspond to the cue types. For starters, a cue does nothing until it is triggered. Cues can be triggered in a number of different ways: clicking the GO button, pressing the space bar (or keyboard shortcut assigned to GO) or via MIDI or OSC controls from another device or from a cue within the workspace, Timeclock, hotkeys, or an AppleScript that sends a GO command. Once the cue is triggered, it will perform its pre-programmed action, and the playhead will proceed to the next cue in the cue list.

Cue Lists

Cue lists are the collection of cues organized together for a purpose. When you click GO, the cue list will play back cues in the order they were programmed from the top of the list to the bottom (unless special cues are inserted to change the playback order). The playback position icon shows which cue is on standby, or ready to fire. Once you reach the end of your cue list, hitting GO will perform no action unless the playback position is reset to a cue within the cue list. Any workspace can have one or multiple numbers of cue lists within it.

Cue Sequences

Cue sequences essentially mean the order in which cues progress and how they interact with subsequent cues. As described in the cue properties above, each cue has a continue mode. Cues can be set up to have no continue, auto-continue, or Auto-follow. For some projects, you could link together every cue in the cue list to play automatically after the first cue has been fired. The image frequently used to discuss this concept is a series of dominoes: tipping the first domino will cause all of the subsequent dominoes to fall until a stopping point is inserted.

In addition to playback cues, there are also special types of control cues that can manipulate the cue sequence. For instance, a go-to cue could redirect the cue sequence to a cue out of the regular order.

Playback Position

There is only one playback position for a cue list. You can select any cue within your cue list and make that your playback position. Once a cue sequence has been fired, then the playback position will move to the beginning of the next cue sequence (skipping broken cues).

3.2 – The Workspace

Within QLab, each new document you create is called a workspace. A workspace is the collection of collection of cues, cue lists, and carts that will be played back for your performance. Understanding the workspace system is fundamental to mastering QLab. In the following section, refer to Figure 3.3 below to identify the various workspace components. The workspace is broken into four separate rows, which each contain subsets of control and information.

A. GO/Standby/Notes Panel

For each workspace, the top row will contain a panel used to both control cues and view information about them. In the left corner is the GO button. This button, when clicked, triggers any selected cue. In addition to clicking the

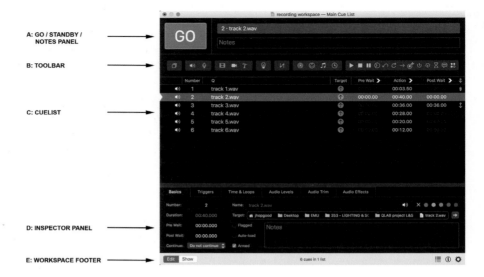

A: GO / STANDBY / NOTES PANEL

B: TOOLBAR

C: CUELIST

D: INSPECTOR PANEL

E: WORKSPACE FOOTER

Figure 3.3
The QLab
Workspace.

button with the mouse, the GO button can be activated by clicking the space bar on your keyboard.

Looking to the right of the GO button will reveal the Standby indicator. This window displays the cue selected to play once the GO button has been clicked. By default, it will show both the cue number and the name.

Directly beneath the Standby indicator is the Notes panel. The function of the Notes panel is to allow for creating a note specific to a cue. While displayed as a small row in the Edit view, once QLab has been placed in Show mode, the window is substantially larger and allows for the programmer to leave notes that might be beneficial or informative for the QLab operator. In addition to text, the Notes Panel allows for inserting pictures, which can be incredibly useful for the operator when triggering playback for a complex piece dealing with dance or fight choreography since there is no script for basing timing on. Another useful tip is the use of copying and pasting into the Notes panel. If you were to create important notes in advance on a cue sheet, you could simply copy and paste them into your Notes. Copy/paste functions will also retain the font, size, style, and color of the original text.

While there are no visible text controls for the Notes panel, if you Command-click (or right-click with some devices) on the Notes panel, the standard Macintosh text editor window will appear as a contextual menu, allowing you to change font, size, color, and style.

B. Toolbar

The second row of the Workspace is a graphic interface called the Toolbar, used for adding cues to your cue list. The Toolbar is visually divided into seven different sections: Groups, Audio, Video, Lighting, Fades, Network/MIDI, and Control Cues. We will delve into the function of these cue types in the following chapters, but the basic use of each category should be relatively self-explanatory.

By clicking on any of the icons in the Toolbar, a cue will be added to your workspace directly after the selected cue. This method essentially leaves the cue as a place keeper until you access the cue and link it to a media file or assign its specific action. In addition, you could also drag new cues into a specific location directly from the Toolbar.

C. The Main Cue List

The third row, which takes up the majority of the workspace, is the main Cue List. Any cue added to your workspace will appear in this cue list. Each cue will be organized in a list fashion, with individual cues on separate rows containing all the pertinent information about the cue (such as cue type, number, file name, target, timing, and cue duration). The organization of all cues into a logical playback order is the foundation of QLab.

Design Tips ▽

Toolbox and Load to Time

There are some functions hidden under the surface of the QLab interface. Previous versions of QLab visibly featured a Toolbox and Load to Time panel. With the release of Version 3, these tools were hidden away to streamline the interface. Use the tips below to access these hidden functions.

Toolbox
The Toolbox is a hidden interface very similar in function to the Toolbar. Pressing ⌘K will open the Toolbox in the left side of the cue list window (Figure 3.4). For beginners, I recommend leaving the Toolbox open while programming for the simple fact that each icon has the cue name typed out beside it. This allows for ease in selecting cues while you are unaccustomed to the icon's meaning. If you are working with a small screen, though, it certainly does eat up a lot of screen space. One incredibly useful function of the Toolbox is the ability to reorder the cues into whatever order you would like. This enables you to put the tools in the most useful order for your purposes and save time with programming.

Load to Time Panel
Load to Time is a function that enables loading a cue or cue sequence to a particular time rather than having to play from the beginning. ⌘T will open

(Continued)

Figure 3.4
The Toolbox is shown on the left side of the cue list window.

the panel, replacing the Cue Bar (Figure 3.5). There are two methods of loading to a time: typing in the desired time on the left side of the panel or using the scrub bar to slide the circle icon to a particular point in the cue. Once you have the desired time selected, pressing the space bar will play the cue from that selected point. A useful, though little known function of the Load to Time Panel, is the ability to input a negative time. By inserting a negative time (i.e., −10) the Toolbar will automatically load up your cue or cue sequence to a point that is 10 seconds *from the end* of playback. This comes in handy for those moments when you just need to go to the end of a sequence.

Figure 3.5
The Load to Time Panel.

It is worth noting that, until you press the "Done" button on the right corner of the Load to Time panel, it will stay up for all subsequent cues. This means that, for those who preferred the old organizational system, you could simply open the Toolbox and Load to Time Panel and leave them open for the duration of your cueing session (though it does cover up the Toolbar).

D. Inspector

The Inspector Panel, located in the third row, is likely the most used component of the QLab workspace, as it describes every available parameter for the selected cue, cue list, or cue cart. Depending on the type selected, there might be anywhere from two to seven different tabs in the Inspector Panel, allowing the programmer to affect every aspect of playback related to the cue. The different uses of the Inspector Panel will be addressed in multiple sections throughout the book. For now, let us address the two tabs that remain consistent for every cue type: Basics and Triggers.

When selecting any cue, cue list, or cue cart, the Inspector will display a series of tabs for control parameters. Each Inspector window will always feature Basics and Triggers. The first tab, Basics, allows for manipulating the baseline information about the selected cue, cue list, or cue cart.

The Basics Tab

There are a number of control parameters listed in the Basics tab related to cue information, naming, continue status, notes, and more. Listed below are the functions as they appear on the tab.

- Number: Assign a cue number
- Duration: This window indicates the length of the cue's playback duration, once triggered.
- Pre Wait: Assign a pre wait to the selected cue
- Post Wait: Assign a post wait to the selected cue

Figure 3.6
The Basics tab contains baseline information and notes.

- Continue: Establish the continue status of the cue as do not continue, auto-continue, or Auto-follow.
- Name: This input allows for the naming of the cue. In addition, beside the name window, there will be an icon that communicates what type of cue it is.
- Color: To the right of the name panel is a row of colored dots. This is the control used to assign a specific color to the selected cue row. Each given cue row can have one of five colors. This allows for ease in assigning a visual representation for certain cue types (i.e., red for sound, yellow for projections, green for MIDI, etc.).
- Target: Assign a specific target file to your cue.
- Flagged: Clicking this button will flag the selected cue, placing a flag icon at the beginning of the cue row. Clicking on this button adds the selected cue to the Broken Cues and Warnings window, a listing of any broken cues or warnings within your workspace. Flagging a cue is a great way to mark a cue that you want to revisit at a later time to correct, as the flag does not change anything about the playback of the cue; it simply marks it for easy reference.
- Auto-load: By checking this box, the selected cue will be automatically loaded when the previous cue is triggered.
- Armed: This button allows you to arm the given cue. Arming a cue means that it will perform its assigned action and pre/post waits. The default is for a cue to be armed. Should you choose to disarm a cue, it will still perform pre and post waits, but not execute the cue action.
- Notes: This tool is used for making notes relevant to the selected cue. Whatever text is entered into this panel appears in the Notes panel for the cue at the top of the workspace. Any notes entered are searchable through QLab's find feature, accessed through the QLab menu under *Edit > Find*.

The Triggers Tab

QLab allows for versatility in control, offering an ability to personalize playback control for different installations. The Triggers tab allows the programmer to expand the control possibilities from simply pressing a GO button to allowing the versatility of Hotkey, MIDI, Wall Clock, or Timecode triggering. Figure 3.7 illustrates functions available in the Triggers tab.

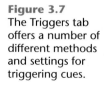

Figure 3.7
The Triggers tab offers a number of different methods and settings for triggering cues.

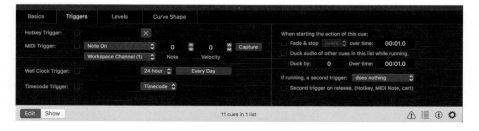

- Hotkey Trigger: This tool allows you to set any key on the keyboard as the trigger for a specific cue. Once assigned, either the space bar or the assigned hotkey will trigger the action. To set a hotkey, simply click in the input window beside Hotkey Trigger and then click the button you want to assign to the action hotkey. Once you do so, this will automatically place a check in the checkbox, noting that the hotkey is active. To deactivate, you can uncheck the checkbox. To remove it altogether, simply click on the "x" button to the right of the input window.

  Note that, when assigning hotkeys, there are certain keys already used by the workspace. In this case a warning message will appear reading "Hotkey used by workspace." These keys cannot be assigned as the action hotkey unless you first go to the Settings window and remove them from the Key Map. In general, you can use any key or key combination on your keyboard excluding the Command key, as it is reserved for other functions.
- MIDI Trigger: This button allows for the programmer to control QLab actions via MIDI either using a MIDI keyboard or another device that sends MIDI control signals. By selecting this function, you could give total control to a performer who could trigger effects from the stage simultaneously with their musical performance.

Design Tips ▼

Assigning a MIDI Trigger

One of the most common functions of using the MIDI triggering is to assign a key on a MIDI keyboard as a trigger for the cue. By clicking on "Note on" in the MIDI Trigger window, this sets the cue to be triggered by a note being pressed on a MIDI keyboard attached to the system. You can input the numeric value for that note in the Note input and assign a velocity to it (meaning the note must be hit with a certain intensity in order to trigger the cue) in the Velocity input. One time-saver is clicking the "Capture" button. After doing so, a message will appear reading "waiting for MIDI" beside the capture button. If you press a MIDI key, it will assign the note and velocity to match this action.

Sometimes velocity can be a sensitive issue in assigning triggers, and you may want to avoid assigning a velocity at all. In this case, simply insert the words "any" or "all" in the velocity input. This will make the cue trigger any time that MIDI note is played on the keyboard. You can also enter "greater than" or "less than" amounts for more precise control (i.e., <10 or >10).

- Wall Clock Trigger: The Wall Clock Trigger allows you to assign an action to a particular time on the computer's clock. To do so, simply input a time in either 24-hour mode (military time) or standard time (selecting either AM or PM). For instance, if you were creating an installation to play a movie at a 6pm every day, you could simply input 18:00:00 or 06:00:00 with pm selected in the drop-down menu. Once checked, QLab would execute the action at that time every day. Should you need to change the event to occur only on a certain day, simply click on the "Every Day" button and select the desired day(s).

• Timecode Trigger: The last setting in the left column of the Triggers tab allows for assigning a trigger based off of the timecode. Every cue in a QLab workspace can be triggered by an incoming timecode – either MIDI Time Code (MTC) or Linear Time Code (LTC). The trigger can be activated by either timecode format or real-time format typed into the window labeled "Timecode Trigger." For Timecode method, the time is inserted in a format of "reel:minutes:seconds:frames." Real-time format uses "hours:minutes:sec onds:decimals." For either method, it is essential to configure your selected cue list to accept incoming timecode.

To do this, open the Cue List Panel (⌘L) and select the desired cue list. The Inspector Panel will now feature three tabs: Basics, Triggers, and Timecode. Click on the Timecode tab, and select the checkbox reading "Trigger cues in this list from incoming timecode." Select the appropriate mode to match your timecode format – either MTC or LTC (see Figure 3.8). Select the Sync source from a drop-down menu of possible input sources and then select the SMPTE fomat that matches your incoming Timecode. When completed, this will allow your cue list to be triggered from an external timecode.

New Trigger Settings

Version 4 introduced a new way for one cue to interact with another, hidden inside of the Triggers tab. The column on the right side of the Triggers tab has a series of checkboxes under the heading "When starting the action of this cue." Each of these boxes allows the programmer to determine how the triggering of the selected cue might affect the playback of other cues in the cue list. The settings are included below:

• **Fade & Stop over time.** If checked, this box will fade and stop other cues over a time inputted into the box. There is a drop-down menu that allows

Figure 3.8
The Timecode tab for a cue list contains options for triggering cues via Timecode.

you to decide which kind of other cues will perform this action. Peers are a way of categorizing cues together into a hierarchy system. Cues in the same Group would be considered peers. If an ungrouped cue is selected, then its peers would be the other cues in the cue list or cue cart that contains this cue.

- **Duck audio of other cues in this list while running.** This setting dictates that the volume of all other cues in the cue list would be decreased upon triggering the selected cue. There are two boxes for inputting control data. The first box is for indicating the number of decibels by which other cues should decrease. The second box is for inputting the duration of time over which the fade should occur.

- **If running, a second trigger.** The final control allows for changing the behavior of the selected cue upon receiving a second trigger. There are five different options within a drop-down menu for how this cue will respond to a second trigger. The first option is **"does nothing."** Previous versions of QLab behaved in this fashion, essentially saying that a second trigger given will result in no action. The **"Panic"** setting indicates that the cue will fade out and stop when it receives a second trigger. This will occur over the default panic time set for your workspace. The **"Stop"** setting means that a second trigger will instantly stop playback of the cue. A **"Hard Stop"** setting indicates that the cue will stop and also immediately stop any audio effects that might remain attached to the cue. Finally, the **"Hard Stop & Restart"** setting will perform a hard stop on the cue and immediately restart the cue upon receiving a second trigger.

    Another interesting setting in this area is the checkbox labeled "second trigger on release." This setting applies to cues that have a hotkey or MIDI trigger assigned to them. When checked, this enables the second trigger to be fired when the hotkey or MIDI trigger is released. In other words, you could program a certain sound to be triggered by pressing down a key on your keyboard and set to stop when the key is released. By doing this, you can set up QLab to function like a sampler.

E. The Workspace Footer

The bottom row of the QLab workspace is a small gray bar that runs along the bottom of the application window. This is referred to as the Workspace Footer. There are three main divisions of information held in the Footer, divided into the left side, center, and right side.

Edit/Show Mode

In the left portion of this workspace footer are two button: one labeled Edit, the other Show. These two buttons indicate the two different modes for QLab function. Edit allows the programmer to access all of the control functions of any cue, whereas Show allows for only playback and locks out the editing of any cue in the workspace. By toggling through these two modes, you will discover a considerable difference in the layout and function of the program.

Cue and Cue List Count

In the center of the Workspace Footer is a short, informational section detailing the number of cues, cue lists, and carts used in your workspace. This is also where certain indicators will appear, such as the override controls.

Warnings Panel

Moving to the right corner of the footer, there will be either three or four icons, depending on your programming. The first icon, Warnings, is present only if there are flagged or broken cues in your workspace. A broken cue is displayed as a red x in the cue row of the affected cue. By clicking on the Warnings button, a window will open with four tabs. The first tab is the Warnings list, showing each cue that is broken or flagged and detailing the warning for those cues. This is a fast way to look over a cue list and determine what errors need correcting. One excellent addition to this tool is the "Copy Warning Text" button.

In addition to warnings and broken cues, this window also houses a great amount of information about your workspace, including logs, Art-Net information, and info such as your workspace ID and Machine ID. This information can be quite useful in trouble-shooting and in communicating with QLab support. If there are no warnings or notes in your workspace, these final three tabs can be accessed by clicking ⇧⌘W.

Lists, Carts, and Active Cues Sidebar

The next icon shown on the bottom right hand corner is the Lists, Carts, and Active Cues Sidebar. By clicking on this button, a sidebar will open in the right corner of the current cue list (Figure 3.9). This panel performs three functions: to show available cue lists and carts; to show which cues are active (currently playing); and to control the playback state of all active cues.

Cue Lists and Carts: The programmer has the potential for creating an unlimited number of cue lists or carts for any QLab workspace. This function allows for a thorough organizational structure. Think of using one cue list for preshow music, one for different acts within a play, intermission, etc. Though this is not necessary, it can reduce the workspace clutter for a particularly large production. In addition to using a cue list for playback purposes, sometimes I will create a cue list as a quick palette from which I copy/paste into my current cue list and then delete it after programming. Cue Carts allow for a more non-linear approach to playback and give a more interactive feel to your workspace. These are covered in detail in Section 3.9 of this chapter.

Figure 3.9
The Lists, Carts, and Active Cues Sidebar.

Upon selecting either a Cue List or a Cue Cart from your list, the main window will be replaced with the chosen cue list or cart. This allows you to explore the different lists and carts in order to edit their functions. In terms of creating cue lists, you can select any cue or number of cues from your current cue list and simply click on the "New List" button to move them from your current cue list into a new cue list. In addition, once a cue list has been created, you can simply drag cues from your current cue list into the desired cue list. If you want to add the cues to the new cue list without removing them from the current list, simply select the files and copy and paste them into the new cue list. If you need to delete a cue list, select the desired cue list and select Edit > Delete from the QLab menu, or use the ⌘ + delete quick key. It should be noted that cue lists are treated as any other cue type in QLab – they are simply a cue that holds other cues within them. By clicking on a cue list, you will notice that a set of options appears in the Inspector Panel called Basics and Sync. These preferences control the basic naming functions, as well as allowing for the triggering of a cue list via Hotkey, MIDI, Wall Clock, or Timecode.

Cue lists are tied to group cues in a fundamental way. If you have a Group Cue created in your workspace and drag it into the Cue Lists Panel, it will automatically create a cue list. Likewise, dragging a cue list from the Cue Lists Panel into the current cue list will result in creating a Group Cue containing the selected cues.

Active Cues: Clicking on the Active Cues tab opens a panel showing the number of active cues (or cues currently in playback on your cue list).

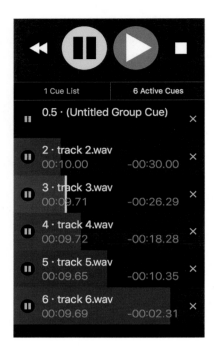

Figure 3.10
The Active Cues
Panel shows
currently active
cues and their
elapsed time.

Depending on your workspace state, there will be a varying number displayed on the Active Cues tab. If nothing is currently active it will read 0 Active Cues, and clicking on it will only show a blank screen. When there are active cues, though, clicking on the tab will reveal a list of active cues and their time elapsed (how long they have been playing) with an x button listed at the end of each row (Figure 3.10). This x represents a panic button which, when activated, will fade the selected cue out over a 5-second duration. This panel can be incredibly useful when using Fade Cues in a cue list. A Fade Cue can mute the volume of an audio cue, but unless it is set to "stop target when done" the audio cue will continue to play, though muted. If you have a series of these cues playing in the background, the CPU usage goes up even though they are muted. Using the Active Cues Panel is a quick way to spot if you have cues playing longer than their desired duration.

Active Cue Control: At the top of the Cue List and Active Cues Panel, you will find four buttons used to control the playback of all active cues. The Reset All button stops playback and resets all cues to their original state (i.e., moving the playback position back to the beginning of the cue, etc.). The Pause All button pauses all currently running cues, while the Resume All button resumes playback of all paused cues. Finally, Panic All, stops the playback of all cues.

Settings – ⌘, (Command-Comma)

The final icon on the right side of the Footer is Settings. Clicking on this icon will open the Workspace Settings window, covered in the last chapter.

3.3 – Adding Cues

New cues are added in one of three ways. The first, mentioned above, is to use the Toolbox or Toolbar to insert a cue place keeper, then assigning a target and attributes within the cue. For media based cues like audio or video, you can simply drag a media file into the cue list. By doing this, the appropriate cue type will be generated and the target will be pre-established. Finally, there is a series of hotkeys for inserting a new cue type. These commands are listed below.

Shortcut	Cue Type
⌘0	Group Cue
⌘1	Audio Cue
⌘2	Mic Cue
⌘3	Video Cue
⌘4	Camera Cue
⌘5	Text Cue
⌘6	Light Cue
⌘7	Fade Cue
⌘8	Network Cue
⌘9	MIDI Cue

3.4 – Setting Targets for Cues

For many cues in the workspace there will be a target. No cue type can have more than one target. As mentioned before, a target is either a media file or another cue within the cue list to be affected by the selected cue. If inserting cues as place keepers, you will eventually need to assign a target for your cue. Like most functions in QLab, there are multiple ways to do this.

For cues that play media files (sound, video, MIDI) the method is different from cues that affect other cues (fades, control cues). For media playback cues, you can click on the upwards-facing arrow icon in the Target column and a window will appear in which you select the desired target file (see Figure 3.11). If this method seems a bit too time consuming, another option is to simply drag and

Figure 3.11
Clicking on the arrow icon in the Target window opens a Finder window for assigning the target file.

drop the desired media file directly onto the cue row. This will automatically target the file. Be careful to actually drop it on the desired cue, though, and not above or below, as this will have the undesired effect of creating a new cue rather than targeting the cue in question.

Some cue types (like the Fade Cue) are used to affect other cues. When inserting a cue such as this, you will see a yellow question mark in the Target column instead of the arrow icon. There are three ways to establish the target for these cue types.

1. Drag the desired target cue (i.e., Fade cue) onto the receiving cue (the Audio Cue to be faded up or down in volume)
2. Drag the receiving cue onto the desired target cue
3. Double-click on the yellow question mark and use your keyboard to input the cue number of the desired target cue

When attempting to set a target via the drag and drop method, the cue will show you if the targeted file is of a type it can affect. If you drag your cue to another and a shaded rectangle appears surrounding the potential target cue, this means that it can be set as the target (see Figure 3.12). If this does not occur, the cue is not an acceptable type for your cue. Examples for this would be trying to assign a Fade Cue to another Fade Cue. In this case, one Fade Cue cannot target another, so the shaded rectangle would not appear.

Figure 3.12
The shaded
rectangle indicates
a targetable file
type.

3.5 – Navigation and View Quick Keys

As with most programs, there are a number of quick keys to increase productivity. Listed below are some of the most useful shortcuts for navigating your workspace.

Shortcut	Description
↓	Select the next cue (when cue list is selected)
↑	Select the previous cue (when cue list is selected)
+	Move to the top of the next cue sequence
–	Move to the top of the last cue sequence
→	Expand the selected Group Cue
←	Collapse the selected Group Cue
>	Expand all Group Cues in the cue list
<	Collapse all Group Cues in the cue list
⌘↓	Select the next cue
⌘↑	Select the previous cue
⌘→	Toggle to the next tab
⌘←	Toggle to the previous tab
⌥⌘↑	Move the Playback position up
⌥⌘↓	Move the Playback position down
⌘I	Open/Hide Inspector Panel
⌘K	Open/Hide Toolbox
⌘L	Open/Hide Cue Lists/Active Cues Panel
⇧⌘L	Toggle between Cue Lists/Active Cues
⌘B	Open the Warnings Panel
⌘,	Open Settings

Design Tips ▼

Searching the Workspace

One great productivity function is the ability to search for text within your cue list. Simply click ⌘F and a search tool will open in the place of the Cue Bar. Insert the text you want to search for, and QLab will search through the cue numbers, cue names, file names, and notes to find the text you inputted. It will highlight all of the results featuring the text, and then you can use the arrow key controls in the search tool to jump from result to result until you find the desired reference.

3.6 – Paste Cue Properties

As a note for users of the earlier versions of QLab, copy/paste functions have moved from the Tools menu into the Edit menu. The ability to copy and paste parameters within QLab 4 has greatly expanded. Dubbed "fancy paste" by the Figure 53 team, this new tool allows you to copy some or all of the properties from one cue and paste it into one or more subsequent cues. This applies to any or all of the parameters available in the Inspector.

By selecting any cue in your workspace and copying it (*Edit > Copy*, or ⌘C) you are placing a copy of all of this cue's parameters onto your clipboard. To paste any or all of these parameters, simply select another cue and paste cue properties (*Edit > Paste Cue Properties*, or ⇧⌘V) onto the selected cue. This will open a window showing you which attributes were copied from the previous cue, allowing you to select the desired attributes to paste into the selected cue. This is done by clicking on a checkbox beside the desired cue attributes (Figure 3.13). It is worth noting that the cues do not have to be the same type of cue in order to paste cue properties. The window will select for you what properties are applicable to the selected cue.

3.7 – The Tools Menu

In addition to the number of functions available via quick keys or buttons, there are also a number of productivity tools located under the Tools heading in the control window at the top of the screen. Of the ten tools listed below, they can either be activated under the Tools menu or by selecting the quick key listed below. It is important to note that some of the Tools functions will change according to the cue type that is selected in your cue list. For instance, selecting a Fade Cue will open another subset of tools not present when examining an Audio Cue. These tools are addressed in the area labeled Fade Tools at the end of this section.

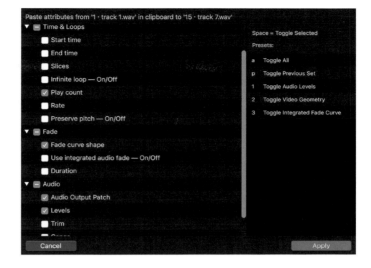

Figure 3.13
The Paste Cue Properties window allows you to select which attributes you would like to paste onto the selected cue.

Load to Time – ⌘T

Using the Command T-function toggles the Load to Time menu with the Toolbar.

Renumber Selected Cues – ⌘R

This tool allows the programmer to select a group of cues and renumber them. Upon pressing Command-R, a pop-up window will appear asking for the start number and increment of change for subsequent cues.

Delete Number of Selected Cues – ⌘D

Similar to the last tool, this one selects the cue numbers of a selected sequence of cues. The main difference is that, instead of renumbering, this tool simply deletes the cue numbers altogether.

Jump to Cue – ⌘J

This tool allows for quickly moving to a cue within the cue list. Simply click Command-J and a pop-up window will appear, asking which cue number you would like to jump to.

Jump to Selected Cue's Target – ⇧⌘J

Like the Jump to Cue tool, selecting this tool allows you to jump to the target of the selected cue.

Record Cue Sequence

The Record Cue Sequence tool is an exciting new addition to QLab 4 that enables you to play through a cue sequence manually and record your specific playback timing as it is triggered. This process creates a Group Cue with Start Cues imbedded within to trigger your cue sequence. These start cues will have pre-waits or post-waits attached to them that enable an exact playback to match your timing. To use this function, click on "Record Cue Sequence" in Tools. This will open a window that gives you two recording options (Figure 3.14).

Both settings essentially create a Group Cue populated with Start Cues to trigger your files. The first setting enables all of the Start cues to fire simultaneously with the appropriate pre-waits attached to them to match your original timing. The second option creates a Group Cue that triggers the first Start cue and then goes to the next cue with pre-waits and Auto-continues attached to each Start Cue. Both will result in identical playback, but you may find one better suits the needs of your particular programming preferences.

It is important to note that the Group Cue created by this process only contains Start Cues. It does *not* have the cues necessary for playback of your media or triggering lights. In the interest of keeping an organized workspace, it might be wise to create another Group Cue inside that you place your cues and triggers. Another option is to create a new cue list and drag these files into that list. The important detail here is that your original media cannot be deleted, or the Start Cues will have nothing to trigger. It can take a bit of getting used to, but it certainly opens up a number of options for programming.

Live Fade Preview – ⇧⌘P

The Live Fade Preview setting enables you to make adjustments to Fade Cue settings and hear the results in real-time (provided that the target cue is

Figure 3.14
The Record Cue Sequence window, with both recording options shown.

START ALL SETTING

START FIRST SETTING

playing). In previous versions, this function did not exist, and any changes made in the middle of a fade did not reflect what the true outcome would be. This new setting is very helpful to the programmer who wants to hear the changes without stopping and restarting a cue sequence with each change. On the other hand, it can prove fairly distracting in a tech or rehearsal setting to make live changes for everyone to hear. If you want to make changes without it affecting live playback, simply click *Turn off Live Fade Preview* or press ⇧⌘P.

Highlight Related Cues

This function is an excellent productivity tool that serves a simple purpose, to highlight all cues that target or are targeted by the selected cue. This will highlight the cues in a gray highlight color.

Black Out and Restore Desktop Backgrounds

The last two tools in the Tools menu are related to the desktop background image on your Mac. By clicking on "Black Out Desktop Backgrounds," your default background image will be replaced with a black screen. This is useful for projections to give a neutral black background and protect your computer's desktop background from being accidentally displayed as part of your projection design. In addition, this function cuts down on ambient light given off by your monitor. You will note that the majority of the QLab screen is in dark gray and black to keep screen glow to a minimum. Blacking out your desktop background will further decrease any unwanted light. To reset the default background, simply click the "Restore Saved Desktop Backgrounds" prompt in Tools.

A. Fade Tools

There are four tools that are only available after selecting a Fade Cue. These tools all function as an extension of the paste properties function listed in Section 3.6, but each is connected to how Fade Cues relate specifically to their target cues.

Set Parameters from Target

The first tool allows you to set the parameters of your fade to match that of the target cue. This is the same "fancy paste" function, but automatically linked to the target of a selected cue. By clicking "Set Parameters from Target," the paste cue properties window will open, showing you the available parameters to be pasted from the target cue onto the Fade Cue.

Set Audio Levels from Target – ⇧⌘T

This second tool is as simple as the name implies. It copies the audio levels from a target cue and applies them to the Fade Cue. Once again, clicking on this tool opens the paste cue properties window with checkboxes preselected for Audio levels and gangs. In addition to using the Tools menu, you can also select the Fade Cue and click the "set from target" button inside the Audio Levels tab of the Inspector.

Set Video Geometry from Target – ^⌥⌘V

Like the tool above, this one will copy certain parameters from the target cue onto the selected Fade Cue. In this instance, it selects the Video properties by default (opacity, translation, aspect ratio, scale, and rotation). Any or all of these parameters can be selected and pasted onto the Fade Cue.

Revert Fade Action

The final tool is used to reset any changes made to a target cue to its state before being affected by the Fade Cue. In previous version of QLab, once the fade action had occurred, the only way to reset the cue to its original state was to stop the cue. This simple addition enables more complex changes to fades without having to constantly stop playback.

3.8 – The Window Menu

The Window menu in QLab 4 is a quick tool for controlling the appearance of your workspace window and accessing any of the various other windows that might be used within your workspace.

At the top, the first two commands are quick methods of accessing the zoom and minimize functions of the workspace. Zoom will automatically make your workspace fill the entirety of your display. Minimize will place the QLab workspace into your dock. This can also be performed with the keyboard shortcut ⌘M. Directly below these options are links to the Workspace Settings and Workspace Status windows.

The Audition Window

While some of the tools in the Window menu can be accessed via icons on the workspace, others are not immediately apparent in looking at the workspace and are only accessible through the Window menu itself. The first of these tools is the **Audition Window** (Figure 3.15). To open the Audition Window, either click *Window > Audition Window* or type ⇧⌘A. The purpose of the Audition Window is to have an onboard method of listening to or watching your cues

Figure 3.15
The Audition
Window allows
for live previewing
of cue playback
without having
a physical
connection to your
audio or video
system.

without having to be directly connected to your system. This is especially useful for situations where you cannot connect to the theatre's sound or video system, but need to edit cues off-site. Once opened, the Audition Window serves as a new destination in which audio and video cues will play back (instead of the normal patch to which it is assigned). Once the Audition Window is open, the GO button will be replaced with an Audition button to indicate this new audition patch.

Override Controls

Another function hidden way in the Window menu is called Override Controls. Clicking on *Window > Override Controls* or ⇧⌘O opens the Override Controls window. This allows you to temporarily halt the input or output of a number of different message types in QLab. These message types consist of MIDI voice messages, MIDI Show Control (MSC), MIDI SysEx, OSC, Timecode, and Art-Net output. Activating these overrides will add certain visual notifications. With input overrides engaged, a message will appear in red text inside of the Workspace Footer. Once outputs are engaged, any cue with a message being overridden will display a red circle with a line through it on the cue's status column. This indicates that the message will not be sent when the cue is triggered. Note that Override Controls will not keep a cue from being triggered, simply disallow the signal from being sent.

Lighting Controls

The following section of the Window menu is devoted to lighting controls. Since we will be covering this in depth in later chapters, it is sufficient to say

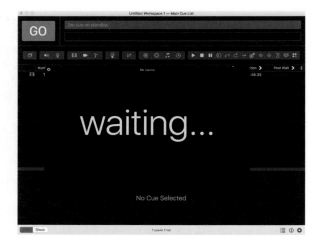

Figure 3.16
The Timecode
window.

that these are the menu items that open the Light Dashboard, Light Patch, Light Library, and DMX Status. Each of these windows serves different functions in creating and editing attributes for light fixtures, establishing control parameters, live control, and observing the status of your DMX universe for diagnostic purposes.

Timecode Window

The next window tool is the **Timecode Window,** a display that shows the incoming timecode for your workspace. By clicking *Window > Timecode,* you will open the window as a moveable screen (Figure 3.16). This window will display the message "waiting…" until the timecode is received. Once a transmitted timecode is detected, the counter will begin ticking away. This is a particularly useful tool in situations where timecode is used as a trigger.

3.9 – Cue Carts

QLab 4 introduces a new way of interacting with cues, outside of the traditional cue list, called **Cue Carts**. A cue cart is a collection of cues that operates in a non-linear function with no Playhead, Auto-follows, or Auto-continues. The layout of the Cue Cart is visually similar to a drum machine, featuring a grid of cells into which you insert cues for playback. It is simply a grid-style interface that allows easy triggering of cues with no regard to sequence (Figure 3.17). The cells in a Cue Cart can hold every type of cue (with the exception of Group Cues).

To view cue carts, click on the Lists, Carts, and Active Cues icon at the bottom of your workspace window. This will open a sidebar on the right side of your

Figure 3.17 Note the number of cue carts shown in the sidebar. This cart is set up with a 3x4 grid layout.

screen. This sidebar will show all cue lists, cue carts, and active cues in your workspace. Click on the button labeled "New Cart" to make a new cue cart in your workspace. You can create multiple cue carts for one workspace, and they will all be listed in the order of their creation on the List and Carts window. It is possible to rename cue carts by double-clicking on the cart and typing in a unique new name. To change the organization of any carts or cue lists, simply drag them up or down inside of the list.

When selecting a cue cart, you will notice that the Inspector has three tabs listed inside: Basics, Triggers, and Grid Size. These controls are used for setting up the parameters of your cue cart. The Basics and Triggers tabs function in the same fashion as previously described in Section 3.2. The Grid Size tab is a quick way of setting up the grid matrix for your cart by assigning numbers of rows and columns. There is a series of 12 check boxes that will change the layout of your grid from 1x1, up to 8x8. When looking at these numbers, keep in mind the first number represents rows and the second represents columns. This means that a 3x4 grid would feature three rows and four columns, as seen in Figure 3.17. The cells of the grid will automatically resize themselves to fit the space given, though there is a minimum size constraint. One interesting side effect can arise when changing the grid size after inputting cues. If you have filled out the grid of your cue cart and then change the grid size to be a smaller format, a certain number of cues will become invisible. For example, changing a 4x4 grid format to a 3x3 format will make one column and one row appear invisible. This can be a bit unsettling the first time you experience it, but rest assured that your cues have not been deleted, only hidden from view. These cues are still a part of your cue cart and can still be activated through a trigger; they will simply not be visible to trigger manually.

Speaking of triggering, there are a number of different ways to trigger cues in a cart for playback. When your workspace is in Edit Mode, there will be a play button located in the upper right corner of each cue. Clicking on this will activate playback. Once the workspace is set to Show Mode, clicking anywhere on the cue will trigger it. Likewise, any cue can have triggers assigned in its Triggers tab of the Inspector. These triggers function in the manner described in Section 3.2, allowing for triggering through Hotkeys, MIDI, Wall Clock, or Timecode. If desirable, a cue within Cue Cart can also be controlled via a Control Cue (start, pause, stop, etc.) or Network Cue inserted into a cue list. These cue types are addressed in detail in later sections of the book.

In a manner of thinking, Cue Carts function similarly to a Group Cue, by holding numerous different cue types inside of them. Each cue added to the grid has a cue name and a cue number, just like in a regular cue list. The cues also function in the same way, meaning that once one is selected you will have an Inspector window open at the bottom of the screen that can be used for editing the cues and their playback functions. Just like a Group Cue, though, keep in mind that deleting the Cue Cart will also delete all of the cues you have created inside of the cart. More applications for the Cue Cart can be found in Chapter 11.

PART II
QLab Audio Control

QLab and Audio Basics

Before one can truly understand the applications of a program like QLab, it is necessary to understand the basics of sound systems and how they function. The following section details some of these core concepts.

4.1 – Audio Systems

For most designers or technicians in the entertainment industry, audio systems fall into three basic categories: recording systems, reinforcement systems, and playback systems. **Recording systems** tend to consist of a Digital Audio Workstation (DAW), a computer running sound editing software in conjunction with audio interface hardware. This audio interface allows the user to convert the analog signal from a microphone into a digital signal for editing in the audio software. With the decrease in cost of computers and the proliferation of mass-market software, such as Apple's Garage Band, most anyone can experiment on their own DAW. Recording systems allow designers to create the audio that will be played back in live performance later.

Typically speaking, a recording system will have a computer running at least one sound-editing program. Many designers utilize multiple programs for their varying strengths. Common applications for this are Apple's Logic or Avid's Pro Tools. Pro Tools or Pro Tools Express comes bundled with a consumer-grade series of digital audio interfaces that allow users to plug in ¼" TRS, RCA, or XLR cables for recording purposes. In addition to analog outputs for speakers, there are also headphone outputs for monitoring purposes. This type of setup is shown in detail in Figure 4.1.

A **reinforcement system** exists to take live sound and amplify it for live perfor-mance. The traditional reinforcement system utilizes microphones to pick up live audio and send it through signal processors (like an audio mixer, EQ, effects processors, etc.), then through amplifiers, and finally out to speakers. Figure 4.2 illustrates this type of setup. Until QLab 3, the software had no integrated

A TYPICAL RECORDING SYSTEM

Figure 4.1
A simple recording
system.

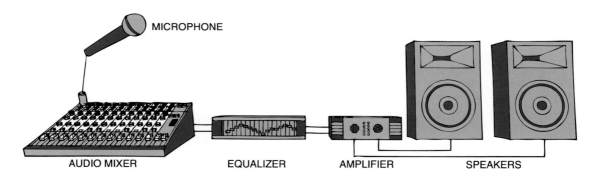

MICROPHONE

AUDIO MIXER   EQUALIZER   AMPLIFIER   SPEAKERS

Figure 4.2
A simple
reinforcement
system with one
microphone.

reinforcement controls. With the addition of the Mic Cue in Version 3, though, QLab added reinforcement to its repertoire. QLab Mic Cues can control up to 24 input signals, activating a microphone, setting levels, assigning Audio Unit effects (such as reverb, EQ, etc.), and more.

Playback systems are a combination of equipment necessary to play back prerecorded audio in a live performance situation. In the past, the audio source files were saved on everything from reel-to-reel, Compact Discs (CD), or Mini-Discs. Today, almost all live performance venues use some type of computer running a software system to play back audio files. Like the reinforcement system, the audio signal might be sent out through an audio mixer and signal processors before being routed through amplifiers before ultimately outputting through the speakers. Depending on the budget and needs of your installation, QLab 4 can function almost totally independently of traditional audio equipment like audio mixers, EQs, and other signal processors. Of course, each setup has its own specific needs, and rarely are any two systems exactly alike.

4.2 – Basic Audio Equipment and Terminology

The world of audio can seem a bit intimidating to the beginner with the vast amount of equipment and terminology. While audio equipment is not the main focus of this book, there are some basic terms necessary to understanding how to set up a sound system. The following section details typical reinforcement/ playback system components and their functions.

Microphone

A transducer that turns audio waves (sound) into electrical signal. This signal is low voltage and not powerful enough to activate a speaker on its own, so it is necessary to send the signal through other hardware components. Typically speaking there are two types of microphones most used in live performance situations: a dynamic microphone or a condenser microphone.

- A **dynamic microphone** utilizes a small moveable induction coil attached to a diaphragm. The coil, positioned in the magnetic field of a stationary magnet, moves when sound waves strike the diaphragm. This movement creates small electrical impulses. These impulses are the signal that will later be translated through a speaker into sound. Dynamic microphones are sturdy and resistant to moisture and require no external power source to operate. These attributes make the dynamic microphone a common choice for live performances, particularly in the club environment.
- A **condenser microphone** utilizes the same diaphragm concept as the dynamic mic, but instead of the induction coil, uses small stationary metal plates and another series of magnets attached to the diaphragm. As the diaphragm moves, the change in proximity of the magnets to the plates creates small electrical impulses that become the audio signal. Condensers are typically much more expensive than dynamic mics, but also have a wider frequency response range – meaning they can capture a wider range of sounds and tend to be more sensitive to volume. Unlike the dynamic microphone, though, a condenser mic requires external power in order to power the microphone. This is typically supplied from the audio mixer in the form of "phantom power," a 48-volt power supply sent from the mixer to the mic.

Input Source

As previously stated, the input source can be any of a variety of different devices. Professional CD or Mini-Disc players were once a common component for their ability to allow the user to cue a CD track to a certain time for playback. Though these still remain in some playback systems, computers have largely replaced them for their ability to run playback software like QLab, which far surpasses the function of a CD.

Mixing Console

Hardware used to combine multiple audio signals and allow the user to create a mix of these signals to output in different ways. The console (sometimes called an audio mixer or sound board) routes signals, sets volume levels, and affects the qualities of the audio signal. Most consoles receive a variety of different signals in a live performance: audio signals from the playback computer, vocals from singers, multiple channels of audio from different instruments in the band, boundary microphones on the stage, and more. The basic purpose of the mixing console is to take all of these different audio signals and combine them into a mix, with all of the levels and effects combined together. There are a wide variety of digital and analog mixers, many of which create multiple sub-mixes and send these out through effects, signal processors, and recording units.

Signal Processors

Devices that affect the quality or timbre of the audio signal. Most typical would be equalization (EQ), audio filters, reverb, delay, and dynamic processing. Some mixing consoles have built-in signal processors whereas some signal processors are standalone devices. In addition to dedicated signal processing units, computers also have the capability of running a plug-in program to affect the quality of an audio signal. In the Mac architecture, these plug-ins are referred to as **Audio Units (AU)**. QLab has the ability to use AU plug-ins as **Audio Effects**, a simple, non-destructive method of adding signal processing within the QLab software.

Amplifier

A device that increases the audio signal to a high enough electrical impulse to power a passive speaker. Amplifiers must be plugged in to an external power source in order to amplify the audio signal.

Speaker

A transducer that changes the electrical signal from the audio source into audio waves (sound). Speakers come in many different varieties related to what frequency of sound they best produce. In general terms, speakers are categorized as either active or passive. In the simplest terms, **Passive Speakers** are speakers that require an external amplifier or powered mixer to work. In contrast, **Active Speakers** (sometimes referred to as "self-powered") have built-in amplifiers in their speaker cabinet so you can plug line level signals directly into the back of the speaker and create sound. These speakers work well for on-location events and have slightly bulkier cabinets due to the additional hardware enclosed. One disadvantage to these speakers is the need to be plugged in to a power source near where the speaker will be positioned.

4.3 – Understanding Basic Signal Flow: Input/Output

Sound systems have a reputation for being confusing. Part of this is due to the fact that often no two systems are designed in exactly the same way. No matter the number of components added to a sound system, though, the same basic concepts apply. Audio signals start from an input source and proceed along the path until they reach the destination of the output (often speakers). This concept is known as **signal flow**, or how the audio gets from its source to the speakers and what happens to it along the way. Think of audio as a flow of water that travels along a series of pipes (audio cables) and through several different faucets (mixers, amps, etc.) along the way to its final destination of the speaker.

For most audio devices, there is both an input that allows the audio signal in and an output that allows for the signal to be passed on to another device down the chain. The most basic sound system would include a microphone, an audio playback device, a mixer, an amplifier, and a speaker. When adding QLab into the mix, there is another layer of routing to consider within the software itself. The following section breaks down the basics of QLab's software signal flow and details how audio is controlled within the QLab software system.

4.4 – Understanding Software Signal Flow

Before delving into the different methods of setup for QLab audio, it might be wise to first discuss in detail the idea of QLab software signal flow. I use the term software signal flow because, as QLab is a program, there is no signal flow in the traditional sense. Instead, the audio signal is routed through many different control functions of the software before outputting to the audio device. Figure 4.3 illustrates the key concepts of QLab's signal flow. Refer back to it often for the following description.

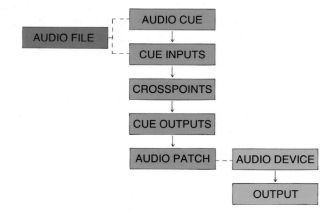

Figure 4.3
The QLab Software signal flow illustrated from file storage to audio output.

Audio File

The audio file is a digital recording of an audio signal saved onto the computer's hard drive. This file is targeted by an Audio Cue for playback but not, strictly speaking, a component of QLab. The nature of the audio file, be it mono, stereo, or multi-channel audio, affects how QLab utilizes it within the Audio Cue. The number of channels in the audio file equate to the number of inputs for the Audio Cue.

Audio Cue

The Audio Cue is the heart of the QLab audio playback system. When inserted into the workspace, the Audio Cue targets an audio file for playback and allows a number of control functions, such as time and looping, volume levels, output patch control, trim, audio effects, and more.

Inputs

Each channel of the targeted audio file is translated as an input for the Audio Cue. Typically speaking, most audio files are either mono (one channel) or stereo (two channels). This means that, unless you are dealing with a multi-channel audio file, most Audio Cues will have only one or two inputs. It is worth noting that, even though most files only utilize two input channels, QLab allows for up to 24.

Crosspoints

Crosspoints can be thought of as a way of routing the audio signal from an input into a Cue Output. In audio engineering terms, this is referred to as bussing. The audio file is bussed down the row to each of the 64 crosspoints. It is up to the programmer to then assign the audio signal to one of the 64 cue outputs associated with the crosspoints.

Levels Faders (Cue Outputs)

The levels faders within an Audio Cue control the amount of the audio signal transmitted into the audio patch. A Cue Output is routed into an Audio Patch, which finally connects to the audio device.

Audio Patch

The audio patch is another layer of abstraction between the audio file and its ultimate destination of the speakers. Essentially, QLab allows for connecting your computer to one or multiple audio devices at once. The patch is the software link between QLab and the audio device or devices.

Audio Device Output Routing

The final layer to the signal flow within QLab is the device routing. By selecting the Edit Patch function within QLab, you can open an interface that then allows you to route the audio signal from the Audio Cue into the desired output channels of the audio device. For this step, the Audio Cue Output from above is now the audio device's input. By using the crosspoints matrix of the Device Routing window, you then route the cue output into one or more level faders for device outputs. Following this, the device outputs the audio signal into the remaining components of your sound system (mixer, signal processing, amplifiers, speakers).

4.5 – A Word About Audio Devices

As mentioned before, QLab can output its audio signal through up to eight different devices in its Audio Output Patch. Though it defaults to the onboard sound card, it will instantly recognize any other digital audio device connected to the system. These devices might be connected via FireWire/USB/Thunderbolt/PCIe or a digital audio network using network protocols, such as Dante or MADI. In the former instance, the digital audio interface outputs either an analog or digital audio signal into your system. The latter method is exclusively a digital signal, transferring audio signals across a network cabling system that provides a pure digital signal from the source to the output. One aspect to consider is the cost of these audio devices. An external audio interface typically costs between $300 and $4000, though you might find some outside this range. The price range of a digital audio network is considerably more expensive.

When working with a limited budget, it might be tempting to try to avoid using an audio interface and simply use the stereo output from your computer's headphone jack directly into an audio mixer. This can lead to complications, however. It is important to consider that the signal from a headphone jack is a high impedance unbalanced audio signal, whereas most professional audio equipment requires a balanced, low impedance input. In addition, you run the risk of accidentally sending phantom power back up the line from your audio mixer into your computer, thereby destroying a port on your computer. Always double-check to make sure the phantom power is disabled before plugging in or, better yet, try inputting into a "line" input that does not supply phantom power. If you absolutely have to output directly from your computer's 1/8" jack, always be sure to include a **Direct Input (DI)** box between the computer and mixer (Figure 4.4). The DI is an audio tool used to change the signal from unbalanced to balanced and minimize distortion, noise, and ground loops (Figure 4.4).

4.6 – Audio System Configurations

There are a number of different possibilities for setting up a sound system with QLab as your playback controller. The following examples illustrate a few of those different configuration possibilities. In addition, these are all examples of relatively simple sound systems. The goal of this section is merely to introduce you to the basics of audio systems rather than provide an in-depth analysis of equipment. For continued reading, I recommend the excellent book *Sound Systems: Design and Optimization* (3rd edition) by Bob McCarthy (Focal Press).

Basic Stereo Playback System with Multiple Speakers

The playback system shown in Figure 4.5 is a simple audio system with four speakers. The computer running QLab is the input source, supplying audio files for playback and allowing the designer to manipulate the file in a number of

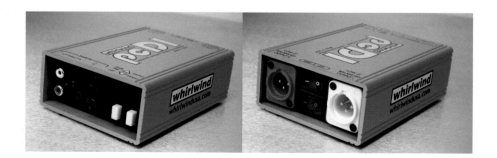

Figure 4.4
The Whirlwind
pcDI Direct Box.

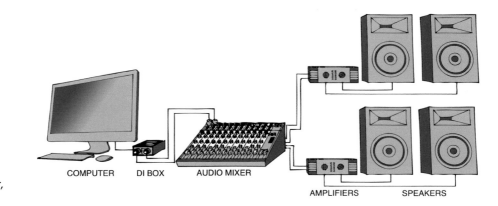

Figure 4.5
Basic playback
system with
QLab, DI, mixer,
amplifiers, and
four speakers.

COMPUTER   DI BOX   AUDIO MIXER

AMPLIFIERS   SPEAKERS

ways. In this configuration, the audio outputs through the computer's built-in sound card via the 1/8" stereo headphone jack. This stereo signal passes into the DI box, and outputs from the two separate output channels (left and right channels) assuring a balanced signal from each channel. From here, the two signals pass into an audio mixer. With a little creative patching, the sound designer would be able to route this signal to multiple speakers through the audio mixer. This would not be automated within QLab, but it is a functional solution when the budget doesn't allow for purchasing an audio interface. From the audio mixer, the signal travels into the amplifiers and then out to the speakers.

Multichannel Playback System with External Signal Processing

In the previous system, the use of stereo output is a definite limitation of QLab's capabilities. QLab 4 has the ability to output its audio feed to up to 64 independent channels (up from the 48 channels available in Version 3). This means that, by plugging in an audio interface, your audio could be routed to any one of 64 separate speakers (providing the device had 64 outputs). There are a number of different types of audio interfaces available, from PCI devices built in to your computer system to external audio interfaces connected via USB, FireWire, or Thunderbolt. Most mainstream external interfaces come equipped with anywhere from four to 16 analog outputs. The system shown in Figure 4.6 utilizes such an external device connected via FireWire, sending out audio signals to six different speakers. In this example, the six outputs from the audio interface go into an audio mixer that allows the designer added control. The mixer then outputs the audio signal to three different EQs, allowing for equalization of each signal. From the EQs, the signal passes through three

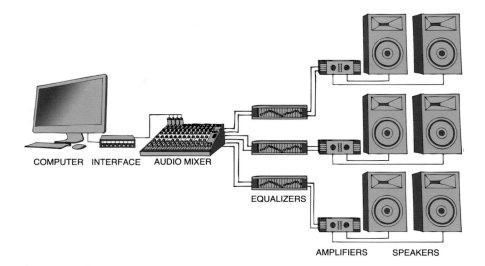

Figure 4.6
A multichannel
system with
QLab, digital
audio interface,
audio mixer,
EQ, amplifiers,
and six speakers.

separate amplifiers and then out into the six speakers. In this system, the use of the mixer and EQ gives a higher level of control to the designer with regards to signal processing.

Multichannel Playback System with QLab Signal Processing

This final system utilizes the functions of QLab 4 in order to eliminate some of the additional external hardware. Like the system above, the computer outputs to an external digital audio interface that outputs the audio signal through six independent channels. In this example, though, using Audio Units through QLab negates the use of an audio mixer and equalizers (Figure 4.7). By assigning Audio Units to individual cues or device outputs, the designer can achieve equalization, reverb, compression, filtering, and more without investing in expensive hardware. Perhaps more importantly, this setup allows a great amount of flexibility for little-to-no additional cost. All of the signal processing can be added, eliminated, or balanced at the click of a button *within* QLab rather than having to physically change settings on hardware.

As you can see, there are a number of different systems to choose from and each has its pros and cons. It has been my experience that the versatility of QLab is its strongest feature. How I use it is exactly that: how *I* use it. As you spend some time getting to know the software, you will likely find other configurations that work best for your individual needs. That's the fun of designing and programming – each project has unique needs and offers up different challenges from the last.

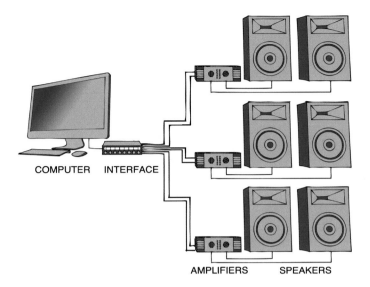

Figure 4.7
A multichannel
system with
QLab, digital
audio interface,
amplifiers, and
speakers.

Design Tips ▼

Redundant Systems

No matter how much money and time you spend setting up the perfect playback system, there is simply no accounting for computer failure or device malfunctions. When every aspect of your sound is coming through one computer, you have left yourself in the unfortunate situation of having no sound at all should your computer crash. A redundant system is the best possible option for protecting your show since it has two QLab computers attached to the same system and firing simultaneously. Should one computer malfunction, you switch from one computer to the other and continue with playback.

The best method for setting up such a system is to not have these two computers connected to each other in any way. Instead, use a MIDI trigger device that sends a GO signal into both computers simultaneously. One excellent choice is the GO Button, listed in Chapter 22. The GO Button 6 allows for control of up to six different pre-programmed commands that can output to two different computers. Should you have a digital console that outputs MIDI from user-defined buttons, you could use that as well.

(Continued)

The next aspect to consider is how to handle switching your signal from one computer to the next. The easiest solution is to use a dedicated mixer that can be used to mute the correct channels. Without a mixer, an external switcher of some type is required, such as the Whirlwind AB-8, an eight-channel audio switcher that allows for quick switching from A-channel to B-channel. What's more, several of these units can be linked together to accommodate for larger setups.

While a redundant system is definitely more expensive and time-consuming to set up, it is an essential factor to consider in setting up your QLab rig. Better safe than sorry.

Setting Up QLab with Your Audio System

As we learned earlier, QLab's default setting is stereo output unless connected to an external audio device. For basic sound systems, this could be all that you need for functional sound playback. In many situations, though, it is necessary to create **directional sound**, sending your audio signal to speakers positioned around your audience so the audio has a realistic feel originating from the correct location. Nothing kills the credibility of a sound design like having music from an onstage record player ring out through the house speakers. We all know that the sound should originate from the object that creates the sound. Luckily, with QLab, an audio device with multiple outputs, and a few speakers, you can make directional sound with ease.

5.1 – Multichannel Sound Systems

A **multichannel sound system** is a type of sound system that incorporates multiple speakers for sound playback, each with its own control channel, thereby allowing for the maximum flexibility of volume and panning. This concept is often confused with surround sound because of its similarity. It is important to note, though, that the concepts we are discussing, while similar, are not the same as the surround sound found in your local movie theatre. Surround sound mixing is a complex process of assigning direction within the DAW. The multichannel method used in this chapter can be a stereo signal routed to individual speakers within QLab or a multichannel WAV file with each channel pre-assigned to an individual speaker. Also, it is important to note that for the purposes of this chapter we will discuss multichannel sound systems specifically for the live theatre environment. Though we will focus on theatre, these principles are applicable for any type of project, from outdoor venues to found spaces or trade-show floors.

When discussing multichannel sound systems, we will use a basic system layout that is common to many theatres (see Figure 5.1). In this system, there are

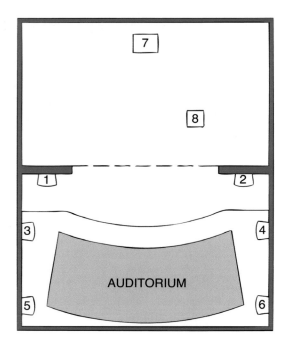

Figure 5.1
A simple,
multichannel
sound setup for a
theatre space.

eight individually controlled speakers – three are stereo pairs, with the last two being used on their own. As you can see in Figure 5.1, speakers 1 and 2 are the stereo pairs (meaning speaker 1 gets the left channel and 2 gets the right channel) located on the proscenium. Speakers 3 and 4 are stereo pairs located in the front sides of the auditorium. Speakers 5 and 6 are stereo pairs located in the rear sides of the auditorium. Speaker 7 is a subwoofer located on the stage – in this case in the rear of the stage, pointed towards the back wall of the theatre to diffuse the sound. Finally, speaker 8 is located inside a prop used onstage during the show – that pesky record player we mentioned earlier. All audio files being used are stereo, but we will configure QLab to send those two channels to any of the eight independently controlled speakers to create directional sound.

5.2 – Audio Settings

As seen in earlier chapters, there are a number of different settings and preferences that can change how you use QLab. These settings are fundamental concepts to setting up a QLab audio system. This section will address how to configure the Audio Settings through your Workspace Settings. Follow along by clicking on the gear icon in the lower right hand corner of your QLab workspace, which opens the Workspace Settings window. After opening this window, click on "Audio" located in the left column.

Figure 5.2
Selecting a device to patch from the device list.

The Audio Setting window is divided into a two by two grid, with two rows and columns. The left column is dedicated to patching audio devices into your system, for either Audio Cues (in the upper row) or Mic Cues (in the lower). In order to output Audio or Mic Cues, QLab must be connected to an audio device – whether the onboard sound card on your Mac or some type of an external device. Any Audio or Mic Cue can be assigned to output to one of the eight different patches, meaning that you can have separate sounds running to up to eight different devices. A friendly reminder though – if you want to output to this many devices at once, you will definitely want to maximize RAM, bus speed, and hardware drive speed. Although QLab automatically recognizes audio devices attached to your system, you must use the patch window to assign particular devices to your patch in positions 1–8. Note that the same devices can be patched in different ways for Audio Cues and Mic Cues.

For the Audio Cues patch, Patch 1 will default to "Built-in Output" (your computer's sound card) until another device is connected. In order to change the device assignment to a patch channel or change a device once assigned, simply click on the drop-down arrow at the end of the middle gray box. This will open a device list, showing which audio devices are connected to your system (Figure 5.2).

Volume Limits

Another important function of the Audio Settings is the Volume Limits tool. This feature is located in the upper right corner of the Audio Settings window (see Figure 5.3). The purpose of volume limits is to allow you to set the peak volume output desired for your system as well as indicating the lowest audible volume levels in your system. These functions are addressed below.

The MAX limit is a simple concept – allowing the user to set a peak level for volume output. This function is best suited to protect equipment and hearing. Before the cueing process begins, it is best to go into the space for your project and test the extreme limits of volume. Start with a good rock song and slowly raise the MASTER slider until the volume reaches an uncomfortable level. This

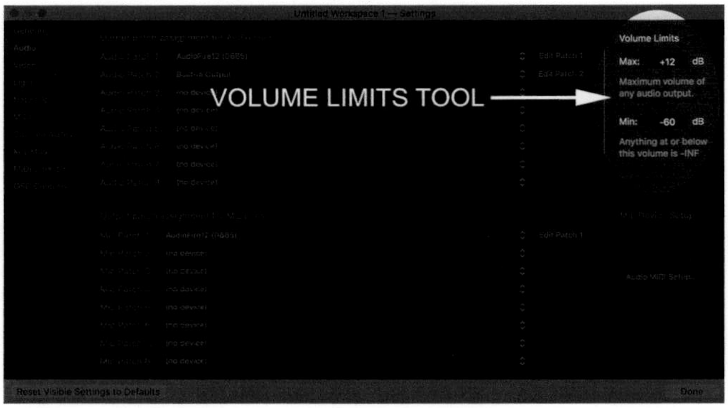

Figure 5.3
The Volume Limits tool is used for establishing a minimum and maximum volume output for your workspace.

is your MAX volume setting. This simple step can save your equipment from being damaged by an inadvertent volume spike.

On the other end of the spectrum, it is important to tell QLab what level is perceived as silence in your system. If QLab thinks –60 dB (the default MIN level) is silent, but your system is silent at –45 dB, then all of your fade-outs will sound too abrupt, as they will reach silence faster than expected. To eliminate this, use the same song as above and slowly pull down the MASTER fader until you cannot hear any volume output. Note the –dB level setting at which you cannot hear sound from your speakers. This number is your MIN volume output. This simple step will save you a lot of time during tech if you take a few minutes up front to set volume limits.

Mic Settings

The bottom row of the Audio Settings deals with Mic Cues. In order to take advantage of the Mic Cue, you need an audio device with inputs for microphones and outputs to send the resulting microphone signal. Due to clocking inconsistencies between separate devices, *Mic Cues must always use the same device for input and output.* It is also worth noting that the audio device used for Mic Cues should ideally have phantom power capability so that you use condenser microphones that require the 48v power signal to operate. Figure 53, LLC has an exhaustive user-created list of audio devices that have been tested in the QLab environment at wiki.Figure53.com.

Essentially, a Mic Cue allows you to insert into your cue list a command that activates the input (or inputs) of an external audio device and/or mutes them. Through the Mic Patch settings, you can route the audio input signal produced by the microphone out through any of the device's outputs.

The settings tab for Mic Cues mirrors that of Audio Cues, without a volume limits control (as the MAX and MIN volumes are the same as those set in the

Audio Cue settings). There are eight Mic Patches that allow you to edit the device in the same fashion as an audio cue.

5.3 – Cue Templates

For those familiar with QLab 3, you will likely recall that the default audio levels used to be located inside of the Audio tab inside Workspace Settings. In Version 4, all default settings for cues (all cue types, not just Audio) are now contained in the Cue Templates window. In the following section, we will address the first step to setting up your QLab show computer with an audio system, creating default audio levels for your Audio Cues. Once you have opened the Cue Templates window, click on Audio. This will open up an Inspector Panel at the bottom of your screen that is used for creating cue templates for all of your Audio Cues. For now, we're only going to address the content in the Audio Levels tab. The other windows in the Inspector Panel will be addressed in Chapter 6.

The Audio Levels control panel (Figure 5.4) is the starting point for setting up how QLab deals with signal flow for Audio Cues. Not only does this panel allow for the creation of default volume levels it also is the method for establishing the path that the audio signal follows on its way to the audio device. When first looking at the screen, you will notice that it is divided into two columns. The left column has three rows inside that control audio patches, default volume levels, and ganging of controls within your mixer.

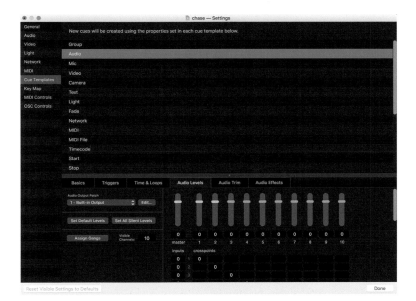

Figure 5.4
The Cue Templates Window is used for establishing all of the default settings for Audio Cues and levels.

Audio Output Patch

In the upper left corner of the window, you will see the Audio Output Patch. As mentioned earlier, an audio patch is the digital path that an audio file takes between an Audio Cue and the audio device. There are eight Audio Patches, which can each be assigned to a different audio device in the Audio Settings tab as mentioned in Section 5.2. Before making any changes to the default audio levels, you must first make sure you have assigned the appropriate patch. The default setting for Audio Patch 1 should be "Built-in Output." This is your computer's built-in sound card and speakers. If you want to select a different patch, click on the arrow at the end of the Built-in Output button and select the desired patch from the drop-down menu (see Figure 5.5).

Figure 5.5
Picking the appropriate Audio Patch through the drop-down menu.

The Matrix Mixer

In the right column is the **Matrix Mixer,** an important interface in the QLab environment that is used to control audio routing and signal flow in multiple different applications (see Figure 5.6). The control structure can seem a bit intimidating at first, but once you understand a few key concepts, you can begin navigating the system with ease.

The Matrix Mixer is a fundamental tool for controlling audio inside QLab, so it is essential for your success to understand how it functions. In short, the Matrix Mixer is a combination of controls that route your audio signal from the Audio Cue to an assigned audio device and control key aspects like volume and output. The beginner might take some getting used to the interface, as its attributes and functions change somewhat for its use in different scenarios. The following section breaks down the Matrix Mixer interface and its use. Refer back to Section 4.3 to see how many of the following components fit within the larger picture of software signal flow discussed in the last chapter.

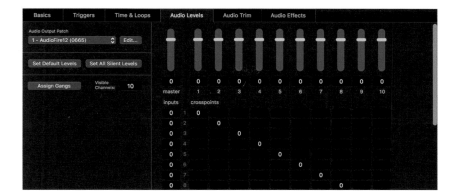

Figure 5.6
The Matrix Mixer
as seen in the
Audio Levels tab.

When looking at the Matrix Mixer (Figure 5.6) for the first time, there are a few keys to understanding how it works. The first important concept is that this is a graphic representation that is meant to resemble a real-world audio mixer. As such, there is a simple grid made up of rows and columns. The horizontal rows represent inputs coming into the mixer, whereas the vertical columns represent outputs from the mixer going to the next step along the chain. Each input can be routed into any of the outputs. Once you understand this basic concept, the rest is simply adapting that knowledge to fit the different ways in which QLab uses the Matrix Mixer. For the following section, we will look at how the Matrix Mixer is used within the Audio Cue to send a signal out to an audio device.

Inputs

The column on the left side of the Matrix Mixer, numbered 1–24, represents the cue inputs. The cue input is the signal coming from the audio file targeted by your Audio Cue. Most audio files are recorded as stereo, meaning they only have two channels of audio, the right channel and the left. In this case, since the signal has only two channels, your setup would only need to address the first two cue inputs (meaning rows 1 and 2). If the recording was mono, then you would only need to have one cue input assigned (row 1). Keep in mind that each Audio Cue has the potential of up to 24 Audio Inputs. In some situations, the audio files might be created as multichannel audio, meaning that you could have multiple input channels. Note that each input is aligned with a series of (up to) 64 cells to its right. These cells, listed 1–64, are referred to as crosspoints.

Crosspoints

Crosspoints are a method of assigning an input signal to a Cue Output. The collection of all of the crosspoints is referred to as the **crosspoints matrix.** Each audio input is bussed to every crosspoint to its right, though they can be set to mute. If the cell is blank, then no signal is being sent onward. The volume

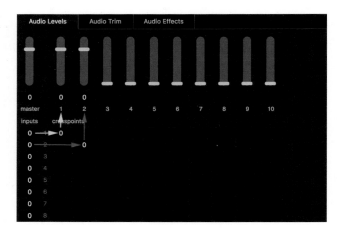

Figure 5.7
In this setting,
Cue output 1
(the left channel
of the audio file)
is routed into
Crosspoint 1. Cue
output 2 (the right
channel) is routed
to crosspoint 2.

settings in these cells determine how much of the audio signal will be sent on to the cue output on a level from –60 (the smallest amount of signal passing through) up to 0 (the full signal being sent through).

Looking at a basic stereo setup with only two speakers, input 1 would be assigned to crosspoint1 in its row. Input 2 would then be assigned to the crosspoint 2 in its row (seen in Figure 5.7). Each of these crosspoints is then connected to the fader shown directly above it at the top of its column. These faders represent the Cue Outputs, the last step the cue takes before going into its assigned audio device.

Cue Outputs

Each Audio Cue has up to 64 possible cue outputs, as represented by the levels faders at the top of the columns. Each column, 1–64, receives any audio signal that is turned on in the crosspoints matrix beneath it. Each cue output can thereby receive an audio signal from any of the 24 Audio Inputs.

By default, input 1 is assigned to cue output 1. This is repeated for each subsequent channel, with input 2 connected to cue output 2, and so on. This typically means that the left channel of audio is in fader 1 and fader 2 controls the right. For a multi-speaker system, though, it is common to reassign the signal so that input 1 outputs through multiple crosspoints, allowing the audio signal from channel 1 to be passed into multiple speakers.

Setting Levels Faders

The sliders at the top of the window are referred to as the levels faders. These levels faders control the amount of audio signal that goes through the cue outputs and into the audio patch. This slider is a graphic representation of classic faders on a soundboard. The cell directly beneath the slider is a numeric representation of the volume output in decibels (dB). As you slide the fader up and down, you will notice the numbers change from +12 (at the highest) down to −59.9 (at its lowest). −60 will automatically default to a MUTE setting, with no number in the cell.

In audio, the term *UNITY* is an important concept to understand. On a traditional soundboard, there is a point roughly 2/3 of the way up the slider that will be labeled as +0 dB or UNITY. Essentially, this means that you are neither adding to nor taking away from the original audio signal. This is why the faders always default to the 0 position in QLab.

Another key concept that can be confusing to the beginner is that 0 *does not* mean no volume. To take the volume all the way to silence, pull the slider down to the bottom and notice that it now has no text in the box below it. This means there will be no audio signal passing through the channel – or that it is MUTED. A quick key that can help you in setting levels is to ⌥click on the slider. This will toggle between MUTE and UNITY.

Master Fader

You will note that there is a **master fader** on the left of the screen (positioned above the inputs column), in addition to the sub-faders in a row to the right. The master fader controls the mix of all outputs, relative to their original levels. In other words, the master controls the overall volume output of the combined group of faders, allowing for the increase or decrease of all cue outputs from one fader.

Design Tips ▼

Balancing Audio Output

A goal of any audio project is to create a well-balanced sound mix, with the appropriate amount of audio coming out of each speaker. Frequently, different amplifiers (even those of the same make and model) will output at differing volume levels. Outputting an audio file with the same output levels on each channel will, in this situation, lead to an unbalanced mix where some speakers output at louder levels than others. To eliminate this problem, it is best to set up default levels for each of your outputs so that each speaker outputs at an ideal volume (even if this means that it needs to receive more or less of an input).

The simplest way to set default levels would be to go into QLab and play an Audio Cue on infinite loop. Pick something that has a nice range of audio

(Continued)

with low, mid, and high-frequency sounds. Also, make sure the volume levels in the original recording are neither too loud nor too soft (look at the waveform to see if this is the case). Next, go to the Audio Levels tab of your Audio Cue and pull each of your output sliders all the way to the bottom to mute their output. Slowly bring them up one at a time until you get your desired mix. Once you have done this, write down the levels and open the Workspace Settings window. Select Cue Presets, Audio, and then Audio Levels to access the default audio levels settings. Set these sliders to match those from your notes. This will guarantee that each Audio Cue you add to your workspace will begin at the appropriate preset audio levels. If you find a need to change the individual cue, you can do so within the Audio Levels tab for the cue in question.

Keep in mind, you will need to have a different type of mix for each space and show you work on. Sometimes it is preferable to have all speakers outputting at the same volume. At other times, it might be advantageous to have the house front speakers at a louder level. The designer must determine the needs for each given project.

Default, Silent, and Gangs

Another set of tools for setting default levels is located in the left column of the Audio Levels window in Cue Templates. These settings allow you to Set Default Levels, Set All Silent Levels, and Assign Gangs. The first two need little explanation. **Set Default Levels** takes the current audio settings in the Matrix Mixer and saves them as your default levels. Keep in mind that this function changes somewhat when used inside of the actual Audio Cue. When you have an Audio Cue selected in the workspace, clicking the Set Default Levels button will assign the default levels to that cue rather than recording it as a default. **Set All Silent Levels** simply removes all routing and volume levels from the Matrix Mixer.

The final tool, **assign gangs**, allows you to pair faders or even crosspoints together into groups so that any action taken by one will affect the ones linked together. For instance, once you have set your default levels for audio cues, you might want to gang together all of your stereo pairs so that the front of house speakers are paired together and will either increase or decrease together. This may not work for all installations, but many times it will save you lots of work to do so. To assign gangs, simply click the Assign Gangs button and then insert a naming system into levels window beneath faders. For instance, if you wanted to pair together stereo pairs in your system, you might insert the letter A into the cells under Faders 1 and 2. Once you click Assign Gangs for a second time, this ganging will apply to your Matrix Mixer and any volume changes made to Fader 1 will also affect Fader 2.

5.4 – Editing Audio Patches

After having set the default levels for new Audio Cues and assigned the signal routing, the next step is to look at the audio patch. To this point, we have looked at simple two-channel systems. When using an external audio device, especially one with more than two outputs, you will need to fully understand the process of assigning device routing for your audio device. These controls are found in the Audio Patch Editor, by clicking on the Edit button to the right of the chosen audio patch.

Audio Patch Editor: Cue Outputs

Upon clicking the Edit button, a window will open called the Audio Patch Editor. This tool is used for assigning the routing from Cue Outputs to Device Outputs, which are the physical connections for outputting to your sound system. The Audio Patch Editor has three tabs: Cue Outputs, Device Routing, and Device Outputs. The Cue Outputs and Device Outputs tabs are used almost exclusively for adding global audio effects. As such, we will examine these in detail in later chapters. There is one important aspect of the Cue Outputs tab to examine at this point, though. The Cue Outputs tab features a list of 64 separate Cue Outputs, each in a separate row with information beside it. Located to the right of the Cue Output # is a cell with a number inside ranging from 1–64. This is the default name for your cue outputs. One interesting feature of cue outputs, however, is the ability to name them whatever you want. To do so, simply delete the number and type the individual name into the box. This is useful for creating a logical naming system, such as Stage Right Proscenium, Stage Left Proscenium, and so forth. Doing so will replace the number of the cue output in your workspace with a specific name, making it easier to program levels quickly and know exactly which speaker you are controlling.

Audio Patch Editor: Device Routing

The second tab of the Audio Patch Editor is called Device Routing. This allows for routing your audio to the output of the audio device. Built-in Output will only be stereo (meaning there will be only two channels of output – one for left and one for right). The window is similar to the Matrix Mixer in audio levels, though it functions slightly differently (see Figure 5.8).

When looking at the Matrix Mixer inside the Device Routing tab, the layout remains the same as audio levels, but the corresponding labels are a bit different. First, look to the left of the screen in the Matrix Mixer. You will notice that there are 64 inputs rather than the 24 seen when setting up default audio levels. This is because *the Cue Outputs serve as inputs for the Audio Device*

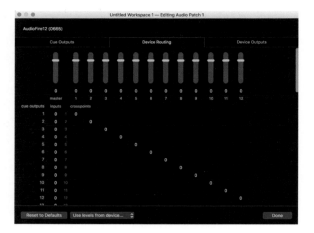

Figure 5.8 The Device Routing Tab is used to assign cue outputs to the appropriate device output or outputs.

Routing. The column to the left of the screen labeled **inputs** corresponds to each of the 64 cue outputs from an Audio Cue and indicates how much of the audio signal will be transmitted into the crosspoints matrix to the right. Again, if the input level is set to 0 (which is the default), then this means that channel 1 of the crosspoints will receive the full signal strength of the audio signal. If necessary, you could decrease the amount of signal so that one or more of your crosspoints received a diminished signal. To set the level on this, simply click the box to highlight the number 0 and then slide your mouse down to decrease volume or up to increase (noting that 0 dB is the maximum amount).

Crosspoints

Using the crosspoints matrix, you will select a device output (or outputs) for each of the inputs and assign the level of signal from 0 db UNITY all the way down to –60 dB. The most common configuration would be to assign input 1 to output 1 input 2 to channel 2, and so on. In this configuration, each Audio Cue's level fader corresponds directly to the same number of device output. Since the intention for this example is to create a basic stereo output, then input 1 will be routed into output 1 at 0 dB and input 2 into output 2 at 0 dB (see Figure 5.8). In this configuration, Fader 1 will control the left channel, and Fader 2 will control the right channel.

Audio Patch Editor: Device Outputs

The final tab in the Audio Patch Editor is called Device Outputs. You will notice that this window looks quite similar to the Cue Outputs tab. That is because the Device Outputs and Cue Outputs work in exactly the same fashion. The key difference is that Device Outputs deals specifically with the physical outputs of your audio device, so there will only be as many outputs listed as are present on your audio device. The second key difference is that Device Outputs cannot be renamed. They will always be represented simply as numbers.

5.5 – Setting Up QLab with an Audio Device

Now that we understand the basics of how to create patches and set default levels for Audio and Mic Cues, the next logical step is to set up QLab to "talk" to the interface in question. There are a few steps to go through in order to make it work correctly, but once you have done so, programming for your multichannel sound system in QLab becomes a snap.

For all of the following examples, we will address the use of an audio device with multiple outputs and show how to set up QLab to send out eight channels of audio to the eight independent speakers in the multichannel system illustrated in Section 5.1. Since many of you might not own such a device, I have included a number of photographs in this section to make it easier to follow no matter what type of device you have at home.

If you are working from the free version of QLab and/or only using your computer's built-in output, you will only be able to see two output channels in QLab. This is because your basic computer sound card likely only has stereo output. You can, however, use the free version of QLab with an external audio device and experiment with these settings – just remember that you won't be able to open a previously saved multichannel output file without upgrading to Pro Audio.

Customizing Your Audio Patch

In Section 5.4, we examined the basics of editing the audio patch. For the following sections, we will explore the application of these concepts and set up our own multichannel sound system with QLab. The following project breaks down how to configure the Audio portion of Settings in order to create a basic stereo output.

Project 5.1 ▼

> ### Setting Up Your System
>
> **Step 1:** With QLab turned off, plug in your external audio device.
>
> **Step 2:** Open a new QLab workspace and save it. I've called mine Multichannel template, with the idea that I will be using this same configuration for other projects in the future.
>
> *(Continued)*

Step 3: Click on the Gear symbol in the bottom right corner to open up your Settings window and then select Audio. Your audio patch 1 will likely be assigned to either "no device" or "built-in output." Click on the arrows at the end of this button and change audio patch 1 to be assigned to your external audio device. In my case, it reads "Audiofire 12." See Figure 5.9 for a screenshot of this step.

Figure 5.9
Select the appropriate audio device from the drop-down menu and assign it as Audio Patch 1.

Step 4: Click on the button at the end of the row labeled "Edit Patch 1." This will open up an interface for routing signals and setting the volume levels for your device. Click on the center tab, labeled Device Routing (Figure 5.10).

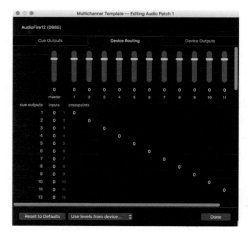

Figure 5.10
The Device Routing tab for Audio Patch 1.

Step 5: For the following step, our goal is to set up the signal flow so that the correct side of the stereo signal arrives at the appropriate speaker destination. In Figure 5.10 you can see that the default setting for signals is a 1-to-1 routing, meaning input 1 from the audio signal goes to channel 1 of the device and so on. This would be ideal for a multichannel audio file with eight different channels, each dedicated to an individual speaker. In our case, though, we want to direct a two-channel signal (stereo) out to eight different speakers. For this reason, we will only be using inputs 1 and 2. Go ahead and option-click on the levels sliders 9–12 at the top of the screen (Figure 5.11). This will toggle the levels to mute – since there won't be a signal coming to them, there is no reason to have them turned on.

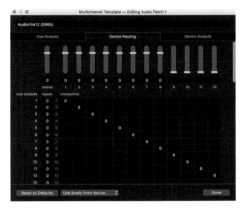

Figure 5.11
In this example, sliders 9–12 have been muted.

Step 6: Now that we are dealing with only eight speakers, let's look to see which signal is assigned to which speaker. The first thing to do is deactivate the signals coming from inputs 3–12. Again, by option-clicking on the window showing the zero, it will toggle it from 0 dB UNITY to off (Figure 5.12). Once you have done this, the next step is to assign the signal from input 1 and input 2 to the appropriate speakers.

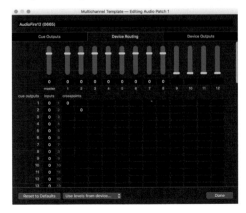

Figure 5.12
Note that the cue outputs have been deactivated for device outputs 3–12.

(Continued)

Step 7: In order to make certain your audio files sound correct in the space, you should have a good understanding of the inputs and which output channel is assigned to which speaker. In QLab, input 1 will be the left channel of an audio signal whereas input 2 will be the right channel. This means that any output needing the left signal should have input 1 assigned in the crosspoints matrix. Conversely, any output needing the right signal should have input 2 assigned to it in the crosspoints matrix.

If you refer back to Figure 5.1, you will see that the speakers correspond to numbers 1–8. Speakers 1, 3, and 5 are all house speakers that receive the left channel of the audio signal, whereas 2, 4, and 6 are the house speakers receiving the right channel. Speakers 7 and 8 will both receive the right and left channels so as to not lose any side of the audio signal. In our setup, the speaker number corresponds to the output channel in QLab – meaning slider 1 controls speaker 1 and so on.

Understanding all of that, look at Figure 5.13 for the default patch to make certain that the correct channel emits from the corresponding speaker. This configuration assures that each speaker is independently controlled and receiving either one channel (in the case of our stereo pairs) or both channels (in the case of the subwoofer and the onstage record player special).

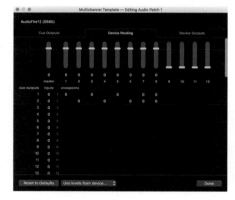

Figure 5.13
This figure illustrates the precise routing necessary to set up individual stereo control for your speakers.

5.6 – Audio Device Volume Levels

As a sound designer, you might frequently find yourself working on one type of audio interface for your programming and then going into a performance space with a different type of audio interface altogether. This can lead to some interesting changes to the volume settings for your show, as different audio interfaces will invariably output at different volumes from location to location. If you were unable to change the output levels on the new audio interface, it would mean hours of reprogramming to get the show set to the appropriate volume levels. Luckily, QLab addresses these differences between audio devices by allowing for the editing of volume settings of the device in question.

Like setting the default Audio Levels inside Cue Templates, this process is simple, but will require some quiet time alone in the theatre to fine-tune the volume settings for that particular location. One might ask why it is necessary to set the volume levels through the device if there are default level settings for each audio cue. The simplest answer is that the purpose of setting the volume output for your audio device should be to make certain that there is an equal amount of audio coming from each speaker in the theatre. In this way, any subsequent level changes can be done within the individual Audio Cue and the balance (or unbalance) occurs through manipulating the Audio Cue in question.

Balancing Audio Device Output

1. To make changes to the output settings of any audio device, open Cue Templates inside the Workspace Settings window and select Audio, then Audio Levels. Next, click the Edit button in the Audio Output Patch. Alternately, you could click the Audio Levels tab in the Inspector of any Audio Cue. On the left side of the window, you will see the Audio Output Patch and an edit button beside it. Click on this button to open the Audio Patch Editor.

2. Upon selecting the Audio Patch Editor, you will need to select the Device Routing tab. Once you have done so, you will see the same interface used in Section 5.4 above to assign input channels to outputs. Instead of focusing on the crosspoints matrix, though, this time we will look at the volume faders at the top of the window. These faders control the output from each physical channel on your audio device. As mentioned before, they are a graphic representation of the classic faders on a soundboard. By default, the master and subsequent output channels will be set to 0 dB, or UNITY. This means that the signal coming into the audio device will be output exactly as received. There is the potential, though, to either amplify or decrease the amount of audio signal going out of each channel. It is by adjusting these faders that you overcome any differences in the default speaker volume levels and create a balanced mix in your theatre.

3. In order to get a balanced mix on the speaker output, first position yourself in the center of the auditorium of the theatre so as to get a realistic perception of what your audience will be hearing. The process will likely require getting up and moving around some, but the center is a good place to start.

4. Pull a test song into your workspace as an Audio Cue set to Infinite Loop. Press GO. At this point, go back to the Device Routing tab and pull all but the MASTER volume sliders down to mute. For the following steps, it is

best to either (a) set up a private network between a laptop and your QLab control computer so you can screen-share and control QLab live, (b) use the QLab Remote app to access QLab and control the settings live, or (c) bring in an assistant to run QLab for you while you give them thumbs-up or thumbs-down signals from the auditorium for setting levels. In either case, it is essential to actually listen to the changes being made *in real-time* rather than running back and forth and trying to remember what it sounded like before.

5. Slowly bring up your slider for channel 1 until the volume reaches a level that is almost uncomfortable, but not too loud. This process is fairly subjective. The purpose of setting it louder than the desired playback level for the show comes from the fact that the theatre's acoustics will change when you have an auditorium full of patrons. Each body will serve to absorb and dampen the overall sound, thereby decreasing the volume. This is why it is always a good idea to make your initial settings a bit louder in the programming.

6. Once you have achieved the desired volume level for channel 1, repeat these steps for each of your auditorium speakers. This can be a time-consuming process, but it is well worth the wait to ensure your design sounds the same from throughout the house. The ultimate mix is the designer's preference. Some designers might prefer the proscenium speakers to be louder than the house speakers in their mix, but I find it easier to set all of the levels at the same volume, then change the standard mix through the default audio levels inside of Cue Templates. Like most things in QLab, there are a number of ways to achieve the end goal. The process should ultimately be the one that makes the most sense to the designer and best fits the project.

5.7 – Audio Effects and How to Use Them

QLab 4 has the ability to use **Audio Units (AU)** to affect the audio signal in some useful ways (i.e., equalization, pitch-bending, hi-pass filtering, reverb, delay, and more). An AU is a software plug-in version that replicates the effects of signal processing devices, like an EQ or a "stomp pedal" for a guitar. Every Mac comes with some Audio Units preinstalled. It is also possible to purchase new Audio Units or obtain freeware versions. As a note, QLab can only use 64-bit Audio Units defined as effects that report a "tail time." There are three common methods of using Audio Units: either as an individual effect on one Audio Cue, as a global effect applied to a Cue Output, or as an effect applied to a device output in which all sound going through those outputs is affected. In this section, we will discuss the last two methods.

Audio Effects and Cue Outputs

Applying an Audio Effect to a Cue Output allows you to either add effects to a cue output currently used in your workspace or to create a slider that you designate as an Effects Run. In the example of the eight-channel sound system shown in Project 5.1, for instance, you could add a reverb effect to any or all of the eight speakers. Another approach would be making a special cue output with a reverb effect applied to it that is patched into your eight speakers. This would create a special fader in your workspace that is used only for adding the reverb effect. In this way, adding effects to Cue Outputs is a versatile way to deal with signal processing.

To add effects to a Cue Output, you will first have to open the Audio Patch Editor. The Editor's first tab, labeled Cue Outputs, allows for assigning an Audio Effect to each of the 64 possible Cue Outputs. Applying Audio Units to a Cue Output is comparable to the use of an AUX, or EFFECTS RUN, in traditional recording terminology. Typically speaking, an AUX is used to create a sub-group controlled by one fader. This is often referred to as an EFFECTS RUN since one of the best uses for the AUX is to assign certain effects (like reverb) to a group of signals.

In QLab, assigning an effect to a Cue Output creates a digital path for your sound system that routes your signal through one or more Audio Units assigned to it. These Audio Units act as signal processors, affecting the sound quality of the audio signal leaving your Cue Output. The possibilities are nearly limitless on how one might use this in a live theatre environment.

One of the best uses for this comes in applying reverb to an Audio Cue. In the following example, we will create a reverb effects run and properly route it so that the QLab workspace will then have a slider to add reverb to any cue in a given cue list.

Project 5.2 ▼

Creating a Reverb Send in QLab

The purpose of reverb in a recording is to recreate the acoustical ambiance of a particular environment. Producers have been using reverb on recordings for years to give a fuller sound to music recorded in the studio. For the purposes of theatre, we use reverb frequently to create a richer environment in conjunction with the scenic design. For instance, what if one of the scenes in your play occurs in a cave? How would the quality of the actors' voices and sound effects differ from that in an office? With QLab 4 Audio Effects capabilities, you can apply effects to Cue Outputs so that these effects are always at the ready for any cue in your cue list. By doing so, you

(Continued)

can add reverb to one scene by simply raising the assigned Cue Output fader. The following project takes you through the process of creating a reverb effect to emulate that cave sound we discussed earlier.

Step 1. Download Project 5.2 from the companion website and open the workspace. The Cue Output assignment is a component of the Audio Patch Editor, so the first step is to select your desired output patch and click the Edit button. Once you have opened the Editor, look at the first tab labeled "Cue Outputs" as seen in Figure 5.14. For this project, we will use a two-channel stereo example, just to keep things simple.

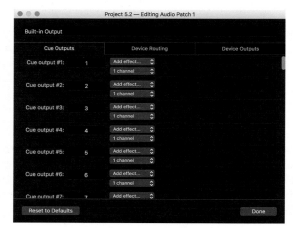

Figure 5.14
The Cue Outputs tab of the Audio Patch Editor.

Step 2. In order to assign an effect to your Cue Output channels, select Cue Output #3 in the Cue Outputs list. Looking down the right of the row, you will notice two drop-down menus that read "add effect" and "1 channel." The top drop-down menu allows you to assign an effect to the selected Cue Output. By clicking on this button, a drop-down menu opens labeled Apple. If your computer has other Audio Units installed, they will automatically be listed here as well. By clicking on this, you will see a list of all of the available AU plug-ins for use. By clicking on AU Matrix Reverb, you will assign the Matrix Reverb Audio Unit plug-in to the selected Cue Output.

One important aspect to remember is that some Audio Effects support one channel of input, whereas others may require two (stereo). For an example like AU Matrix Reverb, it is necessary to set the lower drop-down menu to "2 channel" instead of "1 channel." If you fail to do so, the audio signal will be passed through without any sort of change. In some instances, the audio will not pass through at all. By selecting

2 channel, you will notice that the effects window disappears from the row in Cue Output #4 (Figure 5.15). This is because those two cue outputs have now been paired together for this purpose.

Figure 5.15
This illustration shows the AU Matrix Reverb audio unit applied as an effect onto channels 3 and 4.

When you select AU Matrix Reverb, the control window for this Audio Unit will instantly open (see Figure 5.16). This window is not a part of QLab, rather the control window designed by Apple for this AU. This is the same window you would see in any application using the plug-in. You can think of the control window as an external device with knobs and sliders on the front for you to adjust. For now, close this window. We will return to it in a moment.

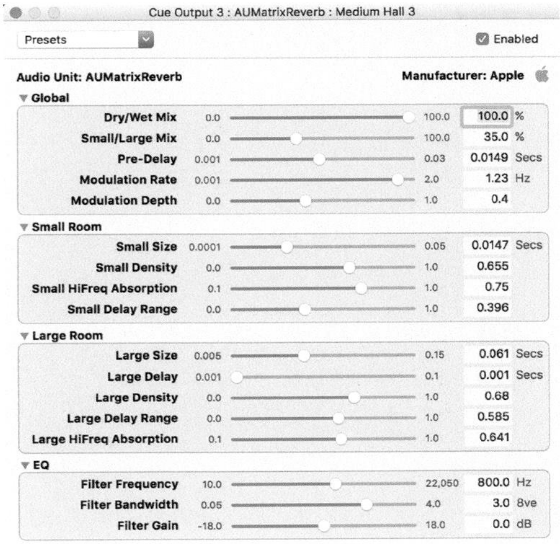

Figure 5.16
The AU Matrix Reverb control interface.

(Continued)

Step 3. In the black box to the right of Cue Output #3, delete the number 3 and replace it with the word "REVERB (Figure 5.17)." This will label the third Cue Output fader as reverb for all cues in your workspace.

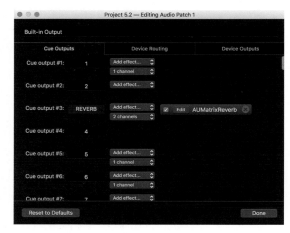

Figure 5.17
Re-naming the cue output as "REVERB" will apply for all cues in your workspace.

Step 4. The next step requires opening the Device Routing tab inside the Audio Patch Editor. This window allows you to assign which Cue Outputs will be sent to the crosspoints matrix and out to the Device Outputs. Type the number 0 into the two black boxes to the right of the Cue Output labeled as "REVERB." This will route your Effects Run through the right and left outputs of your device (Figure 5.18).

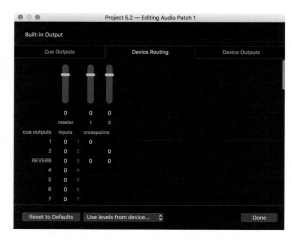

Figure 5.18
Assigning the reverb effect to both device outputs of your system.

Step 5. For the next section, leave the Audio Patch Editor and return to your workspace. Select the Group Cue 1. This Group contains a set of Audio Cues that play simultaneously. This setup allows for individualized control of the separate tracks. We will use these Audio cues to test the reverb settings. In order to use the reverb effect, though, you must first assign it to an Audio Cue. Select any cue in the group and click on the "Audio Levels" tab of the Inspector. This will open a tab that shows the audio inputs, crosspoints, and output levels in the lower right hand corner. If you have followed the steps to this point, the third cue output should be labeled "REVERB." This is your reverb effects fader.

Step 6. Currently, this fader has no audio input assigned to it. In order to activate the effect, you must first assign an input, thereby sending the audio signal through the effect fader. In order to accomplish this, click on the two crosspoints under the Reverb fader and type in a 0. This allows the right and left channel of the audio to pass through the Audio Effect (Figure 5.19). If for some reason, you only wanted reverb on one channel, you could assign it to one and not the other. Repeat this process for every cue in Group 1.

Figure 5.19
In this example, I have assigned reverb to Audio Cue 4, the horn track, as well as a few others within the workspace.

Step 7. Select Group Cue 1 and press the space bar or GO button in the upper left hand corner. Next, re-open your AU Matrix Reverb control window. With your Audio Cue playing, you will now be able to affect the amount of reverb in your mix.

Step 8. Instead of focusing on the minutiae of the control attributes, let us instead look at the presets Apple created for the AU. If you click in the upper left corner, you will see a button labeled "Presets." If you click on this button, a drop-down menu will appear listing a number of options. If you hover over the one called "Factory," you will find a number of factory settings for different types of reverbs created to

(Continued)

emulate certain size rooms (i.e., small room, large chamber, cathedral, plate, etc.). Click through a number of these and you will hear a dramatic difference in the reverb and see which sliders affect what types of sounds. This is one of the quickest and best ways to understand how to create your own custom reverb.

Step 9. If you use one of the factory settings as a starting point and make changes, you can then save this as your own customized reverb by clicking on the presets button, then "Save." A dialog will appear enabling you to name the custom preset, which will be available to you in any application using the AU Matrix Reverb plug-in.

Step 10. Finally, if you want to compare the new reverb you created to the original unaffected audio, simply click on the "Enabled" checkbox in the upper right corner and you can toggle between having the AU on or off.

Step 11. Once having gone through all of these steps, the reverb slider will be available for any Audio Cue in your workspace. Simply slide it up to add the reverb effect inside the Inspector. Try out different amounts of reverb on different cues in this project until you have a nice balance.

5.8 – Using Multichannel Audio Files

One final thought to consider once you have set up QLab 4 as the playback component of your Audio System is the use of multichannel audio files. If you have an audio device with more than two channels of output, you can configure your system for directional sound playback through the individual output channels. In this type of system, you can either route an individual Audio Cue through the chosen outputs on a cue-by-cue basis, or you can create a **multichannel audio file**, a specific type of audio file (typically WAV) that contains a number of channels imbedded within it. In this case, QLab automatically recognizes the number of channels present in the audio file and assigns them to the respective output channels of your device. Simply put, by using a multichannel audio file, you can create a directional mix at your DAW (digital audio workstation) rather than spending the time assigning multiple files to outputs within QLab.

As for the creation of these files, there are a number of DAWs on the market that can output multichannel WAV files. Audacity is one such program – downloadable free for Windows, Mac, and Linux available under the GNU General Public License. You can record live audio or edit audio files in Audacity and save as mono, stereo, or multichannel audio formats. In addition to DAWs, there are also programs available that can take individual mono sound files and combine them together into a multichannel audio file. One such program is SoundFilesMerger, which combines multiple audio files and exports them as either AIF or WAV format.

Like any system, there are pros and cons to using multichannel audio files. On the positive side, you can use one file that contains several outputs imbedded within it. This means that one could create a complex sound effect with multiple layers, each coming from a different direction, without the need to input multiple different audio files. This makes it much easier to organize. On the other hand, let's say you created a complex car crash sequence in this fashion and everything works perfectly – except for the fact that your director hates the car horn. In this case, you would have to go back to your DAW and redo the entire file to correct that one component. Had you created a group cue with each section imbedded as a child within, you could simply replace that one sound effect on the fly and play it back for the director. So, even though programming a group cue might be more work up front, it allows for flexibility and has the potential to save time in the tech process. Another consideration might be the computer used for playback. Multichannel audio files use a considerable amount more CPU than running multiple mono or stereo audio files concurrently. If you don't have an abundance of RAM, perhaps the multichannel route is not best for your given situation. As with many of the other QLab features, versatility is the key. What is right in one situation will not be true in another. Knowing that you have the ability to achieve the same goals in multiple ways is a cornerstone of the QLab platform.

Audio Cues

Audio Cues are the foundation upon which QLab was built. The first versions of the software dealt specifically with audio playback, though soon there- after incorporated a number of new features. The purpose of an Audio Cue is simple, to play back an audio file. Though the function of it is simple, the complexity with which the Audio Cue can be manipulated is quite impressive. The following chapter delves into the Audio Cue in detail and explores its use.

6.1 – Inserting an Audio Cue

Like any other cue, an Audio Cue can be inserted via the Toolbar, Toolbox, or dragging an audio file directing into the cue list. QLab 4 supports a wide range of audio file types, including WAV, AIF, CAF, AAC, MP4, MP4A, and MP3 (though the use of MP3 files is not recommended due to timing issues that may arise). Likewise, the audio file can be either mono, stereo, or multichannel audio.

6.2 – Inspector: Basics

Once an Audio Cue is inserted into your cue list, the Inspector can be used to access a wide range of control functions related to the cue. There are six tabs within the Inspector that house a number of these functions: Basics, Triggers, Time & Loops, Audio Levels, Audio Trim, and Audio Effects. Each of these tabs contains specific control functions that affect the playback of the given Audio Cue. The first tab, Basics, allows for manipulating the baseline informa- tion about the audio cue. These functions are identical to those covered in Chapter 3 (Section 3.2 D). As a reminder, this area is used for inputting infor- mation such as cue number, cue name, cue row color, cue duration, target, pre-wait/post-wait, flagging the cue, auto-loading, arming, and notes. Figure 6.1 shows the Basics tab with the notes panel in use.

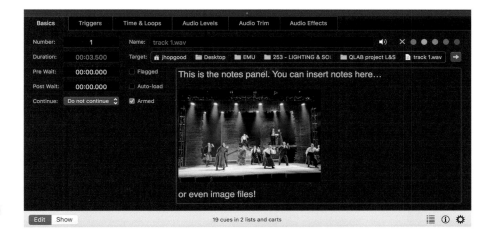

Figure 6.1
The Basics tab
contains baseline
cue information,
color coding, and
notes.

6.3 – Inspector: Triggers

Like the Basics tab, Triggers was also covered extensively in Chapter 3 (Section 3.2 D). This tab is used for assigning trigger functions in addition to the normal GO button, allowing for versatile control to personalize playback options for different installations. The Triggers tab enables MIDI, Hotkey, Wall Clock, or Timecode triggering.

Affecting Other Cues

As a reminder, the right half of the Triggers tab contains a new function for assigning how your selected cue affects the playback of other cues, once triggered (again, seen in Section 3.2). In short, this list of options will make certain changes to the playback of other audio cues by either fading and stopping their playback or ducking their volume level over time.

6.4 – Inspector: Time & Loops

The Time & Loops tab contains a number of different functions for manipulating the playback of an Audio Cue (see Figure 6.2). In short, these functions control start/end time of an Audio Cue, number of times it is played, integrated volume levels (dynamics), and rate of playback (tempo/playback speed).

The Waveform Display

The waveform display visually takes up the majority of the Time & Loops panel. In fact, all of the other control functions in the Time & Loops panel directly

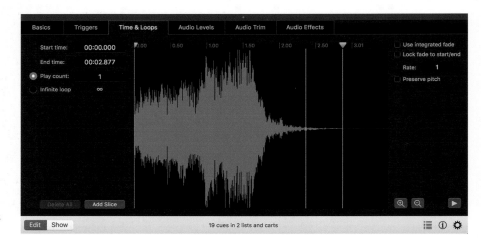

Figure 6.2
The Time & Loops tab.

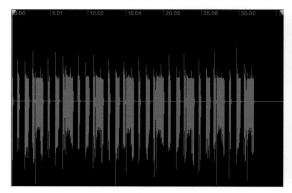

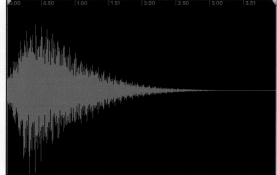

Figure 6.3
The two waveforms offer up a lot of information about their audio files.

affect the waveform, so it is wise that we address this before moving on to the other tools in Time & Loops.

For those unfamiliar with the concept, a waveform is a graph that illustrates the change of amplitude (volume) of a sound over a certain period of time. In an audio waveform, the x-axis (horizontal) represents elapsed time, whereas the y-axis (vertical) represents volume. Waveforms have been an essential component of audio editing software for years. A waveform can give a lot of information to the user without having to even listen to the recording. For instance, look at Figure 6.3 to see the comparison of two waveforms.

The first waveform shows a sound file with a consistent pulsing sound. There are several sections of silence within the track as well. Looking at the second waveform, it is obvious that the sound is louder at the beginning and tails off pretty quickly. The QLab waveform display also shows the elapsed time

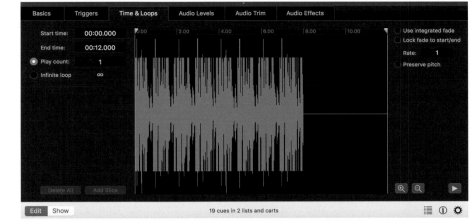

Figure 6.4
The Waveform start/end times are indicated with the yellow line and downward pointing arrows at the beginning and end of the waveform.

of an Audio Cue, listed at the top of the display. Comparing the two tracks from Figure 6.3, you can see the first track is approximately 32 seconds long, whereas the second one is considerably shorter at 3 seconds. The elapsed time can help in determining exact timing on fades and cuts within the track.

The waveform display also offers the ability to modify an Audio Cue's start time or end time. When a new Audio Cue is inserted, the waveform will show a faint yellow line with a downward-pointing arrowhead at the beginning and end of the waveform (see Figure 6.4). This indicates the start time and end time of the cue.

All Audio Cues default to the start time and end time of the inserted audio file, though you might find it useful to change this for your playback purposes. One of the best examples of this function comes when importing sound files from compact disc. There might be a brief pause recorded into the beginning of the file, which would cause the Audio Cue to appear late, even if triggered at the appropriate time. By setting the start time at the true start of the audio file, this problem can be averted. To achieve this, simply slide the start icon to the appropriate location on the waveform and this will become your new start time. This process is quite simple, given the ability to visually see where the audio begins on the waveform. It might take some slight adjustment to get your timing precise, but it is infinitely simpler than the old method of editing the file, burning it to disc, then trying again. As you might have guessed, the process is identical if you want to change the end time of a cue. Simply slide the end time icon to the desired stopping point in your waveform.

The process of changing the start/end time of an Audio Cue (and all other changes made to an Audio Cue within QLab, for that matter) are non-destructive, meaning the original file is not changed in any way, only the manner of its playback. Even though the unwanted audio occurring before the start time or after the end time is trimmed away, the data still remains part of the original audio file.

Waveform Zoom

One of the important control functions of the waveform is the zoom in and zoom out buttons. By clicking on the zoom in button, the waveform is magnified, giving the programmer the ability to view it with more precision. You will note that, as the waveform is magnified, it no longer fits in the window in its entirety. In order to view the entire timeline of the waveform, simply grab the scrub bar at the bottom of the waveform window and slide it to the right or left. When magnified, you might notice that what seemed like a millisecond of time may be more substantial than originally thought. This is why the zoom controls are essential to accurate editing for trimming, especially if the intention is to create a seamless loop-able file.

Design Tips ▽

Multitouch Gestures

Like many other Macintosh-based programs, QLab incorporates the use of multitouch gestures for many functions. If you have a track pad, either on your laptop or the external Bluetooth variety, you can use Multi-Touch gestures to accomplish the waveform zoom without clicking the magnify or reduce buttons. Simply position your cursor in the waveform display and perform a two-fingered scroll to zoom. Slide two fingers up to magnify or two fingers down to reduce. In addition, a mouse scroll-wheel will function in the same fashion.

Preview Cue

The Preview Cue button (the small play icon shown in the bottom right corner of Figure 6.2) is a useful tool used for testing the playback of an Audio Cue without having to press the GO button and advance to the next playback position. When inactive, the icon is the standard play icon (a right-pointing triangle). Once activated, you will notice it changes to a pause icon, enabling you to pause playback.

Times, Loops, and Slices

To the left of the Time & Loops panel, there is a column made up of five rows (Figure 6.5). These five rows control the basic functions of start time, end time,

Figure 6.5
The Time, Loops, & Slices area houses many control functions related to timing and repeats.

and number of times the Audio Cue might loop. The areas below describe the use of each function:

- Start Time: This panel allows for the programmer to type in the exact start time of the Audio Cue, down to thousandths of a second. This allows for trimming off unwanted audio at the beginning of a sound file.
- End Time: This panel offers the same type of control function as start time, except it allows for trimming off any unwanted audio at the end of a file. The input process is the same and anything after the inputted time code will not play back (once again, in a non-destructive fashion). This function is particularly useful when you need to have one cue Auto-follow into another, but the first cue has "dead air" at the end. By manipulating the end time, you can create a seamless Auto-follow scenario.
- Play count: The play count establishes the number of times a cue will play back. By default, all cues default to one, meaning that they will only play once. One can easily set the play count to loop two or more times. Note that the action of the cue will increase for each loop cycle, meaning the action of a 1-second audio cue looped four times would become 4 seconds.
- Infinite Loop: Sometimes, you will find yourself in a situation in which a cue must be looped endlessly until faded out. To accomplish this, simply click the infinite loop button. This function is particularly useful for ambient noise loops like crickets (something every designer should have in their collection) without actually using a 30-minute audio recording. Special attention must be paid to the original audio file, though, to make sure it is truly "loop-able." Having even a tenth of a second of silence or difference in the end of the file versus the beginning will draw attention to the loop and destroy the intended effect.

- Slices: Slicing is a function within QLab that allows for the looping of internal sections of an Audio or Video Cue. This simple addition adds multiple layers of flexibility to sound playback, particularly in the tech situation. Frequently, sound designers are called on to create music or effects to play over scenic transitions in a play. One common problem is in the timing of how long it takes for the shift from one scene to another. Often, the sound designer must lengthen a particular piece of music to match the complexity of the scenic shift. In the past, this always meant going back to the DAW to record a new, longer section of music. With slices, though, a designer can feasibly locate a section within the music to repeat, thereby lengthening the music.
- In order to insert a loop into a cue, simply click the location in the waveform to place the end of your slice. Likewise, if you created the file in an audio editing software with markers, those markers will translate into slices automatically when imported to QLab. If you want the first 3 seconds of an Audio Cue to repeat, place your cursor at the 3-second position in the waveform viewer and click the "Add Slice" button, or simply click the "m" button on your keyboard (for marker). Once you have done this, you will notice a handle appears at the top of the waveform timeline of a downward pointing arrow. This indicates the end of the slice. To fine-tune the ending position, simply grab the slice position icon in the timeline and slide it to the desired location.

Once a slice is inserted, two numbers will appear at the bottom of the waveform, both reading 1. This indicates the number of times your slice will loop before proceeding to the next slice. Click on the first number and change it to 2. This will create a slice that plays back twice before progressing to the next section in the Audio Cue. Likewise, if you want to make the loop repeat an infinite number of times, simply insert "inf" instead of a number and the infinity symbol (∞) will replace it.

If you wish to remove a single slice, simply change the number back to 1 and it will function like it is not there. Likewise, you can grab the handle and pull it out of the workspace to delete it. If you wish to delete all slices, click on the button labeled "Delete All." Be careful about simply trying to delete the number from the slice, though. If you delete the number an infinity symbol (∞) will replace it, giving you an infinite loop cycle within your cue.

To end an infinite loop cycle, you must use the Devamp Cue in conjunction with your Audio Cue. Once triggered, a Devamp Cue tells a cue to stop repeating and progress to the next slice once the next loop cycle has completed. This is addressed in depth in Chapter 9, Control Cues.

One final use for slices is simply to insert visual markers in your waveform that make it easier to identify key spots during tech. If, for instance, there is a spot in

Design Tips ▼

Looping Sliced Tracks

In previous versions of QLab, there was no quick method for looping an Audio Cue with slices (infinite or otherwise). With the release of Version 4.1, however, you can now loop an entire cue, even if there is a slice added. Once the slice has been added, you can select the waveform and either insert a play count number or set it as an infinite loop. Once this has been done, the Devamp Cue can be used to either devamp the selected slice or the entire Audio Cue, itself. Because of this new function, the Devamp Cue now has two modes under its Settings tab: Devamp currently looping slice, or devamp looping cue. This new addition allows for a complex use of slices in arranging flexible playback for both Audio and Video cues.

the middle of a song where a certain instrument enters and you want to note that location, simply insert a slice and keep the loop number set to 1. There will be no function to the slice, other than serving as a visual marker for your own use at a later time.

Integrated Volume Levels and Playback Rate

The last two functions of the Time & Loops panel offer further non-destructive editing options for your audio file. The first of these functions allows the programmer to insert volume changes within the audio cue. In musical terms, this is referred to as dynamics. In QLab, it is referred to as the **Integrated Fade.** When you click on the "use integrated fade" button, a yellow line will appear placed horizontally across the top of your waveform with a circle at the beginning and end of the line (see Figure 6.6). For users familiar with the volume automation in programs such as Apple's Garage Band or Logic, the same basic principles apply to the integrated fade envelope. Like the waveform, the fade envelope works in an x/y axis fashion; the horizontal line represents elapsed time, whereas the vertical represents the master volume of the selected Audio Cue. The straight line at the top of the waveform represents 0 dB (UNITY) with no changes to the output of the audio file. The bottom of the waveform window represents –INF dB, or silence. In order to add integrated fades to the sound cue, just click on the yellow line at the point in the timeline where you want the volume to change. This will insert a control point, represented by a solid yellow dot on the yellow line. You can now pull this control point down and to either the left or right in order to create a fade curve. By inserting multiple control points, it is possible to create a variety of different

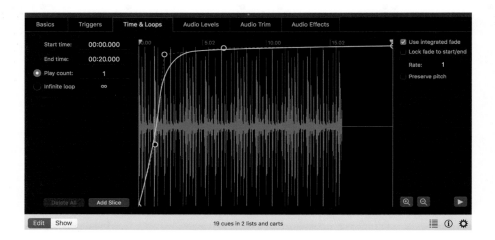

Figure 6.6 The integrated fade tool allows for controlling the volume levels of the cue without using an external Fade Cue.

fade curve options. The closer together the control points, the quicker the changes in volume. The best way to learn how to shape a fade curve is by experimentation.

Beneath the integrated fade checkbox is a new addition called "lock fade to start/end." If the box is unchecked, an integrated fade curve will be locked to the start and end time of the selected sound file. Once checked, the fade will instead be linked to the start and end time of the cue in question.

Controlling Playback Rate

The final control function of the Time & Loops panel is called **Rate**. This button allows for the programmer to change the rate at which the audio file plays back. In essence, this allows for control of the tempo (if music specific) for playback of an audio file. This function is quite useful due to the ability to control pitch shift. Traditionally speaking, when an audio file is sped up the pitch of all notes within the file would become higher or vice versa if slowed down (think of the effect of playing changing the rpm settings on a record player). Today, most sophisticated audio editing software allows for the increase or decrease in playback speed without this pitch shift occurring. In QLab, by using the checkbox beneath the Rate controls, one can choose whether to have the pitch shift occur or not. By clicking the "Preserve pitch" checkbox, the playback rate will change without affecting the pitch of the audio file.

Many plays often feature music or sound effects playing over scenic changes. Consider that you need to cover a 15-second scenic shift, but only have 12 seconds of music. By using the rate function, you could simply insert a rate of 0.8 and what once took 12 seconds to play would now take 15.

Make sure to select the preserve pitch checkbox, though, or the pitch of your audio recording will be quite different from the original. Always keep in mind that there is a limit to the amount of rate change one can apply without sounding too fake. Depending on the type of instrumentation, it might not work for some music, but it is a great tool for a number of different applications.

Project 6.1 ▼

Manipulating Start/End Times

The following project details the process of setting start time and end time of a file, inserting slices, and changing the playback rate.

Step 1: Download Project 6.1 from the companion website.

Step 2: Cue 1 is an Audio Cue that contains music with "dead air" at the beginning and end of the file. Select Cue 1 and click on the Time & Loops tab in the Inspector Panel. Note the waveform that shows a flat line at the beginning and end of the audio file.

Step 3: Using the waveform zoom tool, zoom in to look at the beginning of the Audio Cue. You will see that the audio signal does not begin until almost 2 seconds into the recording.

Step 4: Slide your cursor to the top left corner of the waveform timeline (where it reads 0.00). You will notice a triangular point at the beginning of the timeline pointing down. There should be a yellow line directly beneath its point. When you hover over this icon, your cursor will change into a new icon: a black vertical line with arrows pointing to the right and left. This controls the placement of the Audio Cue's start time. Slide it to the right, stopping just before your audio signal begins in the waveform. You will notice that the area before the yellow line will now turn blue, indicating that it will not be played back as part of the Audio Cue. Releasing the icon will move the start time to this point.

Step 5: Move to the end of the waveform. There is roughly 5 seconds of silence at the end of this cue. Slide the arrow icon at the end of the waveform back to the end of the audio signal. Again, you will notice the area past the yellow line will be highlighted in blue. Releasing the icon here will move the end time to this point.

Step 6: Notice that the Start Time and End Time listed to the left of the Time & Loops tab will now list the exact time in the audio file that playback begins and ends.

Project 6.2 ▼

Adding Slices

The following project details the process of adding slices to an audio file to create loop-able sections.

Step 1: Download Project 6.2 from the companion website.

Step 2: Select Cue 1 and click the space bar. This will fire the cue for playback. The music begins with an introductory phrase that is easily repeatable. For this portion of the project, let us assume that we need to add a few more seconds to the length of the Audio Cue. In this case, it can easily be accomplished by adding a slice that will create a loop within the Audio Cue.

Step 3: Zoom in to the waveform. The first musical phrase is ideal for creating a loop. If you zoom in to around the 6-second mark, you will see the phrase ends around 5.95 seconds. This would be an ideal location to add a slice. To do so, simply click at this point on the waveform to place your marker. A yellow line will appear where you clicked.

Step 4: Click on the "Add Slice" button on the left corner of the window. This will add a slice at the location marker. You will see a white number 1 in the center of the slice. This indicates the loop count of the slice, the number of times the slice will repeat. Click on the number and change it to 2.

Step 5: Select the Audio Cue and click the space bar. You will hear that the slice repeats twice now. Slice placement must be precise or you might hear a slight "hiccup" at the point of repeat where the end of the slice does not correctly align with the beginning. If this occurs, simply go back to the waveform and slide the yellow line at the slice end until it aligns appropriately to accomplish seamless looping.

Project 6.3 ▼

Manipulating Playback Rate

Sometimes you might find that the Audio Cue playback is slightly too short or long. In the past, this meant going back to your DAW to create a new file. With QLab 4, there is the possibility of changing the playback rate of the Audio Cue to make it either faster or slower. The following steps detail the process of making an audio file play back at a faster tempo.

Step 1: Download Project 6.3 from the companion website.

Step 2: Select Cue 1 and click the space bar. This will fire the cue for playback in its unchanged state. In the Time & Loops window, click on the "Rate" panel to the right of the window. It should read 1. This indicates that the file will play back at its recorded rate. Changing this number will make the playback rate either faster or slower. For instance, insert .9 into the rate panel. Click Go again and you will notice the Audio Cue plays back at a slower rate. By inputting 1.1, the same file will play back faster.

Step 3: In these instances above you will notice that the checkbox labeled "Preserve pitch" was not selected. This is why the audio file sounded very different from the original when fired. If you check the checkbox, you will notice that the pitch remains unchanged from the original when played back at a different rate.

Step 4: By inputting 1.05 and checking the "Preserve pitch" box, the resulting Audio Cue will be slightly faster than the original but with an unchanged pitch. Notice that the Start Time and End Time remain the same in the Time & Loops window, but the Action Time in the Cue Row will change to match the true playback time of the Audio Cue.

6.5 – Inspector: Audio Levels

Figure 6.7
The Audio Levels tab houses controls for the audio output patch, volume settings, gangs, and signal routing.

Earlier chapters covered in detail the process for setting up and editing audio devices, audio patching, ganging channels, and creating default levels for new cues. As such, you should be familiar with every function in the Audio Levels tab. Figure 6.7 and the following information should serve as a quick refresher.

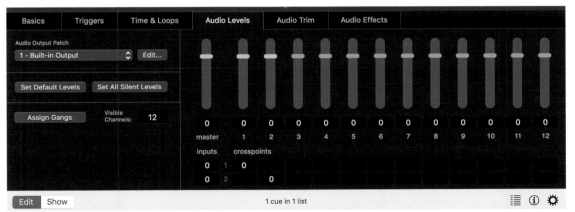

Audio Output Patch and Device Edit

Note that the Audio Output Patch allows you to assign which audio device you want to use for this particular Audio Cue. The button to the right of this allows for the editing of the Audio Device.

Set Default Levels

By clicking on this button, you can set the levels to the pre-assigned default levels set in the Settings window.

Set All Levels Silent

Clicking on this button will mute all channels.

Assign Gangs

Ganging is a function that allows the linking of control of multiple cue outputs or crosspoints. Simply click on the Assign Gangs button and insert either a number or letter in the open space beneath any slider (in the window where volume levels normally reside). For instance, place an "A" in the space beneath cue output channels 1 and 2, then click the Assign Gangs button again. This will now have paired output channels 1 and 2, making them move in unison. You will also notice that the two channels have a similar color. Additional gangs will have unique colors as well.

Visible Channels

This window allows for the change in visible channels. If, for instance, you are only using stereo output, there is no reason to see channels 3–64. Instead, type "2" into the Visible Channels window and only output channels 1 and 2 will remain visible.

Audio Levels and Crosspoint Matrix

This area of the window is identical to the levels settings seen in the Audio Settings earlier in the book. The Master and all audio inputs are shown in the left column. The cue outputs are situated to the right of the Master, with the crosspoints matrix shown beneath for assigning an input channel to the appropriate cue output. Once patched, the sliders control volume and the Master controls the volume of all other outputs.

Had an Audio Effects been assigned to a cue output, as detailed in Chapter 5, the slider (or sliders) for this effect would be listed, provided you gave the effect a unique name.

The true ability to establish directional sound resides in the Levels control panel. Thinking back to our multichannel sound system seen in Figure 5.1, let us imagine that you are designing sound for a play in which a gunshot occurs in the auditorium. The purpose of this should be twofold: to startle the audience and direct their attention to the location in which the actor will enter. If the sound rings out through the rear House Right speaker, then you would want to bring the slider up for Channel 6 and mute all of the other sliders. Let us assume, then, that during the tech rehearsal period the director changes the blocking to have the actor now entering from House Left. Obviously, the gunshot cannot still come from House Right, or the effect would only lead to confusion as the audience looks back and the actor enters on the opposite side. To remedy this, simply mute Channel 6, and bring up Channel 5 instead. Now the gunshot will appear to come from the rear House Left position.

6.6 – Inspector: Audio Trim

Trim allows for the adjustment of the volume levels of all cues and fades within a given Fade Cue series (Figure 6.8). We will cover this concept in detail in Chapter 8. For now, simply imagine the trim setting as a way to increase or decrease the volume setting of the target Audio Cue, thereby affecting the volume levels through all of the subsequent Fade Cues.

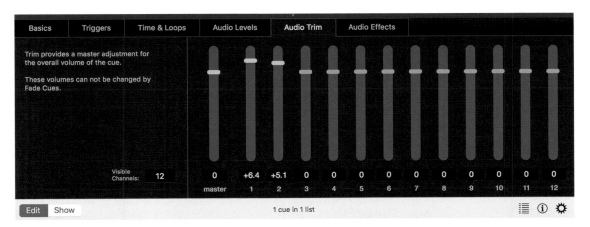

Figure 6.8
The Trim tab allows the user to adjust volume levels of cues over a Fade Cue series.

6.7 – Inspector: Audio Effects

Like other audio effects explored earlier, the Audio Effects tab allows for assigning an Audio Unit (AU) as an effect (Figure 6.9). Unlike the other instances examined earlier, though, the Audio Effects tab will only affect the selected Audio Cue. This is particularly useful in a number of situations.

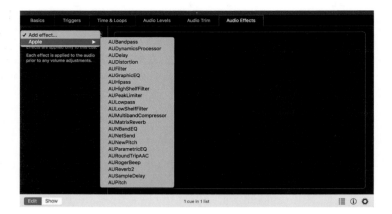

Figure 6.9
The Audio Effects tab is used for assigning Audio Units (AU) to a cue as an effect plug-in.

As a sound designer, the sound of a distant bell is one that often pops up in productions. Quite often, the number of bell peals provided by the designer is not exactly what the director had in mind. For this example, let us look at a recording of a church bell with three peals. Once in tech, the director decides that two would be more appropriate. The only problem with this scenario is that, in cutting off the last peal, you lose all of the reverberation of the bell as it fades out to silence. In this scenario, the Audio Effect would be an ideal choice. The following project will examine how to easily cut this audio file and still maintain the reverberation needed.

Project 6.4 ▼

Editing with Audio Effects

The following project details the process of editing the end time of a file while using Audio Effects to disguise the edit.

Step 1: Download Project 6.4 from the companion website.

Step 2: Play Cue 1. You will notice it has three bell peals. For this project, we will be changing the end time of the file back so as to cut off the final peal.

Step 3: Select the Time & Loops tab in the Inspector Panel. In the Waveform Editor, you will see the three distinct peals of the bell. Grab the slider at the end of the waveform and pull it to the left until the yellow line is placed just previous to the third peal.

Step 4: Play Cue 1 again. You will notice that the sound file ends quite abruptly, without the reverberation of the bell left ringing.

Step 5: Click on the Audio Effects tab in the Inspector Panel. On the left side of the screen click the "add effect" button. A drop-down menu will appear. This should display any Audio Units installed on your computer. In this case, select the Apple button, and then select the AUMatrixReverb button. This will open the control interface for the plug-in.

Step 6: Click on the "Presets" button in the upper left hand corner of the AUMatrixReverb control interface. The drop-down menu will reveal several options. Click on the button labeled "Factory." There will be several options that appear in a drop-down menu to the right of the button. Select one of them.

Step 7: Go back to the workspace and click GO to activate playback of Cue 1. Listen to the effect. Go back to the control interface for the AUMatrixReverb plug-in and change it to a different factory preset, or make adjustments of your own with the sliders. Keep experimenting until you get the right sound.

Mic Cues

Two of the most important functions of any sound system are playback and reinforcement. QLab 3 integrated Mic Cues to add reinforcement capabilities. Mic Cues allow for adding live microphone control, routing, and signal processing effects. The following chapter deals with the use and control of Mic Cues in the QLab 4 workspace.

7.1 – Understanding the Mic Cue

At its core, the Mic Cue functions in much the same way as an Audio Cue. It receives an audio signal, outputs the signal through an audio patch, allows for application of audio effects to the signal, and then routes the signal to the patched outputs of an audio device. The main difference between a Mic Cue and an Audio Cue is that, with the Mic Cue, the patch is an audio input and output patch (I/O) in contrast to being output only. By setting up the I/O patch, you can assign input channels of your audio device to be the signal source and then route them to the appropriate output path. If you plug a microphone into the assigned input channels of your audio device, once the Mic Cue is triggered the audio sent from this microphone will be the audio signal for the cue. There are a few more steps for setup but, once accomplished, the function of the Mic Cue is remarkably similar to what you have already learned in Audio Cues.

Signal Flow

Signal flow for the Mic Cue is similar to that of an Audio Cue, with the exception being there is now an external device (a microphone) inputting signal rather than simply targeting an audio file as the input. Refer to the descriptions below in conjunction with Figure 7.1 to see the signal flow path from the Mic Cue through speaker output.

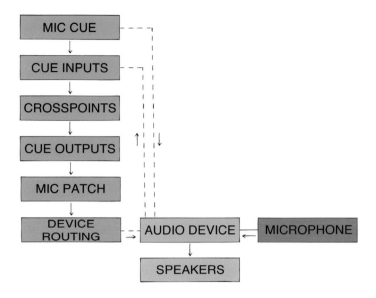

Figure 7.1 Mic Cue Signal Flow Chart.

1. **Audio Device:** The audio device takes input signals from one or more microphones connected to its input channels and then samples these signals to send them back to the computer via the digital connection (FireWire, USB, Network, etc.).
2. **Mic Cue:** When triggered, the Mic Cue sends a signal that activates the assigned input channels of the audio device.
3. **Cue Input:** The digital output from the audio device becomes the Cue Input for the Mic Cue.
4. **Crosspoints Matrix:** The cue input signal is bussed into all 64 channels of the crosspoints matrix. It is up to the operator to assign the amount of signal that will be routed into the corresponding levels fader. Once assigned, this signal becomes the Cue Output for the Mic Cue.
5. **Mic Patch:** The Cue Outputs are then routed through one of eight possible mic patches, which are each assigned to an individual audio device.
6. **Device Routing:** The last layer of routing is the audio device output routing. This is a signal routing within QLab that assigns the cue outputs to one or more specific device outputs on your audio device.
7. **System Output:** Finally, the signal leaves the output device and travels out of your QLab system into external devices (i.e., mixer, signal processing, amplifier, and speaker).

Buffering

A buffer is a region of memory storage on your computer that is used to temporarily hold data while it is being moved from one place to another. All external audio devices use some level of buffering because the device must hold at least one sample of the audio going into it in order to play it back. Essentially, the buffer is how many of these samples the device holds at one time before asking the computer to provide more for playback. For this reason, buffering affects how much of your CPU is utilized when interfacing with an audio device. The lower the buffer number, the more frequently the device has to ask the computer for sampling, thus the higher drain on CPU resources. The higher the buffer, the less frequently it asks, therefore less taxing on the CPU.

While it might seem advantageous at first to use a high buffer setting, the down side to large buffers is that it causes **latency** or delay in the audio signal from input source (microphone) to output source (speakers). In a live setting, it is essential that a lower buffer be used in order to reduce latency. While zero buffering is impossible, you ideally want to get as close to zero as possible. QLab accesses the buffer sizes specific to your audio device and allows for adjusting the buffer within that range of possibilities. To access these settings, click on **QLab** > **Preferences** and a window will open showing buffer size preferences for any audio device connected to your system (see Figure 7.2).

Typical range for buffer settings would be 16–1024. This unit refers to the number of samples held as the buffer before asking the CPU another set. The process of determining which buffer size to use is simple – go with the lowest buffer setting possible that does not either create a scratchy sound or cause your device to "clip." Keep in mind, though, that for ultra-low buffer settings it is always a good idea to use a rig with multiple core processors and lots of RAM.

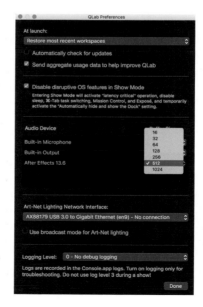

Figure 7.2 The preferences window includes audio device preferences to set buffer sizes for any audio device connected to your computer and, in some cases, other applications on your Mac.

7.2 – Setting Up Your Audio Device

It is worth mentioning at this point that all audio interfaces do not operate in the same fashion or with the same level of dependability. There are some devices that simply do not function well in the QLab environment. Others might work perfectly well for playback, but will not be the ideal choice for microphone reinforcement purposes. This book is not intended to serve as a tool for equipment selection. My best advice for purchasing any equipment for use with your QLab system (be it audio, video, or networking) is to go to the QLab Tested Hardware page at wiki.figure53.com to see user-submitted information about QLab-tested hardware and software. Also, visiting the QLab forum on the Figure 53 website is a great way to interact with the QLab community, both users and developers. Ask a question and, in most instances, you will get lots of feedback quickly.

For the purposes of microphone control, you will need an audio interface with input/output capabilities (and phantom power if you intend to use a condenser microphone). In addition, you will obviously need a microphone and at least one speaker connected to an output on your audio device. The reason for inputting and outputting from the same device is that audio input/output must use the same clock so that audio flows cleanly between the two. You can, however, create an aggregate device – the combination of multiple audio interfaces through one control – in your Audio MIDI Setup application. By doing this, you can use more than one audio interface in the same application, all sharing the same clock.

Design Tips ▽

Getting to Know Your Equipment

There is no overstating the importance of getting to know your equipment and understanding how its use differs from other pieces of hardware. As mentioned above, each audio interface tends to function in a similar way. The one aspect of each interface that tends to drastically differ is its software interfaces. Most every audio interface will have software that must be installed onto your computer in order to use the interface properly. Typically, these interfaces mirror classical audio mixers in some way and allow for the control of levels, routing signals, creating sub-mixes, and adding effects. If your audio interface is not set up to route the audio signal to the correct outputs, then you will never get QLab to communicate properly with the interface. Since there are hundreds of different interfaces on the market, clearly there is no way to cover all of the possible software interfaces in this text. Make sure to read all of the appropriate documentation that comes with your equipment and visit the manufacturer website as well. Frequently, the manufacturer will have Frequently Asked Questions, user forums, and how-to videos on their website. These resources can be invaluable to understanding how best to use their equipment.

Mic Settings

Like the Audio Cue, the Mic Cue has a number of settings that should be established before inserting a cue into the workspace. There are three basic areas of concern to get up and running with Mic Cues: default audio levels for new Mic Cues, Mic patch assignment, and device routing. To access these settings, click on the gear-shaped Settings icon at the bottom right hand corner of the workspace. This will open the Settings window. First, we will look at creating the default audio levels for Mic Cues. To do so, select *Cue Templates > Mic* and then select the Audio Levels tab.

Setting Default Levels for New Mic Cues

Though the look of this window is similar to that of the Audio Cue, the interface is a bit different (Figure 7.3). The first item of difference is located in the left column of the Audio Levels tabs, just underneath the Audio Input & Output Patch. This row is used for setting the inputs. There are two drop-down menus used for this process. The first drop-down asks how many input channels you want to assign from your audio device. The second drop-down menu represents what channel on your audio device should be mapped into the first input of your Mic Cue. As an example, if you assigned "2 inputs starting at channel 1," the matrix would respond by showing two rows. The first row (input one) would have input channel 1 of your audio device patched into input one of your Mic Cue. Like the Audio Cue, each of these signals is then bussed down the entire row of crosspoints to its right. It is then up to the programmer to assign which crosspoints should receive which signal. These signals then become the Cue Output that will be sent into the Mic Patch.

For a simple Mic Cue setup, with only one microphone that needs to be sent out to all of the speakers in your system, an Audio Levels setting would look like

Figure 7.3 The Audio Levels tab inside of Mic Cue Templates is used for setting default levels for new Mic Cues.

Figure 7.4
Setting for Mic
Cue assigned to
Cue Outputs 1–6.

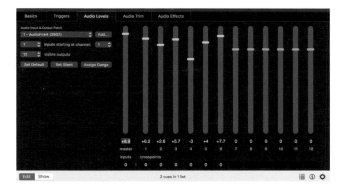

that shown in Figure 7.4. For this configuration, the mic input is assigned to crosspoints 1–6. This means that, for this Mic Cue, cue outputs 1–6 will receive the full audio signal sent from the microphone plugged into the first channel of the audio interface. These signals will then leave the cue and go to the next step of the signal flow: the Mic Patch.

Mic Patch

Like the Audio Cue before, the Mic Cue must be connected to a Mic Patch that sends the signal back to the audio device. Unlike the Audio Cue, though, the Mic Patch must interface with the same audio device for output as input. In order to edit the Mic Patch, select a Mic Cue in your workspace and click on the Audio Levels tab. Once here, select your audio device in the Audio Input & Output Patch area and then click on the "Edit" button beside it. This will open the Audio Patch Editor. Once you have done this, you are ready to move on to the next step: assigning the output patch for your audio device.

Device Routing

Once you have opened the Audio Patch Editor, you can experiment with device routing. This is the final step of the Mic Cue signal flow, allowing you to assign a path from the Mic Cue's cue outputs to one or more given device outputs. This screen will look similar to the device routing interface for Audio Cues and be controlled in a similar fashion. There will be 64 possible cue outputs shown in the left column, representing the 64 cue outputs of the Mic Cue. For this example, we are only concerned with the first six, since we only assigned the signal from input 1 into crosspoints 1–6 in the Cue Template for new Mic Cues. As there are only six speakers used in this configuration, the easiest thing is to set the patch in a 1-to-1 configuration (meaning that cue output 1 is assigned to crosspoint 1, cue output 2 to crosspoint 2, and so on) as seen in Figure 7.5. In this fashion, the sliders 1–8 in the Mic Cue's Audio Levels tab will control speakers 1–8 respectively. This will allow for the operator to choose to which of the eight speakers the signal should be assigned.

Figure 7.5
Setting up 1-to-1
Device Routing.

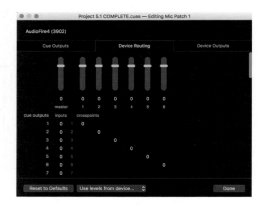

7.3 – Inserting and Editing a Mic Cue

After following the steps above, your sound system should be set up to allow for a Mic Cue to be inserted and all basic volume controls achieved through the Audio Levels tab of the Mic Cue. To insert a new Mic Cue, click on the Mic Cue icon or drag it into the workspace. This will place a Mic Cue place keeper into your cue list in keeping with the default levels for new Mic Cues established in your Cue Templates. The following sections detail the specifics of using the Inspector with a Mic Cue.

Inspector: Basics

The Basics tab is almost identical for the Mic Cue with that seen for the Audio Cue. Again, there are controls for cue numbering, naming, color assignment, duration, pre-wait and post-wait, continue status, flagging, auto-load, notes, and arm state. The only difference is that the Target is not applicable to the Mic Cue, as Mic Cues don't target another file type – rather they take their signal directly from a live audio input.

Inspector: Triggers

Like the Audio Cue, the Triggers tab allows for triggering the Mic Cue via Hotkey, MIDI, Wall Clock, or Timecode. Likewise, it also has controls for affecting other cues upon triggering the Mic Cue.

Inspector: Audio Levels

The Audio Levels tab allows for the control of volume output from the audio device. As this is almost identical to that of Audio Cues, you should be familiar with every function. The following should function as a quick overview:

Figure 7.6 The
Mic Cue Audio
Levels tab
resembles the
Audio Levels tab
for Audio Cues.
In this example,
note that the cue
output channels
are ganged into
groups of two.

Audio Input and Output Patch

For the Mic Cue, the patch is referred to as the Audio Input & Output Patch,
unlike the Audio Cue for which it was output only (Figure 7.6). The idea
remains the same, though, as this patch allows you to assign which audio
device you want to use for this particular Mic Cue. The Edit button to the
right of the Input and Output Patch allows for the editing of the Audio Input
& Output Device. As mentioned in Section 7.2, the two drop-down menus
beneath the patch control the number of input channels for the cue and the
start point on the audio device for input.

Visible Channels

This window allows for the change in visible channels. This is an important tool for Mic Cues, as you typically only ever need to see the number of
outputs available to your audio device (unless assigning an audio effect to a cue
output). If, for instance, your device only has eight outputs, there is no reason
to see channels 9–64. Instead, type 8 into the "Visible Channels" window and
only output channels 1–8 will remain visible.

Default Levels

By clicking on this button, you can set the levels to the pre-assigned default
levels set in the Cue Templates window.

Set All to Silent

Clicking on this button will mute all channels.

Assign Gangs

Ganging is a function that allows the linking of control of multiple cue outputs.
Simply click on the Assign Gangs button and insert either a number or letter
in the open space beneath any slider (in the window where volume levels

normally reside). For instance, place an "A" in the space beneath cue output channels 1 and 2, then click the Assign Gangs button again. This will now have paired output channels one and two, making them move in unison. You will also notice that the two channels have a similar color. Additional gangs will have unique colors as well.

Levels and Crosspoint Matrix

This area of the window is identical to the levels settings seen in the Audio Cue earlier in the book. The Master and all audio inputs are shown in the left column. The cue outputs are situated to the right of the Master, with the crosspoints matrix shown beneath for assigning an input channel to the appropriate cue output. Once patched, the sliders control volume and the Master controls the volume of all other outputs. Had an Audio Effect been assigned to a cue output, as detailed in Chapter 5, the slider (or sliders) for this effect would be listed (if you gave the effect a unique name).

Inspector: Audio Trim

Trim for the Mic Cue behaves in the same fashion as that of the Audio Cue. Mic Cues can be affected by Fade Cues in the same way that Audio Cues can. Using the Trim sliders in the Mic Cue will affect volume settings for all subsequent Fade Cues targeting the root Mic Cue.

Inspector: Audio Effects

Mic Cues can use Audio Effects in the same way as Audio Cues: either within the cue itself or globally through a cue output or device output. To assign an Audio Effect to a particular Mic Cue, simply click the "Add effect" button in the Effects tab. The chosen effect will be applied to only the selected cue. Common uses of this function might be the addition of EQ, reverb, or compression to a particular Mic Cue. Like volume settings, Mic effects can also be changed by subsequent Fade cues.

7.4 – Audio Effects and Mic Cues

As mentioned above, there are a number of methods for applying an Audio Unit effect to a Mic Cue. The easiest way is by adding the effect directly to the cue by using the Effects tab in the Inspector Panel of the Mic Cue itself. This only works on that specific cue and does not affect the playback of any other Mic Cue. While this is particularly effective, there are two other methods to globally apply Audio Unit effects to Mic Cues: by assigning it to the Cue Output or assigning it to a Device Output.

Cue Output

Cue outputs are the signals sent out from the Audio Cue or Mic Cue that get routed into the audio patch before finally outputting from the device. The signal from an audio or mic input is routed directly into the cue output via the crosspoints matrix. For the purposes of applying a global audio effect, though, an unused cue output can have an effect assigned to it. This process of assigning an Audio Effect to a cue output was discussed in depth in Chapter 5 – Section 5.7. Assigning an audio effect to a cue output for a Mic Cue is nearly identical to that of assigning it to an Audio Cue. The complete process is described in detail in the following project.

Project 7.1 ▼

Creating a Global EQ Send with Cue Outputs

An equalizer, or EQ, is used to adjust the individual frequencies of an audio signal in order to affect the resulting sound. There is any number of reasons to use an EQ on an audio signal. One might be to create a generic equalization for a male voice, or one for the female voice. In the following project, we will examine how to use a cue output to create a global EQ send in your workspace. Please note that this project cannot be done without an external audio device that supports microphone input. As such, there is no project file on the companion website. Simply open an untitled workspace to begin this project.

Step 1: Make sure your audio device is properly connected to your system before starting QLab. Once in the workspace, there are two ways to access your device:
If in Edit mode, click on Edit Device in the Audio Levels tab; if in the Audio Settings window, click on the edit button beside Mic Patch 1 (or whatever device you are using for Mic Cues). Once you have opened this interface, look at the first tab labeled "Cue Outputs."

Step 2: Select an unused cue output. In this case, it would likely be the first number past the number of useable outputs on your device, so I have selected cue output 7. In order to assign an audio effect to a cue output channel, click Add Effect, then select Apple, then AUGraphicEQ (see Figure 7.7).

Step 3: When you select AUGraphicEQ button, the control window for this Audio Unit will instantly open (see Figure 7.8). This window is not a part of QLab, rather the control window designed by Apple for this AU. This is the same window you would see in any application using the plug-in. If you are familiar with traditional graphic EQs this window

(Continued)

Figure 7.7 Adding a graphic EQ through Audio Effects.

Figure 7.8 The AUGraphicEQ Control window, used for manipulating frequencies.

will look quite familiar to you. There are 32 sliders, each representing a section of frequency that can be either increased or decreased by the device. The sliders to the left represent lower frequencies (bass), while the sliders to the right represent the higher ones (treble).

Step 4: One great feature of the Cue Outputs editing window is the ability to re-name a cue output. Click on the black box to the right of Cue Output #7 and type in the word "EQ." When you click enter or select an area outside the box, the number 7 will be replaced with the word EQ. This will be useful in the cueing phase, as all your sliders will now be labeled with their function. Keep in mind that a named cue output for Mic settings will not appear for Audio Cues, as this setting is dedicated to Mic Cues only. In this way, you can have distinctly different global effects sends for Mic Cues and Audio Cues.
Leave the settings window, and return to the Mic Cue in your cue list. Click on the Audio Levels tab of the Inspector for this cue, and you will see that Cue Output 7 has been renamed "EQ" (see Figure 7.9).

Step 5: The process above effectively set up cue output 7 as an EQ effects send. Two final steps must be done in order to enable this function. Currently, the audio effect is applied to cue output 7, but there is

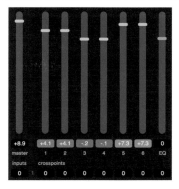

Figure 7.9 The Cue Output fader is re-labeled as "EQ."

no input signal routed into the fader. To assign an input, insert a 0 in the crosspoint matrix beneath the newly labeled "EQ" fader. This routes the Mic Cue signal through the EQ effects send.

Step 6: Finally, you need to route the EQ effects send into all of the device outputs for your audio device. To do so, click the edit button beside your Audio Input and Output patch. Once the window opens, select Device Routing. Now, select the bottom row labeled "EQ" and route it into each space on the crosspoints matrix by typing a 0 into the slot (as seen in Figure 7.10). This will route your EQ effects send into all six channels of your device. Now, the fader can be used to increase or decrease the amount of equalized audio sent out into the mix.

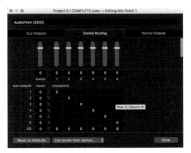

Figure 7.10 Assigning the EQ send to the audio device.

Step 7: Once having gone through all of these steps, the EQ effect will be available for any subsequent Mic Cue added. This process can be replicated for any type of audio effect desired. Simply add an AU effect to another cue output, re-name it, and it will also be available for all cues. It is worth noting that multiple AU effects can be applied to one given cue output. For instance, you could combine together a graphic EQ, reverb, and hi pass filter to one cue output. Keep in mind, though, more effects added to the system can begin to tax your computer's resources.

Device Output

Assigning an audio effect to a device output is the second method of applying effects in a global sense. The process of assigning the audio effect to a device output is quite similar to that of a cue output.

Project 7.2 ▼

Assigning an Audio Effect to a Device Output

One great example of an audio effect that might be used on a device output is a delay. In audio terms, a delay is a type of device that records an input sample and waits a predetermined period of time before playing it back. For many sound installations, digital delays are used to compensate for the passage of sound through air. The use of straight delays in a sound reinforcement system allows for multiple speakers to be used in a large space and makes it appear as if the sound is originating from the stage. This allows for adding speakers in the back of the space that provide sufficient volume without overloading the volume from the front of the hall. In the following project, we will examine how to use a device output to create a delay send for certain speakers in your sound system.

Step 1: If in Edit mode, click on Edit Device in the Audio Levels tab. If in the Audio Settings window, click on the edit button to the right of Mic Patch 1 (or whatever device you are using for Mic Cues). Once you have opened this interface, look at the last tab labeled "Device Outputs."

Step 2: For the purposes of a reinforcement system, the goal would be to add a delay to speakers in the back of the theatre so that the signal is perceived to be originating from the stage. For these purposes, let us assume that the device outputs 5 and 6 are the rear speakers of the theatre. In order to assign an audio effect to these two channels, simply scroll down to the rows labeled Device Output 5 and Device Output 6. Click on the button to the right of the device outputs labeled "Add effect." Select the AUDelay button.

Step 3: When you select the AUDelay button, the control window for this Audio Unit will instantly open (see Figure 7.11). This window controls the functions of the AUDelay plug-in. A delay works in one of two ways: by either delaying the signal and replaying it over itself, thereby creating an echo effect, or by creating a "straight delay" by sampling the audio signal and simply waiting a period of time before playing it back. For reinforcement purposes, a straight delay is preferable. To achieve this, click on the yellow line in the grid. The line represents delay time and feedback. Delay time means how long it waits

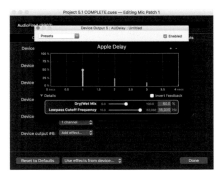

Figure 7.11 AUDelay control interface.

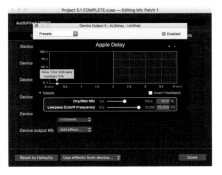

Figure 7.12 AUDelay straight delay settings.

before playing back the sample. Feedback means the amount of time the sample is added onto itself. In order to achieve a straight delay, the yellow dot must be pulled all the way to the bottom of the grid, thereby changing the feedback to 0%. This will create the desired straight delay (see Figure 7.12). Play around with the actual delay time, but keep in mind that anything above 0.03 seconds will start to have an unearthly quality to it. Repeat this process identically for both device outputs 5 and 6.

Step 4: The process above effectively sets up a delay on any Mic signal outputting through Device Outputs 5 and 6. Once having gone through all of these steps, the delay effect will be applied to any subsequent Mic Cue passing audio through device outputs 5 and 6. This process can be replicated for any type of audio effect desired. Simply add an AU effect to another device output and it will also be available for all cues. As with Cue Outputs in the previous project, multiple AU effects can be applied to one given device output. As mentioned before, though, a high number of effects added to the system can begin to tax your computer's resources.

Fade Cues

The Fade Cue is a core component of controlling cues within the QLab system. A fade is a change in the attributes of a cue over a predetermined period of time. Initially, the purpose of the Fade Cue within QLab was simple; to change the volume settings or to stop an Audio Cue. In the newest versions of QLab, Fade Cues have the ability to control a number of different cue types – Mic, Video, Camera, Text, and Network Cues are all targetable by Fade Cues. In general, for audio-related cues a Fade Cue will affect volume levels, whereas with video-related cues a Fade Cue will affect attributes like opacity, image position, and object geometry. This versatility means that the available options for a Fade Cue will change depending on the type of cue it targets. Since we are focusing on audio in this section of the book, the following chapter will detail the differing functions of the Fade Cue for audio purposes only.

8.1 – Inserting and Editing Audio Fade Cues

Audio Fade Cues are used for a number of different functions: to either increase or decrease the volume level of an Audio Cue; to change the output of the audio signal from one speaker to another (panning); or to change how audio effects are applied to an Audio Cue. Fades themselves work within a number of cue types, predominately including Audio, Mic, Video, and Camera. Once you learn the basics of how to use a Fade Cue, though, its application is similar across the different cue varieties.

An Audio Fade Cue must have an Audio Cue assigned as its target or it will not function. In order to have a Fade Cue accept an Audio Cue as its target, simply drag the Audio Cue onto the Fade Cue's line on the workspace and release. This will automatically assign it as a target. Once the target has been assigned, then the Fade Cue is active. For its most basic use, simply open the Audio Levels tab in an Audio Fade Cue and either increase or decrease the volume from that set on the targeted cue. This will either increase or decrease the volume of the cue over the Fade Cue's duration.

One important feature of note regarding the Fade Cue is that, regardless of creating a fade-in or fade-out, **the fade cue should always be placed after the targeted Audio Cue.** This feature often confuses first time QLab users. The reason for this is that an Audio Cue must be playing for a Fade Cue to affect its output. It has been my experience that most people intrinsically understand fade-outs, but are confused by the process of creating a fade-in. To create a fade-in, first insert an Audio Cue and set its levels at –inf (or whatever initial volume desired). Next, insert a Fade Cue and assign the Audio Cue as its target. The volume set in the Audio Levels tab of this Fade Cue will be the final volume for the Audio Cue once faded in.

Design Tips ▼

Cue Naming

One important thing to remember about the use of Fade Cues is that, without looking at the details in the Inspector Panel, it can be very difficult to discern the action of said cue. I find it is good to always be in the habit of naming my Fade Cues according to their function as soon as I input them into the workspace. For instance, if I have a Fade Cue that increases the volume of a police siren, I might call it "Fade up siren." Using descriptive names up front can save you lots of time later on in the tech process.

There are a number of controllable functions for a Fade Cue in addition to the basic levels setting. To change the parameters of the Fade Cue, look into the Inspector. There will be five tabs shown for the Audio Fade Cue in the Inspector Panel. Similar to the Audio Cue itself, these tabs are used for changing the attributes of the Fade Cue. The attributes for each of the Inspector tabs are shown below.

8.2 – Inspector: Basics

The Basics tab remains essentially unchanged from its layout for an Audio Cue. The only substantive difference between the Basics panel for fades is that the file name shown in the Name row is that of the file being targeted by the Fade Cue (see Figure 8.1).

One of the most used functions of the Basics window is setting a pre-wait time for a Fade Cue. By using this function, the programmer can effectively create a crescendo (volume increase) or decrescendo (volume decrease) within an Audio

Figure 8.1 The Fade Cue Basics tab.

Cue. The addition of dynamic changes such as these can add depth to an audio recording and make canned music sound a bit more realistic.

8.3 – Inspector: Triggers

Like the Audio Cue, the Triggers tab allows for triggering the Fade Cue via Hotkey, MIDI, Wall Clock, or Timecode. Likewise, it also has controls for affecting other cues upon triggering the fade.

8.4 – Inspector: Curve Shape

Many attributes of Fade Cues have remained consistent in the transition from QLab 3 to QLab 4. The Curve Shape controls, however, offer up quite a few advances over previous versions in controlling your levels over the duration of the Fade Cue. For an Audio Fade Cue, the fade curve is a graphic representation of audio levels and cue duration. If perceived as a basic graph, cue duration is represented in the x-axis with audio levels (volume) represented in the y-axis. The default cue duration for a Fade Cue is 5 seconds, but can be changed to any desired time in the Cue Templates section of Workspace Settings by selecting Fade and then Basics. The duration is labeled along the top edge of the fade curve window. Understanding this, one can see that each vertical line within the graph represents 0.5 seconds.

When looking at the Curve Shape tab, there are two graphs for setting fade curves. The graph on the left represents any audio fade for increasing levels, whereas the right graph represents a decrease in levels. Like the timing, default fade curves are established in the Cue Templates settings. To choose a different curve type, however, you can simply select a type from the drop-down menu on the left side of the screen. QLab 4 offers four different options for fade curve shapes: S-Curve, Custom Curve, Parametric Curve, and Linear Curve. Each of these types is addressed in the following list.

1. S-Curve

The default curve shape is the S-Curve, a parabolic shape that resembles an "S" on its side (see Figure 8.2). The S-Curve has a slower "attack," meaning that

Figure 8.2 The S-Curve has a slower rate of change at the beginning and end of the fade.

it takes longer to perceive the increase or decrease in volume. This attribute makes the S-Curve suitable for many fade-ins or fade-outs of music. Looking at the curve over the 5-second duration, you can see that the volume remains fairly consistent for 0.5 seconds, and then gradually begins to increase. Once it hits 1.5 seconds, the rate of increase remains constant until around 3 seconds, then begins to slow until the 5-second mark is reached. Sliding your mouse along the S-Curve shape will indicate the percentage of change vs. elapsed time over the duration of the Fade Cue. You will notice that in the S-Curve, both levels and duration align at the halfway mark (meaning at 2.5 seconds into the Fade Cue, increases in levels should be at 50% of their established change). Though it works for most gradual fades quite well, you will find yourself in need of fade curves that have an even faster or slower attack. In these cases, simply click on the button labeled S-Curve and select the Custom Curve setting.

2. Custom Curve

The Custom Curve can be manipulated into any number of unique fade curve shapes to meet the needs of the design. To change the consistent curve into a customized shape, simply click on the curve, and it will insert a control point at that location. The control point is represented as a yellow dot on the fade curve. By grabbing the control point, the operator can add either an incline or decline to the fade curve by simply pulling the control handles in any direction. Multiple control points can be inserted into one Fade Cue to create interesting fade curves. Figure 8.3 shows three different custom fade curve shapes that each behave in radically different ways.

The first fade curve illustrates a fade with a quick attack, having the sound fade to 50% by 0.10 seconds and at full by 0.6 seconds. This fade effect would be used to add a slight fade in to the beginning of an audio file, making its

Figure 8.3 Three fade curve types: fast fade-in; slow fade-in; and an oscillating fade curve.

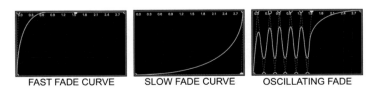

FAST FADE CURVE   SLOW FADE CURVE   OSCILLATING FADE

triggering less abrupt. Sometimes this technique is useful when working from music with a slight aberration at the beginning of the track.

The second fade curve is an example of a particularly slow fade curve. In this example, the audio levels will begin to increase from the moment the Fade Cue is triggered, but at a slow rate. The rate of increase remains constant until about 1.5 seconds into the fade, then begins a more rapid increase, going from 12% at 1.5 seconds to 100% at 3 seconds. This type of fade curve might be useful for creating a sound effect in which something approaches from the distance making sound (like a police siren).

The final example illustrates the potential for adding multiple control points within one fade curve to oscillate the volume changes from increase to decrease. In this example, the audio file's volume rapidly increases then decreases at a regular interval. With a consistency such as this, one could take a constant sound like a horn and make it sound more like a siren used for an alarm.

3. Parametric Curve

The parametric curve is a mathematically precise fade shape that has different control handles than the other fade curve types. When you choose the parametric curve, a window will appear beneath the duration window, reading "intensity." The default intensity will be 1.000. By clicking on this number and sliding your mouse up or down, you can change the intensity to a scale from 0.025 (a gradual fade) to 200.000 (an incredibly abrupt fade). Some experimentation will quickly acquaint you with this function.

4. Linear Curve

Selecting the Linear Curve establishes a straight curve with a consistent rate of increase or decrease in levels over time. The level will reach a 50% change mark halfway through the Fade Cue duration. This fade type creates a simple, straight transition over a predetermined timeframe.

Audio Domain

Directly underneath the Curve Shape selector is a drop-down menu called Audio Domain. This tool allows you to select the scale used by QLab for fading audio. Each of these three settings changes the resulting sound created by a Fade Cue.

1) **Slider Domain.** This audio domain creates a fade type that resembles that of traditional sound consoles and makes for a very smooth-sounding fade. This is the default domain, and creates a similar fading effect as simply grabbing the main volume fade and manually sliding it up or down. It is designed using a logarithmic scale.

2) **Decibel Domain.** The decibel audio domain also uses a logarithmic scale for creating fades. This setting can be used in conjunction with the parametric curve type to create an equal gain fade. This fade type is ideal creating smooth crossfades between phase-coherent sounds, for example two loops of the same sound.

3) **Linear Domain.** The Linear audio domain uses a linear scale type. This setting can be used in conjunction with the parametric fade curve with the default parameter to create an equal power fade. In contrast to the equal gain fade, this fade type is useful in making smooth crossfades between sounds that aren't phase coherent.

Fade Cue Duration

To this point, all of the Fade Cues discussed have had the default duration of 5 seconds. Should there be an instance for which longer or shorter fade durations are needed, simply use the Duration input on the left side of the Curve Shape panel. Input the desired time and press enter. The cue duration and fade curve window will then be changed to match the inputted time.

Reset to Default Shape

The Reset to Default Shape button returns the fade curve to the default setting determined in the Workspace Settings. This will replace any previous custom settings you might have created.

8.5 – Inspector: Audio Levels

The Audio Levels settings in a Fade Cue control the amount of increase or decrease in output volume. This mirrors the Audio Levels tab from an Audio Cue in many ways. There is no device routing, though, since the Fade Cue uses the pre-assigned device routing of the targeted cue. The following section details the many control functions and settings present in the Levels tab.

Fade Type: Absolute vs. Relative

Looking at Figure 8.4, you can see the basic layout of the Levels tab. The first row on the left column of the Levels tab allows the programmer to set the Fade type to that of absolute or relative. These two terms are important to understand for the way in which they affect Audio Cues.

An **absolute fade** adjusts the volume of the targeted Audio Cue to a particular volume level. When triggered, the absolute cue will increase or decrease the volume of the targeted cue to the volume set in the Levels tab of the Fade Cue Inspector. There can only be one absolute fade assigned to one given channel

Figure 8.4 The Fade Cue's Audio Levels tab is used to affect changes to the volume of Audio Cues.

at a time. In the instance of two fade cues targeting the same channel of audio, the second cue fired would control the volume of that channel (Latest Takes Precedence).

A **relative fade**, in contrast, fades the volume up or down relative to the volume of the Audio Cue when triggered. In other words, whereas an absolute fade adjusts the volume *to* a particular level, the relative fade adjusts the volume *by* a particular level. Unlike the absolute fade, an unlimited number of relative fades may be applied to a given channel of audio.

The graphic interface for the levels settings of a relative fade differ from that of the absolute fade. When the relative fade is selected from the drop-down menu, the levels faders in the right column will change from their standard look to hourglass-shaped slider icons (see Figure 8.5).

Stop Target When Done

It is important to understand that Fade Cues only work to affect the overall output levels of the cue. Unless explicitly stopped, an Audio Cue will remain running in the background of your workspace until it reaches the end of its duration. This is true, even if a Fade Cue has lowered the levels to 0%. This function allows for the ability to keep an Audio Cue running in the background and faded back up at a later time, thus allowing for the elapsed time to be perceived. If, upon fading out an Audio Cue, you will not be using the same cue again, it is always best to select the Stop Target When Done checkbox. This function stops the targeted cue from playing in the background after the fade duration. Keep in mind that every cue running in the background (even those which cannot be seen or heard) will continue to engage your computer's CPU. If, over the course

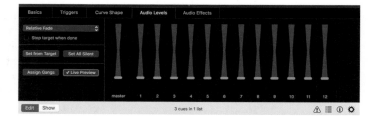

Figure 8.5 The appearance of the levels faders for a relative Fade Cue differ from that of the absolute fade.

of a show, there are multiple cues running at the same time, then your computer's resources will be taxed and negatively affect its playback ability.

The Stop Target When Done checkbox appears in the Audio Levels and Audio Effects Inspector tabs. Note that activating it in either of these tabs will activate it in both.

Design Tips ▽

Fading Group Cues

One great function of the relative fade cue is the ability to control multiple Audio Cues at the same time. If you have created a Group Cue containing multiple Audio Cues, a relative fade cue can be applied to this group, thereby raising or lowering the volume of all Audio Cues within the group at once. Imagine a scene in a play that features a parade passing by. In this case, you could create a Group Cue containing all of the different aspects of the parade (the marching band, applause, talking, car horns, etc.). By simply targeting this Group Cue with a relative Fade Cue, you could increase or decrease volume levels and pan the audio signals to replicate the parade passing by.

Levels and Crosspoint Matrix

The right column of the Audio Levels tab is identical to the control functions for an Audio Cue. By this point, you should be exceedingly familiar with the layout and function of the levels and crosspoints matrix. The Master and all audio inputs are shown to the left, with output channels to the right of the Master and the crosspoints matrix shown beneath each corresponding cue output channel. Once patched, the sliders control volume and the Master controls the volume of all other outputs. This window is used for setting the desired change in levels for a Fade Cue for both absolute and relative fade cue types. It is worth mentioning that Fades will only affect the levels that are activated – not necessarily all levels.

Set from Target/Set All Silent

The middle row of the left column allows for rapid settings of the output levels for the Fade Cue. The Set from Target button sets the levels to be identical to that of the targeted Audio Cue. This is particularly useful to set as a starting point, especially if you are working with multiple channels of audio set at different volume levels. A quick way to set a consistent fade of an audio cue is to click Set to Target, then either increase or decrease the Master output level as desired. Likewise, if the goal is to completely fade the volume out, then click on the Set All Silent button, which will set all of the levels faders to 0.

Assign Gangs

Fade Cue sliders can be grouped together for ease of control using the Gang function. This function is identical to the method shown in Section 5.3 for ganging channels in Audio Cues.

Live Preview

As mentioned in Chapter 3, the Live Fade Preview setting enables you to make adjustments to Fade Cue settings and hear the results in real-time while your cue is playing. The Live Preview button is a shortcut to toggle Live Preview on or off. Another way to access this control is through the Tools Menu or by using the keyboard shortcut ⇧⌘P.

8.6 - Inspector: Audio Effects

The Audio Effects tab features two functions: changing the audio effect attributes of a targeted Audio Cue and changing the playback rate of the targeted Audio Cue. Audio effects, as discussed in Chapter 5, allow for the use of Audio Units to affect an Audio Cue. Fade Cues can also be used in conjunction with audio effects to change the effects settings or remove an audio effect from an Audio Cue. Audio Effects Fade Cues are always absolute fades.

To change the attributes of the Audio Effects, simply add a Fade Cue and target the desired Audio Cue. The targeted Audio Cue must have some type of audio effects applied to it already. You cannot add an audio effect on its own simply by adding a Fade Cue and adding an audio effect. Open the Audio Effects tab of the Fade Cue and check the box beside the desired audio effect and click the Edit button (see Figure 8.6). This will open the control window for the Audio Unit. Make the desired changes to the AU, and then close the window. Now, when the Fade Cue is activated, it will change the playback attributes to those you just set. The Effects Fade allows for either an increase or decrease of effects outputs and can be used for countless different purposes.

Fade Rate

One interesting function of the Audio Effects fade is the ability to change the rate of playback of an Audio Cue. By selecting the Fade Rate to checkbox, you can change the assigned rate of a cue through the use of a fade. This essentially enables you to add variations to the playback rate of an Audio Cue.

Figure 8.6 The Audio Effects tab is used to manipulate audio effects assigned to the targeted cue.

Figure 8.7 The
Fade Rate button
can be used to
change the rate of
audio playback.

Figure 8.7 The Fade Rate button can be used to change the rate of audio playback.

To achieve this, click on the Fade rate button (see Figure 8.7) and set it to the desired playback rate. Increasing to a number value above 1 will speed up the playback, whereas those number values below 1 will slow playback. To make minor changes, simply click in the input window. While holding the mouse clicked down, slide your cursor up to increase the number or down to decrease it. Once the correct rate is inputted, click "enter" to finalize the number. It is worth noting that there is no preserve pitch checkbox with the Fade Rate controls. This means that changing the rate will, by default, change the pitch. If you want to change playback rate without affecting the pitch, you must go to the targeted cue and click the "preserve pitch" checkbox inside the Time & Loops tab.

Stop Target When Done

Like all other Fade Cues, the Audio Effects Fade can be set to stop playback of the targeted Audio Cue when the fade action is complete. To do so, click on the Stop Target When Done checkbox on the left side of the Audio Effects tab. Note that this checkbox is found in the Audio Levels and Geometry tab as well.

Set Audio Effects from Target

This button automatically assigns the Audio Effects of the targeted Audio Cue to the selected Fade Cue. When a Fade Cue targets an Audio Cue, the Audio Effects should be automatically assigned to that fade. Sometimes, during the process of experimentation you might find that you dislike the changes made and want to return to the original state of the cue. This can be easily achieved by clicking the Set Audio Effects from Target button.

Audio Fade Cue Summary

A Fade Cue has many different uses other than simply raising or lowering volume levels. Keep in mind that, even if you are only using the Fade Cue to affect Audio Effects, other attributes of the Fade Cue can be controlled through the Fade Cue Inspector. Curve Shape, duration, waits, and continues all apply to the Audio Effects Fade, like any other cue type.

The following project details the process of adding an audio effect through the Fade Cue in order to adjust audio effects applied to an Audio Cue. The project requires the download of Project 8.1 from the companion website.

Project 8.1 ▼

Pitch Bend to Replicate a Reel-to-Reel Malfunction

Step 1: Open Cue 1 in the Project 8.1 workspace. This file is a recording in the style of old 1940s radio announcers. In order to affect this Audio Cue with a Fade Cue, you must first add an Audio Effect to the cue with no changes applied.

Step 2: Click on the Audio Effects tab in the Inspector Panel. On the left side of the screen click the "add effect" button. A drop-down menu will appear. This should display any Audio Units installed on your computer. In this case, select the Apple button, and then select the AUPitch button. This will open the control interface for the plug-in. **Do not change any attributes!** This will simply apply the AU to the Audio Cue so that a Fade Cue can later affect it.

Step 3: Add a Fade Cue to the workspace. Target Cue 1 with this Fade Cue.

Step 4: Select the Fade Cue and click on the Audio Effects tab in the Inspector Panel. Click the checkbox beside the AUPitch effect. This will activate the AU for your Fade Cue.

Step 5: Click on the Edit button to the left of the AUPitch label. This will open the AUPitch control interface. Slide the pitch knob to the right until it reads "1,800 Cents" (see Figure 8.8).

Figure 8.8 The AUPitch control interface allows for pitch bending and fine-tuning the effect.

Step 6: Select the Fade Cue again and change the fade duration to 4 seconds in the Curve Shape tab of the Inspector Panel.

Step 7: Go back to the workspace. Trigger playback for Cue 1. After a moment, click GO for Cue 2 (the Fade Cue). You should hear a rapid increase of pitch over a 4-second duration.

Step 6 – Bonus: As an added effect, you could find a scratch sound effect to indicate the point of malfunction. Insert this as your second Audio Cue and set it as an Auto-continue with the Fade Cue next in your cue sequence. This would add the sound of a malfunction directly followed up with an increase in tape speed.

8.7 – Mic Fade Cues

As earlier addressed, the Mic Cue is a great tool for adding reinforcement to your QLab sound system. In essence, the Mic Cue sends a signal to your audio interface and activates an input channel. The audio signal then passes through the Mic Patch and into the assigned device outputs on your audio interface. Once the Mic Cue has been activated, it will remain on until either a Fade Cue or another control cue, such as a Stop Cue or Pause Cue, affects its playback. The following section details the use of Fade Cues for affecting the playback of a Mic Cue.

Inserting a Mic Fade Cue

Like all other Fade Cue functions, the process of creating a Mic Cue fade begins with inserting a Fade Cue into the cue list. The second step is then to drag the intended Mic Cue to be affected onto the Fade Cue. This will set the Mic Cue as the target of the Fade Cue. Once you have done this, the process is all controlled from the Inspector of the Fade Cue.

Basics, Triggers, and Curve Shape

The first three tabs in the Inspector Panel remain consistent with other types of Fade Cues. Basics offers up the basic information about the Fade Cue, pre-wait and post-wait, continue modes, and triggering options. Triggers controls the ways in which your Fade Cue can be triggered and affect other cue types upon playback. The Curve Shape tab defaults to the standard S-curve, but also allows for adjusting the curve to other curve types. One important element to note in this tab, though, is the "stop target when done" checkbox. Like other varieties of Fades we have explored, it is essential to note that a Mic Cue will continue to run in the background until stopped. Simply muting all of the channels will not stop the cue by itself.

Audio Levels

The Levels tab is one of the most useful when applying a fade to a Mic Cue. Like applying a fade to an Audio Cue, fading a Mic Cue will most frequently entail increasing or decreasing volume output. The process for doing so is relatively easy.

First, click on the "Set from Target" button in the left column. This will match the levels settings of the Fade Cue to that of the targeted Mic Cue. This assures that you will begin at the preset level of the Mic Cue. To increase or decrease the volume, select the levels fader associated with the Mic you want to change and slide it up or down. If there are changes to be applied to multiple mics, then use each of their individual sliders. Should you want to keep the balance between multiple mic levels consistent as you change the volume of the entire mix, use the master level fader and all will be affected equally.

Audio Effects

Like Audio Cues, Mic Cues can have audio effects applied to them as signal processing. As such, the Fade Cue can be used in a similar fashion to change the audio effects applied to a Mic Cue. This process is identical to the one described in Section 8.1 above for fading audio effects on an Audio Cue. It is important to note, once again, that audio effects cannot be added to a Fade Cue; they only display the audio effects of the targeted cue.

8.8 – Manual Fades

By default, a Fade Cue inserted into a workspace is set as a manual fade, meaning that the QLab operator will trigger it. Manual Fade cues make up a great percentage of the fades used in a typical live performance. Personally, I prefer to give the maximum amount of control to the stage manager and QLab operator in a live performance, as there is no guarantee that a performer will perform in the same fashion from night to night. Any number of factors can change the timing of a performance. For me, this means that I try to limit the instances in which cues are automatically triggered to those for which they are absolutely necessary.

One example that frequently pops up in live performance is an actor answering a telephone onstage. For this type of sound effect, you always want to have more rings available than what you think is necessary. What happens if you have only four rings in your audio file when the actor gets caught backstage in a quick change? For an instance like this, I always set the Audio Cue on an infinite loop so that the phone can ring until the actor picks it up. It is the action of picking up the phone, though, that requires a manual fade set to a zero count. I have seen instances of sound designers providing three ring tones, but the actor accidentally picks up after two. This creates an embarrassing situation for the actor onstage when the audience invariably laughs at being forcibly reminded that they are watching live theatre.

The following project takes you through the process of creating an infinitely looped telephone ring with a manual zero-count fade to end the ringing.

Project 8.2 ▼

Creating a Zero-Count Fade Cue

Step 1: Download Project 8.2 from the companion website and open the QLab workspace. Look at Cue 1. This is a recording of an alarm sounding. In this production, an alarm is activated and must be stopped by an actor hitting a control panel on the wall. The timing for this must be precise and based on the actor's visual cue.

Step 2: Select the Time & Loops tab in the Inspector Panel. Click on the button labeled "Infinite Loop." This will set up the alarm to sound on an infinite loop until stopped by QLab.

Step 3: Using the Toolbar, or Toolbox, insert a Fade Cue as Cue 2. Target Cue 1 with this Fade Cue by dragging cue 1 over cue 2 until it highlights the cue with a blue box.

Step 4: Click on the Curve Shape tab of the Inspector Panel in Cue 2. Using your keypad, insert the number 0 into the Duration window. Press enter. This will make the Fade instantaneous upon pressing GO. You will notice that the words "instant fade" should be printed in the corner of your Fade-curve window (see Figure 8.9).

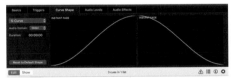

Figure 8.9 Creating an instant fade by changing the fade duration.

Step 5: Select the Levels tab in the Inspector Panel for Cue 2. Pull the master fader all the way to the bottom of the slider. Notice that the rectangle beneath it will now read –INF and have a highlighted background color. This will make the alarm cue fade to –INF (or mute) when the Fade Cue is triggered (see Figure 8.10).

Figure 8.10 Set the Master level to –INF to mute the audio levels.

Step 6: In the area to the left of your screen, beneath the absolute fade button, select the checkbox reading "Stop target when done." This will stop the cue from playing in the background once the Fade Cue has been fired.

Step 7: Test your workspace. Fire cue 1 and then, after a moment, fire cue 2. It should instantly stop the alarm from sounding.

8.9 – Automatic Fades

An automatic fade is one pre-programmed to fire at a predetermined time or is triggered by another cue within the workspace. These types of fades can be quite useful to automate changes of volume levels within an Audio Cue. While it is true that the integrated fade envelope on an Audio Cue can control internal level changes, it is sometimes preferable to combine together a sequence of multiple cues to accomplish an effect. The following project details how to use an automatic Fade Cue to fade in at beginning of an Audio Cue and fade out at its end.

Project 8.3 ▼

Automated Fade-In and Fade-Out of an Audio Cue

Step 1: Download Project 8.3 from the companion website and open the QLab workspace. Look at Cue 1. This is a recording of a piece of music for which we want to create an automated fade-in at the beginning of the song and a fade-out at some interval within the Audio Cue's playback. In the Audio Levels tab of the Inspector, pull the master fader down to the bottom of the slider to mute the audio. This is essential since the sound needs to start at silent in order to fade in.

Step 2: Using the Toolbar, or Toolbox, insert a Fade Cue as Cue 2. Target Cue 1 with this Fade Cue by dragging cue 1 over cue 2 until it highlights the cue with a blue box.

Step 3: Click on the Curve Shape tab of the Inspector in Cue 2. Using your keypad, insert the number 6 into the Duration window. Press enter. This will make the Fade's action occur over a period of 6 seconds.

Step 4: Click on the button labeled S-curve, and select the drop-down option labeled "Custom curve." This will enable you to create your own curve shape. The graph on the left represents the curve for a fade-in, whereas the one on the right is a fade-out. In the first graph box, click on the yellow line at the first line, labeled 0.6 seconds, and pull your cursor all the way up to the upper left corner labeled 0.0 (see Figure 8.11). This will create a fade curve that curves upward fairly quickly over the course of 4 seconds.

Figure 8.11 This fade curve will rise quickly over the 4-second duration.

Step 5: In the Audio Levels tab of cue 2, set the available sliders to 0 (since we are working in stereo, this will be the master and faders 1 and 2). When triggered, this Fade Cue will adjust the playback volume of Cue 1 to 0, or unity, meaning it will play back at the original level of the recording. You should notice that the red x listed in the left corner of the cue row for cue 2 will now disappear, once you have set a level for the Fade Cue.

Step 6: As currently set, cue 1 will play when triggered but cannot be heard since its volume is set to mute. The purpose of the Fade Cue is to bring the volume up to the desired level. In order to automate this function, you must go to cue 1 and set the continue state to **auto-continue.** This can be done at the end of the cue row by clicking in the last column (beneath the arrow icon). Blank means no continue, the triple-arrow icon means Auto-continue (the following cue firing in unison with the first), and the arrow with a circle indicates Auto-follow (the cue firing once the first cue's action and post-wait is completed). Alternately, you could click on the Basics tab of cue 1 and select auto-continue in the continue drop-down menu (located in the bottom left corner). Examine Figure 8.12 to see if your cueing matches.

Figure 8.12 Check to see if your cueing matches.

Step 7: Test the cue sequence. If properly programmed, clicking GO for cue 1 should trigger both cue 1 and 2 simultaneously, and the audio signal will fade in from silent over a 6-second interval.

Step 8: Press escape to end the playback of the cue sequence. The final desired effect is to add an automated cue that will fade out the Audio Cue at a predetermined playback point. To do this, insert a new Fade Cue as cue 3. Target cue 1 with this Fade Cue by dragging cue 1 over cue 3 until it highlights the cue with a blue box.

Step 9: Set the continue state of cue 2 as Auto-continue. This will automatically fire all three cues simultaneously.

(Continued)

Step 10: Since the desired outcome of the final Fade Cue is to fade-out the volume of cue 1, click on the Levels tab of cue 3 and pull the master fader down to –INF. In addition, select the "stop target when done" checkbox in the left half of the Levels tab. This will stop playback of cue 1 once it is faded out.

Step 11: Select the Curve Shape tab of cue 3. Click on the button labeled S-curve, and select the drop-down option labeled "Custom curve." This will enable you to create your own curve shape. This time, you will use the second grid, as the desired outcome is a fade-out. In the second graph box, click on the yellow line at the last vertical graph line (4.5 seconds) and pull your cursor all the way up to the upper right corner (see Figure 8.13). This will create a fade curve that curves downward over the course of 5 seconds.

Figure 8.13 Slow fade-out.

Step 12: If left in its current configuration, cue 3 would automatically trigger resulting in audio signal almost instantly fading out. To achieve the automated fade-out, we must set a **pre-wait** for cue 3. To accomplish this, either enter the pre-wait time in the pre-wait column of the cue row, or insert it in the Basics tab for cue 3. Set the pre-wait as 13 seconds (00:13.00) by typing in 13, and then pressing enter.

Step 13: Test the cue sequence. If properly programmed, clicking GO for cue 1 should trigger cues 1–3 simultaneously, and the audio signal will fade-in from silent over a 6-second interval. After 13 seconds of audio playback, the fade-out programmed by cue 3 should trigger, fading down to silent over a 5-second duration. This will ensure that the song will fade out on its own before entering into the second musical phrase. Figure 8.14 shows how your finished workspace should appear.

Figure 8.14 The finished workspace.

8.10 – Panning

Panning, the ability to "move" an audio cue from one set of speakers to another (right to left, front to back, diagonally, etc.) is one of the bench-marks of a convincing sound design. Historically, panning was either created in the studio and saved into the audio file or performed live through the audio mixer. With QLab, panning can be automated via Fade Cues and saved for playback through your workspace. The following project illustrates the process of doing so.

Project 8.4 ▼

Panning via Fade Cue

One of the best uses of panning is for the creation of "Doppler effect" sound cues, like that of a police siren approaching then passing away into the distance. The following steps detail the creation of such an effect.

Step 1: Download Project 8.4 from the companion website and open the QLab workspace. Look at cue 1. This is a recording of a police siren without the Doppler effect added. In the Device & Levels tab of the Inspector Panel, pull the master fader down to the bottom of the slider to mute the audio. This is essential since the sound needs to start at silent in order to fade in.

Step 2: Using the Toolbar, or Toolbox, insert four Fade Cues (cues 2–5). Use cue 1 as the target for all four Fade Cues. In addition, set the continue state for cues 1–4 as Auto-continue. This is the foundation of the panning effect.

Step 3: Click on the Curve Shape tab of the Inspector Panel in Cue 2. Using your keypad, insert the number 3 into the Duration window. Press enter. This will make the Fade's action occur over a period of 3 seconds upon pressing GO. Make this the cue duration for cues 2 and 3. Finally, set the cue duration for cues 4 and 5 to 5 seconds. This will make for a more realistic progression of sound, rather than making each one identical.

Step 4: Click on the button labeled S-curve, and select the drop-down option labeled "Custom curve." This will enable you to create your own curve shape. Instead of changing the curve, though, this time leave it as a straight line (see Figure 8.15). This will create a fade curve that fades in evenly over the course of the cue duration. Make this the fade curve for all of your Fade Cues (cues 2–5).

(Continued)

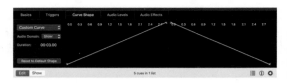

Figure 8.15 The straight curve is the default setting for all custom curves.

Step 5: In the Levels tab of cue 2, set the master fader and fader 1 to 0. Fader 2 should be set to –INF, as we only want the sound to come from the left channel at first.

Step 6: Set volume for cue 3 as follows: master fader +10 dB, fader 1 at 0dB, fader 2 at 0 dB. This will make the sound come from both right and left channels and increase the volume to +10 dB.

Step 7: Set volume for cue 4 as follows: master fader at 0 dB, fader 1 at –INF, fader 2 at 0 dB. This will make the sound come from the right channel only and decrease the volume from the previous cue.

Step 8: Set volume for cue 5 as follows: master fader –INF. This will mute all audio output. While in the Levels tab, select the stop target when done checkbox to end playback at the end of the Fade Cue sequence.

Step 9: Currently, all volume and panning is correct, but since they are all set to Auto-continue, a pre-wait must be set for each Fade Cue in order to make sure the "domino sequence" works correctly and doesn't automatically progress to silence. For correct playback, set the pre-waits in the following sequence: cue 3 and 4 at 3 seconds; cue 5 at 5 seconds. You will notice that the pre-wait for each of these cues matches the cue duration of the previous Fade Cue. This creates a seamless fade sequence.

Step 10: Test the playback sequence. If properly programmed, clicking GO for cue 1 should trigger cues 1–5, and the audio signal will pan in from the left and exit to the right over a 16-second interval. See Figure 8.16 to double-check your cueing.

Figure 8.16 Completed workspace for Project 8.4.

8.11 – Ducking Audio

Ducking is an audio effect used in music and audio production, most frequently involving the addition of voiceover. With ducking, the output volume of one audio signal is reduced in the presence of another. In most musical applications, the music will be decreased when the voiceover is added, then returned to its normal levels when the voiceover ends. In radio or television applications, ducking frequently occurs for foreign language translations. The foreign language speaker often begins at normal volume. Once the English translation is heard, the original speaker's voice is "ducked down" to keep the translation comprehensible and the foreign language speaker softly in the background. This technique is easily accomplished via QLab by inserting Fade Cues that duck audio levels down and then return them to their original state. Alternately, ducking can now also be achieved in the Triggers tab of a cue, by setting other cues to duck once one is triggered. The following project details the process of ducking audio manually through Fade Cues.

Project 8.5 ▼

Ducking Audio

Step 1: Download Project 8.5 from the companion website and open the QLab workspace. Look at Cue 1. This is a Group Cue containing recordings of a thunderstorm with wind and rain effects to set the mood for a scene. The continue state is set to Auto-continue. This will ensure that the next cue automatically triggers when cue 1 is fired.

Step 2: Cue 2 is a voiceover that should play over the thunderstorm effects. In order to better hear this voiceover, though, we will need to "duck" the audio of cue 1 down while the man speaks. In order to do so, we will need to insert Fade Cues to the workspace. Select cue 1 and insert a Fade Cue. This should insert a cue between cues 1 and 4 (2 and 3 are hidden inside the collapsed Group Cue). Name this cue 1.5 and assign cue 1 as its target (see Figure 8.17).

Figure 8.17 Inserting a Fade Cue with a Group Cue target.

(Continued)

Step 3: Select the Levels tab of cue 1.5 and set the volume in the master to –14 dB. In addition, set the pre-wait to 6 seconds and the cue duration to 1 second. Finally, set the continue state of cue 1.5 to auto-continue. This will ensure that the sound will duck down at the same time that the audio from cue 2 begins (see Figure 8.18). Test the cue progression.

Figure 8.18 Decreasing the output levels for the Group Cue.

Step 4: Insert a Fade Cue following cue 4 (cue 5). Set cue 1 as the target for this cue. This Fade Cue will serve the purpose of bringing the volume levels of cue 1 back to their normal level after the voiceover ends. To do so, select the Levels tab of cue 3 and set the volume in the master to +9 dB. Set the duration as 1 second (see Figure 8.19).

Figure 8.19 Resetting the output levels for the Group Cue.

Step 5: In order to automate the end of the ducking with cue 3, set the continue state of cue 2 to Auto-follow. This will trigger cue 3 upon the completion of cue 2.

Step 6: Test the cue sequence. If all of the steps were done correctly, the entire sequence should be automated to begin with the storm sound effects and duck down for the voiceover.

8.12 – Copy/Paste Fade Parameters

As mentioned earlier in the book, QLab 4 now features a wide array of copy/paste tools for all cue types. One of the more useful functions is the ability to copy and/or paste fade shapes from one Fade Cue to another. It can be a cumbersome process to manually set the fade shape for a number of different Fade Cues. One way to simplify this process is by the use of the Paste Cue Properties tool. To do so, select the cue to be copied and then either click *Edit > Copy* or ⌘C. This will copy the cue's parameters. Next select the cue (or cues) to which you want to paste the parameters, and then either click *Edit > Paste Cue Properties* or use the keyboard shortcut ⇧⌘V. This will open the Paste Attributes window, where you can select Fade and decide on what attributes to paste: curve shape, duration, fade mode, geometry fade mode, or stop target when done.

8.13 – Exploring Trim

As we have already seen in the last several projects, one Audio Cue will frequently have a number of Fade Cues affecting its output levels. This instance, where a series of Fade Cues target the same Audio Cue, is referred to as a **fade series.** Trim is QLab's tool for affecting the volume of that fade series without having to individually change levels for each Fade Cue in the sequence.

Unlike the other functions explored in this chapter, Trim is located in the Inspector for the targeted Audio Cue. Trim is always a manual adjustment and cannot be changed by Fade Cues. In short, the Trim settings override the levels set in the fade series and allow for an increase or decrease of volume from one convenient location.

The best example for why one might use trim is the creation of a long sequence tied to a single Audio Cue. Perhaps the play has a moment in which two people argue over the volume settings on a radio, turning it up then down a number of times in a row. Imagine then, the director wants the overall volume for the sequence to be increased. You could go through and individually change the levels of the original Audio Cue and each of the subsequent Fade Cues in the fade series. This process, though, is quite laborious and time-consuming. Another much easier option is to simply open the Trim tab in the Inspector Panel of the Audio Cue and slide the master volume up by 20%. In this way, each Fade Cue in the fade series would be increased by 20% relative to its original settings.

Control Cues

Thus far, we have examined the use of the Audio Cue and how Fade Cues affect their playback. In addition to Fade Cues, there are a group of cues called Control Cues that affect playback of other cues in the workspace. When looking at the Toolbar, the control cues are listed in the seventh grouping located to the right of the screen. The following sections detail the use and function of each of the control cues.

9.1 – Start, Stop, and Pause Cues

No sound system would be considered functional without the ability to start, stop, or pause an audio file. In the case of QLab, these functions are provided in the form of three different Control Cues. When looking at the Toolbar, the icons should be easily spotted, as they are the universal symbols for start, stop, and pause found on all audio/video equipment since the 1960s.

Start Cue

The Start Cue is used to start playback on another cue. Like the Fade Cue, it accepts another cue as its target. Once triggered, the Start Cue will fire the targeted cue. Think of the Start Cue as another method of triggering a cue besides the GO button. It is important to note that the Start Cue will *not* relocate the playback position to the targeted cue. If you need to relocate the playback position to the targeted cue, insert a GoTo Cue following the Start Cue with an Auto-continue set on the Start Cue.

Stop Cue

The Stop Cue behaves in the same fashion as the Start Cue, accepting another cue as its target, except that when fired it will stop the playback of the targeted cue rather than starting it. Stopping a Group Cue will end playback of all cues within the group. Likewise, targeting a cue list with a Stop Cue will stop playback of all cues in that particular cue list. Once stopped, a cue is no longer active and returns to its original state for subsequent playback.

Pause Cue

The Pause Cue can be used to pause the playback of a cue, a Group Cue, or even a cue list. When a Pause Cue activates, it simply halts the playback of a cue or cue sequence, leaving all affected cues in their current state. If a cue is paused, you will still find it located in the Active Cues panel.

To end a Pause Cue, a Start Cue must be inserted into the cue list. It is important to note that the Start Cue should target the paused Audio Cue, *not* the Pause Cue itself. If you target the Pause Cue, then nothing will occur, as the action will essentially create a loop in which pause is pressed over and over again. Once the Start Cue is fired, it will begin playback of the paused cue in the exact location and state in which it was paused. It is important to note that these Control Cues can be used on all cue types – Audio, Mic, Lighting, Video, and Camera.

9.2 – Load Cue

The Load Cue can serve multiple functions in the QLab workspace. The use of the Load Cue can be both subtle and complex. Its primary function enables the programmer to load a cue or cue sequence to a certain time for playback. To insert the Load Cue, simply click on the Load Cue icon (Figure 9.1) in the Toolbar thus inserting the Load Cue place keeper in your cue list. Once this has been accomplished, another cue type must be targeted. Just drag the desired cue onto the Load Cue's cue row and it will automatically target it. Now, once the Load Cue is fired, it loads the targeted cue to the computer's memory. The "loaded cue" status is indicated by a yellow dot placed to the left of the cue's icon (Figure 9.2 a). In this case, the cue will be loaded to its start time.

In addition to simply loading a cue to its start time, the Load Cue can specify an exact start point in the targeted cue's Action time. This is incredibly useful in creating dynamic cue sequences for which you might want to start a cue at a certain point within the audio recording. In order to accomplish this function,

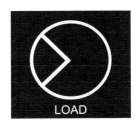

Figure 9.1 The Load Cue icon.

(a)

A LOADED CUE WITH NO TIME

Figure 9.2
(a) A loaded cue
with no load time.
(b) A loaded cue
with a specific load
time.

(b)

A LOADED CUE WITH A SPECIFIC LOAD TIME

open the Load Time tab in the Load Cue's Inspector Panel. Type in the desired load time of the Loaded Cue and, when fired, the cue will be loaded to the predetermined time. When a Load Cue is fired with a load time, a yellow Load Cue icon will appear in the cue row to the left of the Cue icon. In addition, the Action cell on will show the load time (see Figure 9.2 b).

Another function of the Load Cue is simply loading the chosen cue into the computer's memory to ensure seamless playback. In older versions, this function was essential in creating long cue sequences, essentially loading the cues into the computer's memory to enable rapid playback. One would frequently insert a load cue into such longer sequences to ensure proper playback. As the software has advanced, though, this function seems less essential in most instances. One good example of the use of this type of cue, though, is if your computer sits for a long period of inactive time during the show. I have noticed that, depending on the hardware and configuration of some computers, it may take a moment to "wake up" the computer for playback in this instance. I will sometimes program a Load Cue into the cue list for just this function. Just remember to inform the Stage Manager or Operator that the cue will perform no function that they can hear.

Design Tips ▼

Load Cues and Playback Position

One important thing to note is that *a Load Cue does not change the playback position of the cue list*. If you target a previous cue in your cue list, that target will be loaded and remain so until fired, but the playback position will continue to the next cue in the cue list. If you want to use a Load Cue to preload a previous cue and then return to it for playback, you must either manually move the playback position by clicking on the desired cue or insert a **GoTo Cue**. Essentially, a GoTo Cue is used to redirect the playback position to a different point in the cue list. The GoTo Cue is covered in detail in Section 9.5 below.

9.3 – Reset Cue

The Reset Cue (seen in Figure 9.3) is an interesting cue in that it functions slightly differently for different cue types. For example, when looking at Audio Cues, the Reset Cue will change the targeted cue back to its original, unchanged state (resetting volume changes, trim, audio effects, etc.). When applied to an active cue (one playing) it acts as a stop cue and resets the targeted cue to its original state. Like the Load Cue, though, the playback position will remain unchanged and continue to the next cue in the cue list.

Some cues have what we might call "sticky" parameters – meaning that just stopping them will not reset their status. For these cue types, a Reset Cue must be used. When applied to a cue list, a Reset Cue resets the cue list to its original playback position at the top of the list. In addition, when applied to a GoTo Cue that has been changed by a Target Cue (addressed below), the Reset Cue will reset the GoTo Cue to its original target.

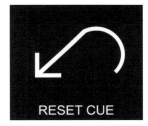

Figure 9.3 The Reset Cue icon.

9.4 – Devamp Cue

The addition of the Devamp Cue (Figure 9.4) to QLab 2 was a defining feature allowing for complex compositional options in contrast to simple audio playback. In musical terms, **vamping** refers to an improvisational musical accompaniment to the solo. In musical theatre, there are frequently sections of the score written in for the musical director with the notation vamp included. These sections are easily repeatable, offering the opportunity to have musical accompaniment under sections of the show whose timing might

Figure 9.4 The Devamp Cue icon.

vary from performance to performance. Within QLab, vamping is accomplished through looping or slices (covered in Chapter 6). When looking at the Time & Loops tab in the Inspector for an Audio Cue, you have the option of looping an Audio Cue based on a predetermined play count or as an infinite loop. In addition, you could create a loop cycle based on slices in the Audio Cue. The Devamp Cue is used in conjunction with a looped Audio Cue to end a loop cycle. When fired, the targeted Audio Cue will play through its final loop and then continue to play the audio file.

The Devamp Cue allows for complex musical composition that matches the action onstage. As an example, I recently designed scenery for a production of *Cymbeline* at the Michigan Shakespeare Festival. In this production, many of the complex battle sequences needed musical underscoring. Since the sound designer for this production was also writing original compositions, she wanted to match the pacing of the music to that of the battle onstage. The score was heavily percussive and featured many sequences in which the drums had to align simultaneously with swords colliding or onstage deaths. In order to accomplish this feat, she created the score in hundreds of short, loop-able sections of music and used Devamp Cues to allow for the music to organically match the action onstage. The effect was stunning and truly made the actors interactive collaborators to the sound design. With QLab 4, the use of slices allows for complex vamping possibilities with even less incorporated audio tracks. A word of warning: This process can be quite time-consuming and requires detailed planning to pull it off. Each loop must be seamless with no "dead air" at the beginning or end, or the timing will vary, making for a fake sound. When done well, though, the process is exceptionally rewarding. The project below details the process for setting up a short composition with internal vamping sequences.

Project 9.1 ▼

Vamping an Audio Cue with Loops

The following project details the creation of an infinite loop sequence and how to use the Devamp Cue in conjunction with this loop. Download Project 9.1 from the companion website.

Step 1: Open the Project 9.1 workspace and select cue 1.

Step 2: Select the Time & Loops tab from the Inspector. Click on the Infinite Loop button. This will create the loop sequence. Click GO to hear the Audio Cue play.

Step 3: Now that the infinite loop is established, the Audio Cue will continue playing until stopped or acted on by another cue type. For our purposes, we will use the Devamp Cue. When fired, the targeted Audio

Cue will play through its final loop and then continue to play to the end of the sequence.

Step 4: Insert a Devamp Cue into the workspace between cues 1 and 2. Set cue 1 as the target for the Devamp Cue. Click on the Setting tab for the Devamp Cue and select the checkbox labeled "Start next cue when target reaches the end of the current slice." This will automatically activate playback for cue 2 at the end of the loop.
It is worth noting that the Devamp Cue can be fired at any point during the loop cycle. In addition, you could set the Devamp Cue to simply stop the target once the loop reaches the end of its cycle without firing a subsequent cue.

Step 5: To test the sequence, trigger playback for Cue 1 and then fire the Devamp Cue after the first loop cycle.

Project 9.2 ▼

Vamping an Audio Cue with Slices

In addition to creating loops, QLab 4 offers the opportunity to create internal vamping within Audio Cues. This process allows the sound designer to create a loop-able section of a file that can vamp (useful for scene changes) until acted on by a Devamp Cue, which will end the loop and let the Audio Cue play on until the end of the file. The following project details the setup of this process, utilizing Project 9.2 downloaded from the companion website.

Step 1: Select Cue 1 from the Project 9.2 workspace.

Step 2: Select the Time & Loops tab in the Inspector Panel. In the waveform display, click on the timeline at approximately the 5.95-second mark. Click on the "Add Slice" button to the left of the screen. You will notice a yellow line will appear with a downward pointing arrow, indicating the slice position. In addition, the number "1" will appear in the slice. This indicates the loop count of the slice. Select this number and type in "INF." This will create an infinite loop cycle.

Step 3: Insert a Devamp Cue following the cue and set cue 1 as the target. Upon firing the Devamp Cue, the loop will end allowing the Audio Cue to play on to its end.
It is important to note that this process can be repeated any number of times. Any Audio Cue can have multiple slices within it set to infinite loop and numerous Devamp Cues may be used to exit the loop cycles.

9.5 – GoTo and Target Cues

GoTo Cue

The GoTo Cue (Figure 9.5) is a simple tool that allows for changing the order of playback in a sequence. Like other control cues, it accepts another cue as a target. Once the GoTo Cue is fired, the playback position is moved to the targeted cue. A GoTo Cue cannot be used to activate playback of a cue. To achieve this, a Start Cue must be used in conjunction with the GoTo Cue (i.e., insert a Start Cue before your GoTo Cue with an Auto-continue enabled).

Figure 9.5 GoTo and Target Cue icons.

Target Cue

The Target Cue (Figure 9.5) is a versatile cue that can manipulate any other cue that uses a cue target (i.e., Start, Stop, Pause, GoTo Cues, etc.). It is intended to work in conjunction with another cue to change the cue target, thereby allowing for even more versatility in changing the order of playback in a cue sequence. The use of a Target Cue can provide some confusion if you are not fully versed in its application.

Like the other control cues we have looked at, a Target Cue accepts another cue as its target (Figure 9.6 a). Once the Target Cue has been triggered, it will override the previous target of the cue and establish a new one. This new target will appear listed in brackets on the target row of the affected cue (see Figure 9.6 b). It is important to note that the target for this cue will remain changed until using a Reset Cue to restore the cue to its original status.

Figure 9.6 (a) A GoTo Cue with a target of Cue 4. (b) The GoTo Cue after a Target Cue is fired, changing its target to Cue 2.

9.6 – Arm and Disarm Cues

The Arm Cue and Disarm Cue (Figure 9.7) are used for the simple purpose of enabling or limiting a cue's ability to perform its action when fired. When a cue is armed, it will perform all of its assigned actions when fired. When it is disarmed, it will still use pre-wait and post-wait functions, but will not perform its assigned action. Like other control cues, the Arm and Disarm Cues both require another cue as a target. Though the purpose of the cue is a simple one, it is a powerful tool that allows for organic control in complex playback situations.

Arm and Disarm cues are frequently used as a component of the cueing and tech process. One possible use is in programming multiple cue options into the cue list before tech. You might have alternate versions of sound cues pre-programmed into your cue list that are disabled. If the director does not like your first choice, simply disable it and enable one of the other choices. This requires additional programming time up front, but makes the tech process go smoothly.

Another possibility is the use of prerecorded materials that might need to change from night to night. Say that there is a prerecorded voiceover for the lead role, but the understudy has to go on for one performance. In this case, the cue list could have two sets of voiceover programmed into it, with the unused files disarmed. To change from the lead role to the understudy, simply arm the understudy voiceover and disarm the lead role.

In addition to individual cues, the Arm and Disarm Cues can target a Group Cue. This is particularly useful for elaborate looping situations – such as a battle or a thunderstorm. In both situations, it is common to create a group of discrete Audio Cues often equipped with Auto-continues and a randomized playback order. Once the Group Cue is playing, the independent cues merge to create a realistic sound effect: explosions, bullets, screams, etc. Fading out a Group Cue such as this would make all of those independent cues fade out over the same duration. This effect would stick out like a sore thumb after the ultra-realistic approach of the previous sound effect. A much more effective technique would be the use of a Disarm Cue targeting the Group Cue. Each inactive cue would be disarmed, whereas the active cues would complete their playback. This effect would create a much more realistic fading of the fight sequence.

Figure 9.7 Arm and Disarm Cue icons.

One important thing to note in this situation is how the Disarm or Arm Cues interact with a Group Cue. The cues will either arm or disarm every cue within the Group Cue. In some cases, you might have previously disarmed one cue within the group. If you disarm this group and then arm it again, all cues will be armed *regardless of the fact that one of the cues was previously disarmed.*

9.7 – Wait Cue

Figure 9.8 The Wait Cue icon.

The Wait Cue (Figure 9.8) is used to insert delays between cues in the cue list. This cue performs the exact same function as the integrated pre-wait or post-wait of an individual cue. It is a matter of preference as to which method you use. Unlike other control cues, the Wait Cue does not target another cue type – it simply inserts a wait period into the cue sequence. The default wait time is set as 5 seconds. Notice that, upon inserting the Wait Cue, the cue will be named "wait 5 seconds." This is a handy function that lets the operator see the action of the Wait Cue. To change the wait duration, simply input the desired wait time in the Action column of the cue row. Note that, upon changing the action, the name of the cue will automatically be changed to match.

9.8 – Memo Cue

Figure 9.9 The Memo Cue icon.

The Memo Cue (Figure 9.9) serves the singular function of inserting a note into your cue list without being attached to another type of cue. This cue has no action associated with it. To use the Memo Cue, insert it into the cue list and write your memo into the Notes panel at the top of the screen. This cue can be particularly useful for adding notes to the workspace that can be later deleted. The Notes panel functions in the same fashion for a Memo Cue as all other cue types.

9.9 – Script Cue

The Script Cue (Figure 9.10) is a function typically reserved for advanced users, or those with previous experience in the AppleScript scripting language. AppleScript is an end-user scripting language that enables users to control applications, exchange data between applications, and automate the control of some repetitive tasks. AppleScripts can be run internally, as a Script Cue or externally through an application such as AppleScript Editor. Within the QLab system, scripting has always been left as an option for those industrious designers who want to create some elements of customized control.

To use the scripting, insert a Script Cue into your cue list. Click on the Script tab in the Inspector Panel and it will open a script window. This window is where you can insert an AppleScript written to perform a given task. AppleScript can be used for a number of different purposes from firing a cue in QLab to opening an Audio Cue's target file for editing in your DAW. One of the great things about the Script Cues is that you can insert a Script Cue into your cue list and assign a Hotkey Trigger for it, thereby giving yourself access to its function at any point. For instance, you could create a Script Cue that automatically muted all active cues and assign it the Hotkey of "M." After creating this cue, pressing the M key would mute all active cues. In addition to using a Script Cue inside of a cue list, QLab 4 now offers the possibility of including a Script Cue in a Cue Cart. This has the potential for creating truly interactive possibilities that are triggered in a more tactile sense.

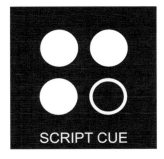

Figure 9.10 The Script Cue icon.

Design Tips ▼

Hotkey Safety

As you might have already guessed, having Hotkeys such as the one listed above could lead to some unintended consequences if your operator accidentally clicked on the incorrect button. Even having the Script Cue in a secondary cue list does not prevent this, as all Hotkeys from any cue list are active. Just to be safe, it is often a good idea to disable or delete any Hotkey activated Script Cues before handing the show over to an operator for the run.

The Figure 53 website features a wiki library of user-generated AppleScripts that have been tested for use in the QLab environment at wiki.figure53.com. Many of these scripts are simple to interpret and can be changed to suit varying purposes. For the next project, we will look at a basic but extremely useful script used to increase or decrease volume levels of a selected Audio, Mic, Video, Group, or Fade Cue. Download Project 9.3 from the companion website to examine this AppleScript at work.

Project 9.3 ▼

Creating a Hotkey Activated Script Cue

Step 1: Open Project 9.3 and select cue 2, the Script Cue.

Step 2: Select the Script tab in the Inspector Panel of the Script Cue. You will see in this dialog an AppleScript. This script effectively increases or decreases the Master volume settings of a selected cue, when triggered.

Step 3: Select the Basics tab of the Script Cue. In the right side of the window, click on the Hotkey trigger checkbox. Once this has been clicked, the next keystroke hit on your keyboard will be set as the hotkey to trigger the Script Cue. (For mine, I use shift+1).

Step 4: Select cue 1 and then click the assigned hotkey. This will open a dialog window reading "Insert + or − Volume Change." To increase the volume insert a + followed by a numeric value (such as +5 to increase the Master by 5 dB). After clicking ok, select cue 1 and note that the Master volume will match the increment inserted in the window.

It is worth noting that the use of such AppleScript Cues with hotkey Assignments might be best stored in a separate cue list or cue cart so as to not add clutter to your workspace. Even when the Script Cue is hidden in a second cue list it can still be triggered via a hotkey.

Group Cues

Other than the Fade Cue, the Group Cue is likely the most commonly used cue type in any cue list. One reason for the prevalence of this cue is its versatility. As the Group Cue is such an essential component to dynamic cueing possibilities, the following chapter both details its use and offers up practical projects for learning how to best utilize the Group Cue in your own projects.

10.1 – Understanding Group Cues

Group Cues are simple to understand, yet have the ability to be utilized to create subtle and complex effects. One key feature of the Group Cue is that grouping cues together does not change the way in which they function; it just provides the ability to control the cues by grouping them together. Though the only true function of the Group Cue is to contain other cues within it, there are many creative uses for creating a group rather than leaving cues independently organized.

1. **Organization:** One of the main reasons for using a group cue is the ability to "hide" some of your more complex cues. This method hides those numerous cues inside one folder on the Desktop, saving the operator from having to look at a large number of cues cluttering the workspace.
2. **Complex cue control:** Group Cues allow for more complex cueing, enabling multiple sub-cues of differing cue types to be fired simultaneously or in sequence. For example, special effects cues are often composed of multiple different cue types with varying continue states, fades, and control cues combined to create one single effect in the show. A good example of this is a rainstorm. The stage manager might simply call one cue to trigger "go rainstorm," but the programming for that cue might entail 10–12 different combinations of Audio Cues, Fade Cues, GoTo Cues, Start Cue, or more. One great use of the Group Cue is to simply drag all of the necessary rainstorm cues into the one group and label it "rainstorm."

3. **Consolidating Control:** Fade Cues and many control cues can affect all "children" within a Group Cue (play, pause, stop). This means a simplified method of controlling one or multiple cues. Keep in mind, though, that some Group Cues will sound fake if faded out as a group.

4. **Randomized playback:** Group Cues can be programmed to play back their internal cues in a random order. One of the most versatile functions of the Group Cue is the ability to program it to fire a random internal cue and then proceed to the next cue in the workspace. By randomizing playback and adding a Play Cue to the group, an intelligent programmer can use this function to get around repetitive loop sounds for things like city street sounds or environmental sound effects.

10.2 – Inserting and Editing Group Cues

Group Cues, like all other cue types, are inserted via the Toolbox or Toolbar. Click on the Group Cue icon to insert a Group Cue place keeper. If using the default hotkey configuration, pressing ⌘0 will also insert a Group Cue. Once inserted into your cue list, simply drag one or more selected cues into the cue line of the Group Cue. You will notice that the cue line for the Group Cue will be highlighted when you have positioned your cursor in the correct location (the highlight color can be changed through your Mac's *System Preferences > General > Highlight Color*). Care should always be taken when dragging and dropping files in your workspace. If you accidentally drag a cue onto another cue (besides a group cue) it can inadvertently replace the cue or, in the case of a Fade Cue, reset the cue's target.

Once inserted, the Group Cue has a limited number of control functions compared to other cue types. The following section details Group Cue control functions found in the Inspector.

10.3 – Inspector: Basics

The Basics panel is similar to that seen on all of the other cue types. The Basics tab includes cue number, name, wait times, and continue modes. Unlike some other cue types, the target function is not applicable to the Group Cue.

10.4 – Inspector: Triggers

Triggering functions are shown in the second tab. Like other cue types, the Triggers tab allows for triggering the Group Cue via Hotkey, MIDI, Wall Clock, or Timecode. Likewise, it also has controls for affecting other cues upon triggering the Mic Cue.

10.5 – Inspector: Mode

The mode of a Group Cue determines how the cue will behave once it is triggered for playback. Figure 10.1 shows the layout of the Mode tab. One key term in discussing Group Cue modes is a **child**. In Group Cues, individual cues contained within the Group Cue folder are referred to as a child. This term is fundamental to understanding Group Cue function. The four different Group Cue modes are listed below.

- The first mode is labeled **Start first child and enter into group.** This mode establishes that when you click GO on the group, it will start playing the first child of the group, then set the playback position to the next child. This is the mode most often used and is useful for creating things like a pre-show playlist. To create a playlist, simply insert a number of cues into a Group Cue and set each audio file as Auto-follow. Note that this Mode will create a folder with rounded edges and a muted violet color.
- The next mode, **Start first child and go to next cue,** allows for the playback position to move to the next cue in the cue list after the Group Cue. This is particularly useful for creating a Group Cue with lots of internal automation when you have a subsequent cue to be fired before the Group Cue completes its action. For instance, you can create a Group Cue sequence ending with a Play Cue that would trigger the first child once the last one had finished, thereby creating an infinite loop. In order to stop this loop, you would have a Fade Cue as the next cue in the cue list. If you set the group mode as start first child and go to next cue, the playback position would be set on the Fade Cue, waiting for your trigger to fade out the infinitely looping Group Cue. This Mode will create a folder with sharp corners and a muted violet color.
- The third mode, **Start all children simultaneously,** means that, upon pressing GO, all of the children in that group will play back at the same time. This is particularly useful for special effects, such as a car crash or an offstage explosion. For the explosion effect, create a Group Cue and drag the

Figure 10.1 The Group Cue Mode tab.

multiple explosion sound files into the group with the mode set to start all children simultaneously. This will enable you to play back multiple audio files at once without having the operator press GO numerous times. Of course, each child can have its own pre-wait settings if desired. This can give a more realistic effect rather than everything beginning at exactly the same moment. This Mode will create a folder with sharp corners and a bright green color.

- The final mode is likely used with the least frequency, but offers flexibility for creating nuanced designs. **Start random child and go to next cue** does just what it says – it will pick a random child within the group, activate it for playback, and then progress the playback position to the next cue in the cue list. This mode will create a folder with sharp corners and a bright violet color. It is useful in creating sound loops that need to have a more random/organic feel to them. One great example, as mentioned above, is creating street sounds for an urban environment. Street sounds are both monotonous and random at the same time. Should you choose to use a prerecorded sound effect for an urban background loop, you run the risk of the audience hearing the same effects looping back. Nothing kills the gravitas of a sound recording like your audience noticing the same car driving by every minute. Short of using a 30-minute-long recording, the random playback Group Cue is the best way to accomplish a more realistic sounding urban landscape.

In order to accomplish this, set up a Group Cue with lots of different sound effects housed within: motorcycles, bikes, people walking, car horns, etc. Make sure that you have these recordings set up to pan from both different directions so you get a realistic interpretation of standing on a street corner. Set up a loop by adding a Play Cue at the end of the sequence and set the mode to start random child and go to next cue. This will create a randomized loop of sound effects for your urban landscape.

10.6 – Workspace Function

One of the last areas of importance to understanding the Group Cue's use is its function within the Cue row. There are two practical functions of the Group Cue within the cue row: notes and hiding contents. Both are simple to understand, yet essential to creating an efficient workspace.

Cue Name

Like all cue types, the Cue Name of Group Cues can be changed to suit the needs of the show. I find it useful to name my group cues in a descriptive fashion since the Group Cue hides a number of cues within its folder. For instance, naming the group cue "Pre-show music" is a useful way for the operator to keep track of the group function without having the folder expanded to see its contents.

Notes

Like all other cue types, the Group Cue allows for inserting information in the Notes panel at the top of the screen. The Notes panel allows for the creation of a note specific to the given cue that might be beneficial or informative for the QLab operator. When QLab is placed in Show mode, the window takes up a large portion of the interface directly beneath the cue name. This information can be useful in communicating the broader picture of what occurs when a Group Cue is triggered if so desired.

Hiding Group Cue Contents

Another useful function of the Group Cue is the ability to hide the contents of a Group Cue. As mentioned above, this is great for reducing workspace clutter. By default, any children added to a Group Cue will be shown in a cascading format beneath the parent cue. The expanded Group Cue features a rounded rectangle box highlighting its children (see Figure 10.2). To hide the internal cues, simply click on the downward facing arrow beside the Group Cue name in the Q column of your cue list. This will change the arrow from downward facing to pointing to the right and hide all of the contents. To expand the Group Cue at a later time, simply click on the right arrow icon to re-open the folder.

Figure 10.2
Two examples of Group Cues. The first is expanded, with the second one closed to hide its contents. Note the difference in the direction of arrows for each one.

10.7 – Group Cue Projects

The following projects detail two common uses of the Group Cue in action: creating a playlist and using a Fade Cue to end playback and simultaneous playback of children for creating effects cues.

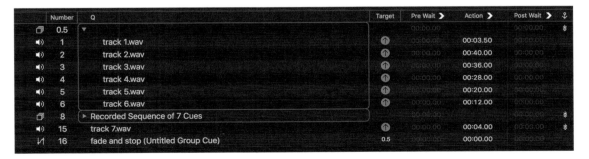

Project 10.1 ▼

Using the Group Cue to Create a Playlist

One of the most common uses of the Group Cue is in creating a sequence of audio files that need to loop. Many shows have pre-show, intermission, or post-show music. Though there is no function of QLab that simply entails dropping audio files into a playlist, the combined use of the Group Cue with multiple Audio Cues and a Start Cue allows for the creation of a loop-able collection of music, which can play indefinitely until faded out. The process is quite simple and one that should be mastered, as it is used in most every production. The following project walks you through the creation of such a playlist.

Step 1: Download Project 10.1 from the companion website. This workspace features three short musical snippets that can be used for the playlist.

Step 2: Click on the Group Cue icon to add a Group Cue to the playlist.

Step 3: Drag the first Audio Cue into the Group Cue. Set the follow status as Auto-follow.

Step 4: Repeat step three for each of the additional Audio Cues.

Step 5: Insert a Start Cue into the workspace and then drag it into the Group Cue as the last cue in the sequence.

Step 6: Set Cue 1 as the target for the Start Cue. This will create a loop that will play the group indefinitely until faded out.

Step 7: Insert a Fade Cue outside of the Group Cue. Set the Group Cue as the target file of the Fade Cue. Under the Levels tab of the Fade Cue, pull the Master fader down to –INF and select the "Stop Target When Done" checkbox (see Figure 10.3).

Figure 10.3 Master fader levels set to –INF.

Step 8: Test your playlist. When the Group Cue is triggered, you will notice that the playback position will automatically jump down to the Fade Cue so you can fade out the Group Cue at any point desired.

Project 10.2 ▼

Simultaneous Playback of Children

Another common use of the Group Cue is the creation of effects cues in which multiple sounds play back concurrently. The benefit of using the Group Cue is unifying control wherein all cues are fired by clicking the GO button only once. Another benefit is removing clutter from your workspace, given the Group Cue's ability to collapse and hide its children. The following project details the steps necessary to create a car crash sound effect. This file contains several different Audio Cues each with its own attributes.

Step 1: Download Project 10.2 from the companion website.

Step 2: You will notice that there are several cues in the workspace. The first is a Group Cue that currently contains no internal cues. Pull the Audio Cues into the Group Cue, keeping them in chronological order.

Step 3: Select the Mode tab in the Inspector Panel of cue 1 and click on the button labeled "Start All Children Simultaneously." This will make all the cues fire at the same time.

Step 4: Select various cues and experiment with how the car crash might sound differently with pre-waits added. For instance, add a pre-wait of 1.5 seconds to cue 3.

Step 5: Test the playback of the cue sequence.

Cue Carts

As mentioned in earlier chapters, QLab 4 marked the integration of the Figure 53 application QCart as a component. QCart is no longer a standalone application, but a completely functional component of the QLab software, now called Cue Carts. A Cue Cart is a collection of cues that operates in a non-linear function with no Playhead, Auto-follows, or Auto-continues. The layout of the Cue Cart is a grid of cells into which you insert cues for playback. Its simple grid-style interface allows for an easy, tactile triggering of cues with no regard to sequence. The following chapter covers the use of Cue Carts and some of the ways in which you can incorporate this tool into your workflow.

11.1 – Understanding Cue Carts

Cue Carts function similarly to a Group Cue, by holding numerous different cue types inside of them. Visually, a Cue Cart looks quite similar to a traditional drum machine, with a series of cells that can be triggered by touch (Figure 11.1). In addition to touch, these cues can be triggered in the same

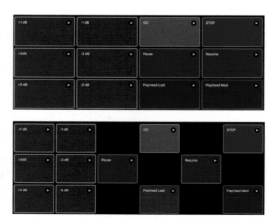

Figure 11.1 The Cue Cart can be arranged in a number of different cell orientations.

way as any other cue type (via Hotkeys, MIDI, Wall Clock, etc.). The cells in a Cue Cart can hold every type of cue, with the exception of Group Cues.

Each cue added to the grid has a cue name and a number, just like in a regular cue list. There is no playhead in a Cart, however, as it functions as a non-linear, interactive method of playback. A cue inside a Cart functions similarly to one in a cue list in that once selected there is an Inspector window open at the bottom of the screen that is used for editing the cues and their playback functions.

Cue Carts can be used for a number of different purposes. One obvious purpose is the ability to make a tactile interface for triggering cue playback. Consider the possibility of a performer onstage making choices for the playback of sound effects or projections and having the ability for those cues to respond interactively. In addition to this use, a Cue Cart could be made to function like a graphic user interface (GUI) within the QLab workspace.

11.2 – Creating a Cue Cart

To create a new Cue Cart, click on the Lists/Carts, and Active Cues button at the bottom right corner of your workspace footer. This can also be achieved by selecting *View > Lists / Carts & Active Cues* in the QLab menu bar or by using the keyboard shortcut ⇧⌘L. This will open a sidebar on the right of your workspace with a number of tools inside. At the bottom of this sidebar, you will see a button labeled "New Cart." Click on this button and a Cue Cart will appear in the place of your current cue list (Figure 11.2). In addition, you will see a Cue Cart listed in the right sidebar, directly beneath the main cue list. By selecting either the cue list or the cart in your lists and carts sidebar, you can navigate between lists and carts saved in your workspace. It is worth noting that there

Figure 11.2 Clicking on the New Cart button will create a cue cart in conjunction with your regular cue list.

are three buttons at the bottom of the sidebar labeled New List, New Cart, and Delete Cue Cart. The purposes of these are self-explanatory, but it is important to recognize that deleting a cue cart will delete all of the cues you create within that cart.

When you have a Cue Cart selected, you will notice that the GO button will be replaced with a new gray button, labeled Preview. This is because Cue Carts have no playhead, so there is no true playback position relative to cue order. This Preview button will function in the same fashion as the traditional GO button, triggering any cue that you have highlighted inside the Cue Cart.

To insert cues into a cue cart, select a cell within the Cue Cart grid and use either the Toolbar or Toolbox to insert a place keeper cue. Likewise, you could drag an audio, video, or image file directly onto the cell, which would generate either an Audio or Video Cue. Once you have added cues to your Cue Cart you can edit them individually by selecting the cue and using the Inspector. Before looking into further uses of the Cue Cart, let us examine how to customize carts through the Inspector.

11.3 – Cue Cart Setup: Inspector

When a Cue Cart is selected, there are three tabs inside the Inspector at the bottom of the screen: Basics, Triggers, and Grid Size. The first tab, Basics, allows you to affect some changes to your Cue Cart itself.

Basics

Keep in mind that this differs from editing a single cue within the Cue Cart. By selecting the Basics tab, you can add a number or name to your Cue Cart, which will be reflected in the Lists/Carts & Active Cues sidebar. Likewise, you can add a color to highlight your Cue Cart on the sidebar. In addition, there are controls to flag your Cart, Auto-Load cues within, and toggle between armed and disarmed. Finally, the Notes panel can be a useful tool for communicating information to the operator. It is important to recognize that there are some functions of the Basics tab that are disabled for a selected Cue Cart, such as Duration, Pre-Wait, Post-Wait, Continue status, and Target. These functions may be available when selecting an individual cue type for which it can be used, though.

Triggers

Similar to other cue types, a Cue Cart can be triggered in unique ways. If you need to brush up on the use of the Triggers tab, look at Section 3.2. As with the Basics tab, though, there are some functions of triggering that are unique

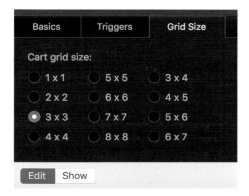

to Cue Carts. Though you can assign a Hotkey, MIDI, Wall Clock, or Timecode trigger to the Cue Cart itself, since there is no true playback order for a Cart, you have to preselect a cue in order for one to be triggered. If there is no cue selected, then any triggering of the Cue Cart will simply load all of the cues.

Grid Size

The Grid Size tab is a tool used for setting up the Cue Cart into a series of columns and rows. There are several options to scale the grid, from a combination of 1x1 to 8x8 (Figure 11.3). In this manner, a Cue Cart can hold anywhere from 2 to 64 cues in a square or rectangular format. One interesting aspect of the grid size is that you can create an 8x8 cart and then change the orientation to a smaller format, such as 5x5. In this case, the other three rows and columns will be hidden from sight, but not deleted. Once you resize the grid to 8x8, these cues will reappear.

11.4 – How to Use Cue Carts

There are numerous ways to use Cue Carts within the QLab workspace. They can function as a playback tool or as a user interface as well. A Cue Cart can hold any cue type other than Group Cues. Once the cue has been added to your Cue Cart, it can be triggered in several ways. If the workspace is in Edit Mode, there will be a play icon located in the upper right corner of the cue cell. Touching this button will activate playback. If in Show Mode, playback is triggered by clicking anywhere on the cue cell. In addition, any cue can be triggered through Hotkeys, MIDI, Wall Clock, Timecode, or the QLab Remote.

The selected Cue Cart displayed in your workspace is referred to as the Active Cart. You can make an unlimited number of Cue Carts, but only one can be the Active Cart. Cue Carts function in a slightly different manner when in Edit

Mode vs. Show Mode. While in Edit Mode, clicking the Preview button (or space bar) will trigger whatever cue you have most recently selected. Once you have changed over to Show Mode, though, using the space bar to trigger the cart will just load all the cues in your cart.

Like so many other functions of the QLab software, Cue Carts are purposefully built with a flexibility to meet the unique needs of each design situation. While the integration of Cue Carts is still a new function to QLab, there are three common trends I already see emerging in the field:

- **Using a Cue Cart as an interactive playback tool.** This use is probably the most obvious one for a cart. Whether having your operator respond to live stimuli onstage (think cartoon-style sound effects connected to physical comedy) or actually allowing a performer to trigger cues in a live setting, the Cue Cart gives a remarkable amount of interactive flexibility to any design. For performer-driven playback, the performer could either use a QLab computer onstage or wirelessly control carts through the QLab Remote on an iOS device.

  For some shows, it might even be advantageous for the operator to actually use a Cue Cart as his playback interface, rather than using a cue list view at all. Consider a movement-based production that toured to different spaces (like juggling, for instance). If there was an Audio Cue that underscores all of one particular section of the show with a number of different sound effects interspersed throughout (rim shots, stingers, trombone riffs, etc.), a strictly linear cue list would not be the best option. Instead, it might benefit the operator to create a cue list *and* a cue cart. The cue list would house the cues whose order never changes, such as the underscoring mentioned above. The Cue Cart could be used for those sound effect Audio Cues with flexible playback locations. In addition, you could add cues that trigger playback, pause, or panic to your cue list. In this way, all of your playback could be controlled directly from one Cue Cart.

- **Using a Cue Cart as a modular programming interface.** Another useful application of Cue Carts is to create an individualized programming interface for your workspace. Lighting consoles, for instance, commonly have an interface with several buttons used for performing programming functions, such as bumps, recording, deleting cues, and more. By creating a Cue Cart with a series of these functions pre-programmed into it, you can expedite your programming workflow at the touch of a button (or a hotkey). One great application for this would be adding a volume bump or dip, allowing the programmer to increase or decrease the master volume of a selected cue by a predetermined number of decibels. Another option might be a quick command for rotating a Video Cue's orientation by a predetermined number of degrees. One of the strengths of this setup is that they can be triggered via Triggering functions (Hotkeys, MIDI, etc.) or controlled by touch, using the QLab Remote to view your cart while looking at the cue list inside your workspace.

- **Using a Cue Cart as a graphic user interface for the operator.** One final use is setting up a Cue Cart as a sort of "if/then" interface for shows that might have changing parameters. One common scenario in academic theatre programs is the student matinee performance, where local public schools come in to see a performance. Often, these performances might be abbreviated versions of the regular show, especially in the case of classical pieces that have a longer running time than what can be allocated for a school matinee. Sometimes, this leads to cutting scenes or certain cues within the performance. If you know well in advance, you could create a series of Network cues that disarm the desired cues through OSC. By placing all of these into a Group Cue, you could simply add a Start Cue in your Cue Cart that targets this Group and disarms the tracks at the click of one button.

11.5 – Integrating the QLab Remote

The QLab Remote is an iOS app that is used to interface with your QLab workspace. As mentioned in earlier chapters, there are a number of ways to use this tool, whether as a remote control for triggering playback, as an editing tool for the designer to work away from the tech table, as a note-taking apparatus, or as a remote interface for triggering cues in a Cue Cart. This last function enables a wide range of flexibility for using Cue Carts and expands the designer's ability to interact with the workspace without having to physically sit at the show computer. The following section takes you through the process of using the QLab Remote in conjunction with your workspace.

- In order to use the QLab Remote, you must first purchase the app through Apple's App Store. This application can be used on the iPhone or iPad in conjunction with a computer running QLab 3 or greater.
- To get started, you must first either create a computer-to-computer wireless network on the Mac that is running QLab, connect the computer via Ethernet to a wireless router, or connect it to a Wi-Fi network. The QLab Remote must then be connected to the same network. Note that your network must allow access to TCP and UDP ports 53000 and 53001.
- Your QLab workspace must have OSC Controls enabled. To enable this, click on the Settings icon in the lower right corner of the workspace and select OSC Controls, then check the checkbox labeled "use OSC controls."
- To connect your QLab Remote to a workspace, open the app and select the desired workspace from the list shown in your "Connect to QLab" menu. You can connect to any workspace open on any QLab computer running on your network. Touch the workspace and it will connect, then open the Remote interface.

- To access your cue lists or carts, click on the Lists, Carts, and Active Cues button in the upper right corner of the app. This icon is identical to the one in your QLab workspace. If you select a cart from the list, you will have touch access to all of the cues, allowing you to remote trigger your cue cart. Keep in mind, this could cause complications if you are triggering cues while your operator is working. Always communicate with your operator to limit the surprise factor.

Once you are connected to your QLab workspace, you can use a Cue Cart running on your iOS device as a programming interface, as mentioned in the previous section. There are several cue types that can be inserted into your Cue Cart for programming purposes. Logical choices are Script or Network Cues programmed to change certain parameters of the selected cue. For instance, increase or decrease master volume levels, add a Fade Cue targeting the selected cue, toggle infinite loop, change play count to an inputted value, change the playback rate, mute all, change the cue row color, or any number of other options that work for your given design. The beauty of the Cue Cart is its modular approach that allows the designer to customize the layout to fit their unique needs.

Project 11.1 ▼

Using a Cue Cart for Flexible Playback

One of the examples mentioned earlier in the chapter mentioned a show situation where the operator had a need for flexibility in controlling certain aspects of the playback, with others following a more rigid linear playback. This can easily be achieved through the use of a Cue Cart. For the following project, we will create a simple playback interface for a circus-style performance. Perhaps there is a juggler or trapeze artist who will be performing stunts. In this type of scenario, it is common to have musical underscoring playing beneath the performer, with occasional "stingers" that emphasize certain daring feats of the act (cymbal crashes, rim shots, trumpet flourishes, etc.). The following project takes you through the steps necessary to achieving this.

Step 1: Download Project Packet 11.1 from the Companion Website.

Step 2: Open the QLab workspace and the folder labeled audio from the Project Packet. Next, you will create a Cue Cart.

Step 3: Click on the Lists, Carts, and Active Cues button at the bottom of your workspace. This opens the right sidebar. Click on the button labeled New Cart. This will open a Cue Cart window, replacing your regular cue list window.

Step 4: Select the Grid Size button in the Inspector and select the 3x3 grid orientation. Once selected, you may need to resize your workspace window in order to see the full grid.

Step 5: For this project, the first two columns of cues will be individual Audio Cues. In order to set this up, simply drag each of the six audio files from the Audio folder onto the six separate cells of the grid. Start by adding the file "Music Loop.aiff" to the upper left cell.

Step 6: Select the top right cell in your Cue Cart and add a Fade Cue into this spot. You can do this by either clicking on the Fade Cue icon or dragging it into the cell.

Step 7: Select the middle cell in the right column. Go to the dropdown menu labeled "Add control cue" and select the Pause Cue from the list. This will insert a Pause Cue into the cell.

Step 8: Select the bottom cell in the right column. Go to the dropdown menu labeled "Add control cue" and select the Stop Cue from the list. This will insert a Pause Cue into the cell.

Step 9: You will notice that each of the control cues added into the right column have a red x on their upper right corner. This is because you have not yet assigned a target for these cues. To do so, simply grab the Cue Cart listed in the Lists, Carts, and Active Cues panels on the right side and drag it onto each cue. This will set the Cue Cart as the target for each cue. Note that you will also have to drag the Master slider all the way down to -INF in the Audio Levels tab of the Inspector for your Fade Cue. Next, click the "Stop Target When Done" check box. This will now create a Fade and Stop for all cues playing in the Cue Cart.

Step 10: Select the first Audio Cue in your cart and open the Triggers tab in its Inspector. The right column of the Triggers tab has a command for ducking audio. Click on the checkbox labeled "duck audio of other cues in this cart while running" and insert the following values: duck by 5, over time 0. This will decrease the volume of any cue playing by 5 dB while the audio cue in the cart is running. Repeat this process for each of the remaining audio cues in the Cue Cart.

Step 11: Test your playback. Trigger the playback of your underscoring music and then try out the audio stingers included in the cue cart. Test the pause and stop cues as well. When you are done, I recommend going back to each of the cells and opening the Basics tab in

(Continued)

the Inspector. Try deleting the cue numbers and renaming the cues to simple, recognizable titles like "GO," "PAUSE," or "STOP." Next, try color coding the buttons (green for go, orange for pause, red for stop). Find a system that works best you. Figure 11.4 shows one possible system for laying out your Cue Cart. Once your cart is set up, you can trigger its playback through the Show Mode or by accessing it through the QLab Remote.

Figure 11.4 This example shows one method for setting up your Cue Cart as a flexible playback controller.

PART III
QLab Video Control

QLab Video System Basics

Like the sound systems mentioned earlier in the text, a video system is a collection of components: media storage unit (computer), cameras, cabling/network, and output devices (monitors, projectors, televisions, LED/LCD panels). The video system deals with both audio and video combined together for the playback of still images, prerecorded video, or live video inputted from a camera. As you might assume, there are a number of different configurations one could choose, based on the needs of the project. The following chapter details the process of using QLab in conjunction with your video system.

12.1 – Understanding Video Systems

As mentioned earlier in the text, QLab is a remarkable tool for a number of different production environments. In addition to live theatre, there is dance, live music, theme parks, museums, trade shows, and more. The use of the video system will invariably change, depending on the environment for which it is designed. Ultimately, there will be two basic types of video systems set up for use with QLab: a playback system and a reinforcement system. After reading the chapter on sound systems, these terms should be familiar to you, as they are similarly used for audio and video systems alike. The following section details the types of video systems and their use with QLab.

Video Playback Systems

Video playback systems are a combination of equipment necessary to play back prerecorded video or still images in a live performance/installation environment. Like audio systems, the video playback system is a combination of one or more computers connected directly either to an output device(s) or into a network. It is much more common in the video system, however, to find a number of different computers each running their own QLab workspace networked into a "master computer" running its own QLab workspace as a controller for all of the component computers and devices.

Again, there are a number of hardware options for a playback system. One major consideration is the number of video outputs available. Some graphics cards have only one video output, though there are many GPUs that offer more than one output. A playback computer might be specially built with multiple graphics cards in order to offer numerous video outputs. In addition, there are other hardware options, such as graphics expansion devices that use the processing power of your GPU, but spread it out across two or three outputs. The Matrox DualHead2Go or TripleHead2Go are two such options that effectively allow for the video signal from your computer to be split across multiple outputs, though there are other products on the market that perform the task as well.

Video Reinforcement Systems

A video reinforcement system is the combination of one or more cameras with QLab and its system of output devices in order to capture and play back live footage from a camera. The reinforcement system is identical to the playback system except in two key features: first, the input video signal comes from a camera, rather than from a video or graphics file saved on the computer's hard drive; second, Camera Cues do not include an audio signal.

The QLab video reinforcement system can receive a digital video signal from any of the following types of devices:

* Any IIDC-compliant webcam
* Any Blackmagic DeckLink device (a high-end cinema-quality digital video input source)
* Syphon inputs (an open-source Mac OS X technology that allows applications to share frames – both still or full frame rate video)
* Any FireWire DV camera
* A FaceTime camera attached to the system

One main consideration in camera playback is latency. Latency will vary drastically between different camera models. As such, it is best to experiment with different cameras until you find the right device for your production needs.

12.2 – Video System Components

Similar to the world of audio, the amount of technology needed for video and graphic systems can be quite extensive. Though our main focus of the text is not equipment, it is impossible to discuss many of the uses of QLab without at least taking a rudimentary look at the equipment necessary to set up a video system. The following section examines some of the basic equipment needed for a video system. While it is by no means an exhaustive list, it should be a good starting point for those new to the world of video systems.

The Digital Video Camera

Video cameras have been around for a very long time. The first video cameras functioned in an analog sense, using a lens to capture moving light, store the impulses on some type of film or tape, and then translate it into a moving image. Digital video camera hardware functions in much the same way as analog technology to capture imagery. Where they vary from their older analog counterparts is the way in which the data is stored. Digital video cameras are made up of two main components: the camera and the recorder. They use a lens to capture the moving light like traditional video cameras, and then send the light through one or more sensors to translate this captured light into images. The captured video image is then translated into computer pixels.

A **pixel** is short for the term "picture element." These tiny dots of color are the smallest element making up a digital image. Typically, thousands of pixels combine together to make an image viewed on a digital monitor. Another important term, **resolution,** can be associated with pixels. Resolution, in video or graphics terms, refers to the number of pixels used to make up a digital image. The higher the pixel count, the higher the resolution, resulting in a higher-quality digital image.

These pixels are sampled by the camera at a predetermined rate and compiled into one set, representing a single still moment in time, referred to as a **frame.** Each video is made up of multiple frames, typically anywhere from 24 frames per second up to 72 frames per second. Playing back these still frames in rapid succession creates the illusion of movement to the human eye. These frames are either stored on the camera's memory unit or directly outputted to an external device.

Computer

For the purposes of a QLab Video System, there are only two typical uses: video playback or live video reinforcement. In either of these configurations, the next logical step in the system is the computer. If recording video for later playback, the computer will be used in conjunction with video editing software to edit audio and video components of the digital video file. Software allows for editing the digital video signal down to single frames and adding multiple effects to the image and/or audio.

If using QLab as a video reinforcement system, the camera is activated by a Camera Cue and streams live video signal directly into QLab to be outputted through the video patch and directly to one or more output devices (monitors, projectors, etc.).

Interface Connections

For any type of audio/video system, physical connections (both hardware devices and cabling) comprise a substantial amount of the necessary components. Each device in your system will require some type of cabling for input and output. Typically, this is one of the commonly overlooked costs of setting up a video system as well. Keep in mind that each project can have considerably different needs, based on the number of input devices, computers, output devices, and the distance between each component in the system. It is often a good idea to sketch or draft out a plan that takes into consideration the distances between each component and the required physical connections between each device. This requires a thorough knowledge of all equipment and the necessary connectors, cabling, and/or adapters required. Listed below are several common types of interface connections.

Interface Connection	Audio / Video		Digital / Analog		Connector Type
Video Graphics Array (VGA)	Video		Analog		D-subminiature 15 pin
Composite (CVBS)	Video		Analog		RCA jack
S-Video	Video		Analog		Mini-DIN 4 pin
Component	Video		Analog		3 RCA jacks
Digital Visual Interface (DVI)	Video		Analog/ Digital**		DVI connector**
High-Definition Multimedia Interface (HDMI)	A/V		Digital		HDMI connector
DisplayPort	A/V		Digital		Display Port connector
Mini DisplayPort/ Thunderbolt	A/V *		Digital		Mini DisplayPort connector
IEEE 1394 (FireWire)	A/V *		Digital		FireWire connector
Universal Serial Bus (USB)	A/V *		Digital		USB connector
Category 5/6 (CAT 5/ CAT 6)	A/V		Digital		8P8C connector

* Indicates BUS power capability
** Depending on cable type, the allowable signal may vary: DVI-A (analog only), DVI-D (digital only), or DVI-I (digital and analog).

Video Only – Analog

Video Graphics Array (VGA)

IBM first introduced VGA to the market in 1987, and it quickly became an industry standard for video transmission. Typically, VGA uses the DE-15 variety of D-sub connecter, with 15 connector pins oriented in three rows (see Figure 12.1).

Composite Video

Composite video, often referred to as CVBS for "color, video, blanking, and sync," is an analog video transmission across an RCA connector. It is a single channel transmission of standard definition video at either 480i or 576i resolution. The standard color coding for a composite video cable is yellow. For home applications, you will frequently see this accompanied with a red and white cable, as well, for right and left audio signals, respectively (see Figure 12.2).

Figure 12.1
A male VGA connector.

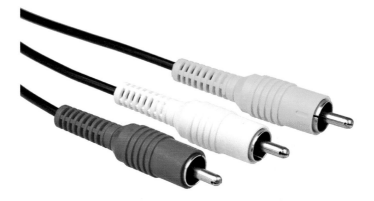

Figure 12.2
RCA plugs for composite video (yellow) and stereo audio (white and red).

Separate Video (S-Video)

Separate video, or S-Video as it is most commonly referred to, is a two-channel analog video transmission of standard definition typically at 480i or 576i resolution. S-Video uses the four-pin mini-DIN connector, seen above. It is a slightly higher quality than that of composite video due to its two-channel separation of the video information (see Figure 12.3).

Component Video

Component video is a common term used to refer to the YP_BP_R method of transmitting analog video across component video cables (see Figure 12.4).

Figure 12.3 A male Mini-DIN S-Video connector.

Figure 12.4 RCA plugs used for YP_BP_R analog component video.

This method transmits an analog video signal that has been split into three channels: Y (which carries luminance, or brightness, information), P_B (which carries the difference between blue and luminance), and P_R (which carries the difference between red and luminance). The component video cable, sometimes referred to as a "yipper" cable, utilizes three RCA jacks in green, blue, and red. The green cable carries the Y channel, the blue carries P_B, and the red carries P_R. Though an analog signal, component video is capable of supporting a number of resolutions up to 1080p.

Video Only – Analog/Digital

Digital Visual Interface (DVI)

DVI was developed in 1999 as an industry standard interface for the transfer of digital video content. The cable is used to connect a video source with an output device, such as a monitor or projector. DVI can support analog or digital signals, meaning that it is a particularly versatile interface when working with a variety of sources. Maximum resolution for DVI video signal is WUXGA (1920 × 1200).

DVI cables come in a number of varieties. There are three different types of cabling for different signal needs: DVI-A (analog only), DVI-D (digital only), and DVI-I (integrated: either analog or digital). In addition, there is another type of cable for higher video resolution bandwidth, called Dual Link DVI. The Dual Link DVI doubles the amount of TMDS pairs, effectively doubling the video bandwidth. Dual Link is only available for DVI-D and DVI-I. All of the connector types are shown in Figure 12.5.

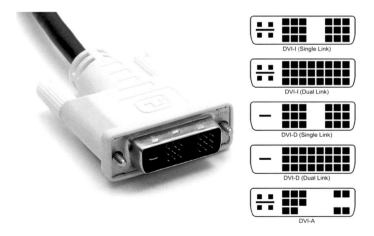

Figure 12.5 A male DVI cable and various connector types.

Video and Audio – Digital

High-Definition Multimedia Interface (HDMI)

HDMI 1.0 was developed in 2002 as a reverse compatible interface for DVI that supported both audio and video signals. Since a consortium of electronics and motion pictures producers developed HDMI, it was quickly adopted as an industry standard in high-definition televisions and projection equipment. The cable was designed to be electrically compatible with DVI signals, so no signal conversion is required nor is there a loss of video quality for the use of a DVI-HDMI adapter. As of 2013, development began for a new HDMI 2.0 specification with the hope of supporting 4K resolution at 60 frames per second, improved 3D capability, and increased audio channels. There are five different types of HDMI connectors. Type A to Type E, Type A (Full size HDMI), Type C (Mini), and Type D (Micro) are the most common connectors currently used. Many Macintosh computers now feature an HDMI output as part of the video card. The HDMI Type A connector can be seen in Figure 12.6.

DisplayPort

DisplayPort was yet another graphics interface specification designed to replace VGA and DVI interfaces. DisplayPort was conceived by a consortium of electronics manufacturers in 2006 and designed to be backward compatible with both VGA and DVI. This is particularly useful in that adapter devices are readily available for use with older interface types. DisplayPort can transmit both audio and video simultaneously or alone. In comparing DisplayPort to HDMI, they are quite similar in resolution, with DisplayPort having slightly more than twice the bandwidth capabilities of HDMI, enabling it to share this bandwidth with multiple streams of audio and video to separate devices. Unlike HDMI, DisplayPort was created as a royalty-free interface, so manufacturers do not

Figure 12.6 An HDMI Type A male connector.

Figure 12.7 A DisplayPort connector.

have to pay a fee to use the technology. This meant a quick industry-wide adoption across a number of computer and A/V platforms. The DisplayPort utilizes a proprietary DisplayPort connector (see Figure 12.7).

Mini DisplayPort/Thunderbolt 2

In 2008, Apple Inc. began development of a new Mini DisplayPort interface, built on the DisplayPort framework, but in a smaller size and with higher possible resolution (see Figure 12.8). Like the DisplayPort before it, Mini DisplayPort was developed to be royalty-free to ensure a widespread industry

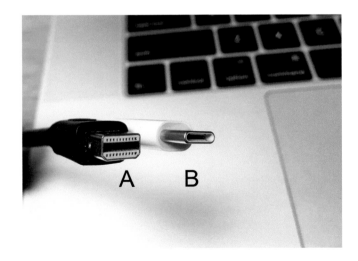

Figure 12.8 A side-by-side comparison of the Thunderbolt 2 Mini DisplayPort connector (A) with the Thunderbolt 3 USB-C Type 3 connector (B).

adoption. One complication of early Mini DisplayPort use in Apple computers (pre-2010) was the inability to transmit both audio and video signals. For these earlier models, audio had to be transmitted via USB, FireWire, or audio line out. Later editions of Apple computers addressed this issue.

Thunderbolt

Thunderbolt is an interface developed between Intel and Apple Inc. Earlier versions of Thunderbolt were electrically identical to the Mini DisplayPort, but combined the function of the PCI Express (PCIe) high-speed serial bus standard with the Mini DisplayPort to create an ultra-high-speed interface (with a data bit rate of 10 GBit/s) capable of powering up to six external devices through the one connection (via hubs or "daisy chaining" devices). Though the Thunderbolt has been used since 2011, there are still a relatively limited number of Thunderbolt devices on the market. The Thunderbolt connector also supplies a DC power signal for bus-powering devices.

Thunderbolt 3

Thunderbolt 3 is a type of interface developed by Intel that uses the USB Type-C connector (see Figure 12.9). This is important for Mac users because, as of 2017, the Thunderbolt 3 is the only port type available on the MacBook Pro line of laptops. It seems that this connector will be implemented into all future Mac computers as the primary interface. A Thunderbolt 3 doubles the bandwidth of the Thunderbolt 2 to 40 Gbit/s, reducing power consumption by half, and adds the ability to simultaneously drive up to two external 4K displays at 60 Hz. At these rates, the Thunderbolt 3 is up to 8x faster than USB 3.0 and offers 4x the video bandwidth than HDMI. In addition to providing ultra-fast data transfer, the USB-C connector also provides power to external devices and can be used to power your Mac, itself. In short, this new connector gives more speed and pixels, offers more power, and supports more types of protocols than previous options.

Figure 12.9 A male Thunderbolt 3 (USB Type-C) connector and the female port on a MacBook Pro.

IEEE 1394 (FireWire)

IEEE 1394 (most commonly referred to as FireWire) is a serial bus interface developed over a period from 1986–1995 by Apple Inc. and a small group of engineers from other technology companies (see Figure 12.10). Similar to USB, FireWire is a type of bus technology for inputting and outputting digital signals and power and the High-Definition Audio-Video Alliance (HANA) standard for communication between A/V equipment. Because of this, most digital cameras (both video and still) utilize this connector. It can be daisy chained to a remarkably high number of devices (up to 63) and used with other connector types, like wireless, fiber optic, Ethernet, or coaxial. The most common industry connectors, though, are known as FireWire 400 or FireWire 800.

FireWire 400 (technically known as IEEE 1394-1995) was the original interface released in 1995. It can transfer data at rates of 100, 200, or 400 Mbps and carry power signals as well.

FireWire 800 (technically known as IEEE 1394b-2002) was introduced in 2002 as a specification that allowed for data transfer of up to 786.432 Mbps, while still remaining backward compatible with FireWire 400 devices. Though compatible, the FireWire 800 utilizes a different connector type, necessitating the use of an adapter to work between the two specifications.

Universal Serial Bus (USB)

Like the FireWire, the Universal Serial Bus (most frequently referred to as USB) is a serial cable used for connecting a wide array of devices and peripherals, both for communication and power supply. Introduced in 1996, USB quickly became the industry standard for computing devices and has since become prevalent in cellular phones, video gaming consoles, audio interfaces, and more (see Figure 12.11). Over the years, USB has introduced various versions: USB 1 (Full Speed) at 12 Mbps; USB 2.0 (High Speed) at 480 Mbps; and, most recently,

(a)   (b)

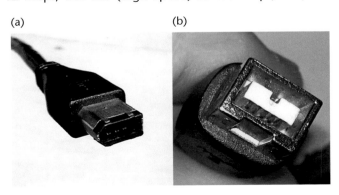

Figure 12.10
(a) FireWire 400 cable. (b) FireWire 800 cable.

Figure 12.11 A
standard USB
Type-A connector.

USB 3.0 (Super Speed) at 5 Gbit/s. There are numerous connectors as well (Type A, Type B, Mini A, Mini-B, Micro-A, Micro-B, Micro-B SuperSpeed, and Type-C), with the Mini and Micro connectors being used most often for smaller devices, such as cameras, tablets, and telephones.

Category 5/6 (CAT 5/CAT 6)

The final interface type that is becoming increasingly prevalent in entertainment applications is that of the CAT 5 or CAT 6. As more control systems become network capable, the use of Ethernet style Local Area Networks (LANs) or Wide Area Networks (WANs) is commonplace. This development has led to the proliferation of CAT 5 and/or CAT 6 cable as an interface. One reason for the use of networking is the ability to send signals over longer cable runs than traditionally possible with the types listed above.

CAT 5 (Figure 12.12), frequently referred to as Ethernet cable, is a twisted pair cable used for carrying signals at high-speed rates (100 MHz). CAT 6 uses the similar Ethernet connector as CAT 5, but is designed to provide a faster data transfer rate (250 MHz) and reduce crosstalk and system noise.

Figure 12.12 A
CAT 5 connector.

A common use of CAT 5/6 cable is for the creation of a LAN for control purposes. QLab 4 is designed to work across a network and communicate with multiple computers running QLab on the network. This function is highly desirable when using QLab as a Show Control system to interact with an audio system, video system, lighting control system, and more. Most digital control devices today are equipped with some type of network port allowing them to be connected to and controlled across a network.

Output Devices

Video output devices can be any of a number of types, from computer monitors, to televisions, projectors, or flat panel displays such as LCD or LED monitors. Essentially, an output device is a transducer that receives the input video signal and translates it into light impulses. The video monitor/television/projector industry is in a state of constant and rapid change, utilizing new technologies to create high definition and 3D capable output devices. The most common devices for entertainment industry applications are digital projectors and flat panel displays. Listed below are some basic considerations to keep in mind in using these types of output devices.

Digital Projectors

Digital projectors, sometimes called video projectors, are digital outputs that accept audio and video signals from a number of different source types, from computers to DVD/Blu-ray or live input from a video camera. The cost of digital projectors has decreased at an incredible rate over the years, making it increasingly common in both professional and academic theatre programs, houses of worship, convention centers, and music venues.

Digital projectors work by receiving a video signal and transmitting it via a bright light source (i.e., a lamp, LED cluster, or lasers) and through a lens to enlarge the image and project it across a distance, known as its **throw**. Common projector types are Liquid Crystalline Display (LCD), Digital Light Processing (DLP), and Light Emitting Diode (LED). The first two types utilize a high-intensity lamp, whereas the latter uses an LED cluster, creating a cooler system with less energy consumption and negating the need for lamp replacement.

Considerations for digital projectors tend to fall into two categories: brightness (lumens) and operating distance (throw ratio). Projectors are, at their heart, lighting instruments that transmit moving light. As such, using a projector in conjunction with other lighting instruments can lead to the image being "washed out" or dim, depending on the spill of other lighting instruments in use at the time. The amount of light in a given space, outside of that created by the projector, is commonly referred to as **ambient light**. The greater the amount of ambient light, the greater the need for a digital projector with high brightness output, typically referred to as "high-lumens."

Throw distance is the second consideration that will influence the type of projector necessary for a given project. All digital projectors have a given throw ratio that describes the ratio of the distance to the screen (throw) to the resulting image width. For instance, if a projector has a throw ratio of 2:1 and the projector is placed 10 feet away from the screen, then the resulting image width would be 5 feet. It is worth noting that, since most projectors have zoom lenses, most ratios will be variable in nature (i.e., 2–2.4: 1). All decisions for projector selection should take into consideration both the need for lumens and throw distance.

Flat Panel Displays

Flat panel displays have been around for some time and now represent a significantly higher share of the market than classical televisions or cathode ray tube (CRT) models. Most flat panel displays today are Liquid Crystalline Display (LCD) technology, with a thin layer of liquid crystal sandwiched between two conducting layers. Most LCD panels are backlit to make them easier to see under ambient light. Another variety of flat panel is the plasma display. A plasma display is so named for being composed of millions of tiny compartmentalized cells housed between two layers of glass. These cells each contain electrically charged ionized gas, making them glow like miniature fluorescent lamps when electrified. The plasma display produces vivid colors and deeper blacks, enabling a high contrast ratio for displayed video. Likewise, it can be manufactured in large panels and is quite thin – typically around 4 inches.

One of the emergent trends in all areas related to lighting and media is the use of Light Emitting Diode (LED) technology. LED displays are quite popular due to their ability to produce incredibly bright, vivid colors while using a smaller amount of electricity and having a longer life than traditional lighting fixtures or projectors. One interesting aspect of LED displays is that, depending on the project, they can function as a component of either the lighting design, the projection/media design, or both. LED displays all utilize clusters of red, green, and blue diodes combined together to make what is known as a color pixel. The technology varies from conventional signage models utilizing discrete LED clusters to Surface Mounted Devices (SMDs) that feature LEDs mounted directly to printed circuit board panels that can be readily connected to one another. One great advantage to the SMD LED display is the ability to curve the display into interesting curvilinear forms.

Still another variety of display is the OLED (Organic Light Emitting Diode). An OLED is a flat light emitting technology that uses a series of flat, organic films placed between conductors. The electrical current passed through the conductors makes the films emit bright light. Since the OLEDs emit their own light, a backlight is not necessary; therefore an OLED display can be considerably thinner and more lightweight when compared to other display types. This also makes them a more energy efficient choice as well.

One final consideration with video displays is the ability to link multiple displays together to create a **video wall**. The term video wall refers to the use of multiple output sources combined to create one large screen. This concept is important to QLab 4, as it uses a model of creating a **surface,** a way of using one or multiple output devices and transferring the data to those individual devices directly from QLab itself. This model makes the creation of video walls from QLab a relatively simple task.

12.3 – Understanding Video Signal Flow

Like other cue types seen before, the idea of signal flow is a bit of an abstraction, considering much of the signal path is contained within QLab itself. It is important, though, to understand the path that a video signal takes from source to output. For the following examples, we will look at the signal path for both Video Cues and Camera Cues. A video file or live video feed is the first point within your system. From there, this signal will be fed into a Video Cue or Camera Cue as their input signal. This signal will then be routed through the Video Surface Patch, an interface within QLab that allows you to assign a path between video signal and video output devices and control certain aspects about how the imagery is displayed. The final step is, of course, video output through a display device such as a projector or video wall. Depending on your playback needs, audio may be included in this as well. The following section breaks down these steps in detail.

Video/Image File/Video Feed

The first step of any type of signal flow is always the source. In this case, the source will be a prerecorded video, a still image file, or a live video feed from a camera. In the case of the first two, a Video Cue targets the files. For the latter, a Camera Cue activates the camera for playback purposes.

Video Cue/Camera Cue

Video and Camera Cues are the place keepers within the workspace that either activate playback of the existing video or graphic file or trigger live video feed from a video camera. In either case, the signal proceeds from the cue directly into the video surface patch.

Video Surface Patch

In order to understand the Video Surface Patch, it might be best to first address the idea of a Surface. In QLab 4, a **Surface** is a programming step that falls between the video source and your output. By adding this step between the media and any display devices, it allows you a greater flexibility for controlling your final product. Another important term to understand is the screen. Any output device connected to your system is referred to as a **Screen.** Every Surface has one or more screens attached to it as a display.

QLab automatically generates a new surface for every display device connected to your system. These are single screen surfaces, meaning that there is only one output screen attached to the surface. This makes for a simple, plug-and-play approach to creating a simple video setup with one display. QLab 4 can also be used for creating a larger video system with multiple displays connected to the system. In this case, you might find yourself wanting to create a multi-screen surface that has a number of screens as outputs. Combining all of the screens together into one Surface allows you to effect a global change to all of your devices and focus on what you see on the stage rather than simply focusing on the signal going to each individual projector. One example of this is using three overlapping projectors to create one large projection surface on a wall. The surface would have three screens assigned to it. In this way, QLab does the work of breaking up your signal and sending out the correct portion of it to each of the screens that make up your surface. This allows you to control each one of them as a whole rather than going through the tedious process of having to control the minutiae of each individual projector. This concept was introduced in QLab 3 and remains a core component of QLab 4 video control.

Design Tips ▼

Surface Control

It is important to understand that changes to surfaces do not actually affect the physical display in question; they simply change the output from that one particular surface. A screen can be connected to any number of surfaces, and the changes made to it are unique to that surface in question. They *do not* carry over to other surfaces that might use the same screen for output.

In addition to parsing up digital signals into component packages, surfaces also have the ability to apply numerous effects to any Video or Camera Cue outputted through a surface patch:

- **Built-In Edge Blending:** Each surface patch can automatically calculate edge blending (a decrease in the intensity of light transmitted on the edges of a projected image) for each overlapping projector on your surface.

This reduces the noticeable appearance of "bright spots" where projectors overlap.

- **Masking:** Masking is the process of adding an image file as a frame around a video or image file. With a transparent center, the video passes through the center, but is masked by the image on the surface edges. This is particularly beneficial for removing the look of "rectangles of light" with projections. In QLab 4, instead of taking the time to create a transparent background image, you can simply upload a graphic file with a white fill where you want video to be visible. It can then be attached to a video surface, and QLab does the hard work of sending the appropriate section of the image out to the component parts of your surface. In addition, QLab watches the mask file for changes, so all you have to do is edit and save in your image editor and QLab will make sure to display the most current version. Though this may seem like a small feature, it is quite a time-saver when editing multiple files.
- **Built-In Adjustment for Projector Orientation:** One aspect of projection that has always been troublesome is determining the placement of projectors and their orientation (rear, front, ceiling, table). For each of these changes, the required image must be different, or it will be reversed or flipped. QLab 4 builds in these changes to the image file at the touch of a button by adding a checkbox for rear projections and a drop-down menu to change the orientation from 0°, 90°, 180°, or 270° in the surface editor.
- **Keystone Correction:** When a projector is not aligned perpendicularly to a projection surface, even by a few degrees, it skews the image to be smaller at the top or bottom. Most projectors have built-in keystone correction to correct this anomaly. QLab surfaces have the built-in **control points,** a common video-editing tool that allows for grabbing a point or points located at key places on the surface and moving them to create a new shape (see Figure 12.13). This resulting shape will then be imposed on the video output, skewing it to match the shape. There are a number of different methods built into QLab to control the warp type for surfaces, such as Perspective, Linear, and Bézier.

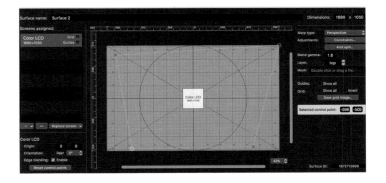

Figure 12.13
Using Control Points to change the video output.

- **Projection Mapping:** Projection mapping, also referred to as video mapping, is the powerful process of editing a projected image to match the surface dimensions of objects (even those that are irregularly shaped with numerous dimensional planes). Through the use of mathematical equations to determine the relationship of a 3D object to the exact placement of a projector, you can skew the image in such a way that the resulting image is perceived without distortion. By using the control points and video grid capabilities of surfaces, projection mapping is much easier in QLab 4 than ever. In simple terms, you can shape a single surface to match the shape of the projection surface, for instance a door. For multifaceted 3D shapes, the combination of multiple surfaces designed to fit the shape of various planes allows for projection mapping on complex surfaces.
- **Layer Control:** In addition to having the ability to create multiple surfaces, QLab allows you to assign different layers to your surfaces. This process enables you to create a hierarchical system in which certain surfaces will always be stacked on top of others. This is incredibly useful in a situation where you have numerous overlapping surfaces and want to make sure the images do not overlap.
- **Support for Graphics Expansion Hardware:** Using the surface patch, you can address individual outputs of graphics expansion hardware, like the Matrox TripleHead2Go or Datapath x4.

Output Device

The final component of the signal flow chain is the device output (i.e., the projectors, monitors, or flat panel displays connected to the surface patch).

Audio

Since Video Cues target video files, it is quite common that the file might contain an audio signal in addition to the video. Audio signals attached to video are treated in the same way as those in Audio Cues. Within the Inspector Panel, there are tabs for Audio Levels, Audio Trim, and Audio Effects. An audio patch is assigned in the Audio Levels tab. The signal then follows the same path as that discussed in audio signal flow earlier in the text.

12.4 – Hardware Considerations

Though QLab has relatively modest minimum specifications to function, most people will find that larger video files or simultaneous file playback will quickly begin to tax a system. One of the first questions many people ask is, "What kind of hardware do I need for video playback?" In short, the answer is, it depends. It depends on the type of system you want to set up. For a single screen, PowerPoint-style system, you will likely be fine with the minimum system requirements. For anything beyond that, though, there are a number of factors to consider: the size of the video files you will be playing back, how many files at one time you will be playing, whether you intend to include live video feed via Camera Cues, and other operations your computer will be running. If you will be asking your computer to complete several operations at once and play back multiple video files simultaneously, then get ready to either drop some money on performance hardware or be frustrated with your productivity.

As with any system, the strength of your video performance will only be as good as your weakest link. While there is no catchall answer for hardware needs, there are some things you can understand to help demystify the process of selecting hardware for your QLab system. The following section will address some of these concerns.

The Bottleneck Dilemma

The main problem in working with video is simple: video files are incredibly cumbersome for your computer. The amount of data that must be transferred across computer hardware to play back even standard resolution video files is large. Add high-definition video into the mix, and change that from large to enormous. Any time you have that sheer amount of digital traffic moving across your system, there is going to be the potential for traffic jams. No matter the speed of most computer hardware, it still tends to operate in an orderly fashion from one operation to the next. When a hard drive, for instance, is asked to access multiple files simultaneously, it still only has access to one point of data at a time. While it spins away, rotating to different physical points of its drive, the other process requests start to pile up – thus the bottleneck term. The question is how can we configure hardware for your system in such a way as to limit that bottleneck? To answer that, let's look at the hardware components for your system and how they are used.

Data Path

Unlike other file types, video is processed and travels along a unique data path, utilizing specialty hardware designed to maximize video playback. Figure 12.14 illustrates the typical data path for a video file, starting with the hard drive and ending with the display device. Each step along the data path has its own unique purpose and affects the playback potential of the entire system.

Figure 12.14 The
standard data path
for video.

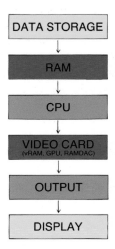

Hard Drive/Data Storage

The three most important questions related to data storage for video are (1) How fast is your hard drive? (2) How fast can your hard drive communicate information (i.e., transfer rate)? (3) What other data traffic is competing with your video file? The first two questions are directly tied to your choice of hard drive. The answer to the final question leads to the next logical question: Is one hard drive enough?

Every computer comes equipped with some type of hard drive. There are multiple types of hard drives on the market. For years, most computers came with the traditional "platter" disk drive, featuring a spinning disk upon which data is recorded and then accessed later by a reading head. This type of drive is referred to as a hard drive disk (HDD). Today, most higher end computers include at least one Solid State Drive (SSD). For QLab purposes, there truly is no comparison between the two types of drives, as the SSD is faster at read/writing, has no moving parts to break, and all data is electronically transferred. Especially for video systems, an internal SSD with a Serial ATA (SATA) connection is preferable. While they vary from manufacturer to manufacturer, the maximum typical transfer rate for SSD is in the range of 100 Mbps–600 Mbps, up to 4.25x faster than the HDD.

External Storage

Today, there are a number of options for external storage that can be used in conjunction with your computer, from flash drives to FireWire or USB external drives. An external drive can be a great addition to any system, but keep in mind that it does present some concerns. The first concern is speed. There are a number of connector types for external storage, and the data transfer rate can vary drastically. As mentioned above, the rate for most hard drives, whether HDD or SSD, is in the range of 100 Mbps–600 Mbps. Older connector types (FireWire 400/800 and USB 1/2) will clock in much slower than this. Newer connector types, USB 3.0 and Thunderbolt, clock in much faster (up to 10 Gbit/s). Obviously, whenever possible you would want to choose the faster variety. One potential problem with external drives, though, is their dependence on an external computer port. In short, they can be unplugged with relative ease. One method of getting around this is configuring a "road box" or rack mount with all external devices mounted inside, but ultimately there is no guarantee that someone will not accidentally dislodge the connector. For this reason, it is typically ill advised to use external storage for running a show.

The Need for Multiple Drives

One question many people ask is whether there is a need for more than one hard drive in their system. The short answer is yes. The more storage options in your system, the more you are reducing the potential for bottleneck. One main consideration for this is the number of video files playing back concurrently within QLab. The third question posed above asked what other data might be competing with the transmission of your video file. If you store your video files on the same hard drive as your OS, QLab software, and any other software that might be running (which should, incidentally, always be kept to the minimum necessary), then your hard drive will have lots of reading and writing constantly occurring while trying to transmit the enormous data of your video file. Adding a separate hard drive (or more) enables storage of your media in a separate location from your system files. In the case of building a system with multiple internal drives, it might be preferable to choose a small-capacity hard drive for your system files and add on one or two large-capacity drives for media storage.

Taking into account all of these variables, a best-case scenario for video playback would be a computer with multiple SSD hard drives, segregating your media files onto a separate physical drive from your system drive. More data paths mean less potential bottlenecks.

RAM

RAM, or Random-Access Memory, is another type of data storage. RAM allows for data to be accessed in any random order rather than the predetermined method used in traditional hard disks and optical media. RAM is a temporary storage method, meaning that when power is removed from the system, all data is removed from the RAM. For our purposes, it is sufficient to say that RAM is used to serve as a temporary storage and workspace for the OS and applications. For video purposes, the more RAM, the better. QLab 4 is a 64-bit program, meaning that it processes data in 64-bit (rather than 32-bit) packets. The main benefit of a 64-bit program is the ability to use a 64-bit address space and thus use a significantly greater amount of RAM than 32-bit programs. With QLab 4, the 64-bit architecture ensures that you can utilize any RAM available to your system.

A common question I hear is, "How much RAM do I need for video playback?" The short answer I always give is, buy as much as you can afford and your computer can hold. RAM has become harder to upgrade in newer generations of laptops and some iMacs. Of course, the best option for maximum upgrade possibilities is to purchase the Mac Pro. This computer is the most modular Mac that allows for upgrading many of the internal components with much more ease than the iMac or MacBook lines. As of the publication of this book, most iMacs start with 12GB RAM and go up to 64GB. It is a good rule of thumb to not purchase less than 16GB if doing video playback.

CPU

The Central Processing Unit (CPU) is essentially the brain of your computer. The purpose of the CPU is to carry out the instructions of computer programs by performing mathematical, logical, and input/output operations of the system. When considering a CPU for your video system, there are two main factors to consider: the number of cores and the processor speed.

A multi-core processor is a type of processor that essentially combines multiple independent CPUs into one single computing component. Originally, all CPUs stood alone as a single core processor. As time progressed, the combination of CPUs into multi-core configurations became prevalent.

The speed of the processor refers to how quickly it can operate those mathematical and logical problems mentioned above. High processor speeds are not always the most important factor in optimizing performance. For video editing, it is typically a good idea to get the combination of the fastest processor with the highest amount of RAM to ensure ideal video playback.

QLab Video CPU Usage

Unlike some other applications, QLab performs much of its image processing of video in real-time on your GPU (Graphics Processing Unit). Compositing, Geometry, and edge blending are performed on the GPU, though most codecs are decoded on the CPU and many video effects use the CPU, as well. What this means is that for video purposes, the CPU speed is not the most important link in the chain. If you are in the position of deciding which is more important for your video system, CPU or graphics card, you can spend a little less and get a medium speed CPU in favor of getting the best graphics card available.

Regarding Codecs and Compression

A codec (derived from the terms coder-decoder) is a computer program capable of encoding or decoding a data stream, in this case a video file. Compressed video files require decompression in order to be played back. This decompressing process is generally performed in the CPU. The more the CPU has to work to decompress files, the greater a possibility for bottlenecking. For this reason, the preferred codec for QLab video is the Apple ProRes 422 Proxy, as it is efficent in low latency / low buffer playback.

Video Card

The video card is an expansion card used to generate a video feed to output to a display. The modern video card is a printed circuit board with mounted components including vRAM, Graphics Processing Unit (GPU), Random Access Memory Digital-to-Analog Converter (RAMDAC), and video output hardware (see Figure 12.15). All of these components are addressed below:

Figure 12.15 A video card with VGA, component, and DVI connections.

vRAM

Video RAM, more commonly called vRAM, is a dual-port variety of dynamic RAM (DRAM) housed on the video card and used specifically to improve video playback speeds and reduce latency. vRAM essentially functions as a buffer between the CPU and the video card. For video to be outputted to a display, it is first read by the CPU and then written to the vRAM. This data is converted from a digital signal to an analog one by means of a RAM-to-analog converter (RAMDAC) housed on the graphics card, before outputting to the display. Unlike typical RAM, vRAM chips contain two ports. This means that two different devices can access it simultaneously. In this way, it can receive new video data from the CPU while simultaneously outputting screen updates.

As you might have guessed, vRAM is another example of more is better. The greater the amount of vRAM, the better the processing ability of your video card and therefore the better your video output. Current high-end video cards (such as the ATI HD 5870 Eyefinity 6) feature 2GB vRAM from fast video RAM capabilities (capable of rendering up to 1 billion pixels per second).

GPU

The Graphics Processing Unit is a programmable logic chip that renders images, animations, and video for output to a display. The GPU is an essential component for decoding and rendering both 2D and 3D animations and video. For QLab purposes, much of the image processing is performed on the GPU in real-time. The GPU handles all image adjustments made by your Video Cue (resizing, opacity, rotation, etc.) and sends the frames to the display.

Output

All video cards contain some type of output hardware, such as VGA, DVI, HDMI, and DisplayPort. This is the final chain before connecting to the display device.

12.5 – Connecting to a Video Display

One major consideration for setting up your video system will be how to physically connect your output devices to the computer or computers in your system. What types of connectors are needed? How long can you run the cable? Will you need a signal booster? With so many questions to consider, the planning of your video system will typically prove to be the most important task.

What Types of Connector(s) Are Needed?

The question of what types of connectors and cables are needed will greatly depend on the type of equipment in your system. What outputs are on your video card? What types of inputs are included on the projector or monitor you want to use? I strongly suggest doing a survey of all of your equipment and detailing the types of connectors and creating an inventory sheet. This will help you later when deciding on cables and adapters.

Typical connectors for Mac computers will be HDMI, DVI-D, DisplayPort, and Mini DisplayPort. Most projectors and monitors will feature at least VGA and DVI connectivity, though many newer projectors will feature a wide array of inputs.

Cable Runs

As you saw earlier in the text, when discussing video there are a number of different cable and connector types. The main consideration when comparing cable types is the question of analog vs. digital signal type. The difference between an analog and digital signal is how the data is transmitted. Analog signals are mechanical representations of the sampled information, whereas digital signals are a series of number sequences of "1" and "0." Thanks to improved manufacturing techniques of analog cabling, there is little difference in the ability of analog and digital cable to transfer high-definition video signals. The resulting difference between the two signal types is the amount of signal degradation that occurs over a run of cable.

HDMI, DVI, DisplayPort, and Mini DisplayPort are all digital video signals, capable of carrying HD signals. Since they are digital, they can carry their signals for a slightly longer distance without picking up interference. VGA is an analog cable type that can also transmit an analog HD signal. The quality is slightly less than that of the digital cabling, but it is slight and likely not noticeable by the layperson. The ultimate question of what types of cabling to use will likely depend on a few variables: How long is the required cable run? What is your budget?

Cable length is always a big concern when talking about video. Longer runs of cable can lead to interference and signal degradation, or even signal dropout. **Attenuation** is a term frequently discussed in video and/or networking conditions. It refers to the gradual loss in intensity of any signal transferring across a medium. In this case, we are typically referring to either copper cabling or fiber. Different types of cable naturally have different attributes that lead to varying maximum cable lengths. The problem in estimating this is that signal transmission is directly related to output resolution.

The smaller the output resolution, the longer the signal can run without debilitating attenuation. The larger the resolution of a video signal, the greater the bandwidth utilized. Because of this, larger resolutions will encounter signal degradation at a significantly shorter span. This variable makes it difficult for a manufacturer to list firm rules for the maximum lengths of cable since it is greatly dependent on the resolution of your signal and other hardware factors. Listed in the table below are a few references for cable length, but keep in mind every situation has variables that no quick reference can account for like cable quality, environmental interference, and hardware quality. The following should be viewed as more of a starting point. Always rigorously test your system before going into a tech setting. Also, note that the types of cables listed below are the standard consumer variety.

Use of cable runs greater than these might work, given the environment, but would not be recommended. It should be noted that the single greatest

Cable Type	Digital/ Analog	Distance (Lo-res*)	Distance (Hi-res**)
Video Graphics Array (VGA)	Analog	65'	25'
Composite (CVBS)	Analog	50'	N/A
S-Video	Analog	65'	N/A
Component	Analog	25'	10'
Digital Visual Interface (DVI)	Digital	50'	20'
High-Definition Multimedia Interface (HDMI)	Digital	50'	25'
DisplayPort/Mini DisplayPort	Digital	50'	10'
Thunderbolt	Digital	10'	10'
IEEE 1394 (FireWire)	Digital	15'	15'
Universal Serial Bus (USB1)	Digital	10'	10'
Universal Serial Bus (USB2)	Digital	15'	15'
Universal Serial Bus (USB3)	Digital	10'	10'

* Lo-resolution is defined as 480i/VGA (640 x 480).
** Hi-resolution is 1080p (1920 x 1080).

determining factor for cable length recommendations is the quality of the manufactured cable. There are a number of professional grade cable options that can be made using coax, category cable, or fiber-optic cable with any number of connector types attached. Using these cable types will expand your options from the tens of feet to the hundreds of feet range. For specs on these, see the individual manufacturer, and always request to see a specifications sheet, whenever possible. For ultra-long cable run requirements, fiber-optic cables might be a good consideration since they can transmit data over thousands of feet.

Signal Amplifiers

Sometimes you might find yourself in a situation where you have to exceed the maximum cable run length for a video system. In these cases, you will need to rely on certain devices designed to boost the video signal to travel over longer distances. One such device, a **distribution amplifier**, takes the video signal and amplifies it to travel over a longer run. These devices are constructed for all types of cabling listed above. In all cases, the amplifier requires an external power supply.

12.6 – Graphics Expansion Devices

For many installations, you will find yourself in need of outputting to multiple display devices. As mentioned earlier, you could outfit a rig with multiple video cards or a single card with multiple outputs. If buying a new computer or upgrading is not in your budget, though, one option remains for multi-screen output: a graphics expansion device. The graphics expansion device is an external electronic device that splits the video output from your computer across two or more outputs. There are a number of devices on the market that accomplish this goal. Chapter 13 features information on how to set up such a device for video output.

Video System Preferences and Setup

In earlier chapters, we discussed the importance of setting up audio preferences in detail. Similarly, when dealing with video, there are preferences that should be set before ever inputting a Video or Camera Cue into your workspace. Though there are many powerful functions related to video in QLab, the setup tends to be quicker than that of audio because there are significantly fewer preferences to address. To begin the process, click on the Settings button in the lower right hand corner of your screen. Next, select Video in the left column. This will open the Video Surfaces list and Camera Patch in the right window.

13.1 – Workspace Settings: Video Surfaces

The Settings window for video (Figure 13.1) is a simple interface with complex possibilities for configuration. This window is divided into two separate lists, one for video surfaces and one for the camera patch.

Video Surfaces

The Video Surfaces list shows a listing of all of the devices currently connected to your computer. As mentioned earlier, QLab will create a single-screen surface automatically for every display connected to your system. These will be the only surfaces displayed when you first open the Settings window. Each surface will have a distinct name, list its display resolution, and tell how many screens are attached to it. If you look to the end of the surface row, you will notice two more icons. One, labeled edit, is used for editing the parameters of your surface. The last icon, an x in a circle, is used to delete the surface from the Video Surfaces list.

Figure 13.1
The Video Settings
screen.

Adding Surfaces

At the bottom of the Video Surfaces portion of the Video Settings window, there is a drop-down menu for creating new surfaces. Clicking on the drop-down menu, you will see the options for making new surfaces. You can select either a new empty surface, a new surface patched to one of the displays connected to your system, or a new multi-screen surface. The specific process of creating surfaces is detailed a bit later in this chapter.

Duplicating Surfaces

There is a button labeled "Duplicate" at the bottom of the Video Surfaces portion of the Video Settings window. This is used for creating a duplicate surface that has identical settings to a selected surface.

13.2 – Editing Surfaces

Each surface in the surfaces list can be edited by clicking on the "Edit" button. This process allows you to add or remove screens, warp the surface output, add masking for the surface, effect edge blending, change the projector orientation, and more. Since there is no limit to the number of surface patches that can be created, you can create multiple surfaces attached to the same projector, each with different variations to accomplish different output effects. For now, let's examine how to edit a single-screen surface inside of the Surface Editor.

Editing the Single-Screen Surface

The single-screen surface is the most basic variety of video surfaces. As mentioned earlier, a surface will be created for any display connected to your system. There are many reasons for editing the surface output, however, such as keystone correction or changing the projector orientation. To edit

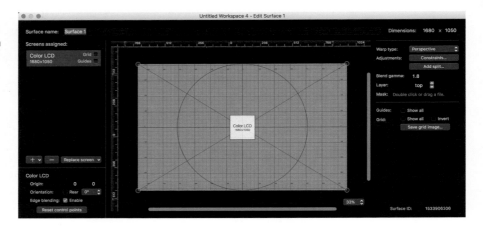

Figure 13.2
The Surface Editor interface features a number of control functions for surface output.

components of this surface, click on the Edit button in the Video Surfaces list. This will open the Surface Editor (see Figure 13.2).

Surface Name and Dimensions

When looking at the Surface Editor, the screen can be broken down into four different areas. The first area, along the top of the screen, is used for editing the surface name and its dimensions.

- **Surface Name:** There will be a generic surface name assigned to any display device connected to your computer, such as Surface 1. If you have a number of different screens attached to your system, it can be advantageous to give each surface a unique name. To do so, simply type in the name in this slot and press enter.
- **Dimensions:** Moving down the row from the Surface Name, you will see an interface that lists the dimensions of your surface. For a single-screen surface, this is the default size of the screen attached to your system. This can be changed, but is typically not necessary for the process of editing a single-screen surface. When creating a new surface, it may be necessary to adjust these settings.

Editor Canvas

The second area of the Surface Editor is located in the center of the screen and takes up the largest amount of space. This grid-like window is called the Editor Canvas (Figure 13.2). The canvas is a visual representation of your surface. This canvas shows the surface as a colored screen with a black grid featuring the dimensions of the surface, broken down in pixels. For instance, if your attached screen was 1680 x 1050, your Editor Canvas would show a grid that matched these dimensions. Located atop this grid will be a translucent colored rectangle that represents the screen attached to your surface. For a single-screen surface, the canvas and screen will match up perfectly, though you could use your cursor and "grab" the screen, moving its orientation around to different portions of the surface. As you do this, you will notice that the origin numbers listed on the left side of the screen will change to reflect the placement of the screen.

The four corners of the screen have circles called **Control Points** attached to them. These control points are used to warp the output of the screen in order to do things like keystone correction or projection mapping. In short, the control points allow for skewing the resulting video output for the surface. By moving the corner pins, you will change the shape of the screen – thereby changing the resulting shape of the projected image for that surface. In order to adjust your control points, simply hover your mouse over a control point and you will see the icon change from an open hand to a closed hand with the index finger pointing. Holding down shift allows for fine adjustments. In addition to moving the control points manually, you can input a numeric value for its placement or select the control point and use the arrow keys on your keyboard to nudge the placement.

When you select a control point, a new interface will appear on the right side of the screen, labeled "Selected control point." There are two text fields for inputting data. The first field represents the control point's placement on the x-plane, where the second field represents the y-plane. By inputting the raw pixel data, you can have precise control over the placement of your control points. To change the placement of a control point, either input a number and press enter or click in the box and hold down the mouse while sliding your cursor up or down to increase or decrease the number. As with moving the control points manually, holding the shift key down allows for fine control of changing your numbers.

Experiment with moving the corner pins and see how the surface shape can change. For single-screen surfaces, there is only one facet window, which fills the entire area of the surface.

Finally, at the bottom of the Editor Canvas, you will see a drop-down menu that allows you to scale your view of the surface from 10% to 400%. This is simply a tool for zooming your view of the surface and will in no way affect your output.

Screens

The third area of the Surface Editor is placed on the left side of the screen. This column is dedicated to screens attached to your surface. As mentioned in the last chapter, QLab refers to any display connected to your system as a screen. The screens area of the Surface Editor shows any screens currently assigned to your surface and allows you to assign additional screens or control attributes of each screen assigned.

- **Screens Assigned:** To the top left side of the screen is a column that lists all of the screens attached to this surface. With a single-screen surface, there should only be one screen listed. The list indicates the type of screen attached, such as Color LCD, as well as the screen resolution. To the right of the screen name are two checkboxes, one labeled Grid and another called Guides. **Grid** is a tool used to project a black-and-white grid image onto the screen. This is most useful for determining the orientation of projectors. By moving the control points for the screen, as discussed later in the chapter, the grid image will be reshaped in real time. Conversely, the **Guide** tool is similar to the grid, but more often used for determining the rough placement of projectors relative to the space. It is a black screen with red guidelines that show the edges and center point of each screen. Guides are related to the full projector output and will not be affected by moving the corner points of the screen.
- **Adding, Subtracting, and Replacing Screens:** Directly below the Assigned Screens list are three buttons used for adding, subtracting, or replacing screens with others. For a single-screen surface, these will not be used. We will explore their use in detail when creating multi-screen surfaces.

Individual Screen Controls

The area directly beneath the screen's assigned tool is an interface used for controlling any selected screen. Again, since you are editing a single-screen surface, there should be no confusion about which screen you have selected. In the case of multi-screen surfaces, always make sure to select the correct screen before changing any attributes in this area. The following tools are used for controlling attributes of the selected screen:

- **Origin** is used for placing the screen on the surface. These numbers are a standard grid format: the first one is for the x-plane, while the second is for the y-plane. Interestingly, though, the point of origin is the bottom left hand corner of the surface. Anything to the left of the vertical axis or below the horizontal axis is a negative number, while anything to the right of the vertical axis or above the horizontal axis are positive numbers. You can either move the canvas by hand or input the numbers directly into the origin interface. Note that there is no button to reset the origin to 0,0, so this must be done manually.
- Projectors are often placed in different orientations, such as rear projection, ceiling mount, or sideways. **Orientation** controls allow you to flip or reverse the video feed to compensate for this. There is a checkbox that will reverse the image feed for rear projection. In addition, there is also a checkbox that will rotate the image orientation to 0°, 90°, 180°, or 270°.
- **Edge Blending.** QLab has the ability to feather out the edges of images that overlap so that there will not be a brighter line where the two light sources

meet. This is referred to as edge blending. Selecting this checkbox will enable edge blending for the selected screen.

- The final tool included in screen controls is labeled **Reset Control Points.** Clicking this button will reset any changes made to the control points of your screen.

Surface Controls

The fourth and final area of the Surface Editor is located on the right side of the screen. This column features a number of controls that affect the surface itself. Each of these allow for nuanced methods of manipulating the surface appearance. Each is listed below.

- **Warp Type:** Warping is the ability to adjust the geometry of the selected surface. As mentioned earlier in the chapter, each surface has control points on the four corners. These control points are used to distort the video output to the surface. This is often used for video adjustments when projecting onto an angled or irregularly shaped projection surface. When warping the video output, QLab follows three different sets of rules to achieve different outcomes: Perspective, Linear, and Bézier. **Perspective** warping is the default mode used for basic keystone correction. By sliding the control points, you can readjust the output to create a perspective-correct surface. **Linear** warping is most often used for adjusting for more complicated shapes. Some applications refer to this as mesh warping. This method of warping allows for making complex splits across multiple faces without interrupting the video. The complication that arises from this warping type is that linear warping can create image distortion in some conditions. Finally, the **Bézier** warping mode is used for projecting onto curved surfaces. Since this mode comes with more control points, it can be used for reshaping the video into complex curvilinear forms.
- **Constraints:** One aspect of the surface window that is exceptionally useful is the ability to adjust the constraints to "shutter down" a surface and create a smaller one. The benefit of this tool is that it allows you to isolate down to a smaller surface while keeping any preexisting warps or splits attached to the surface. If you hover click on the constraints button, a new interface will open with four boxes in which you can enter coordinates. The coordinates represent the number of pixels your surface will be reduced by on the top, bottom, right, or left side. To change the constraints, either input a number or click in the box and hold down the mouse while sliding your cursor up or down to increase or decrease the number. This allows you to "shutter" down from the edges of the surface, creating a smaller surface (Figure 13.3). These masked off areas will appear as darker than the other areas of the surface window. In Figure 13.3, the top and sides have been pulled in, while the bottom was left untouched.

Figure 13.3
The masked area is represented by the "grayed-out" selection.

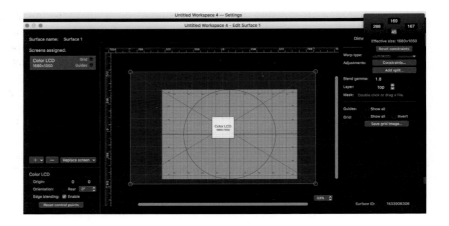

- **Add Split:** Splits are a powerful component of surface editing that allows you to project your video output onto complex projection surfaces. This is commonly used for the process of projection mapping, reshaping video output to match 3D forms like buildings or scenic pieces. Adding a split to your surface subdivides your surface into separate areas known as "patches." To add a split, click on the Add Split button. This will open a pop-up menu that lets you choose where you would like to add a split. By selecting "horizontal," a split will be added along the x-plane, creating two side-by-side patches. Conversely, a "Vertical" split will place a split on the y-plane, creating two patches stacked one over the other.

  To select the location of the split, either input a number or click and drag up or down inside of the number field. The numbers in the field represent a number on your grid along the x- or y-plane and are represented as either a positive or negative number. As you change the placement of the split, a dotted line will appear on the surface canvas to indicate where the split will be placed. When you have placed the split at the appropriate location, either press enter or click on the Add Split button. This will create two patches, labeled A1 and B1. Each patch will have its own unique control points that allow you to warp the patches as needed.

- **Blend Gamma:** When using multiple projectors, it is accepted that there will have to be some image overlap so as to not have gaps of "black" between the imagery. Where two projectors overlap, however, the resulting image will be considerably brighter than the areas around it since two projectors produce the image simultaneously. QLab compensates for this by adding in edge blending by default. The software will automatically decrease the intensity of any overlap between multiple projector surfaces. Blend Gamma refers to the amount of edge blending that occurs for these overlapping screens. The higher the number, the brighter the brightness at the center of the blend region and vice versa for lower numbers. Ideally speaking, you should match this number to the native gamma value of your projector, though it might be useful to actually adjust these numbers while viewing the changes on your projection surface. It is worth noting that this function does not apply to single-screen surfaces – only for created surfaces in which imagery might overlap.

- **Layer:** Layers are an important concept to understand when working with video. QLab uses layers on both surfaces and cues as well. This allows you to control how surfaces stack on top of one another. If you use multiple surfaces that might overlap, it is often a good idea to assign layers to the surfaces so that the appropriate surface will always project atop the other surfaces. This is useful for "patchwork" design surfaces that might have a number of different overlapping projection areas.

- **Mask:** As mentioned in the last chapter, masking is the process of adding an image file with certain opaque and transparent areas that allow for "masking off" areas of your surface. This is often used to "feather" out the edges of an image with some type of gradation so as to avoid "rectangles of light" with projections. In addition, you could mask out any area of the projected imagery (such as in an open doorway where you don't want the imagery to appear). The Mask box in the surface patch allows you to import an image to be used as a mask. To achieve this, simply use a black-and-white image file: black will be interpreted as an opaque area and white will be transparent, allowing the video to show through it. You can also create gradations of opacity inside of your graphics editing program that will allow you to create a gradient mask. Once a mask is assigned to your surface, QLab watches the file for changes, so all you have to do is edit and save in your image editor and QLab will make sure to display the most current version.

- **Guides:** The Guides tool is identical to that seen in the assigned screens list. In this case, though, clicking on the Show All button will bring up the guides for any screen assigned to your surface.

- **Grid:** Similarly, the Show All button will bring up grids for all of the screens attached to your surface. Clicking on the "invert" button reverses your grid color from black on white to white on black.

- **Save Grid Image:** This button saves a picture of the video grid to your desktop. The image is saved in the PNG format. This image is particularly useful for creating mask images. Simply open the image in your favorite image editing software and create new image masks as layers on top of the video grid. This will ensure the appropriate size and proportion of mask images.

13.3 – Creating and Editing New Surfaces

To this point, we have examined the process of editing single-screen surfaces. The backbone of the entire surfaces system, though, is the creation of new and unique surfaces as patches for Video and Camera Cue output. As mentioned before, you can create an unlimited number of surfaces, each with unique display attributes assigned to them. The following section addresses the process of creating and editing these surfaces.

To create a new surface, open the Video Settings tab and click on the plus sign icon at the bottom left corner of the screen. This will open an interface for creating a new surface. There are three options, each with unique functions that are useful for different scenarios. The list below details each option and its purpose.

- **New Empty Surface:** This option creates a new surface without any screens attached to it, allowing you to add screens manually.
- **New with Display:** This option creates a surface paired to one of the displays attached to your system. The dimensions of this surface will match the size of your display.
- **New Multi-Screen Surface:** This final option is used for creating a surface that combines together multiple displays into one combined surface for video output. This is commonly used for combining projectors to create a blended surface, or linking multiple video displays to create a video wall. The benefit of this option is that QLab will ask a few basic questions and create the surface for you, without having to do so manually.

Once you have selected the type of new surface to create, a new Surface Editor will open. This window will look identical to the one mentioned in the previous section, with all of the same functions and layout. Keep in mind that any changes made here are unique to this surface and will not affect any other surfaces, even if they have similar screens assigned.

Tools of the Trade

Remote Control for Your Workspace

One of the things that can create a complication in setting up projections is the need to see and control your QLab workspace, while also having a line of sight for the projections themselves. Often, the projections computer might be hidden away and not offer a view of the stage at all. For situations such as these, it is important to have a method for accessing the QLab workspace while watching the resulting projections.

The first method for accessing the QLab workspace is screen sharing, a native function for Mac computers. By setting up a personal computer-to-computer network, one Mac computer can access and even control another. To enable this, go into *System Preferences > Sharing* on your Mac and enable screen sharing. In addition, you could enable file sharing if you want to be able to drag and drop files from one computer to another over your network. On the remote computer, you will need to log in to the same computer-to-computer network created on the show computer. You will then be able to find the show computer through the Shared tab in your Finder. Click on the show computer in your list of shared computers and click the "Share Screen" button. This should enable you to remotely view and control your QLab show computer.

Another option is the QLab Remote, mentioned several times throughout the book. The QLab Remote allows you to access any workspace open on your show computer and control certain aspects. With projections, one of the best aspects of the QLab Remote is the ability to edit the control points of a surface. In addition to grabbing the control points and manually sliding them, there are also text inputs that allow for more precise manipulation of the control points. The QLab Remote can be purchased through the App Store. One down side is the slight learning curve for editing cues. While you can access many of the Inspector tabs, there are some that are not available. This can make it difficult for editing aspects such as Time & Loops and Video Effects. For remote editing these functions, a screen share is still the best option.

For an inexpensive method of accessing and editing Video Surfaces, there is a free App available on the App Store called Q Surface. The sole purpose of this application is to change the control points of QLab 4 video surfaces. While it does not offer as many of the options of Figure 53's QLab Remote, it is certainly a cost-effective option for remotely controlling your Video Surfaces.

13.4 – Setting Up a Graphics Expansion Device with QLab

The physical attributes of an expansion device tend to be quite simple. It uses the standard video output of your computer as its input source. It might be DVI, VGA, DisplayPort, Mini DisplayPort, or HDMI. In addition to connecting to your computer's video output, some expansion devices use a USB cable to bus power the device and connect to software running on your computer. For older analog models, it might need to connect to an AC power source in addition to these two connections.

The graphics expansion device creates a virtual display that is two or three times wider than the resolution of your display. In the case of the TripleHead2Go, the output dimensions are three times wider than the resolution of your monitor.

Figure 13.4
Multi-screen
output.

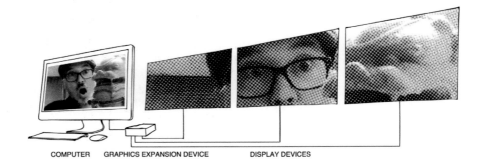

COMPUTER   GRAPHICS EXPANSION DEVICE   DISPLAY DEVICES

For instance, if your monitor were set to SXGA resolution (1024 x 768), then the device output would be three times wider for a resulting resolution of 3072 x 768. An image or video designed to fit these dimensions would be equally split over all of the three separate outputs, the left third going to output 1, the center to output 2, and the right third to output 3 (see Figure 13.4). As seen in Figure 13.4, all images will not necessarily fit within this triple-wide aspect ratio without having some cropping occur or shrinking the image down to fit. This is the basic plug-and-play method covered below. This method is best used when combining multiple projectors or output devices to create a single unified surface.

Project 13.1 ▽

Plug-and-Play Setup

The following project takes you through the process of setting up a graphics expansion module with your QLab system. There is no project packet to download, as it deals specifically with setup.

Step 1: With QLab closed, connect the graphics expansion device to your computer. Make sure to follow the manufacturer's guidelines for installation. Some devices are "hot pluggable" while others will not function in this process.

Step 2: After your device is connected, open QLab. Click on the Workspace Settings icon in the lower right corner and select the Video Settings button. You will see a list on the right side of the screen labeled "video surfaces." Your graphics expansion device should be listed here in addition to any monitors connected to your system (Figure 13.5). This will be displayed as a Surface number (i.e., Surface 2). It is important to note that QLab will not recognize any displays connected to

Figure 13.5
The video surfaces menu, showing the expansion module as an additional surface.

your expansion device as individual surfaces, as they are simply outputs from your expansion device.

Step 3: Click on the "edit" button beside your display. This will open the settings panel for the expansion device. The first attribute to edit should be the surface name. I find it is a good idea to re-name the surface name as something descriptive, like "triple-wide." After typing in the new name, click "enter" and changes will be assigned.

Step 4: Once you have changed the name, you are ready to use this surface as a video surface patch. Any Video Cue sent to this video surface will be outputted to all three displays as if they were one big screen. Images can be displayed on any one or all of the output displays.

The process described above is ideal if you only ever want to use the three outputs as one large display. An especially useful application would be combining three video displays to make a wall. There are, however, many functions such as individual keystone control for projectors, edge-blending, and projector orientation that cannot be used through this single-screen surface method.

Project 13.2 ▼

Individual Screen Control with an Expansion Module

In order to control aspects of each screen individually, you need to go about a different process for setting up your graphics expansion module. The list below describes this process in detail.

Step 1: After your expansion module is connected, click on the Workspace Settings icon in the lower right corner and select the Video

(Continued)

Settings button. In the Video Surfaces list, click the + button at the bottom of the screen to create a new surface. Select New Empty Surface.

Step 2: The Surface Editor window will appear for this new untitled surface. Name the new surface "multi-display." Press enter and it will save the name. This will be the new surface patch used to output to the three outputs of your graphics expansion device.

Step 3: In the upper right corner, there will be two slots for inputting the dimensions of your surface. In this area, input dimensions that match that of your expansion device's output (for this example, 3072 x 768). Inputting these dimensions will create a new surface called "multi-display" that matches the output dimensions of your expansion device (Figure 13.6).

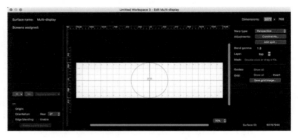

Figure 13.6
The "multi-display" surface is three times the width of our standard output resolution.

Step 4: The process to this point essentially created a new surface that matches the output of your three projectors combined, but with no screen attached to it. That is where the screen's assigned function comes in.

In the left column of the screen, you will see a box labeled "Screens assigned." Click on the + button at the bottom of this column to add a screen. Instead of using one of the single-screen surfaces listed, click on the line labeled "partial screens." There will be a drop-down line that features the name of your graphics expansion device. Click on that and then select the number of outputs your device features. In my case, that is "3 wide."

There will be three choices following this: virtual screen 1, virtual screen 2, and virtual screen 3. Click on virtual screen 1, and a blue box will appear superimposed over your "multi-display" surface (see Figure 13.7). It will be labeled "Display (1/3)" indicating that this is the first of three virtual screens derived from the screen called "Display." The blue screen is the visual representation of the projector connected to output 1 of your expansion devices. It will automatically be placed in the left third of your surface. This means that output 1 of your expansion device will display the left portion of the video output.

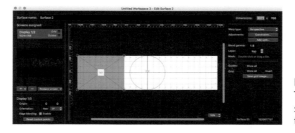

Figure 13.7
The virtual screen is superimposed over the surface canvas.

Step 5: Repeat the process above and insert virtual screen 2. This will then place a new partial screen called "Triple-wide (2/3)" superimposed over the first virtual screen. This virtual screen will have a green color to distinguish it from the first one. Grab it and move it over until it is aligned in the center of the "multi-display" surface. This means that output 2 of your expansion device will display the center portion of the video output. To make sure the facet window is aligned properly, input an origin of 1025 and 0 at the bottom of the screen.

Step 6: Finally, repeat this process a third time for the final virtual screen, "Triple-wide (3/3)." Move this virtual screen, a red one this time, all the way to the right third of the "multi-display" surface. The origin settings for this screen should be 2049 and 0. This means that output 3 of your expansion device will display the right portion of the video output. At this point, your surface output should look like that seen in Figure 13.8.

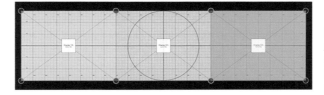

Figure 13.8
All three virtual screens are now appropriately placed.

Step 7: By following the process detailed in the steps above, you will have three individual screens that can be controlled by your surface patch. Select any of the three screens on the left of the screen, and you can control many of the attributes for each screen, such as origin, projector orientation, or corner pin control. Please note that masking, gamma, and shutters affect only the overall surface, *not* the individual screens.

13.5 – Creating a Surface with Edge Blending

When using two or more projectors with overlapping areas, there will be bright spots where the images overlap. In order to combat this, QLab uses a technique called edge blending that reduces the brightness in the overlapping pixel area of both projectors so that the resulting image has the same brightness as other areas of the projection. The following section talks you through the process of creating such a surface.

Project 13.3 ▼

Creating a Surface with Edge Blending

The following project takes you through the process of setting up a surface that utilizes edge blending. There is no project packet to download, as it deals specifically with setup.

Step 1: Go to the Video settings window. In the Video Surfaces list, click the + button at the bottom of the screen to create a new surface. For a quick setup, select the "New Multi-Screen Surface."

Step 2: The Surface Editor will open with a dialogue asking some setup questions. The first input asks the resolution of the connected projectors. It is assumed here that all projectors have matching resolutions. The next input asks your projector arrangement. The first box represents the number of displays wide, and the second one refers to the number high. For creating a triple-wide surface as mentioned above, then you would input "3x1." Finally, the third input asks the screen overlap. The default is 20%, though you can input any number desired. In the example shown here, I created a surface that combines three screens with a resolution of 1920 x 1080. Since I programmed an overlap of 20%, the resulting surface has a size of 4992 x 1080 (Figure 13.9)

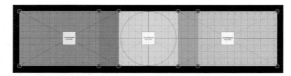

Figure 13.9
A multi-screen surface with 20% screen overlap.

Step 3: In the left column of the screen, you will see a box labeled "screens assigned." In this list, there will be three screens labeled as (unassigned). This means that you will have to assign the desired display to each screen. To do so, select the screen and click on the Assign screen button at the bottom of the list. This will allow you to select from all of the displays attached to your system. Keep in mind that the resolution will change to match that of the selected display, so your layout may change if you select a differing resolution.

Step 4: Once you have assigned your screens to your surface, each one will have separate control points for warping their output and can be repositioned as described in previous exercises.

Step 5: Finally, in order to match the screen orientation and test out the edge blending, click on the grid checkboxes beside each of the three screens. This will bring up a grid on each projector and allow you to move control points as needed to match the grids up perfectly. If you need to adjust the brightness of the edge blending areas, click on the blend gamma button on the right side of the screen, and slide the numbers up or down to increase or decrease until it looks correct.

13.6 – Workspace Settings: Camera

In addition to Video Cues, QLab also has workspace settings for Camera Cues. Directly beneath the Video Surfaces list in Video Settings is the Camera Patch. This is where you assign different camera devices to a specific patch within QLab. The QLab video reinforcement system works with any iSight or FaceTime camera attached to your Mac, most varieties of USB or FireWire webcams, and Blackmagic camera devices. In addition, it can accept input signals via Syphon (a Mac OS X technology used to share video between applications on the same computer). The section below details the process for setting up your camera patch.

Camera Patch Settings

The camera patch shows a list of eight possible camera options (see Figure 13.10). Each one should automatically have a camera assigned to it from

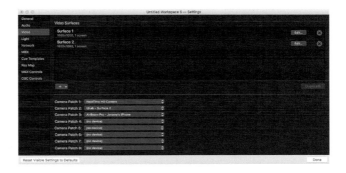

Figure 13.10
The Camera Patch.

the list of available supported cameras attached to your system. If you do not see the camera you are looking for, click on the drop-down menu to view a list of possibilities. You can move camera assignment between patches to meet your programming needs. The purpose of the camera patch is to have a readily available list of cameras that can later be assigned to a Camera Cue as an input.

In addition to traditional cameras, a Syphon feed can be used as a camera input. Syphon allows a computer to share either images or live video stream from one application to another. In this case, a Syphon-capable program on your computer could function as a camera input for a Camera Cue. If you are running a Syphon server on your system, you will see this available in the drop-down menu for your camera patch, in addition to standard cameras.

Tools of the Trade ▼

Syphon Output

Syphon is an open-source Mac OS X technology that allows applications to share either full-frame videos or image stills with one another in real-time. It is important to note that Syphon works on your computer's graphics card to share video and images between applications **on the same computer.** Syphon is *not* intended for use across a network or between separate computers.

QLab 4 offers Syphon integration in two key ways. One, which we have already covered, is the ability to use a Syphon video feed in the place of a camera input for Camera Cues. The second method is to allow the assignment of a Syphon output as a screen assigned to a surface. In other words, any surface can output its signal to a display device, as a Syphon output or as both simultaneously. These Syphon outputs can then be routed into other Syphon-capable programs, such as MadMapper, a program designed to video map images. Visit http://syphon.v002.info for more information about Syphon supported software.

To assign a Syphon output as a screen, open your Surface Editor for the desired surface and click on the plus button in the screens assigned list in the same way you would add any other screen. At the bottom of the drop-down menu, though, you will see a button labeled "Syphon." Clicking on this will create a screen that mirrors the entire surface and outputs it as a Syphon signal. Note that there will be no discernible action to triggering the Video Cue with only a Syphon patch (unless you have a Syphon client running). It will simply output the cue and then proceed to the next cue in the cue sequence.

Video, Camera, and Text Cues

Video Cues are the foundation for QLab's video playback capabilities. They allow you to display either video files or still images through any screen attached to your system. As we have explored in previous chapters, there are a number of ways in which QLab can be configured to display your imagery. In order to truly appreciate the nuances of video playback, though, we should dedicate some time to examining the function of Video and Camera Cues exclusively.

Though you can experiment with all of the video tools in the free version, a video license is required to truly utilize all of the functions available. Full screen video can be played to the default single-screen surface from the free version. A final note before jumping into Video Cues: video editing and playback is a taxing process for most computers. A number of the video functions of QLab will require a lot of processing power. Look over the hardware concerns listed in previous chapters if your computer is having difficulty keeping pace.

14.1 – Inserting a Video Cue

Video Cues are QLab cues specially designed to play video or image files through a video patch. In simple terms, a Video Cue accesses a video or image file saved on your computer and outputs this file through a Surface that can have one or more screens attached to it. In addition to simple playback, there are a number of built-in filters and video effects that can be applied to the video or image files to affect their appearance and behavior. Like any other cue, a Video Cue can be inserted via the Toolbar, Toolbox, or dragging a video file directly into the cue list. Since video files frequently have imbedded audio, the cue also features a number of settings for audio in addition to video. The following section details the numerous tabs found in the Video Cue's Inspector Panel.

Before delving into the finer details of the Video Cue, though, it is wise to look at one final setting. QLab outputs video atop the desktop of attached displays, meaning that if there is no video output, the default image shown would be your computer's desktop. To disable this, you want to use a useful built-in feature that blacks out the desktop background. Click on *Tools > Black Out Desktop Backgrounds*. After activating this function, your desktop background will be replaced with a plain black background, thus ensuring that when all videos are done there will be no visible desktop image.

14.2 Inspector: Basics

Once a Video Cue is inserted into your cue list, the Inspector can be used to access a wide range of control functions related to the cue. There are eight tabs within the Inspector that house a number of these functions: Basics, Triggers, Display & Geometry, Time & Loops, Audio Levels, Audio Trim, Audio Effects, and Video Effects. Each of these tabs contains specific control functions that affect the playback of the given Video Cue. The first tab, Basics, allows the same function seen in examining the Audio Cue. Like the Audio Cue, Video Cue Basics deals primarily with cue information, notes, and organizational tools.

Cue Info

Aligned to the left half of the screen, Cue Basics deals with information related to cue numbering, naming, targeting, and playback. The inputs in this area are identical to that of the Audio Cue.

Design Tips ▼

A Word About File Formats

When creating or finding content for your Video Cues, it is important always to consider the file formats. QLab supports a wide range of moving image and graphics formats. For video, QLab 4 can play any file supported by AVFoundation. The following group is listed in order of preference.

- ProRes 422 Proxy
- ProRes 422 LT
- PhotoJPG
- Hap
- H.264

In the past, ProRes 4444 was the only supported format for video transparencies, sometimes referred to as **Alpha Channel**. QLab 4 has expanded the available format options by adding support for the popular Hap and Hap Alpha codecs through Vidvox.

Finally, for still images QLab supports playback of most standard graphics file types. For a number of reasons, the JPG and PNG formats are an ideal choice. Of particular note is the fact that PNG files support transparency. This offers the ability to layer multiple Video Cues atop one another and create rich compositions whose various layers are individually controllable. It bears mentioning that Figure 53 recommends against the use of PDF and PSD files.

14.3 – Inspector: Triggers

Again, the triggering functions of the Video Cue match that of the Audio Cue. The triggering window allows the programmer to establish MIDI, Hotkey, Wall Clock, or Timecode triggering, as well as affecting the playback volume of other cues when starting the action of the selected Video Cue.

14.4 – Inspector: Display & Geometry

Display & Geometry deals specifically with video surface assignment and affecting the display geometry of a video output. Looking at Figure 14.1, you will notice that the tab is divided into two columns. The left column contains the video surface assignment and video mode, whereas the right side contains the video stage, a graphic representation of your assigned video surface.

The Video Stage

The Video Stage is a great tool for seeing your image placement on the video surface in real-time. The translucent blue shape on the Video Stage represents your assigned Video Surface. Even though the surface might be composed of several individual screens, these screens will not be shown, only the surface.

Figure 14.1
The Display &
Geometry Tab.

When first adding a Video Cue, the Video Stage will show a yellow QLab icon in the center of its area. Once you assign a target file, this will be replaced with a representation of your Video Cue with a yellow bounding box around it. This Video Cue can be moved anywhere inside, or even outside of the surface, by simply grabbing it and moving it with your mouse (provided that you set the mode to Custom Geometry, which we will explore in a moment). There are a few interesting multitouch gestures imbedded into the video stage as well. For instance, the scale can be zoomed in or out by doing a "two-finger scroll" up or down. By using the two-finger scroll from right to left, the z rotation can be easily toggled.

Video Surface

As previously addressed, the QLab video engine allows for the use of video surfaces rather than simple screen patches. A surface is a user-defined area of a predetermined size that can have one or more screens assigned to it. The idea of the video surface is that it frees you up to think about your design in a more artistic and holistic sense rather than focusing on the nuts and bolts of screen output.

When an output device is attached to your system, a single-screen surface will automatically be created and added to your list of available video surfaces (in the Video Settings window). Depending on your design needs, you can either output a Video Cue to a single screen or create a multi-screen surface composed of multiple screens and send the signal to that surface. If you choose to do this, QLab will do all of the necessary calculations behind the scenes to route the video components out the appropriate display devices. Either method, the output patch is selected in the Video Surface drop-down menu.

If you want to edit the assigned video surface, just click on the edit surface button (the button with three dots to the right of the video surface), and it will open up the Surface Editor window. This window allows for naming the surface, changing its dimensions, assigning screens and masks, edge-blending, and more. All of the details for this are covered in depth in Chapter 13.

Mode: Full Surface

The "Mode" control, located beneath the video surface controls, addresses the geometry for controlling image output. When a Video Cue is assigned to a video surface, it can either be full screen or custom geometry. Full surface does exactly what you might suspect – it enlarges or reduces the image or video file to fill the entire width of your surface. In choosing full screen, you can either select "preserve the aspect ratio" (to keep the original proportion of the image upon enlarging or reducing) or deselect this checkbox (to disregard the original proportion of the image and stretch it to fill the entirety of the surface).

Mode: Custom Geometry

Upon selecting the Custom Geometry button in the drop-down menu of the Mode control, a new set of input windows will appear (see Figure 14.2) that allow for adjusting the placement, size, and rotation of the video or image file in the surface output. These controls offer a wide range of tools to affect the image output in a number of ways.

- Translation: Translation refers to the placement of the image or video file in the surface. It is important to think of the concept of a graph for video controls. In translation, the first input represents placement in the horizontal plane (or the x-axis). The second input represents placement in the vertical plane (or the y-axis). The center of your surface represents the 0,0 position. Movement up or to the right of this is a positive number, whereas movement down or to the left is a negative number. There are two methods for changing translation. You can either input the numbers manually or simply grab the image in the video stage and move it to the desired position.
- Scale: Scale refers to the size of the image. The default scale is 1 for any image. To enlarge the image, change the scale to a number greater than 1. To reduce the image, change the scale to a number less than 1. Again, the first input represents the x-plane (width), while the second one represents the y-plane (height). You will notice that changing one will also change the other. This is because the lock aspect ratio is enabled, making it so any change in width affects a change in height and vice versa. To disable this function, simply click on the padlock icon, unlocking the fixed aspect ratio. As mentioned above, a quick method for zooming in and out of scale is the two-finger scroll up to enlarge or down to reduce scale.
- Rotation: Rotation refers to the image placement in relation to the x-, y-, and z-coordinates of the surface. Until this point, we have only discussed the x- and y-axes. In a two-dimensional drawing, x- and y-coordinates refer to right and left or up and down. In a three-dimensional drawing, a third axis, the z-axis, refers to the vertical coordinates lifted above the surface. For QLab, these coordinates refer specifically to the way in which an image can be rotated on the surface.

Figure 14.2
The Custom Geometry window is used for resizing the output image. Notice the aspect ratio of this image has been unlocked to allow for stretching the size.

By clicking on any of the three inputs (x, y, or z), a dialog window will pop up asking for rotation coordinates. The x-rotation tool rotates the image on the x-axis ("flipping" the image head over foot). The y-rotation tool rotates the image on the y-axis ("spinning" the image like a top). Finally, the z-rotation tool rotates the image on the z-axis (turning it in a clockwise or counter-clockwise fashion). To input rotation changes, click in the input box and slide your mouse up for a positive number or down for a negative one. As you do so, look to the image in your video stage to the right and you will see how the numbers affect the image output. To return the Video Cue to its original rotation state, simply click on the reset button, and all axis rotations will be set back to 0.

Design Tips ▼

Rotation Options

The Rotation settings for a Video Cue refer specifically to the original placement of an image. Rotation does not indicate an animated movement. In order to accomplish this, a Fade Cue must be used in conjunction with a Video Cue to allow for 3D rotation around the x-, y-, or z-axes. For more information on using these options, look at Project 14.2.

- Layer: This function allows for the "stacking" of multiple Video Cues atop one another. The lower numbers remain on the bottom of the stack, while higher numbers are arranged above. There are 1,000 numbered layers to choose from. In addition, you can assign any Video Cue to be "bottom" or "top" by selecting this in the Layer drop-down menu.
- Opacity: Opacity is the setting that allows the programmer to change the video image from opaque to translucent. 100% opacity means that the image is perceived as "solid." As the numbers decrease, the resulting image becomes more translucent, allowing the layers or background behind it to be visible through the image. This setting is useful for creating interesting layered imagery seen in tandem. Likewise, combining opacity settings with a Fade Cue creates a fade-in or fade-out of a Video Cue.
- Anchor: The anchor point is the location on the Video Surface around which the Video Cue rotates, moves, or scales. The default position is 0,0 – the center of the video surface. It can be advantageous to change the anchor position, particularly when creating animated movement of video cues. Project 14.3 later in this chapter addresses the use of adjusting your anchor position to create an animation of a ticking clock.

Project 14.1 ▼

Fade Controls for Video Cues

One of the most common requests for Video Cues is the ability to fade in at the beginning or fade to black at the end of the cue. These functions are accomplished via Fade Cues. The following project takes you through the process of creating a fade-in and fade-out for a Video Cue.

Step 1: Download Project 14.1 from the companion website.

Step 2: Select cue 1 from the workspace. Click ⇧⌘A to open the Audition Window. Click GO to fire the Video Cue featuring a young girl on the beach. Press escape to end the playback.

Step 3: Insert two Fade Cues following the Video Cue and assign cue 1 as the target for both.

Step 4: Select cue 1 and open the Display & Geometry tab in the Inspector. Set the opacity to 0.0%. This will make the Video Cue invisible when fired, showing only the black background.

Step 5: Select cue 2 and open the Geometry tab in the Inspector. Click on the opacity checkbox and set the opacity to 100%. You will notice that the red x will disappear from this Fade Cue's status.

Step 6: Set the opacity for cue 3 to 0.0% in the same fashion as Step Five. Likewise, the red x should disappear from the cue row.

Step 7: Test your programming. Clicking Cue 1 should activate the Video Cue (though you will not see it). Firing cue 2 will fade in the image, and firing Cue 3 will fade to black.

Step 8: In order to automate this cue sequence and eliminate the need for extra GO clicks, set the continue status of cue 1 to Auto-continue. This will make the image fade in when the first cue is fired. To further clean up your workspace you could even place both of these cues into one group so as to hide the unnecessary programming.

Step 9: The final step is to make sure the Video Cue will stop playing once faded to black. Remember, like Audio Cues, a Video Cue will continue to play until stopped. In order to free up system resources, remember to click the "stop target when done" checkbox on cue 3. This will assure that the cue will stop playing once faded out.

Project 14.2 ▼

Animating Image Rotation with Fade Cues

QLab 4 offers many different options for rotation. The first method, 3D rotation, allows for rotation of one image along the x-, y-, and z-axes simultaneously. This method is excellent for doing basic 3D changes of image rotation, so long as you do not need multiple spins around any given axis. It is important to note that there is currently no method for creating a 3D rotation that revolves around an axis more than one rotation.

For instances in which multiple spins around one axis are required, you can choose either x-, y-, or z-axes for individual axis rotation. This is effective for rotation effects that revolve numerous times around one axis (like the spinning newspaper effects of classic black-and-white films).

The Spinning Headlines Newspaper

Step 1: Download Project 14.2 from the companion website.

Step 2: Select cue 1 from the workspace. This is an image of a classic newspaper headline. Click ⇧⌘A to open the Audition Window.

Step 3: To create the desired effect of the newspaper zooming in from the distance, we must first start with the Display & Geometry tab. Select the drop-down menu labeled "Full Screen" and change it to "Custom Geometry." After doing this, change the Scale from 1 to 0. This will shrink the image so much as to make the image disappear. Your settings should mirror those seen in Figure 14.3.

Figure 14.3
The Display & Geometry tab settings.

Step 4: Set the continue status of cue 1 to Auto-continue so that it will automatically fire cue 2.

Step 5: Insert a Fade Cue and set cue 1 as its target. Select the Geometry tab in the Inspector Panel. First, click on the Scale button and slowly slide the scale up until the image almost fills the screen of your video stage (see Figure 14.4)

Figure 14.4
Scaling the image.

Step 6: Test the sequence by firing cue 1. The resulting effect should be the newspaper zooming in from the distance.

Step 7: In order to get the newspaper to spin, you must once more select the Geometry tab of cue 2. This time click on the drop-down menu beside rotation and select "Z rotation." Type in –1080 in the box and make sure to remember to select the checkbox to the left of "rotation." Figure 14.5 illustrates how your screen should look.

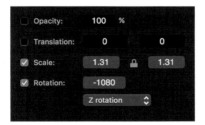

Figure 14.5
Inputting image rotation.

Step 8: Test your cue sequence. It should now successfully spin in from the distance. One last option is customizing your fade curve settings. To do this, select Curve Shape from the Fade Cue's Inspector Panel and click on "custom curve" in the drop-down menu instead of "S-curve." Play around with different curve shapes until you feel comfortable that you understand their use.

Project 14.3 ▼

Using the Anchor to Your Advantage

One of the benefits of using the anchor in animations is the ability to make more realistic movement options. A great example of this is a ticking clock. By combining together a few layers on top of a clock face, setting an anchor point, and adding some fade cues, you can create a realistic animation effect. The following project takes you through this process.

(Continued)

Step 1: Download and open Project 14.3 from the companion website. Click ⇧⌘A to open the Audition Window.

Step 2: You will notice there are three cues in the Workspace. Select cue 1 and trigger playback. This is an image of a clock face with no hands. Cues 2 and 3 are images of clock hands with transparent backgrounds. When I made these files in Photoshop, I made sure to start off with one picture of the clock face and the two hands added as layers on top. I centered the hands on the clock face and aligned them appropriately. By turning off all but one layer and saving each layer as a separate file, I am assured that each graphic has the same dimensions. This means that I know the layers will align with one another once stacked into QLab as separate Video Cues. I also saved each file in the PNG format with a transparent background. Since QLab can use these files with transparencies, it allows you to stack them atop one another and create interesting layered compositions for animation.

Step 3: Select cue 2 and look at the anchor position. You will notice it is not centered on the clock hand. To align this appropriately, all you have to do is either grab the crosshairs of the anchor and slide it or input the number manually. In this case, the anchor should be at the 0,0 coordinates. This is because I centered my image files upon creation. If I had not done this, the task would be a bit more work.

Step 4: Repeat the process in Step Three for cue 3, making sure the anchor is centered at 0,0.

Step 5: Insert two Fade Cues after cue 3. These will be named 4 and 5, respectively. Drag cue 2 onto 4 to set it as the Fade Cue's target. Repeat this process by dragging cue 3 onto cue 5 as well. Now, each Fade Cue will have the previous cue set as its target.

Step 6: Select cue 4 and click on the Geometry tab. To rotate the hour hand, you will have to change the Z rotation value. To do so, first select the checkbox beside the word "rotation." Next, click on the drop-down menu labeled 3D rotation and select "Z rotation." Finally, input −360 as the value into the rotation field (Figure 14.6). Once you have done this, you are free to trigger playback for cue 4. If you have done everything correctly, you should see the hour hand circle the clock.

Figure 14.6
The Geometry tab is used for adjusting the rotation of a Video Cue.

Step 7: Repeat the same process for Fade cue 5, setting the Z rotation as −30. If you also set the continue status of cue 4 as auto-continue, both hands of the clock will rotate simultaneously.

Step 8: Of course, the programming for the clock would change slighting for doing more than a one-hour progression. To do this, you simply have to adjust the rotation and duration of your fade cues to make the hands rotate at the appropriate speed and duration. Have fun playing around with some of the different options until you get the right look.

14.5 – Inspector: Time & Loops

The Time & Loops panel for Video Cues (Figure 14.7) is identical to that in Audio Cues and mirrors the functions seen in Chapter 6, with the exception of one function that can hold a video cue up on the screen at the end of its play-back. The following section addresses a few of the ways that the Time & Loops tab can be used.

Waveform Display

The waveform display is blank for Video Cues with image files or silent video targets. When using a video file with an audio track, the waveform will display in the same fashion as that for an Audio Cue. Likewise, the start time/end time of the Video Cue can be changed by simply grabbing either of the handles at the beginning or end of the Video Cue and scrubbing them to the desired start or end point. Again, this is a non-destructive process that can be changed as frequently as necessary without damaging the target file.

Preview Cue

For the Video Cue, it is especially important to master the use of the **Audition Window** for previewing cues. Click on ⇧⌘A to open the audition window, a special window that serves as a temporary surface for viewing Video Cues or listening to Audio Cues. While you can press the preview button for Video Cues,

Figure 14.7
The Time & Loops tab for Video Cues.

the problem arises when the computer is not connected to your additional output devices. If your computer does not have an external display, the video cue will play in full screen mode and cover up your workspace. This makes it impossible to edit the cue, as you cannot see the controls. By using the Audition Window, the Video Cue preview will be exported to the Audition Window and can be resized or moved anywhere on the desktop for preview purposes.

Times, Loops, and Slices

Again, the column to the left of the Time & Loops tab mirrors that seen in the Audio Cue. There is a start and end time dialog for inserting the times manually. In addition, there is a play count dialog for the number of times the Video Cue will play (looping). Likewise, the infinite loop enables an infinite number of playback loops.

Slices are enabled for video playback as well as audio. Like the Audio Cue, slices allow for the looping of internal sections of a Video Cue. In many ways, video looping is much more complicated to achieve than audio due to the visual nature of videos. The video must be created in such a way that it can loop back to a point without a noticeable "hiccup."

In order to insert a loop into a cue, simply click the location in the waveform to place the end of your slice. Likewise, if you created the file in a video-editing software with markers, those markers will translate into slices automatically when imported to QLab. If you want the first 3 seconds of a Video Cue to repeat, place your cursor at the 3-second position in the waveform viewer and click the "Add Slice" button. Once you have done this, you will notice a handle appears at the top of the waveform timeline similar to the playback position icon in your cue list. This indicates the end of the slice. To fine-tune the ending position, simply grab the slice position icon in the timeline and slide it to the desired location.

Once a slice is inserted, two numbers will appear at the bottom of the waveform, both reading 1. This indicates the number of times your slice will loop before proceeding to the next slice. Click on the first number and change it to 2. This will create a slice that plays back twice before progressing to the next section in the Audio Cue. Likewise, if you want to make the loop repeat an infinite number of times, simply insert "inf" instead of a number, and the infinity symbol (∞) will replace it.

If you wish to remove a single slice, simply change the number back to 1, and it will function like it is not there. Likewise, you can grab the handle and pull it out of the workspace to delete it. If you wish to delete all slices, click on the button labeled "Delete All."

To end an infinite loop cycle, you must use the DeVamp Cue in conjunction with your Video Cue. Once triggered, a DeVamp Cue tells a cue to stop repeating and progress to the next slice once the next loop cycle has completed. This is addressed in depth in Chapter 9, Control Cues.

Like in Audio Cues, the slices can also function as a visual marker in your waveform that makes it easier to identify key spots during tech. If, for instance, there is a spot in the middle of a song where a certain effect occurs and you want to note that location, simply insert a slice and keep the loop number set to 1. There will be no function to the slice other than serving as a visual marker for your own use at a later time.

Integrated Fade Envelope and Playback Rate

The integrated fade envelope allows for inserting fade curves attached to the audio component of your Video Cue. When you click on the "use integrated fade" button, a yellow line will appear placed horizontally across the top of your waveform with a circle at the beginning and end of the line. This is the fade line that allows for inserting level increases or decreases to automate volume changes.

Beneath the integrated fade checkbox is a new addition called "lock fade to start/end." If the box is unchecked, an integrated fade curve will be locked to the start and end times of the selected sound file. Once checked, the fade will instead be linked to the start and end times of the cue in question.

The rate control changes the rate of playback for the Video Cue in the same manner as the Audio Cue. Likewise, the preserve pitch button keeps the pitch of the audio track unchanged with rate changes. When using a Fade Cue in conjunction with a Video Cue, the rate can be manipulated through the Audio Effects tab of the Fade Cue. It is important to note that this only works for video files with an audio track.

At the bottom of the right side of the Time & Loops tab is a checkbox labeled "Hold at end." Clicking this box will keep the final frame of your Video Cue on the screen once it reaches the end of its playback. Without this checked, the cue will instantly fade to black.

14.6 – Inspector: Audio Levels, Audio Trim, and Audio Effects

The following three tabs in the Video Cue Inspector Panel are identical in function to those seen in the Audio Cue Inspector, though the tab names are slightly different.

Audio Levels for the Video Cue functions in the exact same fashion as the Device & Levels tab in the Audio Cue Inspector. The purpose of this tab remains the assignment of the audio output patch, setting volume levels, and ganging outputs.

Audio Trim mirrors the Trim tab in the Audio Cue. As with the Audio Cue, the trim controls allow for the increase or decrease of volume across a series of Fade Cues that target the same cue. In this case, it is specifically related to the audio track of a Video Cue, though, rather than an Audio Cue.

Finally, the Audio Effects tab shares both the name and function of that seen in the Audio Cue Inspector Panel. Again, this tab allows for the addition of audio effects to change the audio output of a Video Cue. All of the same Audio Units are available for a Video Cue as those for the Audio Cue.

All three of these control tabs offer a great amount of flexibility to how a Video Cue can be used in your workspace. By using these in conjunction with Fade Cues, you can truly create dynamic playback effects and offer a wide array of non-destructive editing effects built in to your Video Cue.

14.7 – Inspector: Video Effects

One of the strengths of the QLab video system is the wide array of built-in video effects available for manipulating video and image files. For those used to working with graphics and video-editing programs, many of these effects will already be a part of your working vocabulary. Currently, each Video Cue can apply only one video effect to its output, so there are some limitations to the ways in which video can be manipulated. Nonetheless, video effects add a great level of versatility to Video Cue options.

To access the video effects, click on the Video Effects tab in the Inspector and click on the drop-down menu beside the "Apply Effects" button. You will notice that the drop-down menu features a number of effects, each separated into seven different groups (see Figure 14.8). Listed below are the video effects

Figure 14.8
The Video Effects drop-down menu features many options for affecting video output.

categories and basic descriptions of their use. Video effects are such a large component of the Video Cue structure that Chapter 15 is dedicated to fully exploring their functions.

- **Color and Exposure Effects:** The first category of video effects offers up a number of options in changing the video output related to color, gamma, exposure, and more. Included in this group are features like creating a sepia or monochromatic image.
- **Titles:** The title effect allows for the insertion of text as an overlay on your video cue. There are a number of options, such as font type, font color, size, and blend mode, that affect the look of inserted titles.
- **Blur/Sharpen Effects:** This category of video effects offers a number of blurring (box, disc, Gaussian, motion, zoom) and sharpening effects.
- **Texture and Edge Effects:** Texture effects, such as pixellation, halftones, pointillization, and comic effect, allow for a drastic change to the appearance of the video or image file.
- **Distortion Effects:** This category of effects deals with warping the image output in some fashion to make the image appear to be wrapped in a 3D form.
- **Tile Effects:** Tiling is the duplication of your image feed across multiple areas or "tiles" within your video surface. There are five tile effects, each with numerous output variables for creating interesting tiles.
- **Custom Compositions:** Quartz Composer is the visual programming environment created by Apple for processing and rendering graphical data.

Tools of the Trade ▼

Quartz Composer

Quartz Composer is an application provided with the Macintosh developers tools. It comes as part of a download called Graphics Tools for Xcode, a toolkit of applications needed to create software for the Mac, iPhone, and iPad. This download is not on the App Store, but must be downloaded from developer.apple.com/downloads (free Apple developer account required).

Quartz Composer is a node-based, visual programming platform that allows the user to connect a number of patches with "noodles" that send a signal from one patch to another. The end result is displayed in a viewer, which displays any changes made in real-time. It is useful for creating sophisticated motion graphics compositions without writing any code. One of its strengths is that it allows users to explore all of the graphic technologies available through macOS without taking the time to learn a programming interface. Though QLab does support custom compositions, it does not support every type of composition. In order to work with QLab, a

(Continued)

composition must be an effect type. In addition, it must have specific inputs and outputs programmed within. _protocolInput_Image is used to publish an input that QLab uses to send video into the composition, whereas _protocolOutput_Image is the output used to send the video into QLab post-composition.

QLab has long allowed the use of custom Quartz Compositions for image output. In QLab 4, this function is included as part of the video effects tab.

14.8 – Camera Cues

In addition to playing back prerecorded video, QLab also has the capability to insert a live video feed directly into the workspace via the Camera Cue. A Camera Cue functions in exactly the same fashion as a Video Cue, except it does not have an audio feed. The QLab video reinforcement system works with any iSight or FaceTime camera attached to your Mac, most varieties of USB or FireWire webcams, and Blackmagic camera devices. In addition, it can accept input signals via Syphon. Once the camera patch is set up, pressing go will activate the camera, sending a video feed out to the assigned video surface. The following section details the setup and application of the Camera Cue.

Camera Cues are QLab cues specially designed to activate an external camera connected to the video system and send its signal out through a video surface patch. In addition to simple playback, there are also a number of built-in filters and effects that can be applied to the video feed to affect its appearance and behavior. Like any other cue, a Camera Cue can be inserted via the Toolbar or Toolbox. Since the video feed does not feature audio, the Camera Cue has fewer tabs within the Inspector than the Audio or Video Cues. It is possible to run a Camera Cue in conjunction with a Mic Cue to have both audio and video feed, though there are a number of difficulties in making the audio line up correctly with the video feed due to latency and clocking issues between separate interfaces. The following section details the functions of the tabs found in the Camera Cue's Inspector.

14.9 – Inspector: Basics and Triggers

Once a Camera Cue is inserted into the cue list, the Inspector is used to examine the control functions and settings related to the cue. Unlike the Video Cue, the Inspector for the Camera Cue features only four tabs: Basics, Triggers, Display & Geometry, and Video Effects. The first two tabs, Basics and Triggers, allow the same basic function seen in examining the Audio and Video Cue. Like those other cue types, Camera Cue Basics deals with cue numbering, naming, targeting, notes, and playback options. The Triggers tab deals with options such as MIDI, Hotkey, Wall Clock, and Timecode triggering, in addition to how triggering of this cue may affect playback of others in the cue list.

14.10 – Inspector: Display & Geometry

Like the Video Cue, Display & Geometry for the Camera Cue (Figure 14.9) deals with input assignment (camera patch) and output assignment (video surface patch). As seen in Section 14.4, the Display & Geometry tab contains both patch and geometry functions (on the left side of the screen) and the video stage on the right side of the screen.

Camera: The camera patch is the first menu located on the left column of the screen. By clicking on the drop-down menu, you will see all of the available cameras attached to your video system. Select the desired camera, and it will automatically be assigned as the input source for your Camera Cue.

Video Surface: The video surface patch is located directly beneath the camera patch and is used to assign the display output for your Camera Cue. Like the Video Cue, you can output the video feed to either a single screen or a multi-screen surface. If you choose to do this, QLab will do all of the necessary calculations behind the scenes to route the video feed out the appropriate display devices. With either method, the output patch is selected in the Video Surface drop-down menu.

Video Display Mode: The "Mode" control, located beneath the video surface controls, addresses the geometry for controlling image output. When a Camera Cue is assigned to a video surface, it can either be full surface or custom geometry. For full surface, the image is either reduced or enlarged to the correct size to fill the entire width or height of the assigned surface. By selecting or deselecting "preserve aspect ratio," you can keep the original proportion in mind or disregard it, giving you the ability to stretch the image's height or width

Figure 14.9
The Display & Geometry tab for Camera Cues.

disproportionately to completely fill the surface. Custom geometry allows for changing the size, shape, and geometric rotation of the image around the x-, y-, and z-planes. For a detailed exploration of this process, look at Section 14.4.

Layer and Opacity: Again, the layer settings for a Camera Cue determine the order in which video frames get stacked. A cue with a higher number will always be stacked atop a layer with a lower number (0–999). Assigning "Top" means that this cue will be layered above any previous Video or Camera Cues. The most recent cue labeled top will always be displayed on top.

Finally, opacity is the setting that allows the programmer to change the video feed from opaque to translucent. 100% opacity means that the image is perceived as "solid." As the numbers decrease, the resulting image becomes more translucent, allowing the layers or background behind it to be visible through the image. This setting is useful when combined with the layer function. Imagine the possibility of overlaying a Camera Cue atop a second Camera or Video Cue. This would be particularly useful in the creation of a "ghostly apparition" effect. The following project details the process of tackling this effect.

Project 14.4 ▼

Creating a Ghostly Effect

As a reminder, Camera Cues must use a camera connected to your system. Without one you cannot do this project (though the built-in FaceTime camera on your iMac or MacBook will work).

Step 1: Download Project 14.4 from the companion website.

Step 2: You will notice the workspace contains only one cue. Cue 1 is a Video Cue featuring a crinkled paper background. This will be the background image. Open the Audition window (⇧⌘A) so you can preview the cues live.

Step 3: Insert a Camera Cue into the workspace as cue 2. Check your camera patch under the Display & Geometry tab to ensure the appropriate camera is patched to your cue. Also, while in this tab, set your opacity to 48%. Finally, ensure that the Camera Cue is set to the Top layer (see Figure 14.10).

Figure 14.10
Use the Display & Geometry tab to input the camera patch, change the opacity of your Video Cue, and establish its layer.

Step 4: As currently programmed, the Camera Cue will play atop the paper background, but it will hardly look ghostly. In order to accomplish this goal, there will be some requirements of both lighting and Video Effects settings. As for lighting, make certain to darken the room to black and use a bright light at a harsh angle on your actor (if sitting at your laptop, this will be particularly easy to experiment with – simply turn off the lights and use a flashlight beneath the chin).

Step 5: Open the Video Effects tab in cue 2 and select "Bloom and Gloom" from the drop-down menu. Click on the checkbox beside "Apply Effects" to ensure the effect will be applied. Finally, set Bloom as the effect with Radius at 17.500 and Intensity at 1.000 (see Figure 14.11).

Figure 14.11
Bloom and Gloom settings.

Step 6: Test the cue sequence. If programmed properly, a ghostly face should appear superimposed atop the paper texture (see Figure 14.12).

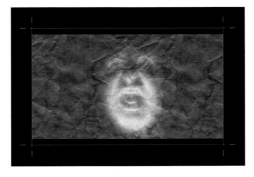

Figure 14.12
The resulting ghostly figure.

14.11 – Inspector: Video Effects

The final tab in the Camera Cue Inspector is called Video Effects. The video effects for Camera Cues function in exactly the same fashion as those for Video Cues. To access the video effects, click on the drop-down menu beside the "Apply Effects" button. You will notice that the drop-down menu features a number of effects, each separated into seven different groups as seen earlier in Figure 14.8. Once you are familiar with the use of video effects in Video Cues, the execution for Camera Cues is identical.

Quartz Composer Integration

QLab 4 allows for the use of a custom Quartz Composer file as an image filter for the camera feed. An original composition can apply Core Image filters complex animations and more to your live video feed. QLab provides Quartz Composition frames to your video feed in real-time to affect the image output.

14.12 – Text Cues

The Text Cue (formerly known as the Titles Cue in QLab 3) is used for inputting text as an individually controllable cue in your cue list. You can insert a Text Cue through the Toolbar or Toolbox and control a number of the cue's attributes through the Inspector. The Inspector offers five tabs: Basics, Triggers, Display & Geometry, Text, and Video Effects. All of the tabs except for Text function in exactly the same fashion as that seen in Video and Camera Cues, shown earlier in this chapter. As such, we will focus specifically on the Text tab of the Inspector and how to use this tool.

Inspector: Text

The Text tab is a simple interface for adding and manipulating text. The largest area in the tab is a rectangular black box, used for inserting the text you want to display as a cue. You can either type directly into this field or copy and paste. Keep in mind that copying and pasting will include the text data, such as font, size, and color, from the application in which it was written. To change these attributes, select the text and click the button on the bottom left of the screen featuring an A icon. This button opens the fonts panel, which allows you to adjust the font type, size, color, and style attributes. To the right of this icon are four separate buttons used to control the justification of your text field: left aligned, center aligned, justified, or right aligned.

QLab uses a method of rendering the text as a PNG file format with a transparent background. This process creates an image file the exact size necessary for displaying the text as inputted in your text field. Sometimes, it might be desirable to change the width of your text field to create a larger invisible bounding area around the text. This might be useful for manually adjusting the placement of text within the field or creating patterns for instance. In order to adjust this image width, use the **Width** field and enter a number to represent the desired width in pixels. Keep in mind that choosing a smaller width can create text wrapping that might not be desirable in all situations. Finally, the **Preview** drop-down menu allows you to adjust the display size of text in your Inspector, allowing you to choose between sizes from 10% to 200%.

14.13 – Text Cue Projects

The Text Cue is useful in a number of different scenarios for live performance. The following section includes three simple projects for using the Text Cue in different ways. The first of these is a "follow the bouncing ball" singalong approach, in which the production calls for providing the audience with song lyrics and an indication of when to sing.

Project 14.5 ▼

Singalong Lyrics

Picture a production in which the audience is invited to sing along with a moment in the show. One method for inviting participation is projecting the lyrics in a visible location and animating a change in the text that works in time with the song. This "follow-the-bouncing-ball" approach is a time-tested method that might show up in pantos, comedies, or other production styles that commonly break the fourth wall. The following project takes you through this process.

Step 1: Download Project 14.5 from the companion website.

Step 2: The workspace for this project contains two Text Cues. Each one has a simple body of text included in it. Select cue 1 and copy the cue (⌘V). Next paste the cue three times in a row. This should create three new duplicate cues between cues 1 and 2.

Step 3: Next, copy cue 2 and paste two copies after cue 2. This should create a total of seven cues in your workspace.

Step 4: Select the first four cues by holding down the shift button and clicking each one. After they have all been selected, click on the Group button in the Toolbar. This will group all of the cues together. Repeat this process for the last three cues.

Step 5: Select the first Text Cue, and open the Text tab inside of the Inspector. Highlight the text "sing," and click on the A button at the bottom of the screen. This will open the font tool. With the text selected, click on the font color button. This opens the color picker. Click on the Image Palettes tab and select yellow towards the bottom of the list. Your text should change color from white to yellow (Figure 14.13).

(Continued)

Figure 14.13
The selected text can be changed by using the Font and Text color tools.

Step 6: Repeat this process for each of the text cues, highlighting the next word in the list as yellow and making sure all of the other words are white. For each cue, there should be one yellow word.

Step 7: Re-name the cue names for all of your cues, making them the word that will light up yellow. In this way, the operator should be able to look at the cue list and know exactly which word they are triggering. Your subsequent cue list should resemble the one seen in Figure 14.14, though your numbering might be slightly different. At this point, you should be able to open the Audition Window and test your playback. You will notice that the second group of cues appears over the first cue, creating an illegible mix-up of the words. This is because each Text Cue is an image that renders atop the previous one. For the first cues, each subsequent cue covered up the previous one because they all had the same placement and size. Once the second group appears, however, it will render atop the previous one.

Figure 14.14
Your cue list should resemble this setup.

Step 8: In order to fix this problem, you must insert a Fade Cue as the first cue of your second group. Target the first group with this Fade Cue. Open the Geometry tab inside the Fade Cue and set the opacity to 0%, and then click "Stop Target When Done." If you set the Fade Cue duration to 0 and set its continue status as Auto-continue, then the first group of Text Cues will all disappear simultaneously as the next one appears.

Step 9: Repeat these steps as many times as necessary to create your singalong lyrics. It requires the operator to be on point, but the result is a fun application of the Text Cue.

Project 14.6 ▼

Intergalactic Title Effects

One of the most popular title effects in film history is the opening sequences of the Star Wars® franchise films. This interesting effect, called the "opening crawl," shows the text scrolling upward from the bottom of the screen, while getting smaller as it moves off into the distance. This effect has been often parodied and could easily be replicated through QLab with the creative use of a Text Cue and manipulating surface geometry.

Step 1: Download Project 14.6 from the companion website.

Step 2: The workspace for this project contains one Text Cue. If you were to play this cue, the text would trail off the bottom of your screen. To create the scrolling effect, you must first select the Display & Geometry tab. Using the translation controls, move the text down so it is just below the perimeter of your surface. In my case, this was –1024.

Step 3: Insert a Fade Cue after cue 1 and target the Fade with the Text Cue. Set the continue status of the Text Cue to Auto-continue.

Step 4: Open the Geometry tab for your Fade Cue. Click on the Translation checkbox and move the Y translation up until the text is placed above the perimeter of your surface. In my case, this was 1024.

Step 5: Open your Audition Window and test the effect. Your text should scroll from the bottom of the screen to the top. Feel free to change the Fade Cue duration and Curve Shape to make it scroll at an ideal pace.

Step 6: In order to truly replicate the opening crawl effect, the text needs to appear to get smaller as it fades off into the distance. To achieve this effect, you must create a special surface that uses control

(Continued)

points to create the depth look. Open Workspace Settings and select Video. In the Video Surfaces list, create a new surface based on your display *New With Display > Your Screen Name.* The Surface Editor will automatically open. First, change the new of the Surface to "opening crawl." Next, grab the upper control points on the editor canvas and pull them towards the center, making a trapezoidal shape as seen in Figure 14.15.

Figure 14.15
Your grid should resemble this setup.

Step 7: Close the Surface Editor and return to your workspace. Select cue 1 and change the Video Surface to the new "opening crawl" surface you just created. This will display the text on your monitor. In order to see this effect, you will have to close the Audition Window. Once you do so, you can trigger playback and see your effect in action. To stop playback, simply click the ESC button.

Video Effects

As mentioned in previous chapters, one of the greatest strengths of QLab video is the ability to apply video effects to both Video and Camera Cues. Essentially, each Video or Camera Cue has a library of video effects to choose from that can be applied to the image/video file or camera feed. There are a number of built-in effects to choose from, all as simple as selecting the effect, applying it to the cue, and changing the video effect control settings. With so many different effects to choose from, the process can be a bit overwhelming for a first-time user. The following chapter details the purpose and process of the seven groups of video effects presets.

For the following sections, download Project 15.1 from the companion website. Open your Audition Window so that you can preview the effects without covering up your workspace. Select the first cue and then click on the Video effects tab in the Inspector Panel. We will use this cue list to examine the various video effects presets.

15.1 – Video Effects Presets: Color and Exposure

The first set of video effects presets deal primarily with changing the color, exposure, gamma, or contrast of the cue output. There are six video effects in the color and exposure grouping. For all effects, you must both select the desired video effect in the drop-down menu and click on the "Apply Effects" checkbox. This will then list the effect controls in the effect inputs window at the bottom of the screen.

Color Controls

The first option listed in the drop-down menu is called color controls. Color controls offer basic video/image editing options of saturation, brightness, contrast, and hue angle (see Figure 15.1). Select cue 1 from Project 15.1 and

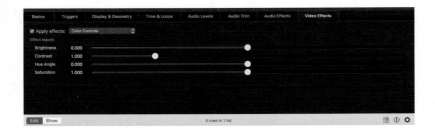

Figure 15.1
The Color controls
subset of Video
Effects.

press the space bar. This will play your Video Cue in the Audition window. Click on the "Apply Effects" checkbox to activate the color controls if you have not already done so. You should notice an immediate, if slight, change to your image. Let's now examine the sliders in the effect inputs panel.

Brightness refers to the amount of light or shadow present in the image. Increasing it will make the image go to a completely white screen. Decreasing it will move towards a completely black screen. **Contrast** refers to the difference perceived between the darks and lights in your image. By increasing the contrast, you will get deep blacks and vivid, glowing highlights. By decreasing it, you will get a washed-out, gray image with little difference between highlights and shadows. **Hue Angle** allows you to enhance the colors present in your image in one range of the color spectrum. Sliding across the scale from −180 to 180 will change the color output from blue (−180) to more cyan tones (180). Finally, **Saturation** refers to the amount of color present in the image. Increasing the saturation will make the image have much more vibrant colors, whereas decreasing it will make it look like a black-and-white photo.

Exposure

Selecting exposure in the drop-down menu will activate the exposure video effects preset. **Exposure** is a photography term that relates to the amount of light that is allowed to transfer onto the film. Exposure is linked to the shutter speed of a camera – the longer the shutter stays open, the more light is allowed onto the film and vice versa. In QLab terms, exposure refers to the method of using a digital effect to simulate film exposure.

Experiment with adjusting the exposure of cue 1. The **Exposure Value** slides from −10 to 10, with values below zero being underexposed (overly dark) and those above zero being overexposed (overly bright white). Figure 15.2 shows the exposure value slider.

Gamma

Moving one step down the list in the drop-down menu, you will arrive at the third effect in the color and exposure grouping, Gamma. **Gamma** refers to a

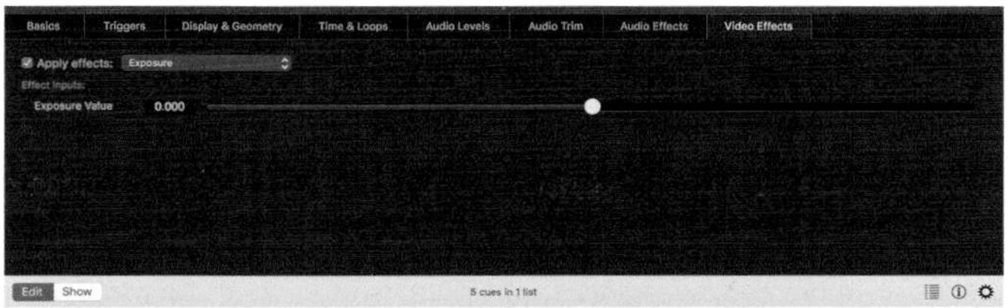

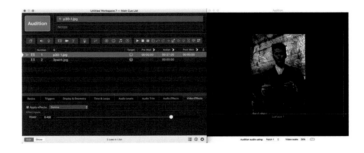

Figure 15.2
The Exposure
value slider.

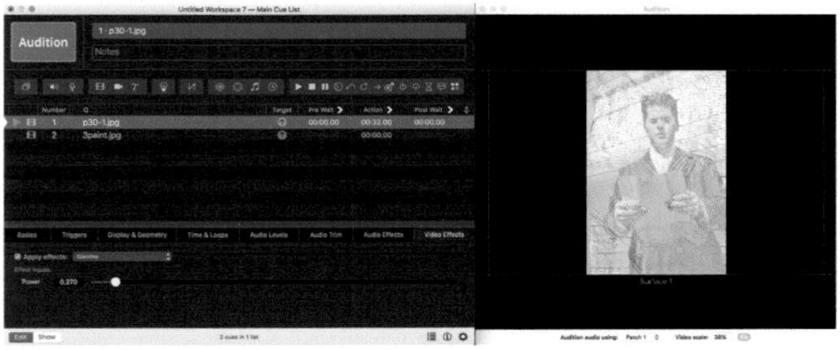

Figure 15.3a
The Gamma
Power slider at a
low setting.

Figure 15.3b
The Gamma Power
slider at a high
setting.

digital method of coding and decoding the brightness values of both still and moving images. In terms of output, each pixel of a digital image is assigned a gamma value. QLab allows for the adjustment of the gamma value from the power of 0.100–3.000. In this case, sliding the gamma power slider down to its lowest setting will brighten the image output, while raising it will darken the image (see Figure 15.3 a and b). Go ahead and adjust the gamma power slider and see the ways in which the image is affected.

Sepia Monochrome

This fourth effect gives the option to change the image output for your Video or Camera Cue to be either sepia or monochromatic. When you first select the Sepia Monochrome effect, the default setting will be sepia. To change to the monochrome effect, select the drop-down menu, and you will see monochrome as the other choice (Figure 15.4).

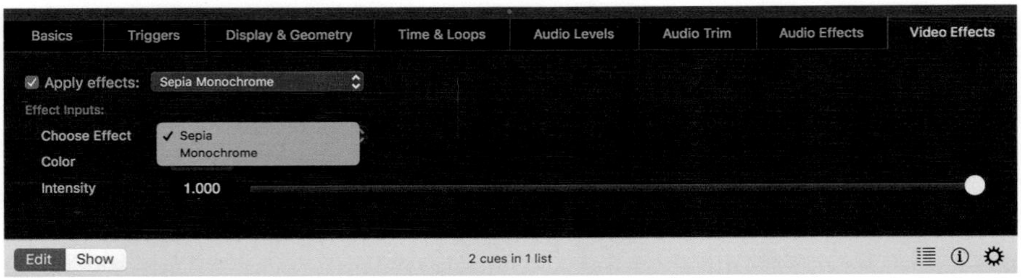

Figure 15.4
The Sepia/
Monochrome
drop-down menu.

Sepia refers to the reddish-brown color of antique photographs. To control the amount of sepia tones added to the image, use the Intensity slider. The intensity scale (0.000–1.000) represents the amount of original color that will read after the effect is applied. 0.000–0.500 will have some of the original color remaining, whereas anything above this will gradually replace all original hues with sepia colors.

Monochrome, or "one chroma," refers to an image in which everything is presented in different values of one color. To use the monochrome effect, simply click on the drop-down menu to select monochrome. After doing this, click on the icon labeled "color." This will open up the macOS Color Picker that gives you several different options from which to choose your color (see Figures 15.5–15.9). The intensity slider will function in the same fashion for monochrome as it did for sepia – meaning the lower half of the slider will allow some of the original colors to bleed through, whereas anything above the 50% mark will begin to replace all original colors with your selected hue.

Tools of the Trade ▼

macOS Color Picker

The macOS Color Picker is a handy tool that was introduced with the first version of macOS. There are a number of different options, but they all serve the same basic purpose of helping you select a color within an application. Along the top of the interface, you will see five icons. Each of these icons represents a different method of selecting colors. The first icon, **Color Wheel**, allows you to select the hue and saturation with the color wheel and the value (or relative lightness or darkness of the color) by using the slider on the right side of the window (Figure 15.5). In the color wheel, moving towards the center of the circle will desaturate your hue selection.

The second icon represents the **Sliders** panel of the Color Picker (Figure 15.6), where there is a series of sliders useful for creating your own

Figure 15.5
The Color Wheel color-picking tab.

Figure 15.6
The Sliders color-picking tab.

color schemes: Gray Scale; Red-Green-Blue (RGB); Cyan-Magenta-Yellow-Black (CMYK); and Hue-Saturation-Brightness (HSB). One very useful function in this window is the Eyedropper tool in the left corner. This tool allows you to select the color from any pixel on your screen, no matter what program is running it. By clicking on a color, it will be selected and placed into your color selection window.

The next icon, the **Color Palette** picker, is a selection tool for using preexisting color palettes and creating palettes of your own (Figure 15.7). The palette picker features four palettes: Web Safe Colors, Crayons, Developer, and Apple. In addition to this, you can use this menu to create your own palettes for a project that needs to use a consistent set of colors. To add a color to your original color palette, simply drag that color down into the row of squares at the bottom of the screen.

The fourth icon is the **Image Palette**. By default, when you select the image palette, it will open a spectrum showing all the colors within the visible spectrum. This is useful by itself, but the truly useful function within

(*Continued*)

Figure 15.7
The Color Palette color-picker tab.

Figure 15.8
Selecting New from File.

this picker is the ability to add any image from your hard drive as a color palette. Click on the Palette drop-down menu, and then select New from File (Figure 15.8). If you have an image on your clipboard, you can also paste it in by using New from Clipboard. To select a color within the image, simply click on the desired color within the image, and it will be added to the color box. Drag that color down into the row of squares at the bottom of the screen to create your own custom palette.

The fifth and final icon is the **Pencils.** It is a simplistic representation of colors with easy to remember color names (Figure 15.9). It has many fewer applications than the other pickers yet is a quick and easy reference at times.

One final thing to keep in mind is that Color Picker is expandable with the addition of plug-ins – some freeware or shareware. Many of these additional color pickers can be added on to use with QLab and allow for a truly customized approach to how you select your colors within the software. Just do a quick search for "mac color selector plug-ins," and you will find a number of options!

Figure 15.9
The Pencils color-picking tab.

Min Max Invert

The Min Max Invert effects preset is actually a collection of three separate video effects: Minimum Component, Maximum Component, and Color Invert.

Minimum Component creates a gray scale version of your image that emphasizes the darker tones by examining the minimum RGB values. **Maximum Component** also creates a gray scale version, but focuses instead on the brighter tones of the image by examining the maximum RGB values. **Color Invert** does exactly what the name implies; it creates an inverted image in which the colors are reversed from those in the original file. There are no variables to these three effects, simply on or off. Click through these three different presets to see the way in which the video output for cue 1 is affected.

White Point

The final effects preset in the color and exposure section of the drop-down menu is called white point. In photography terms, the **white point** is the color value within the photo that is determined to be neutral. This is a key factor that plays into lighting modes on cameras, like incandescent, outdoors, and fluorescent. Each of these light sources produces a drastically different color temperature; therefore, shooting an indoor scene with an outdoor camera setting will result in an oddly discolored photo. White point conversions have been around in photo editing software for years. Essentially, it allows you to select a hue that should be substituted for white. In QLab, once you have selected white point, a color tool will appear in the effects input, allowing you to open the OS X Color Picker and select your white point color. Doing so will create a color overlay that changes your light areas to various values of the chosen hue. Try out this effect by selecting a number of different hues, saturations, and values to see how it affects the image output.

15.2 – Video Effects Presets: Titles

The next section of video effects presets has only one effect included: titles. The titles video effect is a simple yet powerful interface for adding text to a Video or Camera Cue. There are two methods for adding text to the QLab workspace. The first is by using the Text Cue, as seen in Section 14.12 of the previous chapter. The second method is using the Titles video effect in conjunction with another cue. The following section details the process of attaching titles to a Video or Camera Cue as an added effect.

Once more, select cue 1 of Project 15.1 and trigger it for playback. To insert titles, click on the "Titles" button in the effects drop-down menu. An interface will appear featuring a number of options (see Figure 15.10). Unlike the Text Cue, the Titles effect does not integrate an OS X text selection box; rather it provides its own menu of options in the effect inputs panel. The following section details the control options for titles.

Font Placement

The two sliders shown at the top of the effect inputs window control placement of your title. Input X and Input Y refer to the placement of the text within your video surface. One thing you will notice is that titles do not appear in the video stage under the Display & Geometry tab. Because of this, there is no way to simply grab and move the text. Input X and Y controls are the only way to reposition the text placement. Go ahead and adjust the values of each slider to see how they manipulate the size and placement of your title.

Blend Mode

The next control is likely the greatest source of confusion for those unfamiliar with graphics editing programs. **Blend Mode** simply refers to how one object interacts or "blends" with the background when placed atop another layer. There are a number of different options available in the blend mode drop-down menu, and each slightly varies from the other (Figure 15.11).

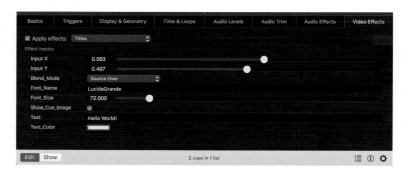

Figure 15.10
The Titles menu in QLab.

Figure 15.11
Blend Modes.

One thing that can lead to a bit of confusion for the beginner is that the blending modes are listed in alphabetical order rather than being grouped by their function. Below is a list of the modes grouped into their functions. It is important to note that working with blending modes is almost always an experimental process. They are, at their core, mathematical processes that change the pixels of your image. The list below will, by no means, make you an expert at blend modes. Rather, it is intended to be a springboard that enables you to better understand where to begin your own experimentation.

Darken Modes	Darken Blend Mode Multiply Color Burn Blend Mode
Lighten Modes	Lighten Blend Mode Screen Blend Mode Color Dodge Blend Mode Addition Mode
Contrast Modes	Overlay Blend Mode Soft Light Blend Mode Hard Light Blend Mode
Inversion Modes	Difference Blend Mode Exclusion Blend Mode
Component Modes	Hue Blend Mode Saturation Blend Mode Color Blend Mode Luminosity Blend Mode
Min Max Modes	Minimum Maximum
Source Modes	Source Atop Source In Source Out Source Over

Darken Modes are so named because they have the effect of darkening the text. Those blending modes in the **Lighten Modes** category lighten the text overlay. Each blend mode in the Darken category has an opposite in the Lighten category. These opposites perform the reverse function of their pair in the other category. For instance, in the Darken Blend Mode, if pixels of your text are darker than the ones in the layer below it, they are kept in the text. For Lighten Blend Mode, it is opposite in that the lighter pixels of the text will remain. The **Addition Mode** is a bit of a subset within the lighten modes. This mode simply adds the pixel value of the text layer to that beneath it. Since this always produces a similar or lighter color of text, this mode is sometimes referred to as "plus lighter." Though QLab does not feature it, the inverse mode in some editing programs is called "plus darker."

Contrast Modes work by lightening the lightest pixels, darkening the darkest pixels, and eliminating the mid-tones of the overlaid text altogether. These blend modes will create a text overlay that is translucent, showing the base image through it.

Inversion Modes are named this for the way in which overlapping colors of multiple layers are treated. For Difference Blend Mode, similar colors that overlap are processed so that the matching colors in the top layer (the text) will be changed to an inverted color. In Exclusion Blending Mode, similar colors cancel each other out and the resulting color on the top layer will be gray.

Component Modes (sometime called HSL Mode for Hue, Saturation, and Luminance) are blending modes that address the hue, saturation, and luminosity of the overlapping layers.

The **Min Max Modes** are an interesting set of blending modes that allow for the use of text as a mask. When using the Minimum function, the color of the font becomes a cutout and the area outside the text functions as a black mask. The resulting effect is that the Video or Camera Cue will be seen through the mask of whatever text is on the screen.

Finally, the last category of blending modes is the **Source Mode.** There are four types of source modes, each of which performs a slightly different function. **Source Atop** places the text over the background image and then uses the luminance of the background to determine what to show. **Source In** uses the background image to define what to leave of the text and sometimes cropping off areas of the text. **Source Out** uses the background image to define what to take out of the text. **Source Over** places the text over the background image. These four modes can be somewhat confusing at first, so I recommend experimentation to see how to best utilize them in your QLab workspace.

Font Name

This input area is where you select the font for your Title. Type in the name of the desired font in the "Font Name" window. QLab will allow you to input any font in your computer's font library. At this point, there is no type of interface that lists the fonts available on your system, though this is not the case for using a Text Cue. As such, when using the Titles video effect, it might be useful to experiment with Font Book (a standard macOS application found in your Mac's Applications folder) beforehand to determine the desired font. The benefit of using this application is the ability to preview fonts but, more importantly, it also tells you the PostScript name of the font. QLab requires the PostScript name in the "Font_Name" window.

Font Size

Font size is on a sliding scale from 1 (almost invisible) to 600 (so large it will likely extend off the borders of your video surface).

Show Cue Image

One of the interesting functions of the title effect is that you can choose to either show or hide the cue's image output. This could be particularly useful if you had a reason to project only text with no image for a background. Of course, you could create a neutral background image to be used for this purpose, but another option is to simply uncheck the "Show_Cue_Image" checkbox, which will make the cue image disappear, leaving only the title behind.

Text

The "text" window is used exclusively for inserting text for title display.

Color

Text color is a simple matter of clicking on the text color box. This will then open the macOS Color Picker for your use in selecting a font color.

One thing to keep in mind with the use of Titles is that there is much less versatility for controlling the appearance than with the use of Text Cues. Text Cues can use video effects and have Fade Cues affect their appearance in a number of ways that simply cannot be achieved through the Titles effect. That said, for a simple addition of text to a Video or Camera Cue, the Titles effects may be a good option.

15.3 – Video Effects Presets: Blur/ Sharpen

Blurs are a specific type of image filtering that creates a blurry image, whereas sharpen does the opposite. Unlike an actual camera, QLab uses a series of algorithms to recreate a traditional blurred look. The following video effects are all used to either blur or sharpen the video output.

Box/Disc/Gaussian Blurs

The first choice in the list of blur/sharpen effects is a series of three basic blurs: the box blur, disc blur, and Gaussian blur. Using cue 1 in Project 15.1 select the Box/Disc/Gaussian Blurs preset from the drop-down menu. You will see that the effect inputs panel features a second drop-down menu to select which blur type you want to utilize and a "radius" slider (see Figure 15.12). The radius slider controls the amount of blurriness for each of the three blur types. In each case, the setting of 0.000 (all the way to the left) indicates no blur, and sliding it upward begins to add more blur effect.

The **Box Blur** creates a hazy quality that does not distort the image shape too greatly. The **Disc Blur** distorts the image quality more than the box blur, but also adds a level of latency to the moving image output as the effect is increased, slowing the resulting image feed and adding a "jumpy" quality to it. CPU load is a factor here; faster machines may not experience this issue, but slower machines likely will. Finally, the **Gaussian Blur** adds the greatest level of "haziness" to the image, resulting in an incredibly blurred image that lacks definition.

Motion Blur

Simply put, the motion blur adds a blur to your Video or Camera Cue in a given direction and radius. When the motion blur is selected, there are two sliders in the effect inputs panel: Angle and Radius. The easiest way to perceive how the motion blur works is to increase the radius all the way to 100.000 and then slowly start sliding your Angle slider to see how this affects the direction of the motion blur.

Sharpen Luminance

In video terminology, **luma** is the signal that represents the brightness of an image, whereas **chroma** refers to the signal that conveys the color information.

Figure 15.12
The Box/Disc/
Gaussian Blur
controls.

Basics   Triggers   Display & Geometry   Time & Loops   Audio Levels   Audio Trim   Audio Effects   Video Effects

Figure 15.13
The Sharpness
slider.

The sharpen luminance effect increases the image detail of the luma without affecting the chrominance. There is only one slider used to operate the sharpen luminance effect, labeled "Sharpness." Sliding the sharpness to the right will increase image detail, whereas sliding it to the left will decrease it. The default level is 1.000, in the center of the slider (Figure 15.13).

Unsharp Mask

The name unsharp mask has confused many beginners into thinking that the purpose of the effect is to "unsharpen" an image. In fact, the opposite is true. The purpose of the unsharp mask is to create a new image that is less blurry than the one you started with. The effect takes a negative copy of the blurry image and superimposes it atop the original, creating a clearer image. To activate the unsharp mask, select it in the drop-down menu. You will notice that there are two sliders for controlling unsharp masking: intensity and radius (Figure 15.14). The first slider, **intensity**, controls how much contrast is added to image edges. **Radius** affects the size of the edges to be enhanced; the smaller the radius, the greater the detail. High radii can lead to halos around the edges of your image. Radius and intensity are inversely connected, as decreasing one allows for increasing the other. Increasing both to high intensities will create a darker image.

Zoom Blur

In photography terms, a **zoom blur** is an effect achieved by activating the zoom on your lens while the shutter is open. The resulting image tends to have

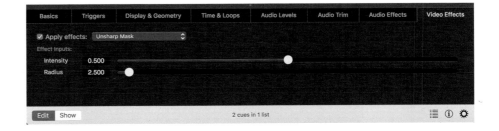

Figure 15.14
Unsharp Mask
controls.

Figure 15.15
Zoom Blur
controls.

one central point of focus, around which the surrounding imagery seems to be moving. In QLab, the zoom blur video effect recreates this look for you. Selecting zoom blur from the drop-down menu will reveal three sliders in the effect inputs panel: Input X, Input Y, and Amount (see Figure 15.15). Input X and Input Y control the direction of the blur on the x- and y-planes. Amount represents the amount of zoom blur desired in the resulting image. This effect can be used with some success to create interesting movement effects.

15.4 – Video Effects Presets: Textures and Edge Effects

For most users, the textures and edge effects will be one of the most useful effects sets and will require the least amount of explanation to use. Essentially, this group of effects takes the image feed and either applies a texture to it or emulates a classic look (like a computer monitor, comic book, or kaleidoscope). This group of effects is the third grouping in the drop-down menu and starts with pixellation.

Pixellation

Pixellation is an effect that breaks down the image feed into a series of squares or hexagons for output. There are four sets of controls: input x, input y, effect, and scale. Effect allows you to choose from its drop-down menu either a square or hexagonal pixel shape. Figure 15.16 shows the same image presented in

Figure 15.16
Both square (left)
and hexagonal
(right) pixel types.

both pixel types. The scale slider changes the overall size of pixels. Smaller pixels give increased image detail, whereas larger pixels add more image distortion.

Screen

The next video effect preset, **screen**, imitates the look of various halftone methods used in printing. This effect features a number of control sliders in the effect inputs (Figure 15.17). The first control function of note is a drop-down menu that allows for the selection between the different screen types: Dot Screen, Line Screen, Hatched Screen, or Circular Screen. Using cue 1, cycle through the four options to get a feel for their different looks. The **Dot Screen**, when first activated, resembles a classic pixellated black-and-white monitor. **Line Screen** features a series of lines running in one direction, whereas **Hatched Screen** has two sets of lines cross-hatching one another for the creation of a moiré pattern. The **Circle Screen** features a series of concentric circles originating from a central point on the screen.

For each of these effects, the five sliders change the appearance of the pattern to some degree. The first two sliders (**Input X and Input Y**) have little visible function for any of the effects except for circle screen. In circle screen, these sliders will move the point of origin for the circles around on the screen. Conversely, the **Angle** slider has no visible effect on the circle screen, but it will rotate the patterns around the z-axis for the other three presets. The final two sliders are applicable for all four presets.

Width controls the size of the pattern and drastically changes the appearance of the effect. For example, the dots screen resembles an older monitor on a small scale, but when enlarged takes on more of a pop art look. Finally, the **Sharpness** slider controls the sharpness/softness of the screen textures. Using cue 1 again, take some time to navigate through these different effects and how the control sliders change their appearance.

Figure 15.17
These four images show how a camera feed would look using the four different screen types.

Bloom and Gloom

The third set of texture and edge effects presets is called Bloom and Gloom. This effect preset is made up of two different effects: Bloom and Gloom. **Bloom** is an effect that creates a glow emanating from light objects in your image feed. This glow will bleed over to other aspects of the image. **Gloom** creates the opposite effect of having a darkness invade from the outer edges of the image and "gray out" the luminance in your image, thus creating a gloomy look. The only two control sliders for both effects are intensity and radius.

CMYK Halftone

Halftone is a reprographic technique used to simulate variations in shade and color in the printed image. The idea is that several halftones are printed, each in a single color. These tones are composed of thousands of circular dots in varying sizes. When combined together this creates the illusion of a continuous range of colors. The CMYK Halftone effect in QLab breaks down your Video or Camera Cue and imposes a CMYK (Cyan, Magenta, Yellow, Black) halftone process to the image output. Like many of the other effects in this category there are the input x, input y, angle, sharpness, and width sliders. By this point you are no doubt familiar with their use. There are two new sliders, though, used to control **Grey Component Removal** and **Under Color Removal**. These two sliders affect the number of black dots versus color in the composition. Sliding both to the right will create an image that is mostly composed of black dots and less CMY (see Figure 15.18).

Color Posterize

Posterization is a classic photographic process used to distill a complex image down to a series of several small regions of color with abrupt changes from one tone to another. This technique was originally used for the creation of color

Figure 15.18
Using high Grey Component Removal and Under Color Removal settings.

Figure 15.19
Low Posterization
levels.

posters. The **Color Posterize** effect in QLab is a simple interface, featuring only one slider called "Levels." The levels slider determines how complex the posterization will be for your video feed. The slider works on a scale from 2.000–30.000. The lower end of the scale will feature fewer layers of tones, whereas sliding it to the upper end will result in thousands of layers of tones (see Figure 15.19).

Crystallize and Pointillize

The sixth video effect is a combination of two effects quite similar to those seen in Pixellation above. Again, you choose the effect between two choices on a drop-down menu. **Crystallize** takes your image feed and imposes a crystalline structure to it, similar to the hexagonal pixellation except that each crystalline pixel is a different shape from its neighbors. **Pointillize** does the same with a series of overlapping circular dots on a white background. Both of these effects have a "shimmering" look to them, as individual random pixels have a slight color flickering to them. Again, the radius slider controls the size of the individual pixels, with a smaller value indicating more detail to the image output. Input X and Input Y control the placement of the effect within the video surface.

Edge Work

The next effects preset has two options: one called Edge Work and the other called Edges. When viewed on its own, **Edge Work** seems to create a simple black-and-white outlined image of your video output. When this image is stacked over another, though, the true function is revealed. The Edge Work effect renders dark tones as transparent and light tones as white with the edges of every object featuring a white outline. This allows for interesting stacked effects of combining one Video Cue with another. Another aspect of this effect is that, for moving images, there is a constant flickering of white dots (similar to

Figure 15.20
The top image illustrates Edge Works, while the bottom is Edges.

the "snow" seen on old television screens without a signal). In this effect preset, the radius slider controls the level of detail and color. The radius slider operates on a scale from 0.000–20.000. The lower ends of the scale produce quite detailed images with an "x-ray" appearance to them. As you slide further up the scale, edges become less defined and the resulting image is more of a series of black-and-white blobs.

The second option, **Edges** creates highly complex images in dark blacks and blues, with the outlines done in various shades of light colors. It also has the "flickery" quality to the image output and resembles a somewhat colorful version of an x-ray. Figure 15.20 shows the same image seen in both Edge Work and Edges.

Kaleidoscope

A real kaleidoscope uses a series of mirrors placed at angles from one another inside a cylinder to create a bizarre fractured and colorful representation of the world. For the kaleidoscope effect in QLab, the image is mirrored on the x- and y-axes without the addition of colorful reflections. This effect preset uses three control sliders: input x, input y, and count. The count slider controls the number of planes upon which the image is mirrored. Sliding it all the way down to 1.000 would result in the image being mirrored across one plane; the x-axis only. 2.000 mirrors the image across two planes: the x-axis and y-axis. Increasing the number begins to create the more recognizable circular kaleidoscope pattern. The input x and input y sliders affect the distance of spread from their axes. This is one of those effects that will truly require spending some time experimenting to find the exact desired look, but the resulting images can be quite stunning.

Figure 15.21
An image with
Comic Effect
applied.

Median and Comic Effect

The Median and Comic effects are both simple on/off effects that create a predetermined look for your image. **Median** is an effect that replaces each pixel with a new pixel having the median value of neighboring pixels. This tends to somewhat darken the image and reduce some levels of noise. The **Comic** effect applies a halftone effect to the image in limited color range, somewhat similar to classic comic book print, but with significantly less detail (see Figure 15.21).

Noise Reduction

Image noise is the appearance of tiny spots of variant color in a digital image, similar to film grain that appeared in pre-digital cameras. Typically speaking, noise is an undesired effect, as it detracts from the image and degrades the overall image quality. The **Noise Reduction** effect allows for manipulating the noise levels and sharpness of an image in order to boost or reduce noise in a cue. There are only two sliders for this effect: noise level and sharpness.

15.5 – Video Effects Presets: Distortion Effects

As the name implies, distortion effects are a set of effects that distort the image output in a number of different ways. These effects are particularly useful in creating dynamic video applications for QLab.

Circle Splash/Hole Distortion

Both the circle splash and hole distortion serve the same basic purpose, to create a circular selection around which the image will be distorted. For **circle splash** the image inside the circular selection remains unchanged, whereas the imagery outside it gets an effect similar to the motion blur applied to it. The

hole distortion, on the other hand, removes any image information inside the circular selection and creates a "black hole" in its place. Like the Edge Work effect, though, this hole is actually a transparent area of your video content, allowing any content on the layer directly beneath it to be seen. The imagery outside this hole is warped in a cylindrical fashion. The three controls for both effects presets are input x, input y, and radius.

Pinch/Bump Distortion

The pinch/bump distortion effect presets have three effects options: pinch, bump, and bump linear. Essentially, these three effects create the appearance that the image is being either pushed down upon to create a depression or pushed up against from the backside, bulging the surface out. **Pinch** is the effect of pushing down on the center of the image to make a depression. **Bump** is the circular appearance of something pushing either up or down onto the image, while **bump linear** creates an effect that resembles the ripple of a flag in the wind. As in others, input x and input y move the point of incident around on the surface. Radius and scale relate to the overall size of the effect. This effect preset also features a slider called "angle_bump_linear_only" that controls the placement of the linear bump effect.

Torus/Lens Distortion

A torus is best described as a 3D form shaped like a donut (with a hole or, in some cases, a concave dimple in the center). The purpose of this video effect is to simulate the look of the refractive quality of light passing through a torus-shaped lens (Figure 15.22). There are numerous control sliders for this effect, but the only new one is the refraction slider. This slider controls the refracted quality of the image viewed through the torus. The effects are not easily described, and this is another of the features best understood through experimentation.

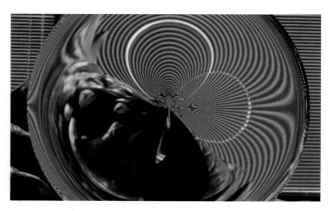

Figure 15.22
The Torus Effect applied to an image.

Twirl/Circular Wrap/Vortex

This effect tab actually has three separate effects presets imbedded within it: twirl, circular wrap, and vortex. All three effects feature the same control sliders: input x and y for moving the effect placement and radius and angle for controlling the size and direction of the effect. Essentially they are all similar effects in that they all deal with distorting the image in a circular or cylindrical fashion. **Twirl** creates a circular selection of the image and spins the contents in either a clockwise or counterclockwise direction, creating a hurricane appearance. **Circular Wrap** creates the appearance of wrapping the image around itself, like rolling a drawing into a tube shape. **Vortex** places a small circular selection at some point on the screen and creates a vortex reaching out from that point to all edges of the image. This creates a strong swirl pattern at the placement and a slight warping of imagery as it reaches the perimeter.

Glass Lozenge

The glass lozenge effect is one of the stranger presets in that it creates a pill-shaped lens through which the image is refracted (see Figure 15.23). When first selecting the effect, you will likely notice a small black semi-circle in the upper right corner of your image. This is one edge of the lozenge. By manipulating the placement of four independent x/y sliders, you can create the desired size and placement of the lozenge. Note that there are two sliders for the x-plane and two for the y-plane. Experiment with moving these sliders around to see what kind of unique sizes and angles you can create. For this effect, the radius slider controls how thick or thin the lozenge becomes. The refraction slider controls the appearance of the refracted image, as seen in the torus/lens distortion effect above.

15.6 – Video Effects Presets: Tiles

Of all of the effects presets, tiles are the hardest to explain. The best way to experience them is to experiment with their use and see for yourself what kinds

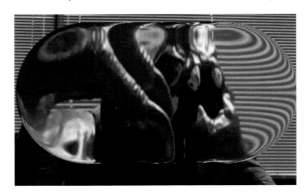

Figure 15.23
The lozenge shape is an interesting effect for creating refracted looks.

of interesting effects emerge. For this reason, the following section will entail only a brief description of each effect and its use. I strongly encourage you to open Project 15.1 and go through each of the effects to see firsthand how they respond. All of the following effects are tiles because they take samples of your image and reconstruct it into some type of tiled fashion. The biggest difference between most of them is the shape or mathematical rearrangement of the tiles for output.

Op Tile

The op tile effect segments the cue image, applies scaling and rotation as inputted in the control sliders, and then reassembles the image to give it an op art appearance.

Perspective Tile

The perspective tile effect applies a transformation to the cue image to give the illusion of perspective and then tiles the result. This effect requires a great number of control sliders, as there are eight interfaces to control the x/y placement.

Quad Tiles

The quad tiles category contains three effects presets bundled into it: fourfold translated tile, fourfold reflected tile, and parallelogram tile. The **fourfold translated tile** effect produces a tiled image from the source by applying four translation operations (x/y placement, angle, acute angle, and width). The **fourfold reflected tile** produces a tiled image from the source by applying a four-way reflected symmetry. Finally, the **parallelogram tile** effect warps an image by reflecting it on a parallelogram and then tiling the resulting image.

Reflected Tiles

The Reflected tiles category contains four subcategories: glide, sixfold, eightfold, and twelvefold reflected tile. Each of them differs only in the planes of symmetry across which the image is reflected. For instance, eightfold reflected symmetry produces a tiled image from the cue source by applying four-way reflected symmetry to the image. Depending on the original image, the resulting image tiles might resemble square tiles, snowflakes, or complex mosaic tile arrangements.

Rotated Tiles

The rotating tile effect looks somewhat similar to the reflected tile effect, but the mathematics to produce it are different. The rotated tile effect is achieved by reproducing a source image multiple times at increments of a common degree. For instance, the sixfold-rotated tile reproduces the image in increments of 60 degrees, thereby creating a resulting hexagonal image output. Within the rotated tiles category, there are three effects: triangle tile, fourfold rotated tile, and sixfold rotated tile.

15.7 – Video Effects Presets: Custom Compositions

One of the greatest strengths of QLab is its inclusion of the macOS native graphic and audio frameworks that enable it to handle graphics, animations, and video effects. Quartz Composer is one of these macOS technologies that work hand in hand with QLab. Quartz Composer is a visual programming environment that allows for sophisticated motion graphics compositions without actually writing code. The software includes preinstalled building blocks of graphics processing that can be combined together to create dynamic visualizations and effects. Once completed, these compositions can be inserted into your QLab workspace to render the video from a Video or Camera Cue.

The custom compositions tab under video effects is the location to insert these compositions. Simply copy and paste the composition into the effect inputs panel at the bottom of the page and that's it. QLab will provide the Quartz Composer frames from the video file as it plays.

Tools of the Trade ▼

Syphon Recorder

One of the complications with QLab video effects is the tendency to tax your computer's processor and create "jittery" playback, especially if you have a large cue sequence with multiple effects playing simultaneously. In order to get around this, it is sometimes useful to create a video capture of an effect created in QLab and use the saved video for playback instead of the original QLab cueing. This has the benefit of reducing the strain on your system resources and even allows for adding other effects onto the video, something that couldn't be done with the original cueing approach.

In order to create a video capture, I often use an application called **Syphon Recorder**, which can be downloaded at http://syphon.v002.info/recorder/. This application can record video or capture screen shots from any Syphon-enabled application. For QLab, this means setting up Surface that uses Syphon as a screen. Any Video Cue that outputs through this surface will

(*Continued*)

then be fed into Syphon Recorder in real-time. To record, simply click on the "snapshot" or "record" button inside Syphon Recorder. Video will be saved through QuickTime, similar to a screen capture done in that software. The resulting video can then be edited, as necessary, and placed into your QLab cue list to replace the old programming. In some instances, this means one Video Cue replacing a Group Cue or cue sequence composed of dozens of elements.

15.8 – Video Effects Projects

Video Effects present a wide range of new opportunities for those using QLab for projection design/integrated media. While there are numerous applications for this aspect of the software, there are only two areas that I would like to cover in projects, as many of the other functions you discover will be based on the foundation of these two techniques. This first technique is using Fade Cues to fade in or out from a Video/Camera Cue with an applied effect. The second is the ability to stack two or more Video/Camera Cues atop one another to create a unique new effect.

Project 15.2 ▼

Video Effects and Fade Cues

Fade Cues are a powerful tool for affecting video playback. One important feature to recognize is that Video Effects cannot be added through a Fade Cue. You can, however, assign a Video Effect to a Video or Camera Cue and then change certain attributes of the effect through a Fade Cue. In order to do so, you must first add a Video Effect on to the target cue. Subsequent Fade Cues will then show the Video Effect attached to this cue and show which parameters can be changed.

The following project details how to fade in a Zoom Blur effect on a Camera Cue. This effect is particularly useful for creating hazy, dreamlike effects. Imagine a production in which you needed to illustrate an actor having an out-of-body experience. To achieve this effect, you could use a live feed of an actor that had a zoom blur applied to it at some point, to illustrate the character jumping to the spiritual plane of existence. The following project takes you through the steps necessary to set up such an effect.

Step 1: Download Project 15.2 from the companion website. Once the project is open, activate the Audition Window to preview your effects.

Step 2: This project includes one Camera Cue. You will need to have a camera attached to your system to test its application. Select cue 1 and click on the Video Effects tab in the Inspector Panel. Select Zoom Blur and click the Apply Effects checkbox.

Step 3: Click GO to preview the Camera Cue feed with the applied effect. Manipulate the Input X, Input Y, and Amount sliders until you achieve the desired ghostly effect on your video feed. Take note of these settings for use later.

Step 4: Insert a Fade Cue after cue 1 and assign cue 1 as its target. Open the Video Effects tab in the Fade Cue's Inspector. You will see the Input X, Input Y, and Amount sliders to the Zoom Blur effect. Match these settings to those seen in cue 1.

Step 5: Go back to cue 1 and pull the Amount slider all the way down to 0. This will make the cue start out with no visible effect applied.

Step 6: Trigger playback of cue 1. You should see a normal video feed. After a moment, trigger cue 2 and you should now see the video feed slowly add the Zoom Blur effect.

Project 15.3 ▼

Combining Video Effects

One interesting feature of Video and Camera Cues is the ability to layer multiple cues atop one another. In the case of the Camera Cue, the feed is identical, thereby enabling the creation of a feed that appears to have multiple video effects applied to one video stream. For the project below, imagine a production with a stylized comic book design aesthetic in which a character is visited by a vision from God. For this production, it might be useful to combine together more than one video effect to achieve the appropriate comic book deity.

Step 1: Download Project 15.3 from the companion website. Once the project is open, activate the Audition Window to preview your effects.

Step 2: This project includes two Camera Cues. You will need to have a camera attached to your system to test its application. Select cue 1 and click on the Video Effects tab in the Inspector Panel. Select Zoom Blur and click the Apply Effects checkbox.

Step 3: Click GO to preview the Camera Cue feed with the applied effect. Manipulate the Input X, Input Y, and Amount sliders until you achieve the desired "supernatural" effect on your video feed.

(Continued)

Step 4: Select the Display & Geometry tab in the Inspector Panel and set the opacity to 0.0%. This will ensure the Camera Cue starts with no opacity so as to create a fade-in. In addition, set the Layer to 1. This will place the camera feed on a lower layer.

Step 5: Insert a Fade Cue (cue 1.5) after cue 1 and assign cue 1 as its target. In the Geometry tab, input an opacity of 100%. This will create the fade-in.

Step 6: Select cue 1 and change the continue status to auto-continue. This will fire cues 1 and 1.5 concurrently. If you test cue 1, you should now see the video feed slowly fade in from a black screen to a ghostly figure.

Step 7: Select cue 2 and activate the Median and Comic Effect setting in the Video Effects tab. In the Choose Effect drop-down menu, select Comic Effect.

Step 8: In the Display & Geometry tab of cue 2, set the opacity to 0%. In addition, set its Layer to 2. This will place the comic effect Camera Cue on a layer above the first camera feed. Finally, set the continue state to Auto-continue.

Step 9: Insert a Fade Cue (cue 2.5) after cue 2 and assign cue 2 as its target. In the Geometry tab, input an opacity of 20%. This will create the fade-in for cue 2 and set the opacity to a low level so it is semi-transparent.

Step 10: Finally, set the continue status of cue 1.5 to auto-continue and then test your cue sequence. Your programming should match that seen in Figure 15.24.

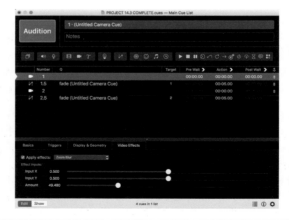

Figure 15.24
A workspace utilizing Camera Cues and Video Effects.

Projection Mapping
and Surfaces

In the world of entertainment design and technology, there are few trends that have made their way into the public consciousness quite so successfully as projection mapping. **Projection Mapping** is the process of using digital projectors to project imagery onto a non-flat surface, often with planes that are not perpendicular to the projector orientation. Traditional projection relies on having a flat, rectangular projection screen that is carefully aligned to the projector so as to eliminate keystoning and distortion of the projected imagery. With the advent of media servers and software used for geometrically mapping the video output from projectors, it is easier than ever for designers to map imagery onto complex 3D shapes. QLab has a number of functions built in for making projection mapping attainable. The following section details some of the ways in which you can begin to address projection mapping through QLab.

16.1 – Mapping vs. Masking

One of the first things to consider when approaching a projection project is what you are projecting onto. When considering projecting onto a non-traditional surface (i.e., anything but a projection screen), the surface will dictate your approach to setting up your QLab Surfaces. If you need to project onto a complex surface, there are a lot of different considerations. Where is your projector placed in relation to your surface? What do you want the resulting image to look like? Should the content be split onto multiple surfaces or spread across one large area? All of these questions will drive choices you have to make regarding your execution. Consider the possibility of a show that has abstractly shaped flats used as projection surfaces. This was the case in a recent production of *Macbeth* staged at Eastern Michigan University. For this production, the scenic designer created a series of organically shaped flats that resembled stalactites and stalagmites that would be used as projection surfaces by the projection designer (see Figure 16.1). For this project, the projections

Figure 16.1
This production of *Macbeth* utilized non-traditional projection surfaces that required the projection designer to mask her surfaces in a unique way. Production credit: *Macbeth*, Eastern Michigan University. October 2016. Directed by Lee Stille. Scenic Design by John Charles. Projection Design by Christine Franzen. Lighting Design by Jeromy Hopgood. Costume Design by Melanie Schuessler.

needed to fit onto the flats and match their organic contours. This type of a design called for masking, more than mapping.

Masking is the process of creating an opaque area attached to your surface that "masks off" the pixel areas where you don't want light to pass through. As discussed earlier, each surface has the ability to use a black-and-white image as a mask file where the white pixels are translated as transparent and the black ones are rendered opaque. In this way, the black area acts as a mask. Some masks are simple geometric shapes to block off areas like windows and doorways, whereas others (like the one seen in Figure 16.1) are complex organic shapes with feathered edges. For a design such as the one seen for *Macbeth*, a crisply masked edge would have looked out of place. In order to achieve something a bit less jarring, the student projection designer used Photoshop to create masks with organic shapes to the edges and used the Blur tool and varying layers of brush opacity to create masking that feathered out towards the edges.

Technically speaking, masking itself is not a form of projection mapping. This is simply one of the more common methods used to create interesting projection surfaces. One thing to keep in mind, though, is that this method does not affect the surface geometry at all, so it is often best used when projecting onto planar surfaces (though we will explore some methods for masking on complex surfaces in the following section).

Design Tips ▼

Gradation and Masks

One positive side effect of using the black-and-white file types for masking is gradations work to create varying scales of opacity within your mask. For example, a radial gradient that is white in the center and black on the edges can be used as a surface mask to create a classical photographic technique called a vignette (Figure 16.2a). Because of the gradated scale from black to white, black pixels will be perceived as opaque, white will be perceived as transparent, and the variations of gray in between will have various levels of opacity. This is a wonderful trick to focus on the image in the center of an area and not notice a big rectangle of light surrounding it. Figure 16.2b illustrates the resulting effect when used as a surface mask.

Figure 16.2a
This shows a mask created with a radial gradient positioned at the center (top).

Figure 16.2b
This illustrates what a Video Cue would look like when sent to a surface with this mask attached.

16.2 – Overlapping Geometric Surfaces

One popular method for integrating projection into a set design is to create a surface made up of a series of interconnected and overlapping geometric forms. By using such a design element as a projection surface, you can essentially create a backdrop for your performance that functions like a video wall. With a bit of creative programming, the wall could function as one giant display or be broken up into several different component screens, each capable of displaying different content. I have included a production photo of a design for Neil Labute's *The Shape of Things* that used this very approach. The scenic design for this production featured a back wall made up of a series of interconnected square and rectangular flats, all with varying surface depths to create a complex patchwork projection surface (Figure 16.3). In order to create a projection design that could maximize each of these flats as a distinct projection surface, I had to create 12 individual surfaces each mapped to precisely fit the shape of the flats. For the following project, we will examine how to create and assign surfaces for a simple geometric backdrop consisting of four separate surfaces.

Figure 16.3
This production utilized a series of overlapping flats in which each became a unique projection surface. Production credit: *The Shape of Things*, Eastern Michigan University. February 2014. Directed by Terry Heck Seibert. Scenic Design by John Charles. Projection Design by Jeromy Hopgood. Lighting Design by Brian Scruggs. Costume Design by Madeleine Huggins.

Project 16.1 ▽

Creating Surfaces for Overlapping Geometric Areas

The following project takes you through the process of setting up multiple surfaces that overlap. There is no project packet to download, as it deals specifically with setup.

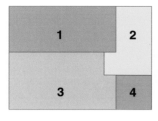

Figure 16.4
This simple surface has four separate flats of varying thicknesses that overlap one another at key points.

Figure 16.4 shows an example of a simple surface made up of four separate flats. For ease in interpreting the makeup of these surfaces, each is numbered and color coded. Each of these flats has varying thicknesses, which make certain surfaces protrude more than others. In addition, there are certain areas of overlap, making some surfaces rectangular and others irregular "L-shaped" hexagons. In order to use each of these areas as distinct display surfaces, we will need to create four separate surfaces and assign different surface layers to each one. The following steps will guide you through this process.

As a basic note, whenever possible it is always the best option to place your projector so that it is aligned in the center of the area onto which you want to project and with as little angle as possible. QLab can achieve keystone correction and compensate for extreme angles, but you begin to lose surface area of your projection in order to achieve this. This can lead to some undesirable effects, especially when projecting text and/or circular shapes.

Step 1: Connect a projector to your system. Open System Settings on your Mac and select Displays and then Arrangement. Make sure to deselect the Mirror Displays checkbox. This will set up your projector as a separate display surface.

Step 2: For this process, let us assume that we will be using one projector that can cover the entire area, with a bit of room to spare. As such, we will be using four separate single-screen surfaces, each attached to your projector. This projector will show up as a single-screen surface in your Video Surfaces list (to view this, select *Workspace Settings > Video > Video Surfaces*).

(*Continued*)

Step 3: To start the process of mapping this wall, let us create five new surfaces based on the projector, one that covers the entire area of the wall and four that represent each separate surface. To do so, click Add Surfaces in the Video Surfaces list and select *New with Display > "Your Projector Name."* This will open the Surface Editor for your new surface. Our first surface will represent the full wall, and we will use this as a template for the four additional surfaces to ensure they will all be based on the same basic geometry.

Step 4: Once you have added your first surface, the next thing to do is rename it. Since we are using Figure 16.4 as our guide, each of the separate surfaces will be numbered 1–4. We will give the full surface a unique name of "full wall" to easily distinguish it from the others. To achieve this, simply type "full wall" into the Surface Name input and press return. Close your Surface Editor and you should see a new surface in your Video Surfaces list named "full wall."

Step 5: Return to the Video Surfaces list and select the Full Wall surface. Click the "Edit" button to open the Surface Editor. Once you have done so, click on the grid checkbox on the left side of the screen. If your projector is turned on, this will display a full-size grid showing the entire display area of the projector. Grab the control points and move them until you have placed the grid to the four edges of your wall. Depending on the placement of your projector, this may take some adjustment to get correct. You will note that the control points will likely create a trapezoidal area in order to compensate for the angle of your projector (see Figure 16.5).

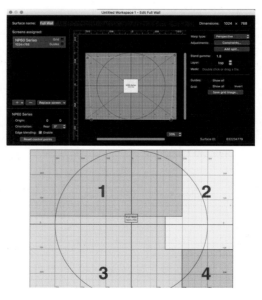

Figure 16.5
This figure illustrates how you might need to adjust your control points in order to match the geometry of the wall. Once you have adjusted the control points as necessary, the grid should resemble that seen on the bottom. Once you have successfully moved your grid to the desired positions, close your Surface Editor.

Step 6: Now that the Full Wall surface is appropriately mapped to the geometry of the entire surface, let's use this as a template for all of the other surfaces. To do so, select this surface in the Video Surfaces list and click the Duplicate button. This will open a new Surface Editor named Full Wall copy. Change the name to 1, and press enter. Close the Surface Editor and repeat this process to create surfaces 2–4. Just make sure to select the Full Wall surface each time before duplicating. After doing this, you will have a Video Surface list that shows surfaces 1–4 and Full Wall (Figure 16.6).

Figure 16.6
Once you have duplicated and re-named your surfaces, you will see them all in your Video Surfaces list.

Step 7: Select Surface 1 from your Video Surfaces list and click on the edit button to open the Surface Editor. Click on the grid checkbox to display your grid from the projector. You will notice that it matches that seen in the full wall surface. Our next step is to isolate the surface down to the area of the wall labeled 1 in our diagram. To do so, you use the constraints button. Clicking on this button opens the constraints tool that allows you to effectively reduce the area of your surface while keeping all of the adjustments made to geometry with control points and warping. In order to adjust to fit the appropriate size, we will be changing the numbers in the right and bottom fields. This represents the right and bottom sides of the Surface. Click on the right field and slide your cursor up to increase the pixel data. In looking at Figure 16.5, you can see that Surface 1 takes up an area approximately 768 pixels wide x 334 pixels tall in the upper left corner. In order to match this, I will adjust the data in the right cell to be 256 and the bottom cell to be 434. This means that the right side will be constrained over 256 pixels, while the bottom will move up 434. The resulting image should match the area of Surface 1 on my back wall perfectly. Figure 16.7 shows what your Surface Editor should look like to constrain the area.

Step 8: Return to the Video Surfaces list and select Surface 2. Open the Surface Editor, turn on the grid, and repeat the process from Step 7.

(Continued)

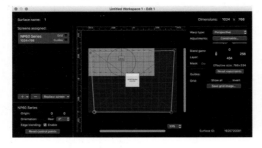

Figure 16.7
The Constraints tool is used to isolate a certain area of the back wall as a unique surface of its own.

This time, though, constrain the surface to match area 2 shown in our diagram of the full wall. To do so, you will adjust the bottom and left constraints. When you make your constrained rectangle, you will notice that Surface 2 overlaps the area of Surface 1. Do not worry about this for the moment, as we will adjust this later.

Step 9: Repeat the process of constraining the area for each of the remaining surfaces. When you are done, you should be able to open the Surface Editor for each surface, select the grid, and see that each one has a unique grid sent to areas 1–4 on the full wall. As I mentioned above, there will be some areas of overlap. For a wall such as this, we can fix that through the use of surface layers. Go back into the Surface Editor for each surface and examine its layer settings. Surfaces 1–4 are numbered in this way because of how they are physically stacked on top of one another. Setting a surfaces layer to a larger number means that it will render on top of other surfaces with smaller numbers. Therefore, we want to set the layer for Surface 1 as the higher number than Surface 2 since it needs to cover up part of Surface 2. Likewise, Surface 2 covers up part of Surface 3, so it must be a larger number as well (refer back to Figure 16.5 to see this orientation). To stack your layers in the appropriate order, set the layers as follows: Surface 1 to Layer 4, Surface 2 to Layer 3, Surface 3 to Layer 2, Surface 4 to Layer 1.

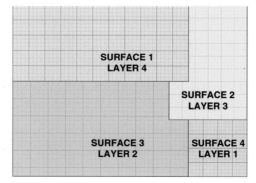

Figure 16.8
Each Surface has a different layer assigned to adjust which surfaces render on top of others.

Figure 16.8 illustrates how assigning layers to these surfaces results in four individually controllable surface patches.

Step 10: One thing you might notice is that all surfaces have a rectangular output and no masking for overlapping edges. This is fine if there is always video on each output, but in the case of sending an image to only Surface 2, for example, there will be an area of overlap where the image is projected onto Surface 1. A quick fix for this is to create a masking cue assigned to Surface 1 that would cover up the area of overlap. To do this, create a Video Cue that displays a small graphic file of a black square. Remember that a projector will interpret black as no light, so there will simply be no image projected in this area. Set the Mode to "Full Surface" and program it to Auto-continue with your other Video Cue. This will fire both cues simultaneously, putting up the black file as a mask for Surface 1 and showing only the video that you want to see on Surface 2.

16.3 – Mapping on Non-Planar Surfaces

In addition to the ability to break up a planar surface into different projection areas, QLab has a robust system of tools for mapping onto 3D, non-planar surfaces such as building architecture or set pieces. You will find that the process of mapping onto these surfaces can be time consuming and requires quite a bit of time for setup. The following section details the process for a very common situation of projecting onto a cube. For our purposes, we will use the example provided in Figure 16.9, a small cube-like protrusion from a larger wall structure. You will see from the illustration that the projector has to be aligned at an angle to be able to hit two planes of the cube, but this creates a great deal of warping and results in some of the projection hitting the floor and back wall. Luckily, QLab has a number of tools in the Surface Editor that will enable correcting the geometry and selecting the appropriate area on which to project. The following project takes you through a step-by-step approach to mapping your surface.

Project 16.2 ▼

Mapping to 3D Surfaces

The following project takes you through the process of setting up multiple surfaces that overlap. There is no project packet to download, as it deals specifically with setup. In addition, it will require the use of a projector connected to your system to work along in QLab. Without a projector, you should still be able to read along and pick up the process for yourself.

(Continued)

Step 1: Connect a projector to your system. Open System Settings on your Mac and select Displays and then Arrangement. Make sure to deselect the Mirror Displays checkbox. This will set up your projector as a separate display surface.

Step 2: As seen in Figure 16.9, we are using one projector that can cover the entire area, with a bit of room to spare. This projector will show up as a single-screen surface in your Video Surfaces list (to view this, select Video Surfaces in the Video tab of Workspace Settings).

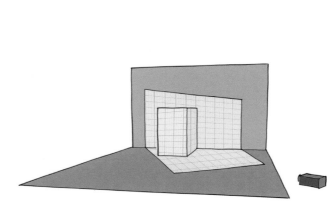

Figure 16.9 The projector in this example has a beam spread that covers much of the wall and floor in addition to the cube protrusion from the wall. You can see how the grid is distorted as it hits the various surfaces.

Step 3: To start the process of mapping this wall, let us create a new surface to map, based on the projector. To do so, click Add Surfaces in the Video Surfaces list and select *New with Display > "Your Projector Name."* This will open the Surface Editor for your new surface.

Step 4: Once you have added your surface, the next thing to do is re-name it. We will give this surface a unique name of "cube" to easily distinguish it from the others. To achieve this, simply type "cube" into the Surface Name input and press return.

Step 5: Check the grid checkbox on the left side of the screen. If your projector is turned on, this will display a full-size grid showing the entire display area of the projector. For the next part of the mapping process, we will be adding a split to the surface. A split divides a surface along either the horizontal or vertical plane. For this example, we would want to add a split that divides our surface on the horizontal plane, making two controllable sub-surfaces beside one another. Where you place the split is determined on your grid location as seen projected onto your wall. As such, it is necessary to have a clear line

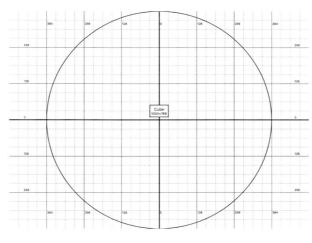

Figure 16.10
This is the grid created for our "cube" surface. Since the projector has a resolution of 1024x768, the surface grid will match these dimensions.

of sight of your grid on the projection surface. For our purposes, I have included an example of the QLab grid image as a reference (Figure 16.10). Imagine that this grid is projected onto the wall shown in Figure 16.9. The vertical line where the two faces of the cube meet aligns with the left side of the grid on the vertical line labeled 256.

Step 6: In order to add a split, you must click on the button labeled "Add split." This will open an interface that asks if you want to split the surface horizontally or vertically. In our case, we will select horizontal since we want to add a split on the x-plane. Next, you need to input the pixel coordinate where you want to place a split. In our case, we said the split should be on the left side of center at the coordinate marked 256. Since QLab uses a Cartesian coordinate system (X,Y), the number used to represent this line would be –256. Once you have inputted this number, press enter and you will see a dotted line appear on the grid as a reference so you can double-check your work. If this is indeed the correct location, click on the button labeled Add Split. Once you have done so, you will see that your grid will now be divided into sub-surfaces called A1 and B1 (Figure 16.11). Note that each side now has its own set of control points.

Step 6: Select the Linear warp type from the drop-down menu at the top right of the Surface Editor. This mode (sometimes called mesh warping) makes your image appear uninterrupted when passing across a surface split. The down side is that there is no guarantee of having correct perspective, so it may take some experimentation to reduce image distortion. Click on the top left control point for A1. This should

(Continued)

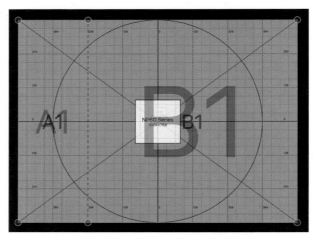

Figure 16.11
The grid is now divided into two sub-surfaces that can be independently controlled.

turn it yellow. Now that it is selected, grab it with your cursor and move it downward and inward until your horizontal grid lines start to align with the plane of your object. An alternate method would involve selecting the point and using your arrow keys. This process requires experimentation and patience. Keep in mind that you are not trying to line up to the edges of the surface yet, just to make your grid align to the plane of your wall. Repeat this process for the B1 sub-surface until you have made this side align as well. Depending on the placement of your projector, this may take some adjustment before it is aligned. You will note that the control points will likely create trapezoidal areas and may even slide off the edge of your grid as seen in Figure 16.12.

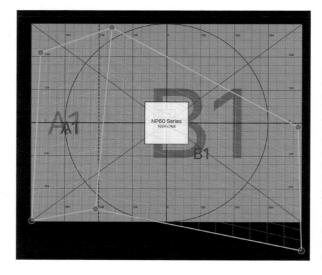

Figure 16.12
This figure illustrates how you might need to adjust your control points in order to match the geometry of the wall. Once you have adjusted the control points as necessary, the grid should match up to the planes of your wall.

Step 8: Once you have successfully moved your grid to the desired positions, click on the Constraints button. As seen in earlier examples, the constraints tool is used to "shutter in" a surface to a smaller area, while still keeping its original warping and splits. Select the left constraint by clicking your mouse inside the box and holding it down while sliding up. This should increase the numbers in the field. You will also notice that the projector's left side will start moving inward. Keep moving this constraint until it touches the extreme outside edge of your wall. In all likelihood, this line will not be perfectly aligned with your surface, but don't worry about that at this point. We will fix it later. Next, repeat this process for the top, bottom, and right constraints. When you are done, you will have the grid appearing almost exclusively on your wall, with a few small slivers of light on any side. When completed, your grid should resemble the example shown in Figure 16.13.

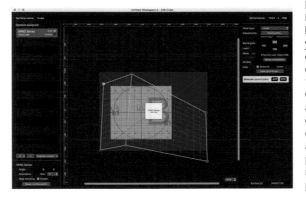

Figure 16.13
Notice the dark blue area around your now smaller grid. This is the constrained area, "shuttered" off. Once you have adjusted the constraints and control points as necessary, the projected grid should match up to the planes of your wall.

Step 9: To fix those additional slivers of light, go back to your grid on the editor canvas and slowly manipulate the placement of the control points until your edges match the object precisely.

Step 10: It is always a good idea to test the practical application of your newly created surface. For this process, I normally create a Video Cue with a graphic that has words and a circular area inside. Assign the Video Cue to your newly created "cube" surface. In the Display & Geometry tab of the Inspector, select custom geometry and then trigger the cue for playback. Grab the image inside the video stage and slide it from left to right. Your image should pass from one plane to the other with minimal warping. If this is not the case, you may need to make some adjustments to your grid and try again.

Tools of the Trade ▼

External Mapping Options: MadMapper

While QLab does have a number of powerful tools for projection mapping and creating surfaces, there are some instances in which it might not be the most practical choice for large-scale mapping applications. One thing to consider is the limitation within QLab that each Video Cue can only output to one video surface at a time. This means that, in situations where you might want to route one video onto three separate surfaces (think of mapping onto a cube, for instance), you would have to play the same Video Cue three separate times, each routed to a separate surface. Often, this type of programming can become time consuming and a big drain on your system resources. It does not take very many instances of high-definition video playing to start bogging down your system and creating a jumpy playback with timing discrepancies between the videos that should be simultaneous playback. In this case, QLab may not be the best choice for your projection mapping needs. Since QLab has a built-in Syphon server, it is a simple matter to output a Syphon video feed to another application serving as a Syphon client. That's where MadMapper comes in.

MadMapper is a simple but powerful application for projection and light mapping. The software can function as a stand-alone method of video/image playback from your computer, or it can function as a Syphon client, receiving a live feed of video content from applications like QLab. To enable this function, you need to create a surface (or surfaces) in QLab that has Syphon assigned as its Screen. If you use this surface as the output patch for your Video Cues, then QLab will output mirror the entire surface as a Syphon feed. This can then be used as a video input inside of MadMapper. By adding mapping elements (such as quads, triangles, and circles), the video feed can then be split out into several different surfaces (Figure 16.14). Figure 16.14 shows a video feed from QLab in the

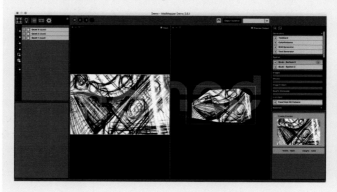

Figure 16.14
A MadMapper interface, showing the Syphon feed as video input on the left, with the mapped output on the right.

left panel. This feed is then split into three separate areas, with the use of quads. The screen on the right shows how the video feed can then be mapped by using control points to warp the feed for projecting onto three non-planar surfaces.

Surfaces within MadMapper can be named and grouped, allowing for moving and rotating multiple surfaces simultaneously. The key advantage here is that you can select and manipulate several surfaces at once, versus QLab's more time-consuming approach of having to adjust each surface individually. Likewise, MadMapper enables using only one Video Cue to play across multiple surfaces, considerably freeing up system resources. For more information on the software, visit their website at www.madmapper.com.

16.4 – Masking Made Easy

As mentioned earlier, masking is a powerful tool that allows you to crop out certain areas of your surface that you do not want to project onto. This could be used for feathering out the edges around the perimeter of your surfaces or as a tool to block off areas of a surface, such as a door, where you don't want to project. Masks are applied to each surface inside of the Surface Editor, so it is possible to have multiple different masks used for differing purposes.

QLab does not have its own image editor; rather it relies on your making it in a graphics editing application such as Adobe Photoshop. It can use any standard image format and watches the source file for any changes that may be made to it along the way. One of the questions that often comes up is how to create an image in another application that matches the geometry of a real-world object. This can prove to be a tedious process when you take into account the image warping that occurs as a result of projector placement. When I am creating masks that have to match real-world elements, I often use QLab as a drawing tool of sorts in order to create a guide that I then use inside of Photoshop. The following example takes you through this process.

Project 16.3 ▼

Using QLab as a Masking Tool

For this process, we will consider the problem of projecting onto the top of an oddly shaped platform on stage. The projector is positioned high above and from behind the actors. The projection designer wants to project onto the top of the platform, but not the floor around it. This can quickly

(Continued)

be achieved through QLab and a graphics editing program by using the following steps.

Step 1: Connect a projector to your system. Open System Settings on your Mac and select the Arrangement tab of the Displays window. Make sure to deselect the Mirror Displays checkbox. This will set up your projector as a separate display surface.

Step 2: Your projector will show up as a single-screen surface in your Video Surfaces list (to view this, select Workspace Settings, then Video, and finally Video Surfaces). To start the process of masking the platform, let us create a new surface based on the projector. To do so, click add surfaces in the Video Surfaces list and select *New with Display > "Your Projector Name."* This will open the Surface Editor for your new surface.

Step 3: Once you have added your surface, the next thing to do is re-name it. We will give this surface a unique name of "platform" to easily distinguish it from the others. To achieve this, simply type "platform" into the Surface Name input and press return.

Step 4: Since this platform is irregularly shaped, you will need to add a number of slices to the surface in order to draw out the perimeter of the surface. For this example, I included three horizontal splits (at -256, 0, and 256 on the x-plane) and one vertical (at 0 on the y-plane). These splits will create 8 sub-surfaces with 15 control points. Keep in mind, you can add as many as necessary.

Step 5: Make sure to click the grid checkbox in your Surface Editor so you can see the change to your grid in real-time. Grab your control points and begin moving them around to match the perimeter of your platform. Don't worry if the grid pattern begins to distort in odd ways; you are only using this as a guide.

Step 6: Once you have matched your grid to the perimeter of your platform, you can use this as a guide for creating a mask. Now, you can take a screen shot of the grid. All Macs are equipped with the function to take a screen shot of either the full screen or a selected portion of your screen. If you press ⇧⌘3 a graphic file will be saved to your desktop of every display attached to your system. This will provide a full-size screen capture of the warped grid, as shown in Figure 16.15. This file will be 100% accurate in terms of resolution and dimensions.

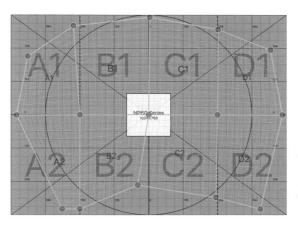

Figure 16.15
The screen shot will be saved to your desktop as an image file, showing the entire canvas editor.

Step 7: Using a graphics editing program, open this file. For this example, I am using Adobe Photoshop, but most graphics applications can be used for this same process. Once you have opened the image file, you will find that it matches the appropriate dimensions of your projector's resolution. This will be the guide for creating a mask image.

Step 8: The next step requires using Photoshop's Polygon Lasso tool. This is a selection tool that allows you to draw polygon-shaped selections. Simply click on the starting point of any control point and carefully trace the yellow perimeter of the shape masked out in QLab. When you make it back to your starting point, click on the same position, and Photoshop will complete the selection for you. You may find it easier to trace the shape by zooming in on the screen to see the image close up.

Step 9: Now that you have created the selection, you will need to create a black-and-white image as your mask. With the area still selected, press the delete button on your keyboard. This should erase the pixels selected inside of the selection. Now, using your Paint Bucket tool, fill the area with white color (Figure 16.16).

Step 10: Right-clicking (control-click) on the selected area will bring up a pop-up menu. Click on *Select Inverse.* This should select all of the area outside of your selection. Press the delete button on your keyboard to delete the content of your selection. Using your Paint Bucket tool, change the color to black and fill this area with black color (Figure 16.17).

(Continued)

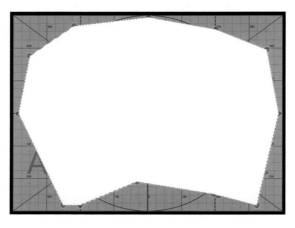

Figure 16.16
The platform area has been replaced with a white color fill.

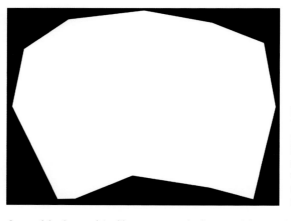

Figure 16.17
The area outside the platform has now been replaced with a black color fill. This will serve as the mask color for our surface mask.

Step 11: Save this file to your desktop with a unique name like "platform mask." I prefer to use PNG file types, but you can use most standard file types (PNG, JPG, GIF).

Step 12: Once you have saved the file, go back to QLab and open your Surface Editor. Click the "reset control points" button at the bottom of the screen. This will return your surface to its original orientation. Now, either double-click in the mask dialog on the right side of your screen, or simply drag the mask file onto this area. The mask image will now be applied to your surface and should match up perfectly to the geometry of your platform.

PART IV
QLab Lighting Control

QLab Lighting System Basics

Lighting design has long been an essential design area for performances and installations. It has only been since the release of V4 that QLab has offered the ability to natively control lighting through your workspace. With the addition of DMX lighting control over Art-Net and USB-DMX interfaces, this opens an entire new realm of possibilities for QLab users that had been impossible until now. In order to understand how to use QLab as a lighting controller, it is important to first learn some of the basics related to lighting control systems. This chapter will give a brief introduction to lighting systems and how QLab interacts with them.

17.1 – Understanding Lighting Systems

A lighting system refers to the collection of equipment necessary to generate and control the lighting for a production. When working in a theatre setting, most of these elements will be included as part of the facility. In the most basic terms, a lighting system must include power, control, and lighting instruments. The following section details common components of a lighting system. For installations, site-specific work, or designs outside of the traditional theatre space, your setup may vary from the basic system described below. The same concepts of power, control, and equipment will still apply though.

Power

For a theatre with a dedicated power system, electrical service will be sent into the building and connected to a dimmer rack. A dimmer rack is made up of several **dimmers**, electrical devices used to regulate the flow of electricity out to specific outlets. The outlet that receives this power is referred to as a **circuit**. In most theatre spaces, these circuits are hard wired into the dimmer rack, creating a system that is referred to as a **dimmer-per-circuit system**, meaning that each dimmer is physically connected to a circuit bearing the same name. In such a system, Dimmer 1 would correspond to Circuit 1, Dimmer 2 to Circuit 2, and so on. For some performances, such as touring shows or non-traditional performance spaces, the production might bring in portable dimmer racks that tie in directly to the main power supply. In this type of an installation, cabling will be run directly from the dimmer to the lighting instruments, eliminating the notion of a circuit altogether.

Conventional stage lighting equipment is typically connected to a circuit by means of a heavyweight electrical cable with a **stage pin connector**, a specialized connector plug that is rectangular in shape with three cylindrical prongs on the male end and three openings on the female receptacle (Figure 17.1).

Control

For every lighting system, there must be a controller used to manipulate the dimmers and lighting equipment. This controller is typically called a **lighting console** or sometimes simply referred to as the lighting board. A lighting console is an electronic device used to send control signals to devices such as dimmers, lighting instruments, color scrollers, gobo rotators, or environmental effects like fogger/hazers. Lighting consoles use a communication protocol called **DMX512-A (often called DMX, for short)** to communicate with these devices. In the QLab lighting system, the console is replaced by your QLab workspace.

Lighting Instruments/Accessories/DMX-Controlled Devices

Lighting instruments are the final component of the lighting system. **Conventional lighting instruments** are lights that remain in a fixed position and whose intensity can be changed by the amount of electrical power supplied to them. **Intelligent lighting instruments** are lights with a number of controllable properties, such as focus position, intensity, color, texture, beam quality, and special effects (such as strobe, bouncing effects, prisms, and more). For conventional lighting equipment, it need only be connected to a

Figure 17.1 The **stage pin** connector, featuring both the male and female connector ends.

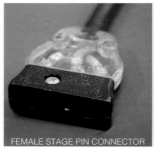

FEMALE STAGE PIN CONNECTOR | MALE STAGE PIN CONNECTOR

dimmer to be controlled. For intelligent lighting, the instrument is typically connected to standard 120-volt power (not a dimmer, as this can damage the equipment) and uses a specific control cable to provide the control signal from the lighting console directly to the lighting fixture. Often, these fixtures will be **daisy-chained** together, meaning that the data output from the first fixture will cable into the data input of the second and down the line into subsequent fixtures. DMX signal is diminished over longer cable runs, so the DMX standard is not to have more than 32 instruments on one cable run. There are a number of variables on this count, such as if all devices are running at full DMX load and number of nodes and controllers. Since different gear can put varying levels of electrical resistance on your signal, my personal rule is not to go in greater runs than 16 fixtures. In order to facilitate multiple instruments on one DMX universe, it is common to use a DMX splitter that enables the distribution of the one DMX universe over multiple outputs, allowing for additional cable runs.

In addition to lighting fixtures, there are also many different accessories, such as color scrollers, gobo rotators, moving mirror attachments, irises, and more, which are all controlled via DMX signal. The same is true of other devices such as foggers, hazers, and even projector dowsers. Since so many of these devices utilize DMX-512, it is important to have a good working understanding of this communication protocol.

What Is DMX?

DMX 512 is a robust communication protocol that has been around for more than three decades. The protocol was first created by the Engineering Commission of the United States Institute for Theatre Technology (USITT), but is now maintained by the Professional Lighting and Sound Association (PLASA). DMX is divided into 512 separate control signals called **channels** that each communicate intensity levels in a numeric range from 0–255. This means that a signal of 128 sent to a dimmer would be translated as approximately 50% intensity. In practical applications, most lighting devices hide this numerical data and simply communicate in a percentage range from 0–100%. The collection of all 512 channels is defined as a **universe.** Many lighting consoles have multiple universes of output. The Pro Lighting license for QLab 4 has an unlimited number of patchable DMX addresses. You are only limited by the number of universes available on your Art-Net node or DMX interface.

What Is an Address?

Every lighting fixture, dimmer, or DMX-capable device must have an address assigned to it. This concept is fundamental to understanding how to set up your lighting control system. In simple terms, an address is the location within a 512-channel universe where a device "lives." This address is a number that indicates the starting point of control signals sent to the device. This address is manually set on the device and often changes from show to show. In addition, you might even set a similar address for multiple devices (provided that each one needed to receive the exact same signal).

Each device uses a predefined number of DMX channels to control its different attributes. With something simple like a conventional dimmer, only one channel is used to control its parameters. So when addressing a series of 24 dimmers, each dimmer would be addressed starting at 1 and going through 24 by single digits. Intelligent fixtures, however, often require multiple channels to control their different attributes (pan, tilt, color, strobe, etc.). Let's consider a simple generic RGB lighting fixture. This type of light often uses three channels for control, the first for red, the second for green, and the third for blue. When addressing a series of these instruments, keep in mind that you will have to leave the total number of channels used by one fixture open before addressing the next. For instance, in a series of three generic RGB fixtures, the addresses would be as follows: Fixture 1 (address 1), Fixture 2 (address 4), Fixture 3 (address 7). When laying out your system, I always find it best to determine the required addressing on paper before jumping into the process. Figure 17.2 illustrates a system with both conventional and intelligent fixtures, showing the method for addressing these different devices.

Figure 17.2 This illustration shows how addressing works in practical terms. Basic devices, such as dimmers, require only one channel of control. More complex devices, such as RGB lighting fixtures, require three channels of control. In this case, it is essential to track which channels are dedicated to which instrument in order to properly address each fixture.

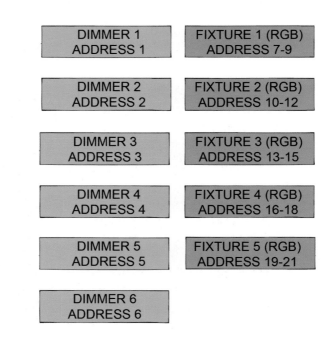

| DIMMER 1 | FIXTURE 1 (RGB) |
| ADDRESS 1 | ADDRESS 7-9 |

| DIMMER 2 | FIXTURE 2 (RGB) |
| ADDRESS 2 | ADDRESS 10-12 |

| DIMMER 3 | FIXTURE 3 (RGB) |
| ADDRESS 3 | ADDRESS 13-15 |

| DIMMER 4 | FIXTURE 4 (RGB) |
| ADDRESS 4 | ADDRESS 16-18 |

| DIMMER 5 | FIXTURE 5 (RGB) |
| ADDRESS 5 | ADDRESS 19-21 |

| DIMMER 6 |
| ADDRESS 6 |

17.2 – Understanding Lighting Consoles

Now that you have a basic understanding of lighting systems and their separate components, it is useful to consider the functions of a traditional lighting console before examining the ways QLab can serve as a replacement.

Input/Output

As mentioned earlier, the lighting console is connected to other components of your lighting system via some form of network – whether that be DMX over XLR cables, over Ethernet, or even via wireless network. All lighting consoles have an input/output (I/O) to facilitate this communication. Many include different methods of connectivity. In addition to DMX, many modern consoles also include Ethernet ports and MIDI connections (Figure 17.3). These interfaces all add a greater level of flexibility for control. With MIDI, for instance, a lighting console can trigger elements of your sound system or vice versa, allowing lighting cues to be triggered by an incoming MIDI signal. Some consoles also allow for transmitting or receiving OSC or UDP over Ethernet.

Channels

In lighting console terms, a channel is a control signal that enables a lighting operator to control one or more components of the lighting system. One important concept to understanding channels is the patch. In older lighting systems before the dimmer-per-circuit system days, most theatres had a patch panel. This was a bay of plugs similar to those used by telephone operators

Figure 17.3 The back of this lighting console features a number of different connection interfaces for numerous methods of I/O.

in the early 20th century. The purpose of this patch panel was to physically connect a dimmer to a circuit. This is referred to as a **hard patch**. When computerized lighting consoles came along, many introduced a function that allowed the console to create a **soft patch**, a computerized patch on the board that connects a channel from the console to one or more addresses in the lighting system. Today, most theatres have done away with patch panels, so the notion of hard vs. soft patch has disappeared. Most lighting consoles simply refer to their soft patch as the **patch**, a function that allows the operator to assign addresses to control channels on the console.

Master Control

Most lighting consoles feature a number of different sliders on the face of the light board. Most often these controls are referred to as **faders**. Each of these faders serves as a tactile control method for increasing or decreasing the amount of signal sent out from 0–100%. Often, these faders are assignable to channels, groups, etc. There is one fader referred to as the **Master** or **Grand Master** that is used to control lighting output on a global scale, meaning the intensity of every other channel on the lighting console is superseded by the Master, allowing the operator to simply dim the lights across the entire system from one fader. This type of control is referred to as inhibitive, meaning that its primary function is to decrease the intensity of all channels coming out of the console.

In addition to the Grand Master, most lighting consoles also feature a button called **Blackout**. A blackout button simply interrupts all signals going out of the board, temporarily setting levels to 0% without actually changing the cueing. This is a useful tool that can also lead to moments of panic if it is inadvertently pushed.

Submasters and Groups

Most every lighting console also includes a series of faders referred to as submasters, or simply subs. A **submaster** is a fader that can have multiple channels at specific levels attached to one fader for control purposes. Consider the possibility of creating a look for an outdoor scene that combines 20 different lights at varying intensities. If you were to save this look into submaster one, then this look could be brought up by sliding up one fader on the console. Each channel would then respond accordingly at its different states, based on the percentage of the sub.

Similar to the submaster is the group function. A **Group** is a collection of channels selected as a single unit. Unlike submasters, there are no pre-programmed states associated with these individual channels; it is simply a method of controlling a group of channels from 0–100%.

Playback

One of the biggest advantages of modern lighting consoles is the ability to have consistent playback of prerecorded cues in a similar fashion show after show. A cue is a recorded "memory" of all of the channels used to recreate a particular look consistently at the touch of the GO button. In addition to channels, each cue has a programmable fade time that dictates the timing to fade in the selected cue and fade out the previous one. This method should be very familiar to QLab users, as it is quite similar to the traditional QLab cue settings.

One important consideration for programming and playback is the idea of precedence. As a design proceeds through a series of cues, the channel values will invariably change. The question is, how does your console deal with this when attempting to control the same attribute? There are two methods of playback control, known as HTP (Highest Takes Precedence) and LTP (Latest Takes Precedence). These two methods dictate how your console organizes its playback of channels. **HTP** means that if you have one channel controlled by multiple faders (two separate submasters, for instance) the channel with the highest value will take precedence and that will be the value sent out to the device. This is an excellent method for simple conventional lighting fixtures where the only concern is intensity. **LTP**, on the other hand, indicates that the latest control signal is the one that will be listened to, no matter the levels. This method is best used when controlling intelligent lighting parameters.

Palettes

Palettes are one of the tools available on intelligent lighting consoles used for programming moving lights. A **Palette** is a method of storing data for moving lights that can be used to speed up programming. For instance, you could create a color palette for all of your intelligent lights set for the color blue. You could also identify a key location on the stage, such as Downstage Center, and program that as a position palette. By having these preconfigured, you could select all of your moving lights and input their position as the Downstage Center palette. This can greatly speed up the programming process. Likewise, should the position need to change for some reason, you can simply update the palette itself, and every cue that uses this palette information will automatically update the position data.

Effects

Most modern lighting consoles have tools for generating lighting effects, like "chase" controls or random channel playback. This is a handy tool for creating interesting visual effects onstage without having to go through the time-consuming process of writing dozens of cues that are linked together to create a simple effect.

17.3 - QLab as a Lighting Controller

Understanding the basics of how a traditional lighting console operates, now we can move forward into examining how QLab can function as a lighting controller and the similarities and differences in the consoles mentioned in Section 17.2.

How QLab Communicates

Similar to traditional consoles, QLab has a number of different methods for input/output. Lighting control has access to all of the same methods mentioned in other sections of the book, such as MIDI and OSC. In addition, it utilizes the **Art-Net** protocol as a method to transmit control data to a lighting system. Art-Net allows QLab to transmit data over an Ethernet or Wi-Fi network to Art-Net enabled devices such as dimmers or lighting fixtures. Many devices cannot receive Art-Net control data, however, and require DMX signals to operate. In order to communicate with these devices, it is necessary to use an Art-Net/DMX interface, called a **node**, that translates the Art-Net signal into DMX. One such popular device is the ENTTEC OpenDMX Ethernet/ DMX 512 interface (Figure 17.4). This small device translates Art-Net signals received via Ethernet into DMX and outputs them through a standard five-pin XLR cable.

USB-DMX Interfaces

The release of the QLab 4.1 update added the ability to communicate through a USB-DMX interface. At the time of writing this book, QLab supports the ENTTEC DMX USB Pro, ENTTEC DMX USB Pro Mk2, DMXking ultraDMX RDM Pro, and the DMXking ultraDMX Micro. By using these affordable interfaces, QLab can communicate directly with lighting equipment through the DMX protocol.

Figure 17.4 The ENTTEC OpenDMX Ethernet interface outputs one universe of DMX signals.

Channels

QLab also uses channels to send control signals out to addressed components of your lighting system. There is a Light Patch that allows the programmer to assign a channel to an address (or series of addresses for devices that require multiple control channels). Once a lighting instrument is inserted into a Light Cue, you can then manipulate the channel or channels to control its attributes.

Master Control

QLab does not have a Master Fader or a blackout button. Cue attributes can be monitored and changed through a window called the Light Dashboard. There is a slider that controls the attributes of all lighting instruments. By sliding this down, you can effectively create a blackout, but the changes will not occur proportionally as they would on a traditional console. Since Lighting Cue follows a similar work flow as other cue types, the easy way to create a blackout is simply to insert a new cue in the workspace with all of the instrument levels set to 0%. Keep in mind that this will update all channels to 0% and does not function in the same way as a traditional blackout button on a console.

Submasters and Groups

Within the current QLab system, there are no submasters. Instead, it incorporates groups, allowing the user to combine together multiple instruments into one group for control. Unfortunately, there is currently no method for the proportional control offered up by submasters on a traditional console. At the time of writing this book, this is a feature being considered by the development team at Figure 53, but it remains to be seen when it might be implemented.

Playback

Lighting playback through QLab follows the same cue conventions as those seen in other cue types. In other words, there is a series of cues stacked sequentially, and playback is achieved through the typical methods (GO button or various triggering options). As usual, you can create multiple cue lists or cue carts for playback options. In addition, Group Cues can be used in conjunction with Light Cues to create a single Group Cue with multiple lighting components imbedded within. Doing this offers the programmer a wider range of flexibility for timing the cues and creating "parts" to the look that can be individually controlled. QLab tracks all cues by default, meaning that it uses the LTP behavior, in which the value of any element in a cue overrides the value established by a previous cue.

Palettes

Currently, QLab deals with palettes by allowing Light Cues to "pull" certain values from other cues. For instance, a Light Cue could pull the position of a particular lighting instrument from a pre-made cue either within the cue list, in a separate cue list, or in a separate cue cart. By creating a series of cues with unique names (i.e., palette 1, palette 2, etc.) you can effectively create your own palettes for programming.

Effects

Effects such as chases and the like are accomplished through programming, using a Group Cue with a series of Light Cues and a Start Cue to trigger loop playback. There are no quick effects presets currently available, though there is discussion of this as an addition to future alpha releases.

Summary

QLab 4 offers up a unique new way to control your lighting system within the standard cue structure of QLab programming. It will no doubt take some getting used to for those coming from the lighting world and having no previous QLab experience. As things stand, the lighting component is not going to be a viable replacement for those controlling a large moving light rig. It is an excellent choice, however, for installations and, especially, touring shows where a single operator needs to control lighting, projections, and sound from one simple interface. In the right setting, a single computer running QLab could replace thousands of dollars of equipment. This no doubt leads to all sorts of logistical questions (not the least of which being the amount of time and planning that goes into cueing a show if there were multiple designers on the same computer), but it will be interesting to see how this new component develops over the coming years and the ways in which the industry embraces it.

Preparing to Cue Lights

Like many of the other cue types in QLab, there are a series of settings and preferences that must be addressed before cueing. In the case of Light Cues, the list is relatively short. The following chapter takes you through the necessary steps to take before adding Light Cues to your workspace.

18.1 – Network Setup

When preparing for working with lights, one of the first steps is setting up a DMX Art-Net interface with your Mac (note that USB-DMX interfaces require no network setup since they work over a direct USB connection, not a network). As mentioned in earlier chapters, this device is sometimes referred to as an Art-Net node. QLab will work with all varieties of network nodes. In order for your Mac to communicate with the node, they must first be connected to the same network. This can be accomplished through several different methods. The easiest method is to physically connect your two devices through an Ethernet cable. This creates a network composed of two devices. If you need to connect other devices to your network (such as other QLab computers or projectors), then it is wise to use an Ethernet switch to connect these devices together. Yet another option is to connect the devices to the same Wi-Fi network and communicate wirelessly.

When setting up QLab to work on your lighting network, there are a few steps to consider. Networking can be a complicated endeavor, particularly for those unfamiliar with the core concepts. These days, it is advisable for most people working in lighting, sound, or projections to have a good working understanding of networking basics. Setting up a lighting network in QLab is relatively simple. For this section, let us assume that the setup will be a wired connection rather than wireless. First, power up your Art-Net node and connect it to your computer via an Ethernet cable. Since nodes are network devices, they will always have an IP (internet protocol) address. An **IP Address** is the identifier assigned to any device on a TCP/IP network that is used for communication between separate devices on the network. They are written as a series of four numbers in a sequence of up to three digits. For example, a common IP address might be 10.0.100.1. In addition to the IP address, networks are also broken down into subnets. **Subnetting** is the process of dividing one network into many smaller "subnetworks." Subnets are also written in the same fashion as an IP address, but communicate different information. With a subnet, the number 255 is used to communicate which part of the IP address represents the network address. The number 0 is used to represent which part of the IP address indicates the machine address. Commonly, for a smaller network, you will use the subnet of 255.255.255.0. This indicates that the first three numeric sequences of the IP address are the network address, whereas the last number or numbers represent the machine's individual address. For our purposes, we will use the subnet of 255.255.255.0, which indicates that each device must have identical numbers in the first three number sets with a unique number in the last area (for instance 10.10.10.1 and 10.10.10.2, respectively). This tells us that the devices are both on the same network and each has a unique machine number.

To set up QLab, you must go into your Mac's System Preferences and open the icon labeled Network. This opens a window that lists all of the available networks on your computer (Figure 18.1). Select the network device you will be using to connect to your node. A column will appear on the right side of the window showing the status and configuration information for this network port. Often, a network port is configured to use DHCP (Dynamic Host Configuration Protocol). **DHCP** is a client/server protocol that automatically provides an IP address for your computer and other information such as a subnet mask and default gateway. This protocol is ideal for large network settings, but can create complications for a show control network. Each component of such a network should have a fixed address, called a **Static IP Address**, that will remain consistent each time the system is powered down. To ensure your Mac uses a static IP, click on the drop-down beside "Configure IPv4" and select "Manually." This will allow you to input your own chosen IP address for your Mac. Just make sure that it is unique and doesn't match anything else in your system. For this example, I chose 10.10.100.1 with a subnet mask of 255.255.255.0. Since we are not using a router for this example, I simply leave the router slot blank. Click the "Apply" button and your configuration will be saved.

In addition to the Mac, you will also need to configure the IP address of your node. In most cases, the node will come with instructions that tell its IP address and methods for changing the address as necessary. If you know the IP address, it might be wise to simply change your Mac's IP address to match the preconfigured node. If you need to re-configure the node, then it is wise to see if the manufacturer makes a utility for this purpose. With the ENTTEC ODE that I use,

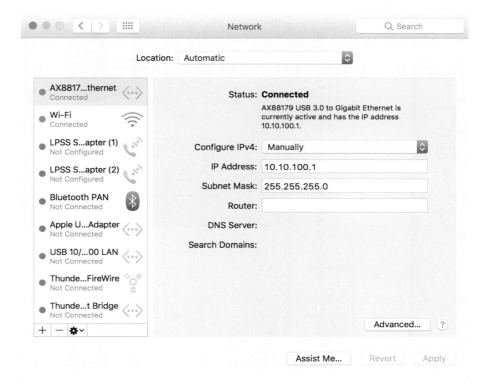

Figure 18.1
The network configuration shown here uses a static IP address of 10.10.100.1. Because of the subnet mask, the node would need to use an address of 10.10.100.xxx.

there is an application called NMU (Node Management Utility) that will identify any node on your network, tell you all of its information, and allow you to re-configure the settings. Using this application, I configured the node to have an IP address of 10.10.100.2.

Once you have reached this point, the next step is to open QLab and check to see if your node is visible. One interesting item of note is that Art-Net is disabled until you have added lights to your workspace. For now, select *Window > Light Patch* (or ⇧⌘I) to open the Light Patch. We will examine this in depth at a later point. For now, go ahead and click on the button labeled "New Instrument ⌘N." By adding one light into your patch, Art-Net will now be enabled in your workspace. Select *Window > Workspace Status* (or ⇧⌘W) to open the Workspace Status window. After the window opens, select the third tab, called "Art-Net." Now, your node should be visible on the list. In my case, it shows that the node is assigned the IP address of 10.10.100.2 and using DMX Universe 1 (Figure 18.2). Once you see your device in this window, you know that it is communicating with QLab and you are ready to move onto the next step.

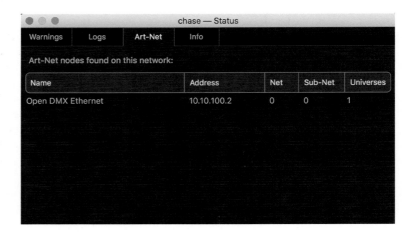

Figure 18.2
The network configuration shown here indicates the node uses an IP address of 10.10.100.2. It is also using DMX Universe 1 to send out data.

Design Tips

A Word About Polling

Art-Net uses a concept called polling, in which the controlling devices send out a message to the system asking all nodes to respond. Not all nodes respond to polling, however. This can lead to a device being properly configured on your network and still not appearing in your workspace status window. If this is the case for your setup, open *QLab > QLab Preferences* from your menu bar. Once opened, you will see a row marked Art-Net Lighting Network Interface; click on the checkbox labeled "use broadcast mode for Art-Net lighting." This enables QLab to transmit data to the entire network without polling. In addition, there is a drop-down menu used for selecting the Art-Net network. In many cases, the default of automatic will work well. If you are connected to multiple networks, however, it might be a good idea to go ahead and select the network being used for Art-Net data.

18.2 – Adding Your Lights

The next step you have to take before programming is adding your lighting instruments into QLab. This process is done through the Light Patch Editor. The QLab patch system assigns an instrument name to an address (or addresses) giving you the ability to then insert this instrument into a Light Cue and control its assigned parameters. The Light Patch Editor can be accessed in numerous ways, by selecting the Light section of Workspace Settings, by using the keyboard shortcut ⇧⌘I, or by selecting *Window > Light Patch*. Once this window is open, click on the tab labeled Patch.

Patch

When you first open the Patch tab, there are two buttons highlighted: New Instrument and New Group. An instrument is the name QLab uses for any type of DMX-addressed device on your system. This could be a dimmer, a scroller, an intelligent lighting fixture, or an atmospheric device such as a hazer. In order to indicate what type of device this is, QLab uses a definition. In QLab terminology, a **definition** is a collection of information about a particular type of instrument, including name, manufacturer, and parameters. When inserting an instrument into the patch, the default definition used is Dimmer. This means that this instrument will have only one controllable parameter, called intensity. In this case, any data sent out by QLab will communicate directly with the dimmer in question and tell it how much voltage should be sent out to the lighting fixture circuited to that dimmer.

There are a number of default definitions saved into QLab's Light Library. Once you click New Instrument, a new instrument will be added with the number 1 as its name. It will also default to the address of 1. In order to see what parameters are attached to this instrument, simply click on the arrow beside the name and a drop-down will appear showing the assigned parameters (Figure 18.3). Addresses can be manually changed in the patch table by double-clicking on the address and inputting a new value. It is worth noting that different instruments cannot share the same address, but QLab will allow you to insert an address that is already being used. In this case, each of the instruments' patch rows would be highlighted in a red color. These instruments will not work until the addressing has been resolved.

Once you have added an instrument, you will also notice an area appear at the bottom of the screen similar in appearance to the Inspector Window (Figure 18.4). In this area, you can change the name of your instrument, add notes, assign its definition, and assign the universe, Sub-Net, and Net. Names can be words, numbers, or single letters. When considering the model of a traditional lighting console, a name within QLab is similar to a channel on a light board. The name is connected to an address and will send out a DMX

Figure 18.3
Since instrument 1 in this list is a dimmer, the only controllable parameter is intensity.

Figure 18.4
The Definitions tab
of the Light Patch
Inspector offers a
number of options
for controlling
instrument
parameters.

control signal to affect change to the addressed device. It offers much more flexibility than a traditional lighting console, though, since you could feasibly name each instrument for its purpose (e.g., Area A: cool front or Area A: warm front). Regarding the DMX universe, it is handy to remember that the first universe is always numbered 0. As such, the default value in the patch will be Universe 0.

MIDI Control

The middle column on the Instrument Inspector is used for assigning MIDI as a control signal to an individual instrument or group. Note on, note off, program change, and control change are all suitable message types. By doing this, you can use a MIDI controller or software to change the light or group's intensity parameter. This allows you to create a fader wing of sorts for a tactile control interface for lighting instruments, akin to that used on a traditional lighting console. This type of control is only active when the Light Dashboard or Light Cue Inspector is open. Finally, in order for motorized MIDI controllers to respond to changes made in QLab, you must select a MIDI output. This is determined in the area at the top of the screen called "Send MIDI Feedback." By setting the channel in the drop-down menu, you can select the MIDI channel that is used for MIDI feedback.

Groups

One final aspect of adding lights is the ability to create Groups and assign different instruments to these groups. To create a group, click the "New Group ⌘G" button. This will create a new group called "group 1." To add lights to this group, select the desired lights individually. In the groups section of the Instrument Inspector, click on the "add to group" button and then select the desired group. This process will keep individual control of the lighting instrument while allowing you to group together several instruments for control. All lights added to the workspace are automatically added to an unseen group called "all," which becomes a controllable aspect of the Light Dashboard.

18.3 – Definitions and the Light Library

To the right side of the Light Patch Editor is another tab labeled Definitions. The Definitions tab lists all of the lighting definitions used in your workspace. When you first open the workspace, this tab will be empty. As you add new instruments, their definitions will also be added to this list. Removing the instruments from your workspace will not remove them from the Definitions tab, however. This must be done manually by selecting the definition and clicking on the trash icon at the bottom of the screen. At the top of the left column, there is a search field labeled "filter," which allows you to filter down the list of definitions by name, a great time-saver should you have an expansive list.

Once a definition is selected from the list, its attributes will appear on the right half of the screen and enable you to make any necessary changes to the name, manufacturer, or parameters (Figure 18.4). There are some workflow tools hidden in this area as well. By selecting the checkbox labeled default, you can set any instrument as the default type to be inserted into your patch. This is useful in a lighting rig that has all intelligent lighting fixtures and no conventional lights or vice versa.

In addition, by clicking on the information icon at the end of the intensity row, a hidden menu appears (Figure 18.5). The default setting for DMX values is

Figure 18.5
This hidden menu allows for controlling percentage data, 16-bit resolution, and home position for a given parameter.

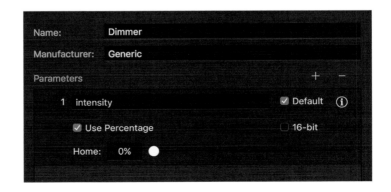

percentage (0–100%), but if you so choose, it can be changed to a raw DMX value (0–255). Some DMX devices use two DMX addresses per parameter in order to give more precision control. If you are using this type of instrument, click on the 16-bit checkbox here. Once you have done so, you will notice that each instance of this definition now takes up two addresses in the patch. Finally, the home slider allows you to set a home position for the control parameter. With devices like a dimmer or a fan on a hazer, the home position should be 0% (meaning it is turned off). Other devices, like an iris, might need a home position of 100% (meaning full open). Many moving head fixtures might have a home position of 50% pan and 50% tilt, meaning the instrument points straight down. If you are unsure, always check with your manufacturer's documentation.

Light Library

The Light Library is almost identical to the Definitions tab of the Light Patch Editor. The key difference being that the Light Library lists all lighting definitions available on your Mac, not only the ones used in your current workspace. To open the Library, select *Window > Light Library*. One interesting connection between the Light Library and the Definitions tab of the Light Patch Editor is the ability to save directly from the Definitions tab into the Library. At the bottom left side of the Definitions tab is a button labeled "Save to library." This will save the selected definitions into the Light Library, provided the definition does not already exist there. Likewise, if a definition from the library has changed inside the definitions tab, you can simply click "Update from library" and the parameters in the definitions tab will be replaced by those already in the library.

18.4 – Putting It All Together

In this section, let us consider a small lighting rig used for an installation. This rig would use four conventional lighting fixtures, four RGB lighting fixtures, a DMX projector dowser, and a hazer for atmospheric effects. For this project, we will patch the instruments and change some of the parameters.

Setting Up Your Lights

The first step to adding these instruments to your QLab workspace is to open the Light Patch Editor. Select the patch tab and then click the "New Instrument" button four times. This should create four instruments listed in chronological order. Provided that dimmer was set as your default instrument, these should each be correct to function as your four conventional lighting fixtures (Figure 18.6).

Figure 18.6
Instruments 1–4
displayed in the
Patch Table.

Next, add another new instrument. This time, though, select the instrument and change its definition in the Instrument Inspector to RGB Fixture with the manufacturer Generic. When looking in the Patch Table, you will see that the address is now set as 5–7. This is because each color uses a specific DMX channel. Repeat this process for instruments 6–8 (Figure 18.7).

For the final two instruments, there is no pre-made definition in the Light Library, so we will need to create one. To do so, first insert the final two instruments into the patch list. Next, click on the Definitions tab and select the plus icon at the bottom of the screen to add a new light definition. For new definitions, be sure to give them as descriptive a name as possible. For my purposes, I will re-name this one Projector Dowser. Next, in the manufacturer field, I will insert City Theatrical. Now, we are ready to add control parameters. To do this, click on the plus icon just above the parameters field. This will assign a new parameter called "empty." Since this value will refer to the position of the flag used to dowse the projector, I will re-name this "Flag Position." Finally, after checking the manufacturer's specifications, I note that the home position should be set at 0%. You can check Figure 18.8 to see if your configuration matches the appropriate setup. When you are satisfied that you've set it up correctly, go ahead and click "Save to library."

The last instrument is a bit more complicated than those we have looked at thus far since it has two control channels that behave in different ways. Most hazers use two DMX addresses: the first one for the hazer output and the second for fan speed. For this setup, add a new definition to the Definitions list and rename it "Radiance Hazer" with "Ultratec" as the manufacturer. Next, click on the add parameters icon and add two new parameters. You will notice the definitions will be highlighted with red until you actually name these parameters. The first one should be named "Haze" and the second one "Fan Speed." Now that these are added, there is one step to make sure it functions

Figure 18.7
Instruments 5–8
displayed in the
Patch Table.
Note that each of
these instruments
requires three
channels of
control.

Figure 18.8
The setup for a
City Theatrical
Projector dowser.

correctly. Open the informational menu for each of the parameters and make sure the home position is set to 0%. If this is not the case, the hazer will blow haze from the moment it receives a signal. For devices such as this, it is incredibly important to double-check the manufacturer's specifications for DMX addressing. In this case, switching the two parameters could mean running the fan instead of the haze and vice versa. Finally, return to the Patch menu and make sure that instrument 9 is assigned to the Projector Dowser definition and Instrument 10 using the Radiance Hazer one. Once this is set up, you should be prepared to begin the process of cueing your show.

Light Cues

Once your lighting system has been set up and QLab is configured to communicate with it, the next step is actually writing some cues. For those who have experience with QLab and are approaching lighting as an extension of the normal QLab command system, the addition of lights is not a difficult leap. If, however, you are coming to QLab for the first time from a traditional lighting console background, there will be a bit of an adjustment period. The following chapter covers how to use the Light Cue and addresses some basic workflow concerns for acclimating yourself to this cue type.

19.1 – Inserting a Light Cue

A Light Cue must first be inserted into your workspace in order to command any attributes of your lighting system. Unlike some Audio or Video cue types, there is no media associated with a Light Cue to drag into the workspace. As such, the primary method for inserting a cue is through the Toolbar, Toolbox, or the keyboard shortcut ⌘6. Once inserted, you are ready to examine the details of a Light Cue in the Inspector.

19.2 – Inspector: Basics and Triggers

Once a Light Cue is inserted into your cue list, the Inspector can be used to access the control functions for this cue. There are four tabs within the Inspector: Basics, Triggers, Levels, and Curve Shape. Each of these tabs contains specific control functions that affect the playback of the given Light Cue. The first tab, Basics, allows for manipulating the baseline information about the Light Cue. The second tab, Triggers, allows for a variety of triggering options. The functions of both the Basics and Triggers tabs are similar to those seen in other cue types examined earlier in the book.

19.3 – Inspector: Levels

The Levels tab shows any active lighting commands and allows you to add new ones or make changes to existing commands. When you first open the tab, it will show an empty window. Here, commands are added to create your lighting looks. The Levels tab is divided into three rows: the Command Line (top), the Lighting Commands List (middle), and the control line.

Command Line

The QLab Command Line is similar in function to the command line of most modern intelligent lighting consoles. In lighting consoles, the command line is a text-driven method of inputting control data. The syntax for the command line varies for different manufacturers. QLab has its own command line language that differs from many consoles. This is addressed in the command line section below.

Add Command

Beside the Command Line entry field is a drop-down menu called Add Command. This is the tactile method of adding lighting commands to a cue. By clicking on the drop-down menu, you will see a list of every lighting instrument or group in your workspace. Selecting one will place a command into the Lighting Commands list for the related instrument or group. Instruments or groups with preexisting commands in the command list will be grayed out.

Prune Commands

Light Cues with a series of commands may have multiple commands that relate to the same instruments. One example is a cue that includes an instrument on its own, as well as being part of a group. In instances where these multiple commands might create confusion, you can use the prune commands function, which removes earlier commands that are superseded by later commands in the same cue. In terms of precedence, commands are executed from top to bottom when in Slider View or left to right/top to bottom when in Tile View.

Safe Sort Commands

Lighting commands added to a Light Cue are displayed in the order they are added to the cue. It can be difficult to find one particular cue if there is a large series of commands. The Safe Sort Commands button will reorganize the commands into alphabetical order based on the instrument name, provided that this sorting does not change the playback. If it would create a change, then the command is left unsorted.

The Lighting Commands List

Once a command has been added to a cue, whether through the command line or the add command button, it will appear in the Lighting Commands List. The list can be viewed as sliders, tiles, or text (Figure 19.1). To change the view type, click on the drop-down menu at the bottom left corner. The slider view shows a horizontal slider with a small circular handle, used for adjusting the parameters. The tile view displays a grouping of cells with a numeric value inside and the instrument number listed below the tile. To change attributes, either click the tile and drag up or down or input a numeric value in the tile and press enter. Finally, the text view is simply a vertical textual listing of the commands using the format x=xx, where x is the instrument name and xx is the percentage. The use of an = is unusual within the context of traditional lighting consoles, which have often used the word "at" or the symbol @ to indicate percentage. The list compiles all commands in the order they are added. This means the oldest commands are at the top of the list when in slider or text view. If in tile view, the order proceeds from left to right. If the command order needs to be changed, you can enter the slider view and grab a command and move it to another place in the list. Finally, commands can be deleted as well. For the slider view, click on the x at the end of the command row. In tile view, hover over the command and an x will appear beside the instrument number. For the text view, simply highlight and delete the command.

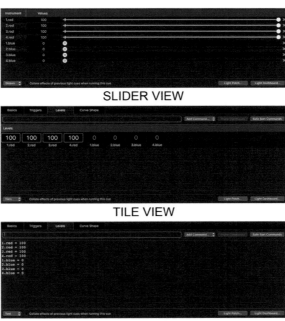

Figure 19.1
Slider view, tile view, and text view.

SLIDER VIEW

TILE VIEW

TEXT VIEW

Design Tips ▼

Live vs. Blind Programming

On conventional lighting consoles, changes added to a cue will be immediately visible onstage. If you want to make a change to a cue without seeing it live onstage, you have to use a blind mode, which changes the cues without displaying the changes live. Within QLab, any changes made to the commands inside of the Light Cue itself will be executed as blind. If you want to see changes in real-time, you have to open the Light Dashboard and make your changes there. In this way, the Dashboard is the "Live" mode controls. The Dashboard will be discussed in Section 19.5.

Collating Effects

At the bottom center of the screen is a checkbox labeled "Collate effects of previous light cues when running this cue." This box enables QLab to run the cue as if all other previous Light Cues have been triggered. Often, the state of a lighting cue is based on a previous cue having been triggered. When running out of order, this might mean that the board operator needs to trigger a certain sequence in order to get a desired look. When using the collated effects setting, this is unnecessary and allows the Light Cue to look the same no matter which cues have been triggered previously.

19.4 – Inspector: Curve Shape

The Curve Shape tab behaves in a similar fashion to other cue types, allowing the programmer to change the curve shape for up fades and down fades while adjusting the fade time. QLab defaults to the linear curve, though custom, S-curve, and Parametric curve options are available as well. Manipulating the custom curve is a process similar to that described in previous chapters as well.

19.5 – The Light Dashboard

As mentioned earlier, the Light Dashboard is used for viewing the live levels of all instruments in your workspace and to make changes that can be viewed in real-time on the stage. As Light Cues are played back, the instrument values are tracked on the Dashboard. To open the Light Dashboard, either select *Window > Light Dashboard*, use the keyboard shortcut of ⇧⌘D, or click the Light Dashboard button in the bottom right corner of the Levels tab. This will open the Dashboard as its own window. Visually, the Light Dashboard resembles some key aspects of the Inspector for Light Cues. Use Figure 19.2 as a reference. Key aspects are listed below.

Figure 19.2
The Light
Dashboard offers
a variety of options
for monitoring
and changing
instrument
parameters.

- **Command Line.** Starting at the top of the window is the Light Command Line for entering command language. This is identical in use to that shown in the Light Cue's Inspector.
- **Over Time.** To the right on the command line is an input labeled "over time." With the command line function, any commands inputted will normally execute with a zero count once you press enter. Sometimes, it is beneficial to insert a command more subtly, over a period of time. By inputting a 3, for instance, the command will gradually fade in over a 3-count after clicking enter. On many lighting consoles, this is represented by the **Sneak** function.
- **Instrument Views.** Like the Inspector mentioned earlier, lighting instruments on the Dashboard can be viewed in different ways. For the Dashboard, this is either Sliders or Tiles (excluding text). Clicking on the drop-down menu allows for selection between the two view types. The Slider view shows the instrument name to the left of the row, followed by the parameter value and a horizontal slider. If a row displays a yellow background, this indicates that a value has been manually adjusted since the Light Cue was triggered. Likewise, if the row selected is a group, there may be multiple yellow ticks that appear on the slider row. This indicates the levels of individual instruments assigned to that group. If an instrument has an arrow beside it, this indicates there are multiple parameters being hidden, and clicking this disclosure arrow will reveal them. With the tile view, changes between cues are indicated by highlighting the entire tile yellow.
- **Latest Light Cue.** In the area below the Lighting Commands List is a note indicating which cue was the latest one fired.
- **Update Latest Cue.** The Update Latest Cue button is used to save any level changes made in the Dashboard since triggering the latest cue. This will make adjustments to the original parameters of the listed cue.

- **Update Originating Cue(s).** QLab operates like a tracking console, meaning that once an instrument is given a value, it will stay at that value until changed by a subsequent cue. Because of this, it is not necessary for every cue to contain control information for every lighting instrument. Even so, the Dashboard will track the status of every instrument whether triggered in the current cue or not. This means that the Dashboard can affect the values started in previous cues. Clicking the update originating cues button will change the values of instruments in the cue or cues that originated the levels, making for a smooth transition between cues.
- **Revert Changes.** The revert changes button simply restores any changed parameters on the Dashboard to those that were previously set to cover the workspace's predetermined panic duration.
- **New Cue with Changes ⌘N.** Clicking this button will insert a new Light Cue into the workspace directly following the selected Light Cue. This new cue will contain parameters for any instruments that have been changed in the Dashboard, disregarding parameters for others. This function allows for a quick method of creating tracking cues.
- **New Cue with All ⇧⌘N.** Clicking on the New Cue with All button creates a new Light Cue following the currently selected cue. Unlike the New with Changes function, however, this one will create a cue with all instruments from your workspace included. This functions similarly to a **Block Cue** on traditional lighting consoles. Any instrument that does not have a current value in the Dashboard will be inputted at an intensity of 0.

19.6 – The DMX Status Window

Another useful tool for lighting is the DMX Status Window, which is accessed through *Window > DMX Status* (Figure 19.3). This window is similar to the active channels view of a traditional lighting console except it lists the activity of all 512 DMX channels in a universe. This window is organized into a table of 32 rows with 16 channels in each row. The purpose of this window is primarily for trouble-shooting any patch issues that may arise. Though you can make changes to DMX levels in this window, these changes cannot be recorded. Note that intensities are listed on a DMX scale of 0–255 rather than a percentage scale.

19.7 – Understanding Lighting Command Language

The textual command language for lighting is a simple approach to setting and changing lighting parameters inside QLab. For every light change, there is a basic text format that instructs QLab how to behave. The basic command

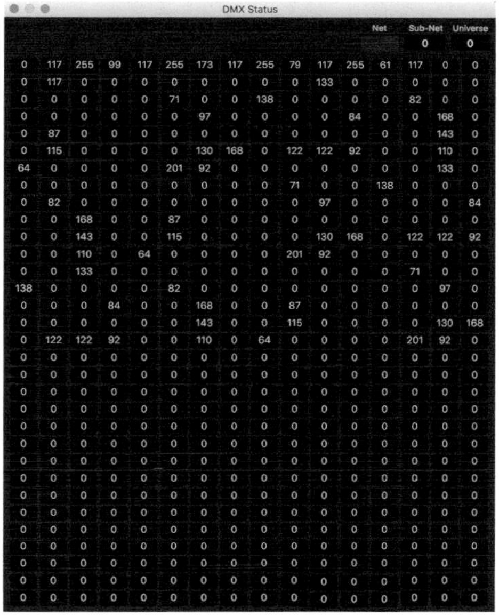

Figure 19.3
The DMX status window tracks the DMX value of all 512 channels of DMX in any given universe. Note that the user can select from separate Nets, Subnets, and Universes.

language follows the format listed below, using either instrument or group as the identifier of what is being controlled. In the case of all instruments or groups, the instrument or group name is used to replace "instrument" or "group." Spaces are optional in the command language. Note that for all examples, the enter key must be pressed to activate the command. In the following examples, this is indicated by [enter] with the brackets used to indicate a hard keystroke on your keyboard, such as [enter] for pressing the enter key or [up] for the up arrow on your keyboard.

instrument = value In this instance, the value will be set for whatever parameter is set as default for the instrument – often intensity. For instance, inputting the command 1=50 would change the default parameter for instrument 1 to 50% (provided you had the instrument set to percentage mode in the patch).
instrument.parameter = value For selecting a specific parameter of an instrument, use this format. Assuming that the instrument in the previous example was an RGB lighting fixture, you could use the command 1.red=25 to set the red cell of this fixture to 25% output. Keep in mind that this uses the precise name of the parameters in the light definition, such as intensity, pan, tilt, edge, zoom, or gobo 1 rotation.
group = value Group behaves in a similar fashion to instruments except it will select all of the instruments inside of the group and apply the parameter to them. For instance, front=50 would take all lights in the Group named "front" and set their default parameters to 50%.
group.parameter = value Finally, using the group.parameter setting allows for selecting individual aspects of a group for control. For example front.green=75 would set the green cells of every instrument in the group named "front" to 75% output.

Selection Ranges and Passing

Selecting a series of instruments or groups is achieved with the dash. For instance, 1–3= 20 indicates instruments 1–3 would be set to 20%. Commas can also be used for a non-sequential range, such as 1,3=50, where instruments 1 and 3 would be set to 50%.

When selecting a range of instruments, it is sometimes useful to exclude certain instruments from your list. Consider the possibility of selecting all of the instruments used for front lighting except for 1, which should remain set at its current levels. Many traditional lighting consoles use the **except** button. For instance, selecting channels 1–20 *except* 3 *at FULL* would then select channels 1–2 and 4–20 and set their intensity to full. With QLab, the **pass** command is used for this function. In the same example shown (Instruments 1–20, excluding 3) the following command would be used: 1–20=100 [enter] 3=pass [enter]. Note that 1–20 must first be entered before inputting the pass for 3.

Pulling Values

One of the features added in V4.1 was the ability to "pull" a value from another cue in your workspace. This is incredibly useful for programming in a style consistent with palettes or presets on traditional lighting consoles. The programming must be done in the command line to achieve this function. I recommend using the pull function to reference cues created in a separate cue list or cue cart so they can be hidden away from your regular cue list. The method for pulling values is shown below.

instrument=cue name In this example, the command tells the named instrument to pull all of its values from cue A, for instance, 15=cue A. Here, Instrument 15 would pull all parameters set for this instrument saved in cue A. To indicate specific parameters only, these parameters must be specified as seen in the next example.
Instrument.parameter=cue name To pull parameters (color, zoom, gobo, etc.) you must indicate the specific parameter from which to pull. In the following example, 1.color=cue A, the command sets the color of Instrument 1 to that used in cue A.
group=cue name Group behaves in a similar fashion to instruments except it will select all of the instruments inside of the group and pull the parameters to them. For instance, front=cue A would take all lights in the Group named "front" and set their default parameters to those found in cue A.

Up Arrow

The up arrow is used for selecting the previous command and experimenting with its levels. For instance, a lighting designer often experiments in bumping the levels of a certain light several times before settling on the perfect level.

In this case, the following command could be used to experiment without inputting as much text: Frontcools=80 [enter]. This sets the output of the Frontcools group to 80%. To adjust this quickly, simply click [up] (the up arrow on your keyboard). This will automatically recall the previous command with the value highlighted. In this instance, perhaps the LD thinks the light is too bright. To change the value, simply type in 75 [enter]. If the value needs to be changed again, simply repeat the process until the values are at the perfect level.

Ad-Hoc Groups

Sometimes, you might need to create an ad-hoc group, a short-term grouping of instruments or other groups for control. To create this, simply enclose the name of the instruments or groups inside of brackets, and QLab will treat them as a group. For instance, [1-4, 10, front]=50 creates a new group slider (or tab) labeled [1–4,front] that can be used to control each of the instruments assigned to this group.

19.8 – Cueing Examples

For the following examples, we will be using the previous lighting rig mentioned in Chapter 18. This setup features four conventional ERS fixtures and four generic RGB fixtures. The design is for an installation piece focusing on a sculpture in the center of a small room. This setup will use the ERS lighting fixtures with gobos inserted to create patterned textures on the sculpture, and the RGB fixtures for their color-mixing capabilities.

Use Figure 19.4 as a point of reference to see how the room is set up. The sculpture is square with four ERS fixtures pointed at it on diagonals and four RGB fixtures, one each side of the square. The four ERS fixtures are each individually controlled by dimmers addressed as 1–4. Each of the RGB fixtures requires three channels for DMX addressing. This means that 16 addresses will be required to control the eight separate instruments.

When creating a traditional light plot, the lighting designer assigns a control channel to each instrument on the plot that corresponds to its patched address. Keep in mind that you can keep this convention with QLab by viewing the instrument name as a control channel, or you could use more descriptive titles, such as "front 1" or "side 1". In my example, I have chosen to name the instruments in the typical channel format, while giving descriptive information in the notes panel of the patch (Figure 19.5). The following steps explain a simple cue sequence for creating different lighting looks. For each step, we will use slightly different techniques to emphasize the flexible approach to programming.

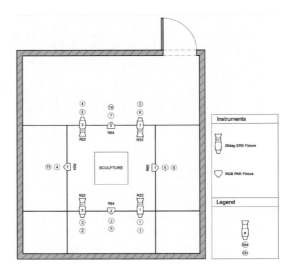

Figure 19.4
The light plot includes the instrument name and other pertinent information to setting up the patch and cueing.

Figure 19.5
The patch for this simple design includes all of the information necessary for QLab to communicate with the dimmers and light fixtures in addition to notes that clarify the purpose of each instrument.

Step One: As the audience enters, there will be two of the ERS fixtures at low levels illuminating the sculpture from opposite angles. To achieve this, click on the Light Cue icon in the Toolbar to insert a new Light Cue into the workspace. To activate two lights opposite to one another on the plot, click the "Add Command" drop-down and select Instrument 1 and Instrument 4. This will add these instruments into the list as either sliders or tiles (depending on the selected view). Select both instruments and increase their value to 30. This will send a signal to the dimmers powering both instruments, telling them to power the lights to 30% capacity (Figure 19.6).

Step Two: The next step of the process involves creating a color wash of blue on the entire sculpture. To create this effect, insert a second Light

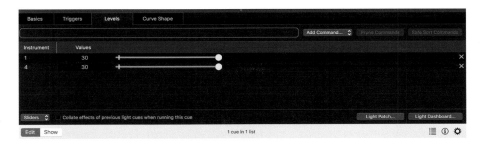

Figure 19.6
Step one adds
two lights at a low
intensity.

Cue into the workspace. In the command line of this cue, insert the command 5–8.blue=65. This will insert four sliders for the blue cells of instrument 5–8 with the value set at 65. Each slider will be named using the instrument name and parameter (e.g., 5.blue, 6.blue, etc.) as seen in Figure 19.7.

Step Three: The next cue needs to change the color of two of the RGB fixtures, take out instruments 1 and 4, and bring up instruments 2 and 3. In order to do this, open the Light Dashboard instead of working specifically in the Inspector of the Light Cue. If you click on the arrow beside each of the RGB fixtures, it will open the grouping and show the individual sliders for each parameter. Unlike the Inspector view of Light Cue, the Dashboard shows every active instrument, whether it was activated in the most recent cue or not (Figure 19.8).

Step Four: In the Dashboard, pull down the levels of instruments 1 and 4 to 0. Notice they will now be highlighted yellow. Next, pull the sliders for instruments 2 and 4 up to 60%. To change the colors of lighting on two sides of the sculpture, select instruments 5 and 7 and then bring down their blue value to 0, while increasing the red value to 100%. To this point, this has only made changes to the current cue. The final step to making a new cue is to click the "New Cue with Changes" button. This will create a Light Cue 3 with value changes programmed in for eight separate parameters.

Step Five: To this point, the programming has used the default fade time of 5 seconds. If you wanted the transition from Light Cue 2 into 3 to be subtler, this might be too quick. In order to change the timing, double-click

Figure 19.7
Step two adds all
four of the RGB
fixtures at 65%,
in a blue wash.
Not shown here
are instruments
1 and 4 from
cue 1, which will
still be running
at 30%. These
lights will stay
on until another
cue changes their
attributes.

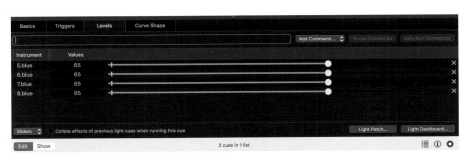

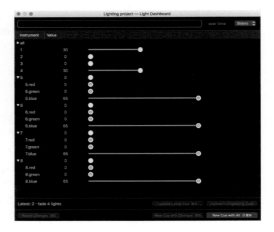

Figure 19.8
The Dashboard shows all of the instruments in your workspace and their current output levels.

on the action of Light Cue 3 in the cue row and change it to 12. This will effectively create a 12-second cross-fade from Light Cue 2 into 3. Experiment with different timing on all of your cues until you get a good feel for what looks right.

Project 19.1 ▼

Creating a Chase Effect

Since QLab does not currently have a lighting effects generator, creating effects like a chase sequence still has to be done manually. This is a relatively simple setup, though it certainly requires many more steps than when using a generator. To create effects, it is often best to create a series of Light Cues inside of a Group and add a Start Cue to loop back to the beginning. Since Fade Cues do not affect Light Cues, you cannot simply Fade and Stop the Group as you would with other cue types. Instead, you have to stop the playback of your loop and trigger a new Light Cue that overwrites the parameters of your previous Light Cues. The following steps take you through this process for a simple RGB color chase using four fixtures.

Step 1: Download Project 19.1 from the companion website. Since you may not have a similar Art-Net interface or one with different settings, many of the cues may show a red X. This is to be expected, however you can still observe how the cueing works.

Step 2: Open the light patch. You will see it is already set up for this project, with four separate RGB fixtures named 1–4. These will be the four instruments used for creating your chase effect. To start programming, create two Group Cues numbered 1 and 2. These will hold all of the necessary cues to create and end the chase. Name the first group "chase" and the second one "fade out chase."

Step 3: Insert three Light Cues and a Start Cue (in that order) into the first Group Cue. Change their cue numbering to 1.1, 1.2, 1.3, and 1.4. These cues will be used to flash from red, to green, to blue, and back to the beginning again. For cue 1.1, select the Levels tab in the Inspector and input the command 1–4.red=100; then press [enter]. This sets the red value of each instrument to 100%.

Step 4: Select cue 1.2. In the command line of this cue, insert the command 1–4.red=0 and press [enter]. This will take out the red from the previous cue. Next, insert the command 1–4.green=100 and [enter]. This will insert green as the color for all four instruments at 100%.

Step 5: Select cue 1.3. In the command line, insert the command 1–4.green=0 and [enter]. This will take out the green. Next, insert the command 1–4.blue=100 and [enter]. This will set the color as blue for all four instruments at 100%. At this point all of the cues are established for changing the colors. There are a few changes that need to be made in order to make the cues loop, though.

Step 6: Assign the target of cue 1.4 (the Start Cue) as cue 1.1, the first Light Cue in your sequence. Finally, add a pre-wait of 1 second to cues 1.2–1.4 and add an Auto-continue to cues 1.1–1.3. Check the programming shown in Figure 19.9 to make sure yours matches.

Figure 19.9 Your programming should match that shown here. Pay particular attention to the pre-wait times and continue statuses.

Step 7: As the programming currently is, there will be a problem once the first loop occurs. This is because cue 1.3 has the blue up at 100% then it loops back to cue 1.1, which does not have a parameter change set for the blue. As a result, if left this way, the loop would keep up the blue color in addition to red once cue 1.1 activates. In order to fix this, you must go into cue 1.1 and set a value of 0% for all of the blue lights. To do so, input 1–4.blue=0 in the command line and then [enter]. This will complete the setup for making your Group Cue function as a chase.

(Continued)

Step 8: Once the chase has begun, you need a way to exit the Group Cue's playback and bring up a new Light Cue. For this, go to cue 2. The first step necessary is to add four Stop Cues. Name them 2.1, 2.2, 2.3, and 2.4. Assign each cue's target as 1.1, 1.2, 1.3, and 1.4, respectively. This will cause all of the cues in your chase group to stop playback.

Step 9: Simply stopping playback would keep the latest triggered Light Cue up as the look. In order to circumvent this, insert a new Light Cue into the "fade out chase" group and set a new look. This will bring up a new overall look to replace the single-color wash left behind. The fade time is set at a default of 5 seconds. You can experiment with setting different times and seeing how this affects your cross-fade.

Step 10: Select cue 2, the "fade out chase" Group Cue. In the Inspector, select the Mode tab. Click the checkbox labeled "start all children simultaneously." This will trigger all of the cues inside the group at the same time.

Step 11: Test your playback. By triggering cue 1, the chase should begin. Once cue 2 triggers, it should stop playback of all cues in Group 1 and bring up cue 2.4, the new lighting look. Check Project 19.1 Complete to see if your programming matches.

PART V
QLab Show Control and Networking

Show Control Systems

The entertainment design and technology industry has evolved over the years to include practices from a number of differing fields. Each area brings its own unique equipment and control systems into the mix, requiring today's practitioners to have a working vocabulary of many fields and the ability to collaborate with more production members than ever before. As production technology has evolved, so too has the need for simplifying methods of control across a wide range of production elements. This is the nature of show control: a method of centralizing control for a number of differing production elements.

20.1 – Terminology

The discussion of show control can be a confusing endeavor without a basic introduction to terminology. The following section covers some of the fundamental terms to understanding show control.

Entertainment Control Systems

For every production, there are a number of different elements that must work together seamlessly: sound, lighting, projections, special effects, etc. For each of these different areas, there will be one or more **systems**, or a set of elements working together as parts of an interconnecting network. An **entertainment control system** is the combination of all of the necessary equipment required to control a live production area. For instance, a lighting control system is traditionally the combination of a lighting console (or any controller), dimmers, circuits, and cabling necessary to power the lighting equipment and send control signals to intelligent lighting.

Standards

When talking about entertainment control systems, we are referring to literally thousands of unique proprietary systems created to work with specialized equipment. This equipment can be anything from sound mixers, to lighting consoles, moving lights, confetti cannons, projectors, foggers, automated scenery/rigging control, and more. Each of these areas also has numerous manufacturers creating equipment that has its own individualized control system architecture.

The one thing that enables all of these systems to work together is standards. Regarding control systems, a **standard** refers to a commonly accepted working practice or protocol that governs how different manufacturers can create products that interact well with one another. The most important type of standard concerning show control is the **open standard**, a standard commonly created by bringing together a group of industry professionals to create a mutually beneficial standard practice publicly available for the market. This standard may relate to how hardware is created or, in the case of a **communication standard**, what type of language is used to communicate between varying pieces of hardware. In the early days of entertainment control, there were many proprietary standards created by and for individual manufacturers that did not work well with equipment from other manufacturers. This practice became costly and frustrating for the end-user, as you would never be guaranteed that equipment would work together at different venues (or sometimes even at the same venue). This led to the creation of entertainment industry standards such as MIDI, MSC, DMX 512-A, and OSC. In addition to standards created for our industry, we obviously benefit from industry standards in the telecommunications and computer industry regarding networking, data transmission, and more. The table below lists some of the most common standards for the entertainment industry that are natively supported in QLab 4, all of which you should familiarize yourself with.

MIDI	**Musical Instrument Digital Interface.** One of the most widely utilized standards for communication within entertainment control systems. Standard maintained by the MIDI Manufacturers Association. www.midi.org.
MSC	**MIDI Show Control.** A subset of the MIDI protocol dealing specifically with triggering and controlling entertainment control systems from a remote source. www.midi.org.
TCP	**Transmission Control Protocol.** TCP is the most commonly used communication protocol used across the Internet. The term TCP/IP refers to TCP sent over an Internet Protocol (IP) network. TCP is a robust communication method that creates numbered packets of data. This numbering method assures that the recipient receives all data transmitted by the sender. In addition, it uses a "handshake" method of having the receiver send a message back to the sender saying it has received the message. If something is lost along the way, the sender simply re-sends it. TCP data packets are also checked for errors. QLab does not currently support outgoing TCP communication, but it does receive TCP for incoming connections.

UDP	**User Datagram Protocol.** UDP is one of the common methods for communicating data over an IP network. With UDP, packets of information are sent from the source to the receiver. Unlike TCP, UDP does not offer a "handshake" or error-checking. As a result, UDP is a faster communication protocol with less "overhead" in your messages. QLab does support outgoing UDP messages through the Network Cue.
DMX 512-A	**Digital MultipleX.** Originally developed by the United States Institute for Theatre Technology (USITT), now maintained by the Professional Lighting and Sound Association (PLASA). This standard describes a method of digital transmission between lighting consoles and equipment. Though originally intended exclusively for lighting, the standard has been adopted for use in special effects (smoke, fog, and haze), video systems, animatronics, and more.
Art-Net	**Art-Net** is a royalty-free communications protocol used for transmitting DMX 512-A and Remote Device Management Protocol (RDM) over an Internet Protocol (IP) network. Art-Net sends data via UDP and allows a server (light console, QLab, computer) to communicate with a node (either a translator device or an Art-Net capable piece of equipment). QLab uses Art-Net to send Lighting Cues.
OSC	**Open Sound Control.** OSC is a protocol for communication between computers, sound synthesizers, and multimedia devices that is optimized for real-time control over networks. www.opensoundcontrol.org. QLab 4 can send and receive OSC commands.

Show Control

In short, show control is the method of linking together multiple entertainment control systems into a master system. It is basically a system that controls other systems. It can be software-based or dedicated hardware.

Network

In basic terms, a network refers to a system of interconnected people or objects that share resources in some way. For technology purposes, we usually refer to a network as a connection of one or more computers that are linked together in order to share files and resources and allow communication/command signals to be transferred in both directions. In the most basic type of connection, a **point-to-point** interface, each device would be physically connected to any device it needed to share information with. This obviously creates a wiring nightmare and is cost-prohibitive. The more common approach would be to create a true network, in which each system device, or **node**, connects to a centralized data pathway to communicate with the **host**, a networked computer that communicates data out the nodes.

There are a number of terms you have likely heard like LAN (Local Area Network) or WLAN (Wireless Local Area Network) referring to networks. These are common in entertainment networks as well. Most of our day-to-day experience with networking comes from the Internet. Whether you use an Ethernet cable or a wireless router to connect to the Internet, you are connecting to a network. With the world of entertainment control systems, though, it is equally common to see our equipment networked through DMX and MIDI cables in addition to Ethernet cable runs. This leads to our next big concept to understanding show control: entertainment control systems.

20.2 – Entertainment Control Systems

Since there are so many different categories of entertainment control systems, it might be beneficial to examine a few of the most common types that can be used in conjunction with QLab. The following section covers three such areas and offers a basic introduction to terminology associated with each system. This is by no means an exhaustive study of these areas, but should serve as a useful platform to discuss control system architecture before delving into show control.

Sound Control Systems

Since much of the first half of the book was dedicated to sound systems, you should already be familiar with many of the basic concepts of the sound system. As we have already seen, QLab serves as a powerful controller for both reinforcement and playback systems. In addition to QLab and a digital audio interface, though, there might be a number of different pieces of equipment connected to your sound system like a mixer, microphones, signal processing, amplifiers, and speakers. Listed below is some of the more common equipment with which QLab might communicate.

MIDI Keyboards/Sequencers: QLab can both receive and send MIDI signals from a variety of sources. In this fashion QLab can either trigger an effect on an external MIDI device or be triggered by a MIDI signal sent from the device.

Sound Mixers: Most digital sound mixers can both send and receive MIDI signals. One great method of utilizing this function is to send a MIDI signal from QLab to change a pre-programmed attribute of your mixer. For instance, you can send a signal from QLab to your mixer to recall a scene from its memory with presets like EQ, reverb, compressions, etc.

Timecode: Timecode is a method of ensuring multiple devices sync with one another for playback. QLab allows for all cues to be triggered by an incoming timecode. In addition, the Timecode Cue allows for QLab to send a timecode out to any MIDI device.

Lighting Control Systems

Lighting control systems can vary in a number of ways, but all share many common attributes. For every system, there will be a lighting controller, dimmers, circuits, and lighting instruments. Lighting control systems utilize the DMX 512-A standard practice for communication. In addition, most lighting consoles also have the ability to send and receive MIDI signals.

Lighting Controller: The lighting controller can be a dedicated console or a piece of software running on a computer. The controller sends DMX control signals that interface with the dimmers and, in some instances, lighting fixtures and accessories. With the release of Version 4, QLab can now function as a lighting console itself (provided you have the Pro Lighting license). All of the Pro Licenses, however, offer the possibility of interacting with your lighting control system via MIDI or OSC.

Dimmers: Dimmers are specialized devices that regulate the flow of voltage out to a circuit. The control signal from the lighting controller tells the dimmers what percentage of voltage to output to the circuits.

Circuits: A circuit is the physical connection through which a lighting instrument receives electricity. There are a number of different connector types, from Edison to stage pin, to twist lock.

Lighting Instruments: Lighting instruments can be either conventional or intelligent in nature. **Conventional lighting fixtures** allow for control of intensity (brightness). These lighting instruments only need electricity to operate. **Intelligent Lighting Fixtures** feature a wide range of control features such as angle, rotation, intensity, color, strobe, textures, and beam shaping. These intelligent fixtures require both electricity and a DMX control signal from the lighting controller to operate. In addition to lighting instruments, there may also be **lighting accessories**, such as color scrollers, gobo spinners, irises, or more that are also controlled by DMX signals.

Video/Projection Systems

Most video systems comprise one or more computers working in tandem to output a video signal to one or more displays or projectors. Video systems typically utilize IP/Ethernet connections for control.

Video Playback Software: Control software like QLab is often used for video playback in video systems. When used as a stand-alone method, the software triggers playback and outputs it through the computer's video card(s).

Video Servers: Video servers are computer-based hardware dedicated to providing video signals. Unlike a typical computer, the video server is utilized for only one function. A high-end video server can play back multiple simultaneous video streams synchronized with one another.

Projectors/Displays: Projectors and displays receive their signal from some type of data input, whether it be an HDMI or DVI cable. In addition, most projectors these days are also equipped with IP connections. By networking your projectors over IP, there are a number of tasks that can be centrally controlled from QLab or proprietary projector management programs, such as powering on/off, adjusting focus, keystone correction, color alignment, brightness, and more.

Dowsers: A dowser is a mechanical method of eliminating the excess light spill given off by a projector even when the screen is blacked out. It often utilizes a flag on a motorized arm that drops over the projector lens to block light output. Many dowsers utilize DMX as a method to trigger dowsing. It is for this reason that you may often find elements of a video system being controlled by a lighting console. Since QLab 4 now offers DMX control, this function can be achieved through QLab itself.

Timecode: Since most video systems must offer synchronized playback with audio feeds, Timecode is an essential component. If using an external time clock, QLab audio playback can be triggered via Timecode to sync with external video playback.

Additional Control Systems

Though the three entertainment control systems listed above are most commonly associated with QLab, there are a number of other control systems that could be controlled by QLab. For example, a number of additional control systems (automated scenery, fog, haze, pyrotechnics, confetti cannons, etc.) are readily controlled by DMX 512-A. Though QLab 4 natively sends DMX signals, it can also interface with another computer or lighting console on the network via MIDI and trigger its control, which would then activate that control system. One example of this might be sending a MIDI signal to a lighting console that would control both lights and special effects via DMX signal transmission.

20.3 – Show Control Systems

QLab show control covers a wide array of possibilities and, as such, features a number of variables regarding how a show control network might be set up. Depending on the nature of your show control needs, you might have one or more additional systems connected to your QLab control computer. At the heart of QLab's show control abilities are two main cue types: the Network Cue and the MIDI Cue. Through the use of these two cue types, QLab can control a wide array of devices. Listed below are some of the common configurations that might be used to set up a QLab show control network for various entertainment control systems.

Sound Control Systems

Regarding sound, QLab has the potential to function as its own sound system or to interface with other sound equipment or computers. The two main methods of control are OSC and MIDI. To control another computer running QLab, network the two computers together via Ethernet and send a QLab or OSC message via a Network Cue to trigger a specific cue number and command type. To interface with other MIDI hardware, you can send a MIDI message across either MIDI cable or Ethernet. Many USB or FireWire audio devices also have built-in MIDI ports for sending MIDI messages. For both OSC and MIDI, a destination must be established in the cue settings to assign which device the signal will be routed to.

Lighting Control Systems

As mentioned numerous times previously, QLab 4 can now function as a lighting console, sending DMX to communicate with various elements of your lighting system. In some instances, this eliminates the need for a separate lighting console altogether. This may not always be the case for your particular production, however. It is still likely that you may find yourself using QLab as a controller to interface with your lighting control system.

Most lighting control systems have the ability to both input and output MIDI messages. This means that these lighting consoles can both be triggered by QLab and/or send MIDI messages to QLab for triggering cues within the workspace. Most lighting consoles feature a standard MIDI connector for both input and output. This provides for the use of MIDI Show Control as well as Timecode. In addition, some lighting consoles offer an Ethernet port for network communication, enabling the use of Art-Net, OSC, and UDP. In this case, QLab could be connected to the lighting console to send and receive MIDI, OSC, UDP, and Timecode control signals.

Video/Projection Control Systems

Video control systems could be set up using a number of different configurations, from using QLab to control displays to networking several computers running QLab together or even sending a control signal to a video server. For all but the most basic needs, your video control system will send and receive messages across a LAN network between computers.

20.4 – Show Control Considerations

As seen above, there are a number of different ways that QLab can interface with various entertainment control systems. The bottom line is assessing the needs for your individual project and considering all the variables: equipment owned by the producing entity, budget to acquire necessary equipment, personnel available for running the show, amount of space available at the performance space for said personnel, or even union contracts stipulating personnel numbers. Not every project is the same, and just because you *can* centralize show control to one computer does not always mean you *should*.

For educational theatre there are often numerous crew members available to run control systems and, though it might be tempting to streamline control, it is beneficial for students to learn how to operate the equipment. For the small storefront theatre, there is often no space for multiple board operators, and you will find one stage manager controlling all control systems from one small booth. In this case, using QLab to control multiple aspects might be desirable. Should you decide that a show control setup is the right choice for your production, there will be a number of steps necessary to integrating control into one network.

The most important step to creating a successfully integrated show control system is planning. Ideally, all designers will meet with stage management and create a thorough list of all cues in the appropriate order. Once all of these cues have been organized, this will be the foundation for creating a master QLab workspace that sends control signals out to various entertainment control systems across the network. As changes occur during the tech process, they must be meticulously noted and changed in the workspace, or else one change might throw off the sequence for the entire system. A preferable option to this might be each design area having its own QLab computer with its separate cue lists being triggered by one central show controller running QLab. Of course, the cueing process for this is still rather time consuming, as every trigger must be programmed into the main computer, but it does free up each design team to program on its own workspace and not have to compete for programming time (or inadvertently damage someone else's cueing).

A word of caution: completely automated show control systems seem to work best in rigidly choreographed productions like dance concerts. In more organic or improvisational productions, this method may not work as well. There are many challenges to creating a successful show control system, but the rewards are well worth it in the long run.

Understanding OSC and Network Cues

One of QLab's greatest strengths is its support for the Open Sound Control (OSC) protocol, a standard for computers and devices to communicate over a network. OSC can be sent or received by QLab, which means that you can use QLab to control other OSC-compliant software/hardware or control QLab from the software/hardware in question. The following chapter examines the relationship between QLab and OSC and some of the ways in which OSC can be used.

21.1 – What Is OSC?

OSC (Open Sound Control) is a protocol for communicating between computers, sound synthesizers, and other multimedia devices across a network. Though somewhat similar to MIDI in function, OSC is a high-resolution content format with a dynamic, URL-style naming convention for versatile control. One of its greatest advantages is the ability to enact real-time sound and media control over both local area and wide area networks (LANs/WANs). OSC was created at the University of California, Berkeley's Center for New Music and Audio Technologies (CNMAT) and has since branched out as a content format used in numerous applications outside of digital music. To read more about the OSC Specification, visit opensoundcontrol.org.

All devices that use OSC have an individual dictionary of their command. For instance, QLab has its own API (Application Program Interface) for OSC that allows it to be controlled by any device or software that can transmit OSC messages. The entire dictionary can be found online at http://figure53.com/docs/qlab/v4/scripting/osc-dictionary-v4/. This function means that you can use programs like TouchOSC or devices like the ETC EOS family of lighting consoles to send OSC messages to QLab.

QLab receives OSC messages through TCP and UDP over a network. All devices must be on the same network, with the same subnet, and using specific IP addresses in order to effectively communicate with one another. Control networks are quickly becoming an essential skill for designers and technicians in the entertainment industry. The subject of networking is far too large a concept to effectively cover in this text. For further reading, I would recommend *Show Networks and Control Systems* by John Huntington and his blog at controlgeek.net.

OSC commands can be used to control simple aspects of your workspace like triggering go, panic, pause, etc. These are referred to as **workspace level commands**, as they are commands directed specifically to your workspace. One of the benefits of OSC is that the language is so easy to interpret. For instance, the command /go sent to QLab from another device will result in triggering GO in your workspace. The same is true of commands such as /panic, or /save.

Using OSC is a no-brainer in a number of different production scenarios. It is a robust, easy to understand communication standard that can be run over wired or wireless networks. In addition, it uses readily available networking equipment such as routers and Ethernet cabling, unlike the specialized MIDI cables used in MIDI installations. It is important, however, to recognize that setting up a network is a specialized skillset that requires knowledge and time to implement. You need to have an understanding of network switching, IP addressing, and subnets. This becomes all the more important if you are coordinating multiple departments together into one network. These days, lighting, sound, media, and more all utilize networking. It seems as if we are approaching a point where it might be advantageous to have a network coordinator as a job description along with our electricians, sound engineers, and stagehands.

One final word of warning related to the use of wireless networks. Though wireless has become increasingly dependable over the years, there is still the concern of wireless interference and security. In a building full of Wi-Fi routers, cell phones, and wireless headsets, interference can prove to be an issue. Always leave plenty of time to test in show conditions and see if interference will be an issue in your space. Also, with an audience who each is likely to have handheld devices that can connect to wireless networks, it should go without saying how important it is to secure your wireless network and keep uninvited guests from logging in.

21.2 – OSC Settings

Like many of the other cue types examined earlier in the text, OSC Cues settings are found by clicking on the Workspace Settings icon in the lower right hand corner of the screen. Once you have opened this, select the OSC Controls

Figure 21.1
The OSC Controls
settings.

button to the left of the screen. When you click this button, a window will open to the right that features a number of control parameters (see Figure 21.1).

Like Hotkeys and MIDI controls, your QLab workspace can be programmed to respond to certain OSC commands. To enable this function, click on the checkbox labeled "Use OSC Controls." Without selecting this box, your workspace will not respond to incoming OSC commands. You can assign an optional passcode by clicking on the "Use Passcode" checkbox. When selected, all clients wishing to access your workspace will be required to give the four-digit passcode. In addition, by clicking the "New" button, QLab will generate a random code.

One important aspect of the OSC Controls window is the display of your computer's current IP address. Knowing this address is essential to setting up OSC patches. In addition to the IP address, this area also tells some important information about ports. When using QLab OSC controls, QLab will listen to TCP and UDP port 53000. If using UDP, QLab will respond using port 53001.

At the bottom of the OSC Controls window, you will see a list of controls that can all be set to respond to OSC commands. In order to assign the desired OSC command, the code can either be written directly into the slot to the right of the control, or you can click the "Capture" button and then send the desired command from the OSC host running on your system. Once QLab "hears" the command, it will be recorded, and the QLab command will be triggered if the message is sent again.

Settings: Network

The second OSC-related setting is located roughly halfway up the list on the left of the screen and is simply called "Network." The Network settings tab controls the output patch for Network Cues in your workspace. In order to send OSC commands from one QLab computer to another, you must set up a network patch in the Network settings window (Figure 21.2). Your local computer running QLab will be listed as "localhost" by default with a port of 53000. In

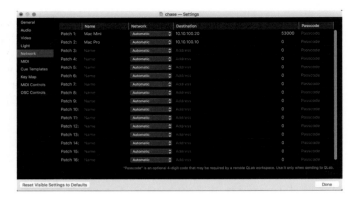

Figure 21.2
The Network
Settings window.

order to set up the patch to communicate with other QLab computers, you will need to open the OSC Controls panel in QLab for each additional computer and note the IP address. In addition, note whether the computer has a passcode assigned. Input the IP addresses into the Network patch row with the port of 53000. If a passcode is required, input this into the passcode column. Once you have managed your list of networked computers, click on the done button and return to your workspace.

Design Tips ▼

Networking Options

There are a number of options for networking together different QLab computers. The following section details three common options.

Ethernet Connection: When using just two computers, the easiest method is to simply connect them with an Ethernet cable. An interconnect cable is unnecessary for newer Macs. In order to network the two computers together, you should turn off the Wi-Fi on both computers to limit interference. After connecting the two computers with the Ethernet cable and inputting the appropriate IP addresses in the OSC Settings patch, you will be able to send OSC controls from one QLab computer to another.

Networking via Router: For instances of multiple computers needing to interact with one another, the best method is to connect the computers with a router. A router is a small device that joins multiple networks together, typically using a wireless or wired IP (Internet Protocol). Essentially, a router works as a gateway device to link together multiple computers in order to communicate with one another on the same system.

One important aspect to remember about routers is that many utilize Dynamic Host Configuration Protocol (DHCP): a network protocol that can change the IP address of devices logged into it from time to time. Since QLab depends on the computers always utilizing the same IP address, it is a good idea to disable DHCP settings on your router or to use manually assigned IP addresses outside of the router's DHCP range. This will guarantee that each QLab machine will have a consistent IP address each time it is booted.

Wireless Networking: Another method for networking is to create a wireless computer-to-computer network (often referred to as an ad-hoc wireless network). In order to do so, click on the Airport status icon in your Mac's Menu Bar (upper right corner). Click on the Create Network button. A pop-up menu will appear reading, "Create a computer-to-computer network." The network name will default to your computer's name or serial number. I recommend creating a specific name for your purposes, like "QLab." If you want to add a password, click on the security button and select either 40-bit WEP or 128-bit WEP. Input a password that fits the parameters listed, and then click the button labeled "Create." This will create a wireless network that can be logged onto from other computers. After all computers are logged into the same wireless network, you will be able to send OSC controls from one QLab computer to another.

21.3 – Network Cues

We have looked at how QLab can be configured to respond to OSC commands, but one of the greatest strengths of QLab 4 is its ability to natively send network messages from one computer to another. This is achieved through the **Network Cue**. The Network Cue allows QLab to send messages through your Mac's network connection. Currently, these message types are restricted to OSC messages, QLab messages (a specific OSC message type for communication within QLab itself), and UDP messages. To insert a Network Message, click on the Network Cue button in the Toolbar or Toolbox. The following section details how to use the Network Cue, once inserted into your Workspace.

Inspector: Basics and Triggers

Like other cue types, the Basics tab features the common naming, pre/post-wait, continue status, and notes. The Triggers tab includes Hotkey, MIDI, Wall Clock, and Timecode triggering options as well as how playback of this cue will affect others in the cue list. These controls do not differ from the ones we covered in earlier chapters.

Inspector: Settings

The Settings tab for Network Cues is the main method for editing your cue information. The first interface listed in the Settings tab is "Destination." By clicking on this drop-down menu, you can choose the routing of your network signal from the entire list of network devices running on your system. Each one will be listed as a unique name, coinciding with the name given in the Network Settings window.

The second interface, labeled "Type," is a drop-down menu that allows for the selection of three message types: OSC message, QLab message, or UDP message. Depending on the message type chosen, the bottom row of the window will change. If OSC message is chosen, then a blank input window will appear in which the OSC address and arguments should be inserted. For QLab messages, there will be a cue number slot and command type. Finally, for UDP messages, there will be a blank screen similar to the OSC command in which raw text is inputted to send UDP messages. Of note, there is a "Send" button in the upper right corner that can be clicked to send a test signal out without actually triggering the Network Cue.

OSC Messages

The OSC message type is used for creating custom messages. With a little experimentation, you can learn how to use these as complex tools for controlling your QLab workspaces. OSC commands are written in the text field as simple plain text, using spaces to separate certain command aspects. There are workspace-level commands, such as /go or /panic, that send out the equivalent of a keyboard command to your workspace. There are also cue-level commands, which are used to send messages specifically to one or more cues. These commands always begin with /cue. The command structure for these cues is always /cue/{identifier}/{command}. In this structure, {identifier} is a bit of text that directs QLab where to send the command, and {command} is the command type, such as go, panic, pause, or delete. For instance, the message /cue/{1}/start would send out a message to cue 1 in your workspace and start the cue's playback. When using the cue-level controls, there are five important identifiers to understand. These are listed below:

- **Targeting a Cue Number:** To target a specific cue, use the command /cue/{x} in which you replace the x with your chosen cue number. For instance, /cue/{12} would target cue 12.
- **Target All Selected Cues:** To target one or more selected cues, use the following command: /cue/selected.
- **Target the Standby Cue:** Using the command /cue/playhead will target the cue that is in the standby position.

- **Using a Wildcard:** In programming terms, a wildcard is a single charac- ter (often an asterisk) used to represent a series of characters or an empty string. This is often used as a time-saving feature in file searches so you don't have to input the full name. In QLab, the OSC wildcard identifier is an aster- isk. When using a wildcard, it can be placed at the beginning or end of a string. For instance, /cue/*3 would select any cue with a 3 at the end of its cue number (3, 43, Tango3). Likewise, using the command /cue/3* would select any cue with the number 3 at the beginning of its cue number, such as 3, 30, or 3blindmice. This can be a time-saver, but don't forget that it could accidentally select unintended cues if you are not specific enough in your wildcard placement.
- **Using a Cue ID:** To target a cue using its Cue ID, use the command /cue_ id/{x} in which you replace {x} with the ID of the cue you want to target.

Commands

There are thousands of commands within QLab's OSC dictionary that can enable a wide range of programming options. Included below are just a few of the more common cue-level commands that can be used in OSC messages. Each would begin with the message /cue/{cue_number}. As mentioned earlier in Section 21.1, the entire OSC dictionary can be found online at Figure 53's website. I would recommend a thorough examination of this document in order to better understand how to implement OSC messaging through QLab.

/cue/{cue_number}/continueMode {number} This OSC message is used to set the continue mode of a given cue. The {number}value sets the continue mode: 0 = no continue, 1 = Auto-continue, and 3 = Auto-follow.

/cue/{cue_number}/load This message is used to load a specified cue.

/cue/{cue_number}/notes {string} This OSC message is used to create a note for a specific cue. When inserting the note inside the {string} value, the note will be saved to a specified cue.

/cue/{cue_number}/panic This message will panic (fade out and stop) the playback of a specified cue.

/cue/{cue_number}/pause This OSC message will pause the playback of the specified cue, allowing any Audio Unit effects to naturally decay.

/cue/{cue_number}/start This message starts playback of a specified cue.

/cue/{cue_number}/stop This message stops playback of a specified cue.

QLab Messages

The second message type in Network Cues is the QLab message. QLab 4 has done the heavy lifting for you in creating a control architecture of pre-programmed OSC commands for communicating with other computers running QLab. Instead of having to research how OSC works and learning how to code it, you can simply click on a drop-down menu and select the desired message type and QLab does the rest. The following section details the use of the QLab message within Network Cues.

Playback Control Commands

When you click on the Command drop-down menu, you will find two types of commands separated by a divider (Figure 21.3). At the top of the menu is what I refer to as playback control commands, as they are used to control some aspect of QLab playback. The list of commands includes Start, Stop, Hard Stop, Pause, Resume, Toggle Pause, Load, Preview, Reset, and Panic. These commands are simple to use. Simply select the command type and input the cue number you want to control. Once the Network Cue is fired, it will automatically find the cue number in the patched workspace and trigger the command.

Parameter-Change Commands

The second section of commands listed in the drop-down menu function to change some parameter of another cue. By inputting the desired cue number and command, you can then input a parameter to change some aspect of a cue, such as Number, Name, Notes, Cue Target Number, Pre-Wait, Duration, Post-Wait, Continue Mode, Flagged, Armed, Color Name. This is an incredibly useful method for changing aspects of a remote workspace without having to actually access it in person.

UDP Messages

This option allows you to send strings over UDP that are not encoded as OSC by QLab. This is a useful method of communication for some applications

Figure 21.3
The Command
drop-down menu.

like Medialon Manager, a Windows® based control software used for controlling audiovisual equipment using any protocol and network. Medialon Manager prefers to receive commands as plaintext strings over UDP, which makes this function preferable to OSC when working with this type of application.

21.4 – OSC and Cue Carts

One of my favorite applications for using OSC messages is to attach them to a Cue Cart. As a reminder, the Cue Cart application within QLab allows you to create a tactile-response system that can be used to trigger cues. One amazing possibility is programming certain OSC commands to cells in a Cue Cart so as to create a remote-control interface for QLab. This makes an excellent programming tool, especially when used in conjunction with the QLab Remote app on an iPad. Since you can open your Cue Carts inside the QLab Remote, it is possible to create a cue cart that is used for manipulating cues in your workspace in real-time through cue carts and the QLab Remote. The following project addresses how to go about setting up your own OSC powered Cue Cart.

Project 21.1 ▼

> ### Creating a Cue Cart Interface
>
> **Step 1:** Open a new workspace and click on the Lists, Carts and Active Cues button at the bottom right of the window. Next, click the button labeled "New Cart." This will open a Cue Cart in place of your cue list.
>
> **Step 2:** Click on the Grid Size tab in the Inspector and select the 3x4 grid. This will resize your Cue Cart to be 9 cells (3 wide x 3 tall).
>
> **Step 3:** Next, click on the Network Cue icon in the Toolbar 12 times. This will insert a Network Cue place keeper into all of the cells. Select each cue, one by one, and insert the following OSC commands into the Settings tab. I have included a brief description of each command function beside the message.
>> **/cue/selected/level/0/0/+ 1** increase the volume of the selected cue by 1dB
>> **/cue/selected/level/0/0/+ 3** increase the volume of the selected cue by 3 dB
>> **/cue/selected/level/0/0/+ 5** increase the volume of the selected cue by 5 dB
>
> *(Continued)*

/**cue/selected/level/0/0/- 1** decrease the volume of the selected cue by 1 dB

/**cue/selected/level/0/0/- 3** decrease the volume of the selected cue by 3 dB

/**cue/selected/level/0/0/- 5** decrease the volume of the selected cue by 5 dB

/**go** Trigger GO for the selected cue

/**stop** Stop playback of selected cue

/**pause** Pause playback of selected cue

/**resume** Resume playback of paused cue

/**playhead/previous** Move playhead down one row

/**playhead/next** Move playhead up one row

Step 4: After inserting the OSC commands, you have a number of options that you can pursue to customize the Cue Cart to meet your needs. I recommend re-naming the cues as something easily recognizable, like −1dB, −3dB, STOP, GO, etc. In addition, color coding the keys inside the Basics tab can make the interface easier to interpret (using green for GO, red for STOP, etc.). In addition, you could program Hotkey or MIDI Triggers inside the Triggers tab.

Step 5: If you have the QLab Remote app, you can now open the Cue Cart inside the app and use it as a remote-control interface. Customize your Cue Cart to include functions you use the most, and then save this workspace as a template. This will include the Cue Cart interface as a component of any workspace that uses this template. An example workspace can be found on the companion website for Project 21.1.

Tools of the Trade ▼

OSCulator

One of QLab's strengths is its ability to use different types of messages, such as OSC, MIDI, or keystrokes, as command functions within a workspace. While some devices, like MIDI keyboards, are logical components of a QLab rig, there are many other types of equipment on the market that may not immediately come to mind as a QLab interface. OSCulator is an excellent tool for connecting these devices with QLab (Figure 21.4). The software functions as a sort of bridge between the different applications that translates one signal type into another.

For example, you can use a Nintendo Wiimote, an iPhone, a WACOM tablet, or other TUIO-compliant touchscreen devices to interface with QLab through OSCulator. The software listens for incoming messages

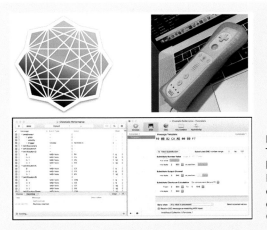

Figure 21.4
The OSCulator interface listens for incoming OSC or MIDI signals. These signals can then be used to trigger events (such as MIDI or OSC messages) as output.

from devices that use OSC or MIDI. Once a message is received, you can program OSCulator to send a new message type out (MIDI, OSC, keyboard commands, or AppleScript). By using this program as an interface between devices and QLab, you could trigger playback of cues within your cue list and even control attributes through OSC or AppleScript. This simple application adds yet one more layer of flexibility to your programming and playback options.

QLab and MIDI

MIDI is one of the most versatile and enduring of communication languages written over the past 30 years. Likely, you have heard the term MIDI before but perhaps not understood exactly what it is or how it is utilized. The following chapter details both the basics of MIDI and how QLab utilizes it as an important component of its show control engine.

22.1 – MIDI Basics

In the early 1980s, a team of engineers and synthesizer designers from various manufacturers devised a method of direct communication between electronic keyboards called **Musical Instrument Digital Interface**, or **MIDI**. Over time, manufacturers adopted this method as a standard, making it a component of most electronic keyboards. In short, MIDI is a digital language that allows musical instruments to communicate with each other, thereby allowing one instrument to control another. Instead of being a musical recording, the MIDI signal is a numeric set of code arranged to send instructions from one device to another. MIDI signals, amazingly compact in size, travel in one direction from one device to another. Within a short time of its introduction to the market, digital musicians quickly branched out to using MIDI with other types of digital devices, like personal computers. By the mid-1980s, MIDI was utilized in music production across several computer platforms.

22.2 – What Is MIDI Show Control?

In 1986, Charlie Richmond debuted one of the first computerized sound control systems for live theatre called Command/Cue. In addition to running Richmond Sound Designs Ltd. a company dedicated to producing a range of commercial theatre sound consoles, Mr. Richmond also served as the Sound Design editor for *TD&T*, the quarterly publication of the United States Institute for Theatre Technology (USITT). It was during this time that he started a MIDI forum through USITT's Callboard network, which used the resources of the early Internet to allow people around the world to communicate. After these early communications, Richmond and roughly two dozen other individuals from across the world (mostly from the lighting manufacturing sector) took on the task of creating a show control standard.

What emerged was **MIDI Show Control (MSC)**. The introduction to the MSC 1.0 Standard defined the purpose of MSC as "to allow MIDI systems to communicate with and to control dedicated intelligent control equipment in theatrical, live performance, multi-media, audio-visual and similar environments." In short, a MIDI interface could send command messages to one or multiple devices in a system, allowing for synchronization in control. The benefits to such a system were reliable and repeatable controls that lacked the errors and inconsistent timing of human controllers. In addition to the immediate application for live performance, MSC quickly became a logical solution for playback and automation in museum installations and audio animatronic shows.

In 1991, both the MIDI Manufacturers Association and the Japan MIDI Standards Committee ratified MSC as an international standard. According to Richmond, this was one of the first international standards created without the members having a single physical meeting since all communication was done virtually. This was certainly a sign of things to come.

22.3 – QLab and MIDI

MIDI has always been an essential component of QLab, both for its use in sound systems and for its show control capabilities. In QLab 4, there are only two MIDI cue types: a MIDI Cue and a MIDI File Cue. Imbedded within the MIDI Cue are a number of different message types, from MIDI Voice Message ("musical MIDI") to MIDI Show Control (MSC) and MIDI SysEx. The first step to harnessing the ability of these MIDI Cues is to set up MIDI within the Workspace Settings. Listed below is the basic information on MIDI setup.

Workspace Settings: MIDI Controls

Look towards the bottom of the settings list on the left side of the Workspace Settings screen in MIDI Controls. By clicking on this, you will open a window to the right of the page that is used to activate MIDI control preferences (see Figure 22.1). There are three rows: one for setting the channel for incoming MIDI, one for MIDI Show Control, and one for "Musical" MIDI controls. The functions for the bottom two are quite similar. By clicking the checkbox to the left of the control, you are allowing your workspace to be controlled by one or both of the MIDI control categories.

Figure 22.1
MIDI Control
preferences.

The first row, Listen on MIDI Channel, allows you to restrict incoming MIDI signals to a specific channel (1–16) or even set QLab to listen on "any." This is used for workspace MIDI controls, lighting controls, or for individual cue triggers.

The next row, Use MIDI Show Control, explains that by checking the box you are enabling QLab to respond to the MIDI Show Control commands: Go, Stop, Resume, Load, All_Off, Standby +/-, Sequence +/-, and Reset. To the right side of the row is a menu for establishing the Device ID for your individual QLab computer. In MSC, there is a possible range of Device IDs from 0–126. Each device in your show control system will have its own unique device ID. In some cases, you can give two devices the same Device ID, but you would lose the ability to individually control either without controlling the other. If an MSC control message with an ID of 127 is sent along the show control network, all devices will respond to the message (if they support the command format). This is a nice "fire all" option.

The final row of control settings is dedicated to "Musical" MIDI Controls. This refers to the type of signal sent out by a MIDI keyboard or device called a message. By clicking the checkbox to the left, you enable the control of certain QLab commands to assigned MIDI messages. Like the Key Map, you can pre-program QLab to respond to certain messages received across the network. To do this, simply click on the drop-down menu to the right of the desired QLab command. After clicking on the drop-down, you will see a list of choices featuring Note On, Note Off, Program Change, and Control Change. These are four of the types of MIDI messages that can be sent by a MIDI device or emulator. Note On refers to the message sent when a note (key) is depressed. Note Off is the message sent when a note is released (ended). Control Change is the message sent when a controller (such as a foot pedal) changes its value. Finally, a Program Change is the message sent when the patch number changes on the MIDI device.

The middle windows, labeled Byte 1 and Byte 2, allow for the insertion of the 8-digit binary code that represents the pertinent data of the note being triggered on the MIDI device. Another method is clicking on the "capture" button to the right of the row. Once depressed, the message "waiting" will appear in the windows for Byte 1 and Byte 2. Once a note is triggered on a MIDI keyboard attached to the system, QLab will record its values and insert them into the row. Thereafter, once that note is triggered under the same conditions, the QLab command will be triggered.

Workspace Settings: MIDI

Roughly halfway up the settings list is a tab labeled MIDI. This serves the function of establishing the output patch for both MIDI Cues and MIDI File Cues.

Both rows function in the same way, by assigning MIDI devices to one of eight different patches. Any MIDI-capable device attached to your system will automatically appear on this list. You can change the order of devices to reorder the arrangement as desired. The top patch is specifically for MIDI Cues, whereas the bottom one is for MIDI File Cues. The MIDI File output patch is identical to the MIDI Cues output patch in every way except for their purpose.

Design Tips ▼

MIDI Across Network

One of the great benefits of the Apple computer has long been its native ability to send MIDI across IP. For QLab, this is a particularly useful application. MIDI interconnect cables are, by their nature, one-way communication. If you want two-way communication between devices you will have to run two sets of cabling to allow for this. In the case of MIDI over IP, though, signals can travel in both directions, making the network an ideal solution for instances of MIDI Show Control. For this application, a program called ipMIDI is indispensable.

ipMIDI is a freeware program for Mac computers that allows the routing of MIDI across an Ethernet network, using ipMIDI ports to send and receive data between computers connected to your network. The driver for the software produces results with less latency than traditional MIDI interconnect cables and eliminates the need for additional cabling between devices. To download the software, visit http://www.nerds.de/en/download.html. Once installed, ipMIDI will be available as a MIDI patch for QLab.

22.4 – MIDI Cues

Once the workspace settings have been established for MIDI control, you are now ready to utilize MIDI Cues. A MIDI Cue can be used in a number of different ways. It could send a control signal to a MIDI device to trigger play-back. It could be used for MIDI Show Control to trigger other entertainment control systems. There are many options. The following sections detail the process of utilizing the MIDI Cue for such purposes. To insert a MIDI Cue, simply click on the MIDI Cue icon in the Toolbar or drag it into your workspace. From there, you can examine all of the functions of the cue in the Inspector Panel.

Inspector: Basics and Triggers

The Basics and Triggers tabs for a MIDI Cue are identical to those seen in many of the other cue types. The Basics tab features the common naming, pre/post-wait, continue status, and notes. The Triggers tab includes Hotkey, MIDI (yes, you can trigger a MIDI Cue with MIDI), Wall Clock, and Timecode triggering options as well as how playback of this cue will affect others in the cue list. These controls do not differ from the ones we covered in earlier chapters.

Inspector: Settings

The settings tab is the primary control method for MIDI Cues. It is impor-tant to recognize that the MIDI Cue function contains three different MIDI Message types imbedded within its control architecture. The look and functions of the settings tab will differ between these three message types. For each of the three message types, the Settings tab is divided into two rows. The top row will always remain the same for each message type (see Figure 22.2).

MIDI Destination: The first button on the top row is labeled "MIDI Destination." This drop-down menu allows you to select one of eight different MIDI patches from the MIDI tab in Workspace Settings. This allows you to determine which MIDI device will receive the MIDI Cue.

Message Type: This drop-down menu allows for the selection between the three different MIDI Message types: MIDI Voice Message ("Musical" MIDI), MIDI Show Control (MSC), and MIDI SysEx Message. Depending on the work-space settings established for MIDI, all MIDI Cues inserted into the workspace default to one of these three:

Figure 22.2
The MIDI Settings tab in the Inspector.

- **MIDI Voice Messages** (also referred to as channel voice messages) are used to carry musical performance data, such as triggering or stopping a sound, selecting a particular instrument, bending the pitch, or sustaining a note. In addition to sending information to MIDI instruments, this type of message can also be used to control certain sound devices, such as a digital mixer.
- **MIDI Show Control Messages** are a specific subset of MIDI messaging used to interact with a wide array of devices in the entertainment industry. These messages include command formats for equipment (lighting, sound, machinery, video, projection, process control, and pyro) paired with specific commands like go, stop, and resume. The purpose of these controls is to decrease the likelihood of errors in cueing and give more precise timing for playback.
- **MIDI SysEx Messages** (MIDI System Exclusive) are one of the biggest reasons for MIDI's longevity. SysEx messages are a subset of MIDI messaging that gives versatility to manufacturers of MIDI devices. Most manufacturers have created their own proprietary messaging system that is more thorough than the standard MIDI and written specifically for one piece of equipment. SysEx messages are addressed to a specific device in the system and ignored by other devices in the same system.

Each of the three message types listed above is contained within the cue architecture for a MIDI Cue. Now that we have explored the difference between these three message types, it is useful to examine how each of them can be used. The following sections address the controls featured in the Settings tab for each message type.

22.5 – MIDI Voice Message

The MIDI Voice Message, sometimes referred to as "musical" MIDI, can be used for a number of different control functions interacting with MIDI devices in your system. Since MIDI is such an exhaustive category unto itself, it is perhaps best to address a few of the basics in this area. The MIDI Voice Message is in a category of MIDI called "channel messages," or MIDI messages that apply only to a specific channel. MIDI has a possibility of 16 channels, so in a MIDI Voice Message, a channel number is included with the status byte for the message to indicate which channel should receive the command. In QLab, the MIDI Voice Message has seven commands that can be sent. Each one has its own attributes listed below.

- **Note On:** The Note On command is the data sent when a key is pressed on a MIDI keyboard. It contains the information of which key is pushed and with what velocity (how hard the key was hit). The QLab parameters include channel, note number, and velocity (Figure 22.3). By assigning

Figure 22.3
The Note On command window.

a note number and velocity, QLab can send a MIDI command across the system to trigger a note on an attached MIDI keyboard.

- **Note Off:** The Note Off command serves the same function as the Note On except it sends the message to release a key on the keyboard. The Note Off interface is identical to that of the Note On.
- **Program Change:** Most MIDI devices have a number of different instrument sounds programmed for playback. The Program Change is a MIDI message that tells the device which instrument to use for playback. There are 128 possible program numbers (0–127). In some cases, some MIDI devices may not have instrument sounds but rather use program change to shift between functions. One example of this might be a drum machine that will change the drum beat when it receives a program change command. In QLab, the Program Change command window includes parameters for Channel and Program Number (see Figure 22.4).
- **Control Change:** A controller is a type of musical device that implements a function other than starting or stopping notes, such as a sustain pedal, modulation wheel, or volume pedal. A Control Change command is the MIDI command associated with the changes created by that device. As with all MIDI commands, the details are strictly defined in the MIDI Specification. For a Control Change, QLab can send a Channel, Control Number, and Control Value. The control number references 128 different possible controller types, whereas the control value is the level (0–127) at which

Figure 22.4
The Program Change command window.

Figure 22.5
The Control
Change command
window.

the controller is operating. One interesting function of the Control Change command in QLab is the ability to fade over a duration (Figure 22.5). In the right corner of the control window, you will see a fade curve window with a time and "fade to control value" setting. This allows you to draw more gradual control changes.

- **Key Pressure (AfterTouch):** The Key Pressure command deals with the ability of MIDI to communicate information regarding the amount of pressure applied to an individual key on the keyboard *after it has been depressed*, leading to the term **AfterTouch.** These messages can be used to vary the pressure on a given key to create a vibrato effect. For the Key Pressure command in QLab, the control window features Channel, Note Number, and Pressure Value. Like the Control Change command, this command can be faded over a duration (Figure 22.6).

- **Channel Pressure:** Unlike Key Pressure, which generates AfterTouch information for each individual key, the Channel Pressure command generates AfterTouch information for *every* key on the keyboard simultaneously. As such, the only difference between the Key Pressure and Channel Pressure interfaces for QLab is that Channel Pressure does not list a note number.

- **Pitch Bend Change:** On a MIDI keyboard, the Pitch Bend Change command is normally sent by the instrument's pitch bend wheel. Like the name implies, this command will bend the pitch either higher or lower, depending on the byte value entered in the MIDI command. For QLab, the Pitch Bend Change command features two control attributes: Channel and Velocity

Figure 22.6
The Key Pressure
command
window.

Figure 22.7
The Pitch Bend
Change command
window.

(see Figure 22.7). The velocity can be viewed as a binary representation of sliding the pitch bend wheel up or down. Pitch bend data has a possible 16,383 values with –8,192 being the lowest bend, 0 being no pitch bend, and 8,192 being the highest bend.

Each of the MIDI Voice Messages can be used in a number of creative ways to interact with other MIDI equipment in your sound system. I recommend a thorough examination of the user's manuals of your equipment, as each manufacturer uses slightly different systems for MIDI communication.

22.6 – MIDI Show Control (MSC)

MIDI Show Control is a useful subset of MIDI dedicated to communication between entertainment controllers and devices in a system. Like MIDI itself, the documentation for MSC is thorough and recommended reading for anyone interested in pursuing show control. The complete document can be obtained from the MIDI Manufacturers Association (MMA) at www.midi.org. For general understanding, we will look at some of the basics below. To specify your MIDI Cue as MSC, simply click on the Message Type drop-down menu and select MIDI Show Control. You will notice that, upon changing the message type, the bottom row will feature new options (Figure 22.8). These options are addressed below.

Figure 22.8
The MIDI Show
Control Message
window.

Though the top row of the Settings tab remains unchanged between MIDI Voice Message and MIDI Show Control, there are a few key differences to the bottom row with the different message types. The first item listed is **Command Format**. In MSC, there are categories to commands specified for different types of equipment. Command Formats fall into three categories: General, Specific, and All-types. For example, in dealing with lighting commands the general command format sent out would be called "Lighting." Within the category of lighting, though, there are a number of other specific command formats, like moving lights, color changers, strobes, lasers, or chasers. The command format "All-types" is reserved for a system-wide broadcast of commands to all devices in the system.

All MSC-capable devices can be assigned a **Device ID**, a number specific to that device so that each can be individually controlled without fear of accidentally triggering the wrong device. That is why each MSC message has a device ID drop-down menu for assigning its patch. Likewise, each cue has the ability to specify Q number, Q List, and Q Path for detailed interaction with other entertainment control systems.

The last term of importance in the Setting tab is **Command**, which indicates the type of control signal to be sent out to a device (such as Go, Stop, Resume, etc.). Like the MIDI Voice Message, MSC features a number of different commands (26 in all) for communicating with devices. The first 11 commands are categorized as general commands that can be used with a range of differing entertainment control systems. The final 15 commands are specific to sound control. The list below briefly explains each command type and its use.

General Commands:

- **Go:** This command starts a cue. Once triggered, the cue will play until complete or until acted upon to stop with another command. If the controlled device has multiple cue numbers or cue lists, this information can be stipulated in the command. If no cue number is indicated, then the next cue in sequence will play back.
- **Stop:** Halts the playback of the running cue. If no specific cue is specified, then all running cues will be stopped. If a specific cue number is given, only that cue will stop.
- **Resume:** Begins the playback of a halted cue at the stop point. If no specific cue is specified, then all stopped cues will resume. If a specific cue number is given, only that cue will resume.
- **Timed_Go:** Starts a cue at a specific point in time, using the standard time specification with sub-frames (Timecode). Once triggered, the cue will play until complete or until acted upon to stop with another command. If the controlled device has multiple cue numbers or cue lists, this information can be stipulated in the command. If no cue number is indicated, then the next

cue in sequence will play back. When the Timed-Go command is selected, a Timecode window will pop up in the right half of the screen for inputting start time.

- **Load:** Places a specified cue into a standby position. If the controlled device has multiple cue lists, a specific cue list must be specified, or all similar cue numbers will be loaded to standby.
- **Set:** This command defines the value of a Generic Control on a controlled device and the time in which these changes occur. Depending on the manufacturer, almost any attribute can be established as a Generic Control (levels, subs, channels, rates, etc.). When using the Set command in QLab, the variables are control number, control value, and send Timecode.
- **Fire:** The Fire command triggers a pre-programmed Macro on the controlled device. QLab features a Macro menu for selecting the desired Macro to trigger.
- **All_Off:** This command disables all functions and outputs of the controlled device without changing control settings.
- **Restore:** Restores the operating status of the controlled device to what it was before the All-Off command.
- **Reset:** This command terminates all running cues and resets them to their original state. The cue order will also be reset, loading the first cue in the sequence.
- **Go_Off:** Starts a cue and immediately places the cue into the off state. If no cue number is indicated, then the next cue in sequence will go. If the controlled device has multiple cue lists, a specific cue list must be specified, or all similar cue numbers will go off.

Sound Control Commands:

- **Go/Jam_Clock:** Starts a cue and simultaneously forces the clock to the "Go Time" if that cue is set as Auto-follow. If the cue is manual, then Jam clock is ignored. If no cue number is indicated, then the next cue in sequence will go. If a cue number is specified, that cue goes, and the clock of the appropriate cue list is "jammed" to that go time.
- **Standby_+:** Places the next cue in the cue list into standby. If no cue list is noted, the current cue list will be used. If more than one cue list contains the same number, then these matching cue numbers will be placed on standby for each cue list.
- **Standby_-:** Places the previous cue in the cue list into standby. If no cue list is noted, the current cue list will be used. If more than one cue list contains the same number, then these matching cue numbers will be placed on standby for each cue list.
- **Sequence_+:** Places the next parent cue in the cue list into standby. If no cue list is noted, the current cue list will be used. If more than one cue list contains the same number, then these matching cue numbers will be placed on standby for each cue list.

- **Sequence_-:** Places the lowest numbered parent cue in the previous parent sequence into standby. If no cue list is noted, the current cue list will be used. If more than one cue list contains the same number, then these matching cue numbers will be placed on standby for each cue list.
- **Start_Clock:** Starts the "Auto-follow" clock timer. The clock will start from any previous value from which it was stopped. If no cue list is noted, the clocks for all cue lists will start.
- **Stop_Clock:** Stops the "Auto-follow" clock timer. When stopped, the clock will retain its value. If no cue list is noted, the clocks for all cue lists will stop.
- **Zero_Clock:** Sets the clock to a value of 00:00:00:00:00 whether or not it is running. Zeroing the clock will not affect its run status. If no cue list is noted, the clocks for all cue lists will zero.
- **Set_Clock:** Sets the clock to a value sent by QLab whether or not it is running. Zeroing the clock will not affect its run status. If no cue list is noted, the clocks for all cue lists will be set to the value sent by QLab.
- **MTC_Chase_On:** Causes the clock to be set identically to incoming MIDI Timecode. If no cue list is noted, the clocks for all cue lists will chase.
- **MTC_Chase_Off:** Causes the clock to stop receiving the MIDI Timecode. It does not reset the clock value. If no cue list is noted, the clocks for all cue lists will stop chasing.
- **Open_Cue_List:** Opens a stipulated cue list and makes it active so that the controlled device can access it.
- **Close_Cue_List:** Closes a stipulated cue list and makes it inactive so that the controlled device cannot access it.
- **Open_Cue_Path:** Opens a stipulated cue path and makes it active so that the controlled device can access it.
- **Close_Cue_Path:** Closes a stipulated cue path and makes it inactive so that the controlled device cannot access it.

22.7 – MIDI SysEx

MIDI SysEx commands, short for System Exclusive, are a type of command used specifically to communicate proprietary information to one particular model of equipment. No two devices use the same SysEx commands, meaning that you need to have access to the owner's manual for your particular device to best understand how to send it commands. The only common factor between all manufacturers SysEx commands is that they must begin with a 0xF0 status and end with a 0xF7 status. This is the only type of MIDI command that has both a beginning and an end status byte. When sending SysEx commands in QLab, there is only an input window for typing in the raw MIDI code (see Figure 22.9).

Figure 22.9
The MIDI SysEx
command
window.

22.8 – MIDI File Cue

One final aspect of QLab's MIDI control is the ability to play back a MIDI file. MIDI files are a collection of binary code that communicates a vast amount of information, including instrument voice, note duration, velocity, volume, and more. Though QLab does not have a built-in synthesizer for hearing MIDI playback, it can send the MIDI file information across its system to another MIDI synthesizer for playback. When the MIDI file is inserted as a MIDI File Cue, you can see the file information in the Settings tab of the Inspector Panel (Figure 22.10). There are no control parameters for the MIDI File Cue other than playback rate.

Figure 22.10
A MIDI file
displayed in the
Settings tab of the
Inspector Panel.

Tools of the Trade ▼

Go Box

One of the advantages of QLab is its ability to integrate with MIDI devices. One such powerful MIDI device is the Go Box, created by Team Sound, a New York-based sound technology company. The Go Box is a USB MIDI remote for use with programs like QLab and other MIDI-capable applications. Instead of pressing the space bar to trigger playback, you can plug in one of these interfaces and save the stress on your keyboard.

There are currently three different remotes, Go Box 1, Go Box 4, and Go Box 6. Each one is designed using high-quality parts, making the Go Box a sturdy component of your rig. The buttons are made from arcade-style switches rated for half a million cycles. The boxes are made from powder-coated aluminum so they are lightweight and durable. The USB jacks come equipped with Neutrik locking connectors that, when used in conjunction with a locking USB cable, really stay put so there are no worries of accidentally pulling the cable out.

Each Go Box is named for the number of buttons it provides – one, four, or six (Figure 22.11). Each model works in a similar fashion, with the buttons serving as MIDI remote triggers. There is no driver software required, so they are simple to set up. Each button sends a MIDI signal through the USB on channel 16. The signal is a Note On message with a velocity of 127 when the button is pressed (Note 1 on Go Box 1, Notes 1–4 on Go Box 4, and Notes 1–6 on Go Box 6) and a velocity of 0 when the button is released.

GO BOX 1

GO BOX 4

GO BOX 6

Figure 22.11
The three current Go Box models. Photos courtesy Sam Kusnetz, of [Team of Sound].

Team Sound offers preconfigured QLab workspaces on its website at www. teamsound.nyc/support. In the basic workspace for Go Box 4, Note 1 is "Go"; Note 2 is "Panic All," which stops all cues over a duration determined by the user; Note 3 is "Select previous cue"; and Note 4 is "Select next cue."

Go Box 6 is ideally suited for a redundancy rig (a collection of two show control computers running their workspaces simultaneously). Both are connected to output to your system, typically including a manual switch to change output from one unit to another should the need arise. Go Box 6 features two USB connectors, meaning that each button sends MIDI signals to both computers simultaneously. By using this unit, there is no need for a separate go button for each show control computer.

One final item of note is that Team Sound is currently working on a wireless version of the Go Box. It is not Wi-Fi or Bluetooth, so there will be no passwords, pairing, or latency issues. The transmitter will have an integrated LiPo battery good for at least 12 hours with a current tested range of around 80 feet. As always, there is no guarantee until the product actually ships, but it does seem to be a very promising development.

Timecode

Timecode has origins tied to the earliest video recorders in the 1960s. The recording of moving images on magnetic tape created a number of problems related to editing video and aligning audio with video. In film-based recordings, each picture on the film was aligned with guide holes that could be counted exactly to clearly define the location of frames. With magnetic tape, there were no such guide holes, creating difficulty in clearly tracking the alignment of frames. By 1967, the Society of Motion Picture and Television Engineers (SMPTE) had created a standardized system for sending audio impulses for recording a picture number parallel to every video picture, thus creating an "electronic guide hole" system. This method was the first Timecode. In the years since the creation of Timecode, a number of interesting uses have emerged, including aligning video and audio signals and triggering cues from a Timecode signal. QLab 4 has the ability to both transmit and receive Timecode signals across an audio output or a MIDI system.

23.1 – How Timecode Works

Traditionally, Timecode is a data signal that runs parallel to image data in a video signal. Each picture is clearly labeled with Timecode data containing clear information of hours, minutes, seconds, and frames. The number of frames used in each specific Timecode is determined by the original video format with the sending and receiving ends set to the same frame rate to be effective for syncing. In modern usage, Timecode may be used independently from a video signal. There are a number of different Timecode frame rates available through QLab to fit any application.

The advantage of using Timecode is the creation of a reference point for playback of separate systems. One great example of this would be running audio from a QLab computer that needs to be synced with a video signal sent from a video server remote to the QLab system. Timecode will ensure that the video will be triggered to follow the audio exactly. This is especially important in instances of dialog lip-syncing to a video. Likewise, it is beneficial to use Timecode to trigger a cue at a very specific point in the Timecode stream. Consider the use of Timecode to send cues to trigger lighting effects in perfect sync with an audio track. Effects like this are particularly useful in theme parks, museum displays, and dance concerts (all situations in which the cueing is particularly linear with a very rigid and inflexible timeline).

One important concept to understand related to Timecode is drop frame. NTSC color video uses a frame rate of 29.97 frames/sec, which means that the frame rate is 0.03 seconds slower than the nearest whole number Timecode of 30 frames/sec. In order to compensate for this, drop frame timing is used to drop Timecode numbers periodically to assure that the Timecode aligns with the true frame rate of the video. Drop frame timing is used relatively infrequently – only for NTSC video.

In terms of QLab, Timecode is typically used in one of two ways: as an incoming signal to trigger QLab cues or as a Timecode Cue that generates a Timecode signal to be sent to other computers or devices.

23.2 – Timecode Settings

Timecode Settings are located in the Workspace Settings window under *Cue Templates > Timecode*. After selecting the Timecode template, select the Settings tab in the Inspector. The first option in this tab is the selection of the default output type, either MIDI Timecode (MTC) or Linear Timecode (LTC). Linear Timecode is the aforementioned audio signal typically recorded to tape and decoded by a synchronizer originally used to synchronize audio and video equipment. With the proliferation of MIDI devices in the 1980s, a new method was required for syncing analog devices with computer MIDI sequencers. MIDI Timecode (MTC) was developed for this reason. For all practical purposes, MTC can be thought of as LTC in MIDI form. QLab can generate both LTC and MTC.

Next, there is a drop-down menu for selecting the Timecode destination. Clicking on this menu opens a list of all the available destinations within your system. Directly following this is an option to select the default frame rate for new Timecode Cues. Choices are 24 fps, 25 fps, 30 fps non-drop, 30 fps drop, 23.976 fps, 24.975 fps, 29.97 fps non-drop, and 29.97 fps drop. Finally, there is a window for inputting the start time of the Timecode to be generated.

23.3 – Triggering Cues from Timecode

One of the strengths of QLab is its ability to allow cues to be triggered by incoming Timecode signals. There are a few steps necessary to enable this process. The first step is to enable the cue list to be triggered by Timecode. In order to do so, first click on the Lists, Carts and Active Cues button in the lower right hand corner of the QLab screen. This will open up all available cue lists in the upper right hand corner of the screen. Click on the desired cue list and then select the Timecode tab in the Inspector. Click on the checkbox labeled "trigger cues in this list from incoming Timecode." This will enable cues within the cue list to be triggered by incoming Timecode.

In order to trigger an individual cue with Timecode, there is one remaining step. First, click on the desired cue and open the Triggers tab in the Inspector. The last row on the left side of the screen is a checkbox labeled "Timecode trigger." By clicking this checkbox, you can insert the Timecode signature at which you want the cue to be triggered. Once a Timecode signal is present, QLab will listen for the appropriate time to trigger the cue. It is important to note that QLab does not "chase" Timecode. It only triggers cues from the start of the cue and does not try to compute a position mid-stream based on the Timecode.

23.4 – Timecode Cues

To insert a Timecode Cue into your cue list, click on the Timecode Cue icon in the Toolbar, or drag it into your workspace. Once the cue has been inserted, click on the Settings tab in the Inspector Panel. The settings are relatively simple and straightforward. First, there is the Timecode type tool that allows you to select between MIDI Timecode and Linear Timecode. After selecting the type, the next step is to select the destination, or output patch, for the Timecode signal. MTC is transmitted across a MIDI patch, whereas LTC is sent out through an audio patch.

Frame rate is the next variable for Timecode Cues. As discussed before, frame rate must match the frame rate of the receiving end's frame-rate setting, otherwise nothing will happen. The frame rates are divided into two separate groups: **Film Speed** and **Video Speed.** Film Speed formats are divided into integer frame rates (such as 24 fps, 25 fps, 30 fps non-drop, 30 fps drop), whereas the Video Speed formats are non-integer frame rates (23.976 fps, 24.975 fps, 29.97 fps non-drop, 29.97 fps drop). Video Speed frame rates are 0.1% slower than their Film Speed equivalents.

Finally, the last variable for Timecode Cues is the start time of the Timecode. Insert into the window the desired start time of any Timecode to be outputted through the system. It is worth mentioning that Timecode can take a few frames to transmit enough data in order to read. If you have to trigger something on a precise frame, it is a good idea to start the timecode rolling a few frames ahead in order to guarantee correct timing.

Index

References to figures are shown in *italics*.

Index